Accountable Government in Africa
Perspectives from public law and
political studies

Accountable Government in Africa

Perspectives from public law and political studies

EDITORS

DANWOOD M. CHIRWA
LIA NIJZINK

United Nations University Press

TOKYO • NEW YORK • PARIS

UCT
P R E S S

BRITISH COUNCIL

Accountable Government in Africa: Perspectives from public law and political studies
Published in 2012 in South Africa by UCT Press
An imprint of Juta and Company Ltd
First Floor Sunclare Building
21 Dreyer Street
Claremont, 7708
South Africa
www.uctpress.co.za
© 2012 UCT Press

Published in 2012 in North America, Europe and Asia by
United Nations University Press
United Nations University, 53-70, Jingumae 5-chome,
Shibuya-ku, Tokyo 150-8925, Japan
Tel: +81-3-5467-1212   Fax: +81-3-3406-7345
E-mail: sales@unu.edu   General enquiries: press@unu.edu
http://www.unu.edu
United Nations University Office at the United Nations, New York
2 United Nations Plaza, Room DC2-2062, New York, NY 10017, USA
Tel: +1-212-963-6387   Fax: +1-212-371-9454
E-mail: unuony@unu.edu

United Nations University Press is the publishing division of the United Nations University.

The views expressed in this publication are those of the authors and do not necessarily reflect the views of the publishers.

ISBN 978-1-91989-537-6 (Southern Africa)
ISBN 978-92-808-1205-3 (North America, Europe and South East Asia)

Library of Congress Cataloging-in-Publication Data
Accountable government in Africa : perspectives from public law and
political studies / editors: Danwood M. Chirwa, Lia Nijzink.
    p. cm.
  Includes bibliographical references and index.
  ISBN 978-9280812053 (pbk.)
  1. Africa—Politics and government—1960– 2. Government
accountability—Africa. I. Chirwa, Danwood Mzikenge. II. Nijzink, Lia.
  JQ1875.A7218   2012
  352.3'5096—dc23   2011040863

Cover design: Comet Designs
Language Editor: Rae Dalton
Proofreader: Lee-Ann Ashcroft
Indexer: Cliff Perusset
Typesetter: Exemplarr
Printed in Hong Kong
Typeset in 10.5 pt on 13 pt Minion Pro
This book has been independently peer-reviewed by academics who are experts in the field.

in memory of
Jwani T. Mwaikusa
1952–2010

Contents

List of Tables and Figures

Acknowledgements

This book is the product of a three-year partnership between the University of Cape Town, the University of Dar es Salaam and the University of Warwick. The objectives of this partnership were to investigate problems of accountability and constitutional implementation in Africa, with a specific focus on formal and informal institutions of accountability and external accountability support; to draw on this knowledge in developing new or revising existing courses in law and politics at the three partner institutions; to encourage interdisciplinary and comparative research; and to stimulate curriculum development in comparative constitutional law and political studies.

We are grateful to all members of the partner institutions who participated in the activities of our partnership. In particular, we would like to thank Professor Christina Murray and Professor Peter Burnell for the leading role they played in establishing the partnership.

With special appreciation, we remember the contribution of the University of Dar es Salaam's leading and most active participant in this partnership, Professor Jwani Mwaikusa. To our great dismay and sadness, Professor Mwaikusa was murdered outside his home in Dar es Salaam in July 2010. We dedicate this book to his memory.

The chapters included in this book were drawn from a conference entitled 'Sources of Accountability on the African Continent' hosted in July 2009 by the Department of Public Law at the University of Cape Town. This conference attracted participants from the three partner institutions and beyond, including academics, judges, legal practitioners, students and members of the press. The contribution of these participants to the success of the conference is duly acknowledged. We would like to extend our special gratitude to Advocate Vusi Pikoli, former National Director of Public Prosecutions of South Africa, who gave the opening address; and to Justice Albie Sachs, then Judge of the Constitutional Court of South Africa, Justice Barnabas A. Samatta, former Chief Justice of Tanzania, and Justice Andrew Nyirenda, Justice of Appeal of the Supreme Court of Malawi, who constituted the panel for a judges' forum discussion at the conference. We would also like to extend our appreciation to Dorothy Lucejko, Sue Wright and Vanessa Stemmet for their assistance with the practical and administrative arrangements for the conference.

All chapters in this book were peer-reviewed. We would like to express our deep appreciation to the anonymous reviewers for both their critical and positive comments. The authors were understanding and appreciative of these comments and of the feedback that we as editors gave on their chapters. We owe all authors our profound gratitude for the work they put into this project and for their cooperation, diligence and patience. We hope that their contributions to this volume and their future work will contribute to the deepening of democracy and accountability on the African continent.

This partnership and consequently this book would not have been possible without the generous financial support of the Development Partnerships in Higher Education (DelPHE) programme of the British Council and the UK Department for International Development. The following organisations provided additional support for the partnership and its 2009 conference:

- British Academy
- Southern African-Nordic Centre (SANORD)
- University Research Committee, University of Cape Town
- Institute of Advanced Studies, University of Warwick
- Department of Politics and International Studies, University of Warwick

Our special thanks go to our publishers, UCT Press and United Nations University Press, and their staff, especially Sandy Shepherd and Deidre Mvula, for their professionalism and diligence, and Rae Dalton for language editing. We also gratefully acknowledge the help of Chacha Murungu in proofreading chapter five and addressing editorial queries and requests for further information.

To our readers, we hope that this book contributes to your own work and understanding of the dynamics and challenges of accountable government on the African continent.

Danwood M. Chirwa and Lia Nijzink
Cape Town
24 August 2011

About the Editors

Danwood M. Chirwa is the head of the Public Law Department at the University of Cape Town. He is also an Associate Professor and Fellow at the same university. He teaches administrative law, international protection of human rights, current issues in constitutional law and children's rights. He is the founding editor of the *Malawi Law Journal* and an expert on human rights in Africa and Malawian constitutional issues. Chirwa's recent publications include *Human Rights under the Malawian Constitution* (Juta Law).

Lia Nijzink is a senior researcher with the Law, Race and Gender Research Unit, University of Cape Town. Previously, she held the same position with UCT's Department of Public Law, where she has coordinated a British Council funded South-North partnership between the universities of Cape Town (SA), Dar Es Salaam (Tanzania) and Warwick (UK). Having obtained her LLM from the University of Maastricht (NL) and her MA in Political Science from the University of Amsterdam (NL), she came to South Africa in 1998 to take up a research fellowship with the Cape Town-based NGO IDASA. Since then, she has worked as a researcher/consultant for various South African and African organisations and travelled extensively in West, East and Southern Africa to conduct fact finding and review missions. Prior to joining the Department of Public Law, Nijzink lectured in UCT's Department of Political Studies in the areas of research methodology and comparative political institutions, was awarded a research fellowship with the Centre for Social Science Research and the Centre for African Studies and served as a principal investigator and project manager of the African Legislatures Project. Her current research interests concern accountable government, parliamentary and party politics in Africa, democratisation, comparative research methodology and comparative law and politics. Nijzink is the co-editor of *African Perspectives on Tradition and Justice* (Intersentia, 2012) and *Patterns of One-Party Dominance in African Democracies: How One-Party Dominant Systems Endure and Decline* (Lynne Rienner Publishers, 2012).

About the Authors

Peter Burnell is a professor of politics and international studies at the University of Warwick, England.

Diana Cammack was born and raised in the USA, obtained her PhD at the University of California, and specialised in South African history (*The Rand at War*: University of Natal Press & James Currey, 1990). As an SSRC-MacArthur fellow on Peace and Security in a Changing World she retrained at Oxford University in the early 1990s in refugee studies, human rights and the politics of aid. She now specialises in contemporary Southern African politics. Diana led the politics and governance team at the Overseas Development Institute in London for three years, and now oversees the local governance stream of the Africa Power and Politics Programme (www.institutions-africa.org). She has worked as a consultant researcher in sub-Saharan Africa and Asia for three decades and has lived in South Africa, Zimbabwe and Malawi for nearly 20 years. Her primary focus is Malawian politics and she has published on, inter alia, transitional justice, elections, conflict, freedom of expression and politics. She has also researched and written on gender, refugees, governance, poverty, human rights, etc, in Africa and parts of Asia. In recent years, Cammack has specialised in political economy studies, with a focus on the link between politics and development in neopatrimonial and fragile states. Work for APPP in Malawi has included a study of 'town chiefs' as a form of peri-urban government, and their role in the provision of public goods. This has fuelled her interest in the relationship between development and forms of legitimacy, authority and accountability in present-day Africa.

Hugh Corder has been professor of public law at the University of Cape Town since 1987. He is a graduate of the universities of Cape Town, Cambridge and Oxford. He has served in many administrative capacities, including a period as Dean of the Faculty, from 1999 to 2008. His main academic interests are administrative justice and the judicial process, in which areas he has published widely, both in scholarly and popular form. He was involved as a technical adviser in the making of both the transitional and final Constitutions for South Africa, in the early 1990s.

Pierre de Vos is the Claude Leon Foundation Chair in Constitutional Governance at the Law Faculty of the University of Cape Town. He teaches constitutional law and has published widely on a variety of constitutional law topics, including social and economic rights, non-discrimination law and constitutional governance issues. He was a special advisor to the South African Parliamentary

Ad Hoc Committee reviewing the work of so-called Chapter 9 institutions. He writes a widely read and quoted blog entitled Constitutionally Speaking. He is also the chairperson of the Board of the Aids Legal Network.

Siri Gloppen is a professor of comparative politics, University of Bergen, Norway and Research Director at the Chr. Michelsen Institute for development research. Her research interests centre on the social and political role of law and legal institutons and spans constitution-making and constitutionalism, institutionalisation of accountability structures, courts and elections, the transformative potential of social rights, juridification and social citizenship, climate lawfare, and transitional justice and reconciliation. Empirically, her research focus is on Southern and East Africa (South Africa, Malawi, Uganda, Tanzania, Zambia) but she has also directed several international research projects comparing the social and political role of courts across regions (accountability functions of courts in new democracies, courts and the poor, the right to health through litigation). Recent publications include *Courts and Power in Latin America and Africa* (Palgrave Macmillan, 2010) and *Litigating Health Rights: Can Courts Bring More Justice to Health* (Harvard University Press, 2011).

Fidelis Edge Kanyongolo is a Malawian national who has taught at the University of Malawi since 1986. He obtained his PhD from the University of East Anglia in the United Kingdom in 2000 and is currently an associate professor of law specialising in constitutional law and jurisprudence. He served as Dean of the Faculty of Law of the University of Malawi from 2008 to 2010 and member of the Council of the Catholic University of Malawi from 2007 to 2010. His research interests focus on the interplay of law and politics in the framework of constitutionalism, democratic governance and development. From 2008 to 2011, Fidelis participated on the Africa Power and Politics Programme managed by the Overseas Development Institute as a part-time senior researcher based in Malawi. Co-editor of *Democracy in Progress: Malawi's 2009 Parliamentary and Presidential Elections* (Kachere, 2009), Kanyongolo has also authored a number of reports on various aspects of governance including *Malawi: Justice Sector and the Rule of Law 2006* (Africa Governance Monitoring Programme, 2007) and *State of the Judiciary Report: Malawi 2003* (International Foundation for Electoral Systems, 2004). He has participated actively in human rights advocacy in Southern Africa, including in his capacity as trustee of the Media Institute of Africa from 2000–2005, member of the Advisory Board of the Africa Programme of Article 19 from 2002 to 2004 and member of the board of directors of the Open Society Initiative for Southern Africa (OSISA) from 2006 to 2009.

Redson E. Kapindu, LLB (Hons) (MW); LLM (UP) and PhD candidate (Wits), is the Deputy Director of the South African Institute for Advanced

Constitutional, Public, Human Rights and International Law (SAIFAC), a legal research centre within the University of Johannesburg. He is also a lecturer in the Department of Public Law at the University of Johannesburg. Kapindu is a former Director of Legal Services at the Malawi Human Rights Commission. He has served as Vice President of the Malawi Law Society and Special Law Commissioner in the Malawi Law Commission's Child Rights Law Reform Commission. Kapindu has published in the areas of socioeconomic rights and the work of national human rights institutions. He is an admitted legal practitioner in Malawi, and has previously been involved in major human rights litigation in that country.

Augustine T. Magolowondo holds a PhD in political science, an MA in development management (both from the Ruhr University of Bochum, Germany), and a BA in public administration from University of Malawi. His main areas of research include democratisation aid, political parties, governance, development cooperation and conflict management. His work has been published in a number of peer-reviewed edited volumes. His 2005 PhD dissertation on *Democratization Aid as a Challenge for Development Cooperation* won him the 2006 Young Researchers Award of the Justus-Liebeg University of Giessen (Germany). He is a member of the African Good Governance Network (AGGN), a network of young scholars that are committed to advancing democratic governance in Africa. Magolowondo works for the Netherlands Institute for Multiparty Democracy as Coordinator of its Africa Regional Programme.

Sifuni Ernest Mchome is a lawyer by profession and has worked extensively in Tanzania on matters related to law, justice, policy and administration. He is currently the Executive Secretary of the Tanzania Commission for Universities which is a regulatory body for university level education in Tanzania. He is the former Dean of the School of Law (formerly Faculty of Law) of the University of Dar es Salaam and was a Fulbright Fellow from 2002 to 2003 in New York, where he used his time to evaluate the refugee system and the way it relates and applies to Tanzania. He has done work related to reforms in the legal sector and has a distinguished record in that regard relating to reform of the police, prosecution, judicial and correctional systems in Tanzania. Mchome is also an advocate and a notary public and commissioner for oaths in Tanzania.

Jwani T. Mwaikusa was an associate professor at the University of Dar es Salaam which he joined in 1986. Before that, he had been a state attorney and assistant lecturer at the Institute of Development Management, Mzumbe University. At the University of Dar es Salaam Mwaikusa was Head of the Department of Constitutional and Administrative Law, member of the University of Dar es Salaam Legal Aid Committee (1988–1992), and chairman of the same committee (1992). Mwaikusa also served as chairman of the Centre for Media

Studies, Research and Networking (2002–2010) and was the lead counsel for the Defence at the UN International Criminal Tribunal for Rwanda (2007–2010). Mwaikusa has published numerous articles and book chapters on a wide range of subjects and was also a poet. Mwaikusa was murdered outside his home in Dar es Salaam on 14 July 2010.

Andrew Nash teaches history of political thought at the University of Cape Town. Before that, he taught philosophy and politics at the universities of Stellenbosch and the Western Cape and was editorial director of *Monthly Review Press* in New York. He is the author of *The Dialectical Tradition in South Africa* (Routledge, 2009).

Nandini Patel is a political scientist by training and holds a PhD from the University of Mumbai, India. She is currently serving as associate professor and Head of the Department of Political Leadership at the Catholic University of Malawi. She has taught political science and international relations in India and in Malawi for over 25 years. She is the co-founder and first coordinator of the Center for Conflict Management at Chancellor College, University of Malawi. She has prepared training modules and conducted training sessions for the youth members of political parties in Malawi and in Zambia. She has facilitated several workshops for political parties focused on the promotion of intra-party democracy. Her research focus is on democracy and governance with emphasis on elections, political parties and Parliament. Patel has published many papers and book chapters and is also the chairperson of an NGO called Institute for Policy Interaction based in Blantyre, Malawi. She is a board member of the Electoral Institute for Sustainability of Democracy in Africa (EISA). Patel was a research fellow at the Institute for Federalism, University of Friburg (Switzerland) and at the Centre for Development Studies, University of Oslo (Norway).

Neo Simutanyi is a political scientist with more than 20 years' experience in teaching, research and policy analysis in East and Southern Africa. His work has focused on issues of democratisation, particularly related to constitution-making, elections and electoral management, political parties and non-state actors; political economy with emphasis on politics of economic reform, policy-making, and politics of development aid. Dr Neo Simutanyi has previously worked as research fellow at the Institute of Economic and Social Research (INESOR) and taught African politics and government in the Department of Political and Administrative Studies at the University of Zambia. He is currently the executive director of the Centre for Policy Dialogue (CPD), an independent, non-profit research organisation based in Lusaka, Zambia. He has published several monographs and articles in international journals and edited volumes on the politics of economic reform, democratisation, corruption, civil society and constitution-making.

Philip C. Stenning is a professor at the School of Criminology and Criminal Justice, and an associate investigator in the Centre of Excellence in Policing and Security, and in the Key Centre for Ethics, Law, Justice and Governance, at Griffith University, in Brisbane, Australia. Prior to this he was a professor in criminology at Keele University in the UK (2006–2010), professor and director of the Institute of Criminology at Victoria University of Wellington, New Zealand (2003–2005), and associate professor at the Centre of Criminology, University of Toronto, Canada (1968–2002). He obtained his doctorate in law at the University of Toronto in 1983. His principal research interests have included: public and private policing; the prosecution process; governance and accountability in the criminal justice system; firearms abuse and gun control; aboriginal justice and policing; use of force by and against police; occupational safety and homicide of police officers and taxi drivers. He is currently involved in research on gender-based violence against female university students in European universities; on the governance of Vancouver's Downtown East Side (one of North America's most notorious 'skid row' areas); and a comparative study of relations between prosecutors and governments in a number of common-law jurisdictions in North America, Europe, Africa and Australasia. He is assembling an international research team to undertake some ethnographic research on the role of transnational private security in the coming years. His most recent book is *The Modern Prosecution Process in New Zealand* (Victoria University Press, 2008).

Martin van Vliet studied cultural anthropology and development sociology at the University of Leiden where he specialised in African politics and research methodologies and wrote a thesis on Mali's decentralisation process. Between 2004–2010 he worked for the Netherlands Institute for Multi-Party Democracy (NIMD), an institute set up by Dutch political parties that supports political actors in young democracies. Besides the management of political party support programmes in Mali and Zambia, he contributed to the development of generic party support strategies and edited NIMD's handbook *Writing Autobiographies of Nations: A Comparative Analysis of Constitutional Reform Processes* (2009). In 2009, he received funding from the Dutch Ministry of Foreign Affairs to initiate a PhD research project at the African Studies Centre in Leiden. The study focuses on local accountability mechanisms in five African countries, the contribution of Malian Members of Parliament in shaping accountability, transformations in Mali's party system over the last decades and current legal reforms in Mali. In addition to his research activities, Van Vliet regularly conducts consultancies for the Dutch Ministry of Foreign Affairs, think tanks and non-governmental organisations and teaches from time to time at different institutions.

Chapter 1

Accountable government in Africa: Introduction

Danwood M. Chirwa and Lia Nijzink

1. Overview

This book addresses a key issue that confronts emerging democracies in Africa: how to make governments accountable. Combining insights from public law and political studies, the specific focus of this edited volume is on various institutions and mechanisms of accountability, their effectiveness in holding governments to account and how these institutions themselves are being held accountable. The judiciary, national prosecuting authorities, human rights commissions, political parties and informal mechanisms are critically assessed in terms of their contribution to 'accountable government'. The book also discusses different sources of accountability that are specifically relevant in the context of Africa's young democracies.

The contributions to this volume fall into two categories: chapters discussing legal and political developments in a particular country and chapters that take a comparative perspective. All chapters benefit from the extensive experience of the authors in the areas and countries of their research interest. Collectively, these chapters present research findings from 10 African countries that are directly relevant to the broader policy goal of developing and deepening democracy and accountable government on the African continent.

The 16 chapters in this book are presented in a way that emphasises the notion of government accountability as a concentric circle. The book starts with a critique of the notion of accountability itself, questioning whether formal mechanisms of accountability are sufficient to ensure accountable government. It then looks at the Constitution as a source of accountability and draws our attention to the importance of the constitution-making process. Why do some processes of constitutional reform fail to produce a Constitution that embodies sufficient values and adequate mechanisms of accountability while others succeed?

The book then moves to the core branches of the state and examines various aspects of the functioning of judicial and legislative bodies. What explains the effectiveness of African judiciaries in facilitating the accountability of governments? What is the role of the judiciary in setting and enforcing norms of accountability in relation to electoral processes? What is the role of judicial review of legislative action in a constitutional democracy?

The circle subsequently expands to include specialised bodies such as national prosecutorial authorities and national human rights institutions. Here, questions arise as to who should determine whether it is in the public interest to prosecute and how those entrusted with such decisions should be held accountable. What conditions are necessary for national human rights institutions to perform their watchdog functions effectively and how have such institutions worked in practice?

The next circle investigates the role of political parties. Does the practice of floor crossing enhance or undermine the accountability of Members of Parliament (MPs)? Why are some political parties more effective than others in holding the executive to account? Is there a relationship between intra-party democracy and the ability of political parties to serve as sources of accountability?

Finally, in the outer circle, informal mechanisms and interventions of international agencies to promote accountability are discussed. What is the interplay between formal and informal mechanisms of accountability, and between domestic and external forms of accountability? How do culture, traditions, customs and local institutions facilitate or impede formal procedures, norms and institutions of accountability? Do external forms of accountability reinforce or undermine internal forms of accountability?

2.   Scope and significance

Africa is arguably a continent where the problem of 'accountable government' remains most stark. The decolonisation process of the 1960s promised an era of self-rule and independence in which the new governments would be both responsive to the needs of the people and accountable to them (see, eg, Jennings 1963). Yet the regimes that decolonisation gave birth to did not meet that promise. One-party and military dictatorships mushroomed throughout the continent (see, eg, Southall 2003). Governments not only retreated from the relatively modest accountability structures that were established by the Constitutions adopted at independence but also undermined the few accountability structures they had decided to retain (see, eg, Okoth-Ogendo 1991). The democratic wave of the 1990s resuscitated the public's yearning for greater accountability and resulted in better constitutions.

However, making governments in African states accountable remains a huge challenge. The reasons for this challenge are legion and complex. Some are historical and revolve around external factors such as the colonial legacy (Owusu 1992), the Cold War (Marte 1994; Laidi 1990) and neoliberal economic policies (see, eg, Mhone 2003). Others relate to internal factors such as civil wars, military dictatorships, ethnic-based politics, corruption, the lack of a vibrant civil society and poverty (see, eg, Shivji 1991; Davidson & Munslow 1990; Adelman 1998). It is not the aim of this book to investigate why 'accountable government' remains stubbornly elusive in African countries. Rather, this book seeks to contribute to an understanding of the dynamics of this problem.

Owing in part to the fact that 'accountability' cuts across many disciplines and subjects within each discipline, the concept of accountable government in Africa tends to be dealt with in piecemeal fashion, often in the context of country or sub-regional studies that focus on select themes. In constitutional law, for example, the issue of 'accountable government' is often considered indirectly within debates about constitutionalism, the separation of powers, judicial independence, human rights, etc (see, eg, Oloka-Onyango 2001; Fombad & Murray 2010; Hatchard et al 2004). In political studies, accountable government features in discussions about political parties and electoral systems, legislative bodies, civil society, etc (see, eg, McNeil & Mumvuma 2006; Nijzink et al 2006; Salih & Nordlund 2007). Other disciplines, such as economics, anthropology and public administration, have also dealt with aspects of accountable governance in African countries, albeit often in isolation from other disciplines.

This book is unique in that it treats the notion of accountable government as a cross-cutting and multi-disciplinary theme. Drawing on the two main fields — public law and political studies — that are by their very nature particularly interested in 'accountable government', it has accountability as its main subject of inquiry. The specific focus of this book is on the nature and workings of various institutions of accountability and the role they play, or ought to play, in holding governments to account. It examines the ways in which institutions — such as the judiciary, national human rights institutions (NHRIs) and national prosecutorial authorities — foster horizontal accountability between different organs of state, while also analysing institutions, such as political parties, which promote vertical accountability of the government to its people. Furthermore, the book examines how governments are held accountable to external or international actors and the ramifications this has for domestic accountability in African countries. While most of the chapters discuss formally established institutions of accountability, some explore the role of informal mechanisms, such as family groups, town chiefs, and local norms and standards, and the interplay between these and formal mechanisms. Finally, this book discusses different sources of accountability that are specifically relevant in the context of Africa's young democracies: Constitutions and constitutionalism, cultural norms and practices, and international accountability assistance. Because of its multi-disciplinary approach and its understanding of government accountability as a concentric circle, this book deals with the notion of accountable government more comprehensively than others do. Although it does not deal exhaustively with all the institutions and sources of accountability, we hope that the book will improve our understanding of accountable government in Africa.

It is axiomatic that an accountable government is inherently good. We need governments to account for the manner in which they allocate and spend public funds, make public policy and take decisions, which affect the people in whose name they govern. Accountability is needed to ensure fairness, equality and equity in public decision-making (Behn 2001). Without accountability, governments cannot respond effectively to the needs of the people or set national agendas that are relevant and address current and important problems. We also need an accountable government to avoid abuses of power and corruption (Olowu 1994), and to break the networks of neopatrimonialism and nepotism, which remain pervasive in African politics. An accountable government is better able to fulfil its constitutional mandate, provide public services, and implement public policies, priorities and legislation in a fair, responsive and efficient manner (Chawatama 2009).

While this book addresses issues of accountability that arise throughout Africa, it does not specifically cover all the countries on the continent. Country-specific chapters focus on Ghana, Malawi, Mali, South Africa, Tanzania, Uganda and Zambia, while comparative chapters include further references to Mozambique, Kenya and Swaziland. The choice of the country studies or mechanisms of accountability is a result of the interests and expertise of the various chapter authors and was largely influenced by the composition of the academic partnership under which this book was conceived: the 2007–2010 South–North partnership between the University of Cape Town, the University of Dar es Salaam and the University of Warwick, generously funded by the Development Partnerships in Higher Education (DelPHE Programme) of the British Council and the UK Department for International Development. The aim of this partnership was to build on existing expertise at the partner institutions to accumulate comparative knowledge that would contribute to deepening democratic governance and accountable government on the African continent. Most of the authors of the chapters in this book are members of the three partner institutions, although efforts were made, within the limits of the funding that was available, to include authors from a greater number of African countries. In July 2009, the partnership organised a conference about 'Sources of

Accountability on the African Continent' at the University of Cape Town, where a range of papers was presented. Selected papers are published in this book.

3. Defining 'accountable government'

What is an 'accountable government'? Despite the ubiquity of the word 'accountability' in common parlance and political rhetoric, its actual meaning is not straightforward. The meaning of 'accountability' depends on time, context, cultural orientation or ideological persuasion. 'Accountability' is also a contested term because of disagreements about the standards that should be used for holding actors accountable and because of the wide range of players and actors to which the term is applied.

However, all the chapters in this book proceed from the premise that 'accountability', in the context of the exercise of public powers, entails at least three major elements. First, it denotes the responsibility of the power holder to answer for the exercise of his or her powers — *answerability.* This, in turn, means two interrelated things: that the power holder must explain how his or her powers were exercised and justify the manner in which they were exercised; and that the power holder must be transparent in the way that he or she exercises his or her powers (see, eg, Burnell 2008; Hyden 2010).

Second, accountability requires public authorities to act in a manner that responds adequately to the needs and expectations of the public — *responsiveness* (Hyden 2010). It does not require or justify a paternalistic interpretation of the needs of the public and a top-down imposition of solutions, as was the case during the dictatorial era in Africa. Rather, responsiveness requires that people participate in public decision-making so that they can express their views and contribute to the design, development and implementation of public policies and laws and to the determination of disputes.

Third, accountability also entails the imposition of some form of sanction if the power holder fails to answer for the exercise of his or her powers or if he or she is unresponsive in the manner described above — *enforceability* (Burnell 2008). Examples of the sanctions that are commonly used to enforce accountability include dismissal, criminal prosecution, civil remedies in courts of law, disqualification from public office, electoral censure through the ballot and public opprobrium.

'Government' can be defined as the body that is vested with the authority to exercise public powers within a state. It includes all organs of government — the executive, legislature and judiciary, and all other institutions, bodies and agencies that exercise public powers. An 'accountable government' is therefore a government whose organs, institutions and agencies are open, transparent and responsive, explain or justify their acts and omissions, and enforce standards of accountability when maladministration, an error of judgement, abuse of power or injustice occurs.

Government accountability in the African context occurs at two broad levels: domestic and external. *Domestic* government accountability is, in turn, of two types: vertical and horizontal. *Vertical accountability* occurs when the government or its organs, institutions and agencies are called upon to explain and justify their decisions to the public. This is typically done through elections, whereby citizens elect their representatives to Parliament in periodic elections — *electoral accountability*; through public decision-making, public participation, public protests, and actions of the media and civil society that expose government wrongdoing — *societal accountability* (Hyden 2010; Smulovitz & Peruzzotti 2000); and at the individual level, whereby public authorities give reasons for decisions that affect specific individuals or groups — *individual or group accountability*. *Horizontal accountability* occurs at the intra-governmental level, when one organ, institution or agency of government holds another to account. For instance, the executive and legislature are subject to judicial control for the exercise of their constitutional and statutory powers, while the legislature provides a check on the executive. Institutions such as the Ombudsperson, Auditor-General and NHRIs serve as important horizontal accountability mechanisms. In practice, the distinction between horizontal and vertical accountability is not clear, because, as the chapters in this book will demonstrate, all institutions that seek to foster government accountability are themselves also required to be accountable to the public for the manner in which they perform their watchdog functions and, indeed, some provide a mechanism by which the government is held directly accountable to the public.

Like domestic accountability, *external accountability* takes different forms. The first is inter-governmental accountability, which happens through international, regional and sub-regional bodies created by states, such as the United Nations, the African Union and the Southern African Development Community. Accountability at such inter-governmental forums occurs within a framework of the norms and procedures specifically agreed to by the states concerned. The more controversial type of external accountability is accountability to international donors. This form of accountability is tied to donor assistance received by African governments from donor countries or international financial institutions, such as the World Bank and the International Monetary Fund. It is a controversial form of accountability, because it occurs on a level unregulated by either international or domestic law and because it has a tendency to undermine or sidestep domestic accountability mechanisms. The nature and implications of this form of accountability are considered in detail in chapter 16.

4. The chapters in this book

The idea of an 'accountable government' is certainly not uncontested (see, eg, Haque 2000). Indeed, this book begins with a critique of contemporary notions of accountability. Andrew Nash (chapter 2) powerfully argues that our current understanding of accountability reflects a neoliberal way of thinking, which reduces accountability to a set of formal processes enforced by professionals such as lawyers and politicians on behalf of ordinary people. As a result, accountability is limited and elitist in character, deepens the chasm between the holders of public power and ordinary people and erodes ethical community. Tracing the transformation of the concept and practice of accountability in South Africa since the 1970s, Nash emphasises the importance of shared ethical values and citizens' active participation in public decision-making.

Neo Simutanyi (chapter 3) echoes this conclusion and underscores the significance of meaningful and active public participation in constitution-making. Constitutions are important sources of government accountability because they are the supreme source of legal authority for the exercise of public powers. A Constitution that vests unlimited powers in public authorities cannot yield an accountable government. Not only do Constitutions define the powers of all organs, institutions and agents of government, they also prescribe the relationship, including checks and balances, between state organs *inter se* (horizontal relationships) and between state organs and citizens (vertical relationships). Simutanyi draws our attention to the importance of the constitution-making process. Tracing Zambia's constitutional history from independence to date, he demonstrates that constitution-making and reform have largely been dominated by the ruling elite and have ignored the views of the public. Simutanyi attributes some of the key accountability deficits that exist in Zambia to its troubled history of constitution-making.

The next three chapters examine the role of an important mechanism of horizontal accountability — the judiciary. Siri Gloppen and Fidelis Kanyongolo (chapter 4) analyse the role that the judiciary in Malawi and Uganda has played in ensuring free and fair elections. Discussing various theories to explain the assertive role of the courts in both countries, they argue for a multi-factor explanation which takes into account the historical and socio-political context, the institutional architecture of judicial independence, and differences in the individual characteristics of judges. Jwani Mwaikusa (chapter 5), looking at the relations between Parliament and the judiciary in Tanzania, examines the role that judicial review has played in holding the legislature to account. According to Mwaikusa, the doctrine of parliamentary supremacy has in the past been used as a smokescreen for abuses of the legislative authority of Parliament.

However, since its adoption in 1984, the notion of constitutional supremacy has enhanced the accountability of the Tanzanian legislature, although it has at times heightened tensions between the legislature and the judiciary. Hugh Corder (chapter 6) follows with a similar analysis of the role of judicial review in South Africa. He demonstrates that the concept of constitutional supremacy has been used by the Constitutional Court in South Africa to hold the government to account for the manner in which it enacts legislation. Significantly, not only has legislation itself been subjected to judicial scrutiny but so too has the procedure of enacting it. South African courts have underscored the need for Parliament to ensure adequate and meaningful public participation in law-making. In a sense, therefore, this chapter echoes Nash's point that formal mechanisms of horizontal accountability should not preclude or undercut direct, participatory mechanisms of accountability.

As noted earlier, there cannot be accountability if the power holders are not liable to some form of sanction in the event of a failure to account for the exercise of their powers. Criminal prosecution serves as an important and ultimate form of sanction. Abuse of state resources can lead to charges for theft, fraud, financial mismanagement and other crimes. Failing to perform a public duty and accepting bribes while exercising public powers also constitute corruption. Through criminal prosecution, abuse of public resources and corruption can be stopped. At the same time, prosecutorial authority is an important public power that is prone to abuse by prosecutors and political leaders. In Africa, examples of the political abuse of prosecutorial powers are legion (see, eg chapter 4). It is therefore important that the prosecutorial authority is independent, effective, fair and efficient.

Philip Stenning (chapter 7) reviews the controversy surrounding prosecutorial decisions in cases of high-profile defendants in a number of countries. His chapter discusses the important questions of who determines whether it is in the public interest to prosecute such defendants and who should have the ultimate authority to determine what the public interest requires in such cases. Is it the independent prosecutors, politicians or the court, or a combination of all, or some, of these? How can we ensure that prosecutorial discretion in such cases is protected from unwanted partisan influence and that prosecutorial authorities are themselves held to account? In chapter 8, Sifuni Mchome examines recent developments in Tanzania concerning the establishment of a modern prosecutorial system. Underscoring the importance of separating the prosecution from the investigation, he draws attention to the practical steps that need to be taken to ensure a truly independent, fair and efficient civilian prosecution system in Tanzania. Although Mchome welcomes the new system, he flags some vital concerns about the independence of the office of the Director of Public Prosecutions in Tanzania.

The next two chapters deal with a relatively new mechanism of accountability, that of NHRIs. NHRIs have become an important mechanism for closing the gap between public authorities and ordinary citizens. Not only are they more accessible to the public than the courts, the procedures of NHRIs are informal, flexible and short, hence better able than judicial remedies to respond to individual and systemic human rights violations proactively and retrospectively. Since they operate as a horizontal mechanism of accountability, NHRIs are well placed to work closely with state organs to address human rights concerns and other accountability problems.

Danwood Chirwa and Redson Kapindu (chapter 9) examine the factors that guarantee an independent and effective NHRI. After an analysis of the experience of the Malawi Human Rights Commission, they propose some ways in which NHRIs can maximise their accountability function and complement other institutions of accountability, such as the judiciary. In a similar vein, Pierre de Vos (chapter 10) discusses the so-called Chapter 9 institutions of South Africa and grapples with two key questions: whether NHRIs can be truly effective in promoting human rights and holding the legislature and executive to account without being guaranteed the institutional independence the judiciary enjoys; and, if not, what kind of independence could guarantee that these institutions perform their accountability function effectively? Drawing on the report of the South African Parliament's Ad Hoc Committee on the Review of Chapter 9 and Associated Institutions, De Vos recommends a robust yet limited model of independence for these institutions.

Chapters 11 to 13 shift to an examination of the role of political parties in fostering government accountability in Africa. Lia Nijzink (chapter 11) considers the implications of the practice of floor crossing for the accountability of political representatives to their political parties and the electorate. Comparing the legal framework and experience of floor crossing in Malawi and South Africa, she argues that floor crossing is inimical to the vertical accountability of elected representatives in both first-past-the-post and proportional representation electoral systems. Augustine Magolowondo (chapter 12) and Nandini Patel (chapter 13) underscore the significance of intra-party democracy as a building block of government accountability. While Patel examines the dynamics of the problem of intra-party democracy in Malawi, Magolowondo investigates the extent to which formal mechanisms, such as party constitutions and party rules governing membership, funding, election of leaders, discipline and other party affairs, enhance intra-party democracy in East and Southern Africa.

Any study on government accountability in Africa would be incomplete without examining the role that informal mechanisms or factors play. Two chapters in this book address the importance of informal norms and local understandings of accountability. Looking at the impact of Mali's decentralisation programme on local communities, Martin van Vliet (chapter 14) explores the interplay between formal and informal incentives for holding local authorities accountable. He demonstrates that, although local elections create opportunities for vertical accountability, culturally shaped informal relations determine local citizens' ability to hold their representatives accountable. Diana Cammack (chapter 15) also emphasises the importance of culturally shaped local forms of accountability. She presents findings from fieldwork about MPs in Ghana and town chiefs in Malawi that demonstrate the existence of a multitude of sources and overlapping forms of accountability, including those rooted in informal, unwritten but shared understandings of culture and tradition. This chapter also suggests that, while factors such as poor information flows, large power differentials and clientelism hinder accountable government in Africa, some hybrid forms of local leadership have the potential to forge a degree of accountability that is comparable to that generated by formal institutions of accountability.

The final chapter by Peter Burnell looks at the external accountability enforced by donor countries, which ironically also aim to strengthen domestic mechanisms of accountability. This chapter investigates the tensions, paradoxes and ambiguities raised by accountability assistance, as conceived and implemented by donor countries. Burnell emphasises the need for international development organisations and African governments to develop relations that advance democratic accountability within African countries, instead of bolstering relations of external accountability or domestic arrangements that do not advance democracy.

These chapters provide valuable insights into the nature of the problem of 'accountable government' in Africa, describe the extent to which various formal and informal mechanisms of accountability work in practice, and identify ways in which African governments can be made more accountable. We hope that this book will be useful to scholars and students in public law and political studies, politicians, civil society, international organisations and other actors interested in democracy and the rule of law in Africa.

References

Adelman, S. 1998. Constitutionalism, pluralism and democracy in Africa. *Journal of Legal Pluralism*, 42: 73–88.

Behn, R.D. 2001. *Rethinking Democratic Accountability*. Washington DC: Brookings Institution Press.

Burnell, P. 2008. The relationship of accountable governance and constitutional implementation. *Journal of Politics and Law*, 1(3): 10–24.

Chawatama, R. 2009. Political accountability. Southern African Catholic Bishops' Conference, Briefing Paper 211. July. Available at http://us-cdn.creamermedia. co.za/assets/articles/attachments/22301_sacbcpolitical_accountability.pdf. Accessed 30 November 2010.

Davidson, B. & Munslow, B. 1990. The crisis of the nation-state in Africa. *Review of African Political Economy*, 49: 9–21.

Fombad, C. & Murray, C. (eds). 2010. *Fostering Constitutionalism in Africa*. Pretoria: Pretoria University Law Press.

Haque, M.S. 2000. Significance of accountability under the new approach to public governance. *International Review of Administrative Sciences*, 66: 599–617.

Hatchard, J., Slinn, P. & Ndulo, M. 2004. *Comparative Constitutionalism and Good Governance in the Commonwealth: An Eastern and Southern African Perspective*. Cambridge: Cambridge University Press.

Hyden, G. 2010. *Political Accountability in Africa: Is the Glass Half-full or Half-empty?* Africa Power and Politics Working Paper No 6. Available at http://www.institutions-africa.org/filestream/20100118-appp-working-paper-6-political-accountability-in-africa-is-the-glass-half-ful-or-half-empty-by-goran-hyden-january-2010. Accessed 16 August 2011.

Jennings, I. 1963. *Democracy in Africa*. Cambridge: Cambridge University Press.

Laidi, Z. 1990. *The Superpowers and Africa: The Constraints of a Rivalry — 1960–1990*. Chicago: Chicago University Press.

Marte, F. 1994. *Political Cycles in International Context: The Cold War and Africa — 1945–1990*. Amsterdam: VU University Press.

McNeil, M. & Mumvuma, T. 2006. *Demanding Good Governance. A Stocktaking of Social Accountability Initiatives by Civil Society in Anglophone Africa*. Washington, DC: World Bank Institute.

Mhone, G.C.Z. 2003. Developmentalism and the role of the state. Paper originally presented for the workshop on Growth and Development for the Premier's Policy Development Unit of the KwaZulu-Natal Provincial Government in February 2003. Available at http://www.sarpn.org.za/documents/d0000437/P378_Mhone.pdf. Accessed 4 July 2011.

Nijzink, L., Mozaffar, S. & Azevedo, E. 2006. Parliaments and the enhancement of democracy on the African continent: An analysis of institutional capacity and public perceptions. *The Journal of Legislative Studies*, 12(3–4): 311–335.

Okoth-Ogendo, H.W.O. 1991. Constitutions without constitutionalism: Reflections on an African political paradox. In Shivji, I.G. (ed.). *State and Constitutionalism: An African Debate on Democracy*. Harare: Southern African Economy Series Trust.

Oloka-Onyango, J. 2001. *Constitutionalism in Africa: Creating Opportunities, Facing Challenges*. Kampala: Fountain Publishers.

Olowu, D. 1994. Organizational and institutional mechanisms for ensuring accountability in Africa: A review. *Commonwealth Law Bulletin*, 20: 329–339.

Owusu, M. 1992. Democracy & Africa: A view from the village. *Journal of Modern African Studies*, 30(3): 369–396.

Salih, M.A. & Nordlund, P. 2007. *Political Parties in Africa: Challenges for Sustained Multiparty Democracy*. International Institute for Democracy and Electoral Assistance. Available at http://www.idea.int/publications/pp_africa/upload/Africa_report_inlay_final.pdf. Accessed 4 July 2011.

Shivji, I.G. 1991. State and constitutionalism: A new democratic perspective. In Shivji, I.G. (ed). *State and Constitutionalism: An African Debate on Democracy*. Harare: Southern African Economy Series Trust.

Smulovitz, C. & Peruzzotti, E. 2000. Societal accountability in Latin America. *Journal of Democracy*, 11(4): 147–158.

Southall, R. 2003. *Democracy in Africa: Moving Beyond a Difficult Legacy*. Cape Town: Human Sciences Research Council.

Chapter 2

Post-apartheid accountability: The transformation of a political idea

Andrew Nash

1. Introduction

Practices of accountability, however sporadic or unsystematic, have existed in some form or other in almost every political system since the ancient Greek *polis*. The vast majority of those accounting for their use of power and resources over the centuries and around the globe have been providing their account to those in positions of greater power. That is likely still the case today. But there has also been a long history of those in power being accountable to those they govern.

That history begins in earnest in the ancient Greek democracies, where elected officials were required to report regularly to the *demos*. They were subject to severe and immediate penalties, including removal from office and banishment from the state, if their fellow-citizens were not satisfied with what they had done with the powers entrusted to them (Roberts 1982). Even rulers wielding absolute power found, at specific moments, that they needed to win the support of crucial allies or subordinates and would account for themselves for this purpose, however reluctantly. The obligations of accountability were often fixed by custom, which could vary from one generation to the next. Since the *Magna Carta* of 1215, there have been formal, quasi-contractual frameworks within which accountability can be required or contested. Parliamentary government has sometimes provided a forum and procedures for doing so. For most of its history, accountability has been unequal, and explicitly limited to accountability within the ruling elite.

A major turning point in the history of accountability was the establishment of capitalist democracies, beginning with the adoption of the United States Constitution in 1787, which acknowledged the political rights not just of nobles, but of the whole body of citizens. As in ancient Greece, this citizen body excluded women and slaves. Unlike in ancient Greece, however, it protected elected officials from the direct supervision of the *demos*. This laid the foundations for our own contemporary mediated forms of accountability, in which those in power are held accountable, but not too accountable, mainly through the intervention of administrative and judicial structures that the powerful themselves have put in place.

We tend to lose sight of this long history today, when accountability presents itself as one more contemporary buzzword, which seems to provide precision and even progress in the broad area of intersection between politics and ethics, sometimes overseen by law. In the last few decades, we have seen a rapid proliferation of codes of conduct, performance indicators, reviews and contracts, ethics committees, bodies of oversight, public protectors, special courts, investigative and monitoring bodies, agencies to rate transparency, corruption and red tape, rules to protect whistle-blowers, institutes of accountability, academic conferences, research projects and the like — all of them making up a vast and growing accountability industry, a thriving subsidiary of the ethics industry, which grows along with the ethical problems it regulates.

It is all too easy for us to think that this is what accountability means, and all that existed beforehand was no more than a primitive and unconscious groping in this direction. This chapter is intended to warn against such historical short-sightedness, by reflecting on the changing meaning of accountability in South Africa from the 1970s to the present.

Today, formal processes of accountability, while claiming to provide equal power to all citizens, are mostly controlled by political and economic elites. Contemporary accountability is a peculiar balancing act, suspended between the contradictory poles of elite accommodation and popular rule. Its place between them varies from one context to the next. But in general, and perhaps unavoidably, it tends to give the impression of responding to popular needs as if indifferent to status, while in reality deferring to the needs of the elite or some part of the elite.

Although South Africa's accountability industry has some of its own quite specific features, it also grows out of a longer history and fits in with existing global trends. Viewed in historical context, it can be seen as a specific neo-liberal form of accountability. Its structures of accountability align with the idea that all value is measured by the capitalist market, making phenomena such as representation and public service anomalous and in need of oversight. Formulated in this way, our contemporary model of accountability presents itself as a cure for all manner of public ethical disease, while structuring itself in such a way as to turn a blind eye to the contemporary causes of the disease.

14

2. Accountability in the independent labour movement after 1973

Accountability became a central term in South African politics with the rise of the independent trade union movement after the Durban strikes of 1973. At the time it was illegal for African workers to strike. The law provided for works committees, which were commonly known as 'tea and toilet committees', as they dealt with minor grievances of that kind and passed on management instructions to workers. When workers walked off the job in January 1973, management found they had no-one to negotiate with. The general manager of Coronation Brick and Tile, where the strike wave began, complained that he was being forced to negotiate 'with 1 500 workers on a football field' (Friedman 1987: 37–38, 55, 62–63). Workers simply refused to elect spokesmen. Management and the police had threatened to punish the 'ringleaders' and workers stuck together rather than putting forward individual leaders for victimisation.

This sense of everyone being equally involved in a collective struggle characterised the labour movement that emerged after the 1973 strikes — first in the form of advice bureaus, benefit funds, training projects and the like, then gradually as unions, and in 1979 as the Federation of South African Trade Unions (FOSATU), which merged with other union structures to become the Congress of South African Trade Unions (COSATU) in 1985. From the outset, this movement 'deliberately sought structures which would ensure that workers took part in decisions' (Friedman 1987: 60). Unions recruited new members gradually and at times even reluctantly, warning that members should not have unrealistic expectations of their union. The movement itself depended on constant debate and argument over its own goals and character. It sought to protect its identity as a worker organisation against the encroachments of nationalist and populist politics, staying out of the United Democratic Front (UDF) and criticising alliances with the African National Congress (ANC) and the South African Communist Party (SACP) (Foster 1982; Erwin 1985).

Unions developed and nurtured this distinctive class identity by focusing on shop-floor organisation and ensuring that its members were constantly involved with issues close to their daily lives, rather than being drawn into policy issues which did not impact on them as workers. Meetings were conducted in African languages rather than in English, and translations were provided when language was a barrier. Union leaders took care not to impose their views on the meeting, often refusing to give their own views so that members could decide on the mandate they would give to their leaders. When important issues had to be decided, debate went on until everyone was satisfied, often all through the night. By the mid-1980s, one unionist estimated that about 150 union meetings were taking place throughout the country on most week nights (Friedman 1987: 497, 504).

Accountability was the foundation on which that union movement was built. It was also, in a sense, the burden which weighed it down, preventing it from realising its vision of a liberated South Africa in which all could speak as equals; but that is another story. Union leaders were constantly made accountable to union members and union members to each other, and unions sought to engage with allies on a similar basis. Accountability was also at the heart of the vision of the society they sought to bring into being, in which 'the free development of each was the condition for the free development of all' (Marx & Engels 1968: 53; in the South African context, see Turner 1978).

Accountability usually took the form of reporting back to a meeting of members. But this report was always located within a three-part structure. Accountability began with a mandate, which provided the basis on which leaders could act on behalf of workers. And it was followed by confirmation or recall of that mandate and creation of a new mandate through discussion of the report. This structure provided an organisational and indeed a philosophical framework for accountability, neither populist nor bureaucratic, but deeply democratic. It provided an ethic which informed the relationships and daily actions of huge numbers of people within the labour movement.

This philosophical framework found its way into the community struggles of the 1980s as well, perhaps most conspicuously in the Cradock Residents Association under Matthew Goniwe, although also in civic associations in other parts of the country. A complex and intricate network of accountability enabled townships in Cradock, Port Elizabeth, Alexandra and elsewhere to withstand the onslaught of state repression:

> Each township is broken down into areas, and the areas into streets. In each street one or two people take responsibility for calling house meetings to discuss issues and problems. The street rep sits on an area committee, which co-ordinates people's actions against whatever common problems there are. There is also an elected executive committee of that area committee. The street committee structures have particular advantages for organising in the current climate. ... They can withstand the most repression. Street reps can be low profile and will be protected by the people in the street. If a street rep is detained, the people can appoint a new rep. In other words, since the community organisation is run at a mass level — rather than being an 'executive organisation' — there will always be people to take over leadership responsibilities. And street committees provide a structure for training (Seekings 2000: 143–44).

In this context, accountability was not just an organisational strategy. It served also to promote shared ethical values. In townships such as Lingelihle in Cradock, during the period of ungovernability and boycott, there was a marked decrease in crime, drunkenness, teenage pregnancy and anti-social behaviour more generally. Members of the community felt responsible for each other. After the murder of Goniwe and his comrades in 1985 and the smashing of community structures, things returned to normal.

Although the idea of accountability was not current at the time, something similar happened in the context of the community projects initiated by the Black Consciousness Movement in the 1970s. When communities in Ginsberg and elsewhere built their own clinics and cultural centres, it was not necessary to impose a set of rules on doctors and teachers, who put their energy into institutions they thought of as their own.

In the crucible of the mid-1980s, however, this philosophy of mandate, reporting back and confirmation or recall could not take root in townships, villages and schools in the same way as they did in the labour movement. Township residents were not protected from repression by their vital role in the economy, as workers were. Foreign investors and bankers had a greater interest in labour peace than in how order was kept in the townships. But the most important difference, from the point of view of understanding the changing fortunes of accountability in South Africa, was that townships and schools lacked the sense of a common class identity, and a common vision of liberation, shared by organised workers. Thus, street committees could become conduits for instructions from above, sanctioned by the imperatives of national liberation and by calls for unity and discipline, rather than forums for genuine debate and democratic decision-making.

3. The emergence of the post-apartheid model of accountability

Increasingly central to the agenda of the nightly union meetings in the mid-1980s was the question of the relationship of the labour movement with the mass uprisings in South African townships, country towns, rural reserves, schools and universities. Workers lived in the townships, their children went to the schools, and the unions could not stand aside from these struggles. As unions were drawn into the insurrectionary currents of the time, so the structure of union accountability was eroded. After the unbanning of the ANC and other organisations and their return from exile, COSATU entered into a formal alliance with the ANC and SACP.

Mandela's decision to begin negotiations with the apartheid government in 1986 was, at the time, a major departure from the ethic of accountability. Mandela himself was at pains to make clear to his comrades that he was not negotiating on behalf of the liberation movement. In his autobiography, he explained his decision as an extraordinary exception to the rule of collective decision-making:

> The ANC is a collective, but the government had made collectivity in this case impossible. ... I knew that my colleagues upstairs [ANC leaders in Pollsmoor prison]

would condemn my proposal, and that would kill my initiative even before it was born. There are times when a leader must move out ahead of the flock, go off in a new direction, confident that he is leading his people the right way (Mandela 1994: 514).

Mandela's unquestionable record of self-sacrifice gave him the credibility to weather the storm when word of his initiative reached activists in the mass movement (O'Malley 2008). Since then, many others have followed his example of deciding for himself, but without any such record to justify them.

In retrospect, the Reconstruction and Development Plan (RDP) was the last gasp of the philosophy of mandate and reporting back that carried the labour movement through 20 years of struggle for a new society and made itself an indispensable part of the mass struggles of the 1980s. The RDP became the programme on which the ANC stood for election in April 1994. And it was on the basis of the RDP that COSATU threw its weight behind the ANC. The RDP was viewed as a mandate given to the ANC, on the basis of which the ANC would be held accountable. Given the history of betrayal of newly independent African states, COSATU argued, it would be mistaken for workers to support the ANC without such a mandate. The general secretary of COSATU, Jay Naidoo, was appointed to cabinet as the minister responsible for the RDP.

However, the RDP mandate was exercised in a new context of accountability, in which there was little or no active and ongoing participation by the electorate, and no real prospect of their recalling their leaders or changing their mandate. In 1996, just two years later, Naidoo was removed from his cabinet portfolio, the RDP was abandoned, and the neoliberal Growth Employment and Redistribution plan (GEAR) became government policy. Naidoo himself later moved into business, as did many other former union leaders.

Strangely, just at the time that the specific ethic of accountability discussed above was dealt its death blow, the idea of accountability was being celebrated as never before. The new Constitution adopted in 1996, the year that the RDP mandate was unceremoniously abandoned, announced in its first clause that the South African state was founded on four central values, including those of 'universal adult suffrage, a national common voters roll, regular elections and a multi-party system of democratic government, to ensure accountability, responsiveness and openness'[1]. It also established as a founding value the supremacy of the Constitution and the rule of law, confirmed the independence of the judiciary and established a host of bodies tasked with different forms of political and ethical oversight and accountability, the Chapter nine institutions,

---

1   Constitution of the Republic of South Africa, 1996, section 1.

including the Public Protector, the Human Rights Commission, the Commission for the Promotion and Protection of the Rights of Cultural, Religious and Linguistic Communities, the Commission for Gender Equality, the Independent Electoral Commission and the Independent Communications Authority of South Africa to regulate broadcasting.

Other such institutions followed. The Moral Regeneration Movement was a government-sponsored venture, briefly chaired by Jacob Zuma when he was Thabo Mbeki's Deputy President. It was recently revived and ran an advertising campaign, encouraging radio listeners to SMS the word 'good' to a certain number, with the aim of making them morally better. Non-governmental organisations have been established to monitor public service accountability and to report on government transparency. Universities have established units of applied ethics, taking on similar tasks at a higher level of abstraction.

In all of this, the main focus was on government, not on business, even though much of the focus of the new accountability is on corruption in which business is almost certainly involved. There has been no real challenge to the idea that business corporations are primarily accountable to their shareholders and their obligation to them is to make a profit. There were numerous laws governing the conduct of business and more have been added. But these post-apartheid laws are generally seen as part of transformation, an area of democratisation, if it is that, which depends on the inclusion of black capitalists, managers and professionals, and not on the inclusion of the majority.

Codes of corporate governance have been promoted at the same time as allegations of corporate price-fixing have increased. The first King report on corporate governance appeared in 1994, perhaps as an attempt at corporate self-regulation ahead of the advent of non-racial democratic government in South Africa. It provides model codes of conduct that would be hard to adjudicate. There has been more reporting on the publication of these codes than on possible violations of them. The architect of this corporate governance regime, Mervyn King, has recently been on record as opposing criminal charges against corporate executives guilty of cartel activities, as this would result in 'fit and proper' people not taking corporate appointments: 'Business is about risk and if people are punished when they get it wrong, then few people would take appointments because they could be prosecuted if they made wrong business judgment calls' (Jacks 2009). The acceptance not only of corporate self-interest, but of the right of corporations to evade criminal liability, is the other side of the coin of the post-apartheid model of accountability.

In a certain sense, the triumph of the rhetoric of accountability over its actual practice is represented by the Zuma government's project of signing performance contracts with cabinet ministers. These contracts will apparently include performance indicators against which ministers can be assessed in order to ensure service delivery. The performance contracts have not yet been drawn up, and there are likely to be many delays while legal teams negotiate their terms. The thinking is that performance contracts will ensure that sufficient houses, schools and clinics are built, electricity, water and sanitation provided, medicines dispensed to the sick, books delivered to schools, etc. The result of this strategy when applied to policing in South Africa was that police stations refused to record crime or falsified recorded crime statistics in order to meet their targets for crime reduction. Now not only police officers will face performance reviews, but their minister as well. And if the minister fails, will the next step be for the president to sign a performance contract?

4.   Two models of accountability compared

The two models of accountability can be contrasted with each other, in a somewhat schematic way. The model developed within the labour movement of the 1970s and 80s saw accountability not just as an organisational strategy but as a virtue, to be exercised and developed in relationship with others in the context of a shared struggle for justice. It was a virtue that required a commitment to democracy and equality for its exercise. The conception of the good society informing it was often socialist. Accountability, in this model, reinforced the bonds between people, and strengthened their commitment to justice and equality. A rigorous practice of debating mandates and accounting publicly for how they are carried out produces a clearer and more articulate idea of justice shared by those involved in the process. It does not reduce members of the union or civic organisation to a homogenous mass, but enables them to articulate their own views in such a way as to contribute to collective goals.

The model of accountability which has developed under the auspices of the South African Constitution of 1996 treats accountability primarily as a set of rules exercised within a bureaucratic structure by professionals, mainly lawyers and politicians, on behalf of the mass of ordinary people. It is possible to engage with or appeal to those rules by making complaints or allegations, by making denials or excuses, by discovering procedural problems or legal loopholes. Structures of accountability often isolate individuals from those around them, as complainants or subjects of investigation. This model of accountability does not so much promote a neoliberal capitalism as take its premises for granted, treating society as an accumulation of acquisitive individuals, whose essential aims are furthered by evading the requirements of accountability. It is consistent with persistent and growing material inequality, often treats it as a given and does not seek to redress it.

The contrast between the two models of accountability might be illustrated by an example of the conduct of political leaders that has recently been in the news: the purchase of new motor cars by members of the provincial executive councils (MECs) and cabinet ministers. The first and perhaps only victim so far of the Zuma government's commitment to ending corruption and mismanagement, former Gauteng MEC for Agriculture Nomantu Nkomo-Ralehoko, was forced to resign for irregular procedure in acquiring her new luxury car (Isaacson 2009). Her colleagues in government, who have paid more attention to procedure, have been able to inflate the costs of their cars massively, as the rules allow them unlimited additional accessories. A report on Minister Siphiwe Nyanda's two new BMWs lists such items as a 'rear-seat entertainment system' (R23 400), an 'innovation package' including a rear-view camera and ambient interior lighting (R35 800) and a 'high-gloss satin chrome' paint job (Davies 2009).

In the participatory model of accountability that characterised the labour movement of the 1980s, one cannot imagine a leader asking for a mandate to pay for all of this from those who elected her or him. In that time, full-time unionists were paid very modest salaries, similar to those of union members. But in the new, procedural model of accountability, this does not matter. What matters is that 'in terms of the cabinet-approved ministerial handbook' the minister was entitled to the cars, and presumably nothing in the handbook set a limit to the extra fittings he could add (Davies 2009). In the first case, the leader must report back to a constituency; in the second, what is needed is a legal loophole.

In the first case, accountability does not depend on lawyers, bureaucrats or accountability experts, or even a handbook. It depends on active participation in political life, informed by a shared ethical standard. Even when the mandated initiative fails, the process of accountability strengthens the capacity of oppressed people to act collectively and consciously take responsibility for their actions. In the second case, it is the handbook and the legal opinion which matters. Whether Siphiwe Nyanda gets his car accessories or not, the report only adds to public cynicism and apathy.

It should be added that the contrast between these two models of accountability does not depend particularly on the moral or political character of the individuals involved. The labour movement surely had its share of rogues and opportunists, and it is equally certain that there are people in government whose intentions are entirely praiseworthy. Many leading figures in the union movement made a quite seamless transition from the one model of accountability to the other, although it is not easy to think of people who have moved in the opposite direction.

5. The limits of accountability in capitalist society

The democratic ethic of accountability which developed in the struggle years has effectively been displaced by a technocratic ethic, which sees democracy as a basis for legitimacy, rather than a living practice based on a shared vision of the good society. But this more limited model of accountability was indeed the basic project of capitalist democracy, clearly announced in the arguments that devised the political form we now treat as definitive of modern democracy, in the adoption of the United States Constitution in 1787. Hamilton, Jay and Madison, the authors of the *Federalist*, could not have imagined the model of accountability implied in the ministerial handbook cited in relation to the new crop of luxury cars for South African political leaders. But the road they opened up leads to that end.

The United States is often described as the oldest modern democracy in the world, so it may be surprising to discover that its founding fathers did not describe the Federal Constitution that they adopted in 1787 as democratic. Indeed, they made clear that they intended it to *prevent* democracy. Above all, they sought to avoid the example of citizen participation offered by democracy in ancient Greece. *Federalist* number 9 describes the proposed Constitution as a 'barrier against domestic faction and insurrection' exemplified by the Greek democracies, whose histories cannot be read without feeling 'sensations of horror and disgust' (Hamilton et al 2003: 35).

Federalist number 10 argues that the Constitution will have the benefit of breaking and controlling 'the violence of faction' (Hamilton et al 2003: 40). A faction is defined as 'a number of citizens, *whether amounting to a majority or minority of the whole*, who are united and actuated by some common impulse of passion, or of interest, adverse to the rights of other citizens, or to the permanent and aggregate interests of the community' (Hamilton et al 2003: 41, emphasis added). At first sight, it seems mistaken to treat a *majority* of the citizens as a faction when they share a common purpose. But Madison makes clear that preventing such a majority from achieving its common purpose is the major problem that the Constitution has to solve. 'To secure the public good and private rights against the danger of such a faction, and at the same time to preserve the spirit and form of popular government, is then the great object to which our enquiries are directed' (Hamilton et al 2003: 43).

The authors of the *Federalist* do not give a clear account of the 'public good' that must be protected against the majority of its citizens. But we get to see what they have in mind when the causes of faction are described. Faction arises because people hold different opinions and have different interests and are at liberty to pursue them. These differences arise in turn from 'different and unequal faculties in acquiring property' (Hamilton et al 2003: 41). Although these can be expressed on many points, there is one issue above all which gives rise to faction, or makes it dangerous. 'The most common and durable source of factions, has been the various and unequal distribution of property. Those who hold and those who are without property have ever formed distinct interests in society' (Hamilton et al 2003: 43). The task of government is to regulate these differing interests.

How then are the majority of citizens to be prevented from carrying out their common purposes, especially when these purposes might impact on the rights of property, while preserving the form of popular government? Various measures are suggested, but the most important and original of them is 'the enlargement of the orbit' of the political system, that is, a large enough state that the role of citizens is reduced and power is exercised by their representatives (Hamilton et al 2003: 36). This is what separates a republic from a democracy. A republic, and especially an extended republic, depends on representation. The effect of representative government, Madison argues, is 'to refine and enlarge the public views, by passing them through the medium of a chosen body of citizens, whose wisdom may best discern the true interests of their country' (Hamilton et al 2003: 44). Put differently, it is not that representation is needed because the state is too large for direct participation of citizens in the government. Instead, it is a large state that is needed in order to prevent the direct participation of the citizens in deciding how they should live.

Critics of the Constitution argued that it was not democratic and its legislative bodies were not truly representative. Representatives, according to Brutus (probably the pseudonym of Richard Yates), 'should bear the strongest resemblance of those in whose room they are substituted. It is obvious, that for an assembly to be a true likeness of the people of any country, they must be considerably numerous' (Hamilton et al 2003: 456). In as small a body as the United States Congress, Brutus argued, the rich would dominate, as wealth creates influence and a 'natural aristocracy' (Hamilton et al 2003: 457). The result 'will literally be a government in the hands of the few to oppress and plunder the many' managed by 'influence and corruption' (Hamilton et al 2003: 458).

Federalist number 35 is largely a response to Brutus' argument. Hamilton argues that 'the idea of an actual representation of all classes of the people by persons of each class is altogether visionary [i.e. illusory]' (Hamilton et al 2003: 159). Indeed, it would be against the wishes of working people who 'will always be inclined with few exceptions to give their votes to merchants in preference to persons of their own professions and trades' (Hamilton et al 2003: 159). The habits of life of working people do not give them the perspective and ability to promote their own interests, according to Hamilton, and 'we must therefore consider merchants as the natural representatives of all classes of the community' (Hamilton et al 2003: 160). Hamilton speaks of the representative body being composed of 'land-holders, merchants and men of the learned professions' (Hamilton et al 2003: 161). Where Brutus sees the domination of the wealthy in the proposed United States Congress as a defect, Hamilton sees it as right and proper. As we know, Hamilton and his allies won the day. They bequeathed us a more honest and unvarnished account of their project than we are likely to hear or even willing to accept today.

6. Conclusion

Our neoliberal model of accountability can be understood largely in the terms provided by the *Federalist*, as a way of providing the façade of democracy without the substance, ensuring that issues around which a 'faction of the majority' might unite against the interests of the propertied are taken out of the political arena and made the subject of bureaucratic procedure instead. It provides a mechanism through which the ruling elite can decide when it is necessary to sacrifice some of their number, often as a way of restructuring the ruling elite. If we ask the isolated question whether some process of accountability is better than nothing, then the answer is often that it is. But as long as such questions are asked in isolation, we remain mystified by them, unable to see how these mechanisms of accountability buttress a larger system of material inequality which continues and often worsens despite the formal equality of rights bestowed upon us by the clauses in a Constitution.

In this context, the transformation of the concept and practice of accountability in South Africa, described in this chapter, can be seen as something more than an oversight or accidental failure, capable of being corrected by the accountability experts. It should be seen as the result of the systematic limitation of accountability that is characteristic of capitalist society and lies within the origins of capitalist democracy. In the last instance, accountability is a political rather than a legal question. More democratic practices of accountability can be established only in the struggle for more democratic forms of society.

References

Davies, R. 2009. Nyanda hits road in R1.1m Beemers. *Cape Times*, 17 July.
Erwin, A. 1985. The question of unity in the struggle. *South African Labour Bulletin*, 11(1): 51–70.

Friedman, S. 1987. *Building Tomorrow Today: African Workers in Trade Unions, 1970–1984.* Johannesburg: Ravan Press.

Foster, J. 1982. The workers' struggle: Where does FOSATU stand? *South African Labour Bulletin,* 7(8): 67–86.

Hamilton, A., Madison, J. & Jay, J. 2003. *The Federalist, with Letters of 'Brutus',* Ball, T. (ed). Cambridge: Cambridge University Press.

Isaacson, M. 2009. Gauteng Premier's message: Don't mess with the rules. *Sunday Independent,* 7 June.

Jacks, M. 2009. King sings different tune on cartels. *Business Report,* 9 June.

Mandela, N. 1994. *Long Walk to Freedom.* Johannesburg: MacDonald Purnell.

Marx, K. & Engels, F. 1968. The communist manifesto, *Marx-Engels: Selected Works.* Moscow: Progress Publishers.

O'Malley, P. 2008. *Shades of Difference: Mac Maharaj and the Struggle for South Africa.* New York: Penguin.

Roberts, J.T. 1982. *Accountability in Athenian Government.* Madison: University of Wisconsin Press.

Seekings, J. 2000. *The UDF: A History of the United Democratic Front in South Africa, 1983–1991.* Cape Town: David Philip.

Turner, R. 1978. *The Eye of the Needle: Towards Participatory Democracy in South Africa.* Johannesburg: Ravan Press.

Chapter 3

The politics of constitutional reform in Zambia: From executive dominance to public participation?

Neo Simutanyi

1. Introduction

A Constitution defines the norms, standards and mechanisms by which holders of public power are held accountable. A Constitution produced by a process which is dominated by the ruling elite is unlikely to contain high standards and strong levels of accountability. Contrariwise, a Constitution which is developed in a consultative process in which the public is allowed to participate is more likely to entrench strong accountability norms and mechanisms. However, the experience in Africa demonstrates not only that constitution-making or constitutional reform processes have almost always been dominated by those in power to the exclusion of the general populace but also that Constitutions have failed to effectively regulate the exercise of public power (Okoth-Ogendo 1991; Mbao 2007a). Essentially, constitutional reform initiatives have not sufficiently limited executive powers, or reduced the scope for personal rule and centralised decision-making. Furthermore, the principles of limited government, the separation of powers and respect for the rule of law, which are the hallmarks of a liberal constitutional regime, have been observed more in theory than in practice. In 1991, commenting on the post-colonial constitutional practice, Okoth-Ogendo (1991: 4) observed that most African countries had 'Constitutions without constitutionalism'. By 2001, this picture had not changed much (Tumwine-Mukubwa 2001: 303) and, as this chapter will demonstrate, constitutionalism remains a challenge in Zambia.

Constitution-making is essentially a political process that involves competing claims and interests of two main groups, those in power bent on preserving the status quo and the ruled who demand that power should be exercised in the interest of all (Oloka-Onyango 2001: 13). As Okoth-Ogendo (1991: 20) correctly observes, constitution-making involves 'struggles for an optimal balance between the few upon whom Constitutions confer power and the vast majority for whose benefit it is supposed to be exercised'. While the practice of the state dominating the constitutional reform process and dictating the reform agenda is now well-established in most English-speaking African countries, it has increasingly come under scrutiny. The debate has mainly revolved around the extent to which the public should be involved in the process.

The idea of public participation in the constitution-making process is now being championed by scholars and civil society across the continent. A Constitution can only be legitimate if the people to whom it will apply participate in its making. Oloka-Onyango (2001: 21) has argued:

> The biggest challenge confronting those involved in struggles for constitutional reform around the continent is how to strike the balance. The balance in question is between ensuring that the path to reform is a participatory and inclusive one, and that it comprehensively addresses both the large and small issues of social, political and economic concerns.

Similarly, Ndulo (2001: 113) has observed:

> [c]onstitution-making structures must be open to views and opinions of all stakeholders who must be given meaningful opportunity to make their views known. ... A constitution that is perceived as imposed on a large segment of the population, or as having been adopted through the manipulation of the process by some of the stakeholders, is unlikely to gain sufficient popularity or legitimacy to endure the test of time.

Mbao (2007b: 17) views constitution-making as an important but painful process that should not be left to one segment of society. Expressing the same view, Odoki (2001: 263) has argued that the constitution-making process must as of necessity be characterised by 'popular participation by the people through consultation and national debate'. In his view, national consensus is essential as a way of promoting the acceptability and legitimacy of a Constitution.

Zambia has had four Constitutions since independence. None of them has met the needs and aspirations of its citizens. A major concern has been that in each instance of constitution-making or constitutional reform, the wider populace was not involved. The constitutional changes that have so far been undertaken were designed to satisfy the needs of the moment, the short-term interests of those in power. To address this concern, late President Levy Patrick Mwanawasa embarked on a constitutional reform process in 2003 aimed at the adoption of a new Constitution that would not only be 'people-driven' but also 'stand the test of time'. However, this constitutional reform process, which was originally scheduled to be completed within one year, took seven years to be completed.

This chapter discusses the politics of Zambia's constitution-making processes with a focus on the Third Republic.[1] First, it will discuss the history of constitution-making in Zambia and identify a number of important legacies that have a bearing on the current constitutional reform process. Thereafter, it will analyse the process of constitutional reform in the period 2003–2010. Finally, this chapter will address the question of the mode of adoption of a new Constitution and the manner in which this question has been addressed in Zambia's latest constitutional reform effort.

2. The history of constitution-making in Zambia

As noted earlier, Zambia's constitution-making processes have been characterised by a lack of involvement of the general public in the debates concerning the design and adoption of the country's Constitution. Within a period of 46 years, Zambia has had four Constitutions.[2] This record translates into an average of one Constitution every 11 years, ranking Zambia among the countries in Africa with the highest rates of constitutional change. Nevertheless, these constitutional changes have neither altered the power map nor reflected the needs and aspirations of the Zambian people.

2.1. The First Republic 1964–1972

The constitution-making process in Zambia has been highly contested since 1964. The Constitution adopted upon gaining independence from Britain was put together in a hurry to enable the new leaders to have a functioning post-colonial government. The new Constitution provided for a Bill of Rights, the separation of powers, multiparty politics and the rule of law. However, the new political elite lacked experience in a functioning democracy. After almost 75 years of colonial rule, the new rulers failed to break the authoritarian and repressive culture of the colonial state and found the new constitutional order to be not only inappropriate but also unsuitable for what they termed the 'nation-building project'.

It was widely recognised that the new Constitution needed be altered to bring it in line with African realities. However, as the new leaders consolidated their power, they became reluctant to modify the Constitution to guarantee accountable government. On the contrary, they found the constitutional

---

1   The Third Republic refers to the period after the end of one-party rule (1991 to the present). The First Republic covered the period 1964–1972, while the Second Republic was the one-party period from 1973–1991.

2   A fifth Constitution should have been adopted by Parliament in early 2011, but instead the Constitution Bill failed to get the mandatory two-thirds majority and was thus thrown out after one of the longest constitutional reform processes in the country's history, which lasted almost eight years.

provisions authorising the concentration of power in the President, the dominance of the executive, coercive powers of the state, and broad discretionary authority to be acceptable. The first act of constitutional reform in Zambia was the 1969 referendum but instead of strengthening the Constitution to enhance democracy, accountability, the rule of law and human rights, the referendum removed a number of constitutional constraints placed on the government and concentrated public powers in the executive (Okoth-Ogendo 1972; Shivji 1991: 29). The referendum gave the ruling United National Independence Party (UNIP) of Kenneth Kaunda the right to make major constitutional amendments through the legislature without consulting the population. The Bill of Rights was the only area where the government was required to consult the people when seeking amendments. Given the fact that the Constitution attached many internal limitations to the provisions in the Bill of Rights, the government could nevertheless restrict fundamental freedoms without having to change the Constitution.

As a result of the 1969 referendum, the President was given extensive powers. While at the formal level the legislature was expected to serve as a check on executive authority, in practice it was subordinate to the executive and often merely rubber-stamped government legislative proposals. Moreover, the President could override decisions of the legislature and had the power to dissolve the National Assembly. The President also controlled the judiciary. He had the power to make all appointments to constitutional offices, including the Attorney General, judges, permanent secretaries and heads of state companies. Internal security laws gave the President unrestrained authority to detain any person suspected to be a threat to public order and internal security without charge, to proscribe political parties, to outlaw strikes, and to criminalise protests and public processions (Burnell 2003).

Thus, by 1970, executive power had been personalised and there was no longer any distinction between the office of the President and the holder of the office. Any criticism of the office was considered a personal attack on President Kenneth Kaunda. With the escalation of internal factional fighting within UNIP, especially after the fractious 1967 UNIP General Conference and the disastrous showing by UNIP in the 1968 general elections in the Southern and Western Province, there was real fear that the ruling party might lose power. Inspired by developments elsewhere in Africa, the UNIP government resolved to abandon the multiparty Constitution bequeathed to it by the departing colonial power and sought to replace it with a one-party Constitution. While there were many factors which might have influenced the Zambian government to pursue this line at the time (including the arguments that multipartyism was an impediment to rapid economic growth and inconsistent with the African tradition of consensus-building), the desire for self-preservation seems to have been paramount in the political calculations.

2.2. The Second Republic 1972–1991

On 30 March 1972, President Kaunda appointed a constitutional review commission headed by the then Vice President Mainza Chona to inquire into and examine changes to the Republican and UNIP constitutions, practices and procedures necessary to create a one-party system in Zambia.[3] It was not within the Chona Commission's terms of reference to inquire into the acceptability or suitability of the one-party system of government, or to entertain petitions against the proposed system of government.

The purpose of the Chona Commission was to investigate how a one-party state would function and to propose the institutions required for its implementation. People's participation in this process was limited to giving their views on how the proposed one-party system would work. The Chona Commission was not empowered to receive public comments on its desirability. The final decision on the content of the revised Constitution rested with the government. Those who opposed the establishment of a one-party system of government — many at the time — did not receive any hearing. In particular, trade unions, the Catholic Church and opposition parties opposed the idea of a one-party system, describing it as a form of dictatorship. Opposition leaders, such as African National Congress (ANC) leader Harry Mwaanga Nkumbula and United Progressive Party (UPP) leader Simon Mwansa Kapwepwe, petitioned the High Court in an attempt to halt the government's plans to introduce a one-party state. However, the courts ruled in favour of the government.

The report of the Chona Commission was not subjected to public debate. However, the government did not accept all its recommendations. It rejected most of the proposals initiated through public participation, including proposals for a reduction of presidential powers and for the creation of the position of Prime Minister. In particular, the government rejected the Commission's recommendations that the President's powers of detention be limited, that an individual should serve a maximum of two consecutive five-year terms of office as President, and that UNIP should present three presidential candidates before the electorate. On 13 December 1972, nine months after the government had partially adopted the Chona Commission report, the revised Constitution endorsing the one-party political system was passed by Parliament.

Various other attempts at constitutional reform were made thereafter. Although these involved a measure of public participation, the views of the

---

3   Chona Constitutional Review Commission (1972).

public were nevertheless not fully reflected in the final amendments. Overall, it is fair to argue that constitution-making in Zambia during the independence period was not informed by national consensus. Neither did the constitutional reform processes reflect a political commitment to the national interest. Rather, they predominantly served short-term interest — in particular, the interests of those in power.

2.3. The return to multiparty politics 1991–1996

A number of events compelled the UNIP government to acquiesce to popular demands for a return to the multiparty system in 1991. Sporadic food riots occasioned by increases in the price of maize meal in December 1986 and a failed coup d'état in June 1991 revealed how unpopular Kaunda and his one-party rule had become (Simutanyi 1996). Following internal demands within the ruling UNIP, demands from organised labour and popular pressure, the UNIP government amended the Constitution in December 1990 to allow for a return to a multiparty system. Thereafter, a constitutional review commission was appointed headed by Solicitor General Patrick Mvunga. The terms of reference for the Mvunga Commission were to inquire into, determine and recommend a system of political pluralism that would ensure the separation of powers.[4]

Among other things, the Mvunga Commission recommended the establishment of a bicameral Parliament and a constitutional court, that ministers could be appointed from outside Parliament, the introduction of a two-term limit for the office of the President, and the introduction of the threshold of at least 50 per cent plus one of all the votes cast for the election of the President. The UNIP government accepted most of the Commission's recommendations, except those concerning the reduction of the powers of the President. The government did not even bother to explain why it had rejected some of the recommendations.

This constitutional review process was boycotted by the main opposition party, the Movement for Multiparty Democracy (MMD), although its objections had little to do with altering the power map. The MMD opposed the idea of a constitutional court and a second legislative chamber, both of which they considered to be unnecessary and a waste of public resources. The MMD also opposed the proposal to appoint ministers from outside Parliament, arguing that this would undermine the accountability of ministers to the legislature. As it turned out, none of these features found their way into the Constitution that was passed in August 1991 by a UNIP dominated legislature. The powers of the President remained unchanged in the new Constitution.

---

4   Mvunga Constitutional Review Commission (1991).

The MMD won the subsequent elections held on 31 October 1991. Frederick Chiluba was elected President and his MMD obtained 125 seats in Parliament against UNIP's 25. Since the MMD had campaigned on a platform of spearheading further constitutional reforms, there was public pressure to deliver on that electoral promise. It was widely acknowledged that the 1991 Constitution was deficient and fell short of meeting the aspirations of the Zambian people. While Mbao (2007a) has suggested that the 1991 Constitution was a product of a broad-based consensus as people 'sat down and agreed to a constitutional text', the evidence shows that this view is not entirely accurate. The Constitution was a product of a bipartisan consensus between UNIP and the MMD and did not adequately reflect popular aspirations. It was in fact a kind of 'elite consensus'[5] meant to facilitate the holding of multiparty elections. The MMD itself acknowledged at the time that the 1991 Constitution was an imperfect document and made a public undertaking to review it once elected to power.[6] This is why on 22 December 1993 President Frederick Chiluba appointed the Mwanakatwe Commission to review the 1991 Constitution.

The Commission was asked to come up with a Constitution that would 'stand the test of time'. In particular, its terms of reference required it to make recommendations for a system of government that would promote the democratic principles of regular and fair elections, transparency and accountability, and that would guard against the re-emergence of a dictatorial form of government. The Commission was also mandated to recommend appropriate arrangements for the entrenchment and protection of human rights, the rule of law, good governance and judicial independence. In addition, the Commission was required to recommend the most suitable mode of adoption of the new Constitution.[7]

In its report, the Commission made many wide-ranging recommendations, including the proposal that the new Constitution be adopted by a constituent assembly followed by a national referendum and the proposal that the President be elected by at least 50 per cent plus one of the votes cast.

However, Chiluba's government rejected almost 70 per cent of the recommendations. Significantly, the government rejected the Commission's proposal concerning the mode of adoption of the new Constitution. The most controversial proposal which was endorsed by the government concerned a new requirement for eligibility to the presidential office: that both parents of a presidential candidate must have been born in Zambia. The inclusion of this requirement in the new Constitution lent credence to the impression that one of

---

5   For a discussion on the concept of 'elite consensus' or 'elite pacts', see O'Donnell and Schmitter (1986); Linz and Stepan (1996).
6   Personal communication with Akashambatwa Mbikusita-Lewanika, December 1992.
7   Mwanakatwe Constitutional Review Commission (1995).

the main objectives of the constitutional reform exercise was to exclude Zambia's former President Kenneth Kaunda from contesting the 1996 elections.

2.4. Legacies affecting the constitutional reforms

All attempts at constitutional reform discussed above had four things in common. First, they were dominated and driven by the executive and reflected executive preferences. Second, they undermined vertical accountability by limiting public participation in the design and approval of the Constitution. Third, the legislature played a minimal role in vetting government proposals or ensuring that public opinions were taken into account in the final draft. Lastly, the constitutional review commissions themselves were more accountable to the executive than to the Zambian people.

The executive dominance of the constitutional reform process is partly a colonial heritage. It is a practice found in most former British colonies. Under this system, the executive appoints a commission of inquiry, determines its terms of reference, and provides it with a timetable and funding. The result of the inquiry is presented to the President who then tables it before his or her cabinet. After studying the report, the executive decides what to accept and what to reject and publishes its response to the recommendations in a white paper. The approved clauses are then presented for deliberation in Parliament which enacts them into law. Under this system, the public's role in the constitution-making process is limited to consultations and the government does not consider itself to be under an obligation to take the views of the public into account.

The other enduring legacy in Zambia's constitution-making process is the absence of vertical and horizontal accountability. The only role Parliament played in all these constitution-making processes was simply to rubber-stamp executive preferences and not to question, modify or debate the constitutional proposals. For example, although the Constitution of 1971 was essentially anti-democratic, it was overwhelmingly approved by a UNIP-only Parliament whose primary interest was in maintaining political stability and consolidating UNIP's political hegemony. Similarly, the 1996 Constitution was approved by an MMD-dominated Parliament mainly to remove former President Kaunda from the political scene.

Public participation in the constitutional reform processes generally takes two forms. The public participates through civil society organisations and/or directly by making oral submissions, writing letters to newspapers, or engaging in public discussions on radio and television. It provides a form of vertical accountability. As argued earlier, all the three constitutional reform initiatives discussed above allowed for very limited public participation. Worse still, the little input made by civil society and opposition parties was mostly disregarded.

Interestingly, most of the rejected proposals demanded greater accountability through the separation of powers, a reduction of presidential powers and an effective Parliament.

3. From executive dominance to public participation?

It is against this background that there has been a constant popular demand for a people-driven Constitution in Zambia. In 1996, civil society organisations canvassed for the adoption of a new Constitution through a constituent assembly and a national referendum. This demand was ignored by the Chiluba government which claimed that it had the electoral mandate to legislate. In 2001, civil society organisations demanded that all political parties commit themselves to implement constitutional reforms after the elections. Some political parties, such as UNIP, the United Party for National Development (UPND) and the Forum for Democracy and Development (FDD), included constitutional reform in their electoral manifestos. The FDD, in particular, promised to institute constitutional reforms within 90 days of assuming power. While the MMD remained less committal on constitutional reform, the events of early 2001, when President Frederick Chiluba pushed for a constitutional amendment to allow him to run for a third term in office, brought the issue of constitutional reform squarely onto the political agenda.

Chiluba's attempt to seek a third term displeased many MPs. Some of them went as far as asking the Speaker to convene the National Assembly to debate a motion to impeach Chiluba for breaching his oath and the Constitution. Over two-thirds of MPs signed the petition but, for more than eight months, the Speaker declined to convene the National Assembly. In the end, a sustained campaign by opposition parties, MPs, ministers and civil society discouraged Chiluba from effecting a constitutional amendment to allow him a third term in office. The departure of Chiluba paved the way for Levy Mwanawasa to be elected the next President of Zambia in December 2001, albeit winning with the narrowest of margins: 29 per cent of the votes against 27 per cent obtained by his nearest rival, Anderson Mazoka of the UPND.

3.1. The Mung'omba Commission 2003–2007

After Mwanawasa's election, civil society organisations demanded a comprehensive review of the 1996 Constitution. It was clear from the outset that piecemeal amendments and executive dominance would not be tolerated, as Zambians no longer trusted those in power.[8] On 17 April 2003, President Levy Mwanawasa appointed a 41-member commission of inquiry headed by a lawyer,

---

8   Personal communication with an Oasis Forum official, 22 August 2007.

Wila Mung'omba. This commission's terms of reference bore close resemblance to those of the Mwanakatwe Commission and included the following tasks:

- To collect views from the general public on a new Constitution which would stand the test of time and entrench and promote the legal and institutional protection of human rights
- To recommend a system of government that would ensure regular free and fair elections, transparency and accountability and guard against dictatorial rule
- To examine functions of government with a view of maximising checks and balances
- To recommend the manner of adoption of the final Constitution.[9]

Unlike Chiluba, who embarked on the constitutional review process barely a year into his presidency when he was still immensely popular, Levy Mwanawasa did not have it easy. He ascended to the presidency based on an electoral mandate of only 29 per cent of the national vote and lacked support even within his own party, the MMD (Erdmann & Simutanyi 2003). Thus, while people welcomed his decision to embark on a review of the Constitution, they were not convinced that a leader lacking popular legitimacy had the necessary mandate to dictate the constitutional reform process.

There were three issues of contention from the very start. First, questions were raised about the need for a new constitutional review commission considering that two previous commissions had made similar recommendations. Second, it was argued that members of the constitutional review commission should not be appointed by the President but by their respective organisations. This proposal was seen as an important measure to guarantee the independence of the commission. Third, civil society organisations wanted the recommendations of the constitutional review to be debated and approved by a constituent assembly and then by a national referendum, as was recommended by the Mwanakatwe Commission in 1995.

While there were consultations before the appointment of the Mung'omba Commission, the government maintained that there was no legal way of undertaking the constitutional review process other than through a commission of inquiry. However, it made one important concession — the inclusion in the terms of reference of the requirement that commissioners review the recommendations of the previous constitutional review commissions. The demand that the President should not appoint commissioners but leave this task to their respective organisations was flatly rejected. In response, organisations demanded that those who had been appointed to sit on the Commission

---

9   Mung'omba Constitution Review Commission (2005).

without the blessing of their organisations either withdraw or be disowned. As it turned out, most of the appointees defied their organisations and sat on the Mung'omba Commission in their individual capacities. For example, the UPND expelled two of its MPs for defying party directives, while the Media Institute of Southern Africa (MISA) also disowned its president for accepting to sit on the Commission. This was a serious political embarrassment for President Mwanawasa. Not only did civil society organisations expel their members for sitting on the Commission, they also boycotted the Commission's sittings.

The issue of the mode of adoption of the new Constitution formed the main bone of contention between the government and civil society. As noted above, civil society groups argued that the draft Constitution should be adopted by a constituent assembly followed by a national referendum. The government did not favour this method. It argued that it would be expensive and would take too long to complete. Furthermore, it argued that a national referendum would require the time-consuming and expensive task of conducting a national census to determine the number of eligible voters.

In its report, submitted in December 2005, the Mung'omba Commission endorsed most of the proposals put forward by civil society. Nevertheless, the government rejected the idea of adopting the Constitution by a constituent assembly as well as other recommendations of the Commission. These included the requirement that the President be elected by at least 50 per cent plus one of the total votes cast; the appointment of ministers from outside Parliament; the election of the President together with the Vice-President (as a running mate); and the inclusion of economic and social rights in the Bill of Rights. However, as elections drew near, the government back-pedalled on the method of adopting the Constitution and promised to honour the wishes of the people. Pleading for more time and resources, it rejected the demand for the new Constitution to be enacted before the 2006 elections.

President Levy Mwanawasa won the 2006 presidential election with 43 per cent of the national votes against his nearest rival, Michael Sata of the Patriotic Front (PF), who obtained 29 per cent of the national vote. In the parliamentary elections, the MMD improved on its 2001 performance by winning 77 seats against the PF's 42 seats. The remainder of the seats were won by five other parties[10] and two independents. Following his re-election with an improved electoral mandate, Mwanawasa announced his constitutional reform plans. He would continue with the constitutional reform process but on his own terms. He reverted to his original position opposing the adoption of the Constitution by a constituent assembly, reiterating that the government would not have the money to establish such a body.

---

10   UPND 22, United Liberal Party 3, FDD 2, UNIP 2, National Democratic Front 1.

A period of ambiguity and contradictions followed. The government envisaged that the constitutional reform process would take at least three to four years to complete. This roadmap was challenged by civil society organisations, which argued that it was simply a delaying tactic by the government. They maintained that the process would take no longer than nine months.

When it appeared to the government that public opinion was in favour of a constituent assembly[11], it announced that a referendum would be organised to decide whether the draft Constitution should be adopted by a constituent assembly or Parliament. President Mwanawasa told the nation that the government would campaign against the proposal. The decision to put the question of the manner of adopting a draft Constitution to the referendum was absurd, not least because it proved that the government's initial objections to a referendum were not made in good faith. Many believed that this decision by the government was part of a wider machination to delay the process even further. It was clear that the government was not committed to the process unless it was in full control of it.

3.2. The National Constitutional Conference 2007–2010

In July 2007, following a meeting of all political parties represented in Parliament under the umbrella of the Zambia Centre for Interparty Dialogue (ZCID), it was resolved that instead of a constituent assembly, a national constitutional conference be convened to deliberate on and adopt the Mung'omba draft Constitution. This decision, made by political parties without the involvement of civil society, was viewed with deep suspicion. The Oasis Forum, a group of civil society organisations, was of the view that the proposed national conference could easily be manipulated by the government. It also wondered why political parties had acquiesced to the idea after more than three years of wrangling.

In August 2007, the National Constitutional Conference Bill was passed by Parliament and signed into law by President Mwanawasa in September of the same year.[12] The National Constitutional Conference (NCC) was to be 'a forum for the examination, debate and adoption of proposals to alter the Constitution as contained in the draft Constitution as submitted by the Commission.'[13] According to section 13 of the NCC Act, the main functions and powers of the NCC included the following:

- To consider and deliberate the provisions of the draft report of the Commission
- To adopt a draft Constitution or part thereof

---

11 A Constituent Assembly defined as an elected body that is tasked with drafting a new Constitution is different from a constitutional conference that does not have any law-making powers.

12 National Constitutional Conference Act 19 of 2007 (NCC Act).

13 Section 3 of the NCC Act.

- To submit the adopted draft Constitution or part thereof to Parliament or to a national referendum.

Section 13(4) of the NCC Act required the NCC to be accountable to the people of Zambia; to recognise the importance of confidence building and developing national consensus; and to ensure that the final outcome of the adoption process faithfully reflected the wishes of the people of Zambia.

Notwithstanding these clauses, some civil society organisations and opposition parties expressed disquiet about the NCC Act and threatened to boycott the process. At issue were the provisions empowering the President to dissolve the NCC at any time, if in his or her opinion it was not fulfilling its mandate. There was concern that the President would dissolve the NCC if the deliberations were not going the government's way. Furthermore, the NCC was dominated by politicians and government officials. Of the 478 delegates, more than 70 per cent were either politicians or government appointed officials, while civil society representatives occupied less than 30 per cent of the NCC seats (Mwenye 2007).

After the death of President Mwanawasa in August 2008 and the election of his successor, Rupiah Banda, the work of the NCC continued. The new President extended the NCC's mandate twice. While the NCC was originally supposed to sit for only a year, its mandate was extended to August 2010. This was condemned by civil society and some opposition parties which felt that the body lacked accountability and was becoming a drain on public funds.[14] There was a perception that members of the NCC were more concerned with their personal welfare and allowances than with serving the Zambian people.

The NCC was established as a mechanism to facilitate public participation in the drafting and adoption of a new Constitution. It was expected that the proposals of the previous constitutional review commissions that had popular support would find their way into the new Constitution. Furthermore, many expected the 1996 Constitution to be completely overhauled to reflect the changed political realities. The NCC was also expected to pay particular attention to the fact that the previous constitutional reforms had all left an executive-dominated power structure intact and failed fundamentally to address the questions of the separation of powers and accountable governance. It was envisaged that the NCC would be a mechanism of accountability, as the legislature was considered incapable of playing this role in the constitution-making process due to its partisan character and that it was dominated by the ruling party. However, after three years, most of the contentious

---

14   The NCC budget amounted to K136 billion (approximately US$27 million) between 2007 and 2010, part of which was funded by donor countries.

issues remained unresolved and the prospects for a durable Constitution that would address Zambia's main governance issues looked rather grim.

On 30 August 2010, the NCC presented its final report and the Constitution of Zambia Bill to the Minister of Justice and Vice President George Kunda. With this submission, its tenure came to an end. The Constitution of Zambia Bill contains a number of new provisions, such as those concerning the enlargement of the legislature from the current 150 seats to 280 seats, a mixed-member proportional electoral system, dual citizenship, and the registration, funding and regulation of political parties. However, it did not alter presidential powers or enhance the role of the legislature as a counter-balance to executive power. The power map remains centralised, with local authorities being mere appendages of the central government and lacking administrative and financial autonomy.

The NCC voted against two proposals that were contentious in the past: the election of the President by 50 per cent plus one of the total votes cast and the appointment of ministers from outside Parliament. The idea that a presidential candidate should be elected by an absolute majority (50 per cent plus one) was a popular recommendation that featured in the reports of all three constitutional review commissions (Mvunga 1991; Mwanakatwe 1995; Mung'omba 2005). In fact, the 1991 Constitution included such a provision until it was amended by the Chiluba government in 1996. In the NCC, the matter was put to a vote and the majority of the commissioners voted against it. The recommendation to appoint ministers from outside Parliament was made by both the Mwanakatwe and the Mung'omba Commissions and was seen as a way of enhancing government accountability. The NCC rejected it with the argument that it would weaken government authority.

A close examination of the Constitution of Zambia Bill shows that, overall, the government got its way. Almost all provisions that did not have government support did not find their way into the new draft Constitution. This has raised questions as to the independence of the NCC and whether its decisions reflect popular aspirations. Clearly, the NCC, although relatively representative, failed to write a new Constitution which addresses the governance deficits that have plagued the Zambian polity since independence. Instead, the NCC sanctioned the continuation of the status quo. As a result, the draft Constitution ignored too many popular demands to be accepted by the Zambian people. To the extent that a significant number of civil society organisations, including church bodies and the opposition PF, boycotted the NCC, the new draft Constitution lacked popular legitimacy. A national referendum would have given a clear indication of the extent of popular support for the constitutional draft.

On 29 March 2011, the Constitution of Zambia Amendment Bill failed to get parliamentary approval as it fell short of the mandatory two-thirds majority. The opposition PF voted against the Bill, while UPND MPs walked out. The

Bill failed to pass because there was no consensus on four key opposition demands: the 50 per cent plus one requirement for the election of the President; the Vice President as running mate; the appointment of ministers from outside the legislature; and a three-month transition period before a new President is sworn in. On these demands the ruling MMD government simply refused to concede, because doing so would have meant abrogating its authority and hold on power (*The Post* 30 March 2011). The failure of the Constitution of Zambia Amendment Bill, though surprising, demonstrates that the legislature can exercise its oversight function and hold the executive to account. In this case, parliamentarians rejected being used as mere rubber stamps by the executive and threw out the Bill that they felt mainly served the interests of those in power. Thus, eight years of constitution-making came to an abrupt end on account of a lack of popular consensus on the one hand and government intransigence on the other.

As noted above, the Mung'omba Commission, as did the Mwanakatwe Commission before it, recommended that the draft Constitution be adopted by a constituent assembly followed by a national referendum. After initial opposition, the government established the NCC. Although the NCC was relatively representative of the Zambian people, it was expected that it would not be the final arbiter on all constitutional issues and that the general public would be given a chance to decide whether to accept the new Constitution or not. The NCC itself decided that proposals concerning matters on which it had reached consensus would be sent to Parliament for enactment while those pertaining to issues on which there was no consensus, such as the issue of the threshold for the election of the President and the appointment of ministers from outside Parliament, would be put to a national referendum. This decision departed from the original expectation that the whole Constitution would be put to a referendum.

The fact that the Constitution Amendment Bill failed to be approved by Parliament means that the constitutional reform process will have to be re-started. It is no longer conceivable that a national referendum will be held over the contentious issues. Unfortunately, the Zambian people will have to wait longer for an opportunity to directly participate in decisions about their Constitution.

4. Conclusion

The current constitutional reform process in Zambia remains incomplete. While the government has made some concessions to the people's demand for a people-driven Constitution, the NCC process has not produced a draft Constitution which addresses all concerns raised by the public. The NCC aligned itself with the government's preferences. It is therefore not surprising that the Constitution of Zambia Bill presented to Parliament in February 2011 retained all the provisions that undermine the principles of 'accountable governance'. The Zambian experience shows that incumbents continue to be reluctant to cede the vast amount of powers and privileges accumulated during the dictatorial era. The resistance to a genuine constitutional reform process can be explained as an effort by those in power to remain in power.

The Zambian constitution-making processes have not been fully open and transparent, partly because those who advocate for change have been excluded from the process or their views have simply been ignored and partly because those processes have all been dominated by the executive. Proposals by civil society to bolster the accountability mechanisms under the Constitution have been rejected by an executive preoccupied with retaining its power. Ideally, constitution-making in the context of a multiparty system involves contestation between political parties offering different policy alternatives to the electorate, but whether constitutional change will remain on the agenda of the opposition parties after the 2011 elections is unclear. What is clear is that popular demands for greater accountability are not shared by the political elite including those in the opposition, who seem to look forward to benefiting from the broad executive powers and privileges when they themselves come to power.[15]

References

Legislation

Constitution of the Republic of Zambia Act 18 of 1996.
Draft Constitution of the Republic of Zambia, 2005.
National Constitutional Conference Act 19 of 2007.

Reports

Chona Constitutional Review Commission. 1972. *Report of the National Commission on the Establishment of a One-Party Participatory Democracy in Zambia*. Lusaka: Government of the Republic of Zambia.

Mung'omba Constitution Review Commission. 2005. *Report of the Mung'omba Constitution Review Commission*. Lusaka: Government of the Republic of Zambia.

Mvunga Constitutional Review Commission. 1991. *Report of the Mvunga Constitutional Review Commission*. Lusaka: Government of the Republic of Zambia.

Mwanakatwe Constitutional Review Commission. 1995. *Report of the Mwanakatwe Constitutional Review Commission*. Lusaka: Government of the Republic of Zambia.

---

15 In 2006, Michael Sata of the PF advised UPND president Anderson Mazoka not to press for limiting presidential powers because they may both need them if they come to power. Personal communication, July 2006.

Articles, books, chapters in books and other works

Burnell, P. 2003. Legislative-executive relations in Zambia: Parliamentary reform on the agenda. *Journal of Contemporary African Studies*, 21(1): 47–68.

Erdmann, G. & Simutanyi, N. 2003. *Transition in Zambia: The Hybridisation of the Third Republic*. Lilongwe: Konrad Adenauer Foundation.

Linz, J.J. & Stepan, A. 1996. *Problems of Democratic Transitions and Consolidation*. Baltimore/London: John Hopkins University Press.

Mbao, M.L. 2007a. Constitutional reforms in Zambia: Some lessons in constitution making and development. Paper presented at the ANCL Conference on Constitutionalism in Africa, Nairobi, 18–20 April.

Mbao, M.L. 2007b. Popular involvement in constitution making: The case of Zambia. Paper presented to the Seventh World Constitutional Congress, Athens, Greece, 11–17 June.

Mwenye, M. 2007. 'Is the National Constitutional Conference Act adequate to enable Zambians to attain a people-driven Constitution?' Paper presented at the Zambia Congress of Trade Unions National Conference, Protea Hotel Cairo Road, Lusaka, 15–16 October.

Ndulo, M. 2001. Constitution-making in Africa: Assessing both the process and content. *Public Administration & Development*, 21(2): 101–117.

Odoki, B.J. 2001. The challenges of constitution-making and implementation in Uganda. In Oloka-Onyango, J. (ed.). *Constitutionalism in Africa*. Kampala: Fountain Publishers.

O'Donnell, G. & Schmitter, P.C. 1986. *Transitions from Authoritarian Rule*. Baltimore: John Hopkins University Press.

Okoth-Ogendo, H.W. 1972. The politics of constitutional change in Kenya since independence, 1963–1969. *African Affairs*, 71(9): 9–34.

Okoth-Ogendo, H.W. 1991. Constitutions without constitutionalism: Reflections on an African political paradox. In Shivji, I.G. (ed.). *State and Constitutionalism in Africa: An African Debate on Democracy*. Harare: Southern African Economy Servies (SAPES) Trust.

Oloka-Onyango, J. 2001. Constitutionalism in Africa: Yesterday, today and tomorrow. In Oloka-Onyango, J. (ed.). *Constitutionalism in Africa*. Kampala: Fountain Publishers.

Shivji I.G. (ed.). 1991. *State and Constitutionalism in Africa: An African Debate on Democracy*. Harare: SAPES Trust.

Simutanyi, N. 1996. The politics of structural adjustment in Zambia, *Third World Quarterly*, 17(4): 825–839.

Tumwine-Mukubwa, G.P. 2001. Ruled from the grave: Challenging antiquated constitutional doctrines and values in Commonwealth Africa. In Oloka-Onyango, J. (ed.). *Constitutionalism in Africa*. Kampala: Fountain Publishers.

Chapter 4

Judicial independence and the judicialisation of electoral politics in Malawi and Uganda[1]

Siri Gloppen and Fidelis Edge Kanyongolo

1. Introduction

One of the most significant features of the development of accountable government in Africa in the past two decades has been the growing relevance and importance of the judiciary in setting and enforcing norms of accountability. However, the accountability performance of African judiciaries is uneven, between countries as well as within countries over time, raising the question of what explains this variability. This chapter seeks to contribute to a better understanding of the courts' accountability role, by exploring the performance of courts in the context of Ugandan and Malawian elections. It focuses on the independence of the judiciary as an important condition for the effective discharge of its accountability role.

In new or weakly institutionalised democratic systems, elections represent a form of crisis, testing the strength of the institutions established to secure fair and peaceful political succession and representation. In African countries like Uganda and Malawi, where political office is crucial to social and political mobility, the stakes of gaining and retaining political positions are high, which increases the need for dispute resolution and the enforcement of the legal electoral framework. Courts thus have an important accountability role in relation to electoral processes. To understand what enables courts to fulfil this role is important because it assists us in understanding broader processes of institutionalisation of democratic accountability.

---

1   This chapter builds on previous work by the two authors (particularly Gloppen & Kanyongolo 2006) and work on Uganda, conducted as part of a collaborative project between Chr. Michelsen Institute and the University of Makerere. The authors would like to thank Emmanuel Kasimbazi and Alexander Kibandama for their collaboration on the data collection and analysis. The chapter also draws substantially on Gloppen et al (2010), especially chapters 2 and 5.

Elections are not only about election day or the campaign period. They are also about establishing (and changing) electoral rules, (re)drawing constituency boundaries, registration of voters and candidates, and the resolution of disputes during and after the electoral process. As we shall see, the courts in Malawi and Uganda have been involved in electoral processes at all stages and are used by all sides.

Theoretically, competitive elections should work to strengthen judicial independence since political actors — both those in power, who fear losing office in the future, and the opposition — need the insurance that an independent judiciary affords to the loser. Uncertainty, it has been argued, creates incentives for politicians to encourage independent behaviour on the part of the judiciary.[2] It has also been argued that the uncertainty as to who will be the future political rulers increases the motivation of judges to act independently. When deference to the sitting government is no longer a rational strategy for securing their careers and their institution, judges are more likely to rule for the opposition or take on a politically independent arbiter role.[3] How well do these explanations, which focus on the rational self-interest of the actors, capture the African experience?

Compared to many African countries, Malawi and Uganda have had reasonably competitive elections where the judiciary has played a significant role. How well do the strategic models referred to above explain the patterns that we see here? To start answering this question, we outline the role that the courts of the two countries under study have played in electoral processes since the mid-1990s.[4]

2. Courts and elections in Malawi

In Malawi, the formerly marginal judiciary contributed significantly to the 1993–1994 democratic transition and has been central to the political process since. The courts have made a substantial, though at times uneven, contribution to accountability around elections and political succession. In a context where the quality of the country's political institutions has declined,[5] the judiciary became, despite its weaknesses, a democratic stronghold (Gloppen et al 2010). An indication of the relative independence of the Malawian judiciary is that between 1994 and

---

2   See VonDoepp and Ellet (2008); VonDoepp (2009); Gloppen et al (2010) (chapter 2).
3   The 'strategic defection model' of judicial independence, starting from the judges' motive for acting independently, is developed by Helmke (2002; 2003; 2005). See also Gloppen et al (2010).
4   Malawi had a relatively swift transition to a democratic dispensation. Pressure from a broad pro-democracy movement led to a referendum in 1993 and the adoption of a new Constitution and holding of general elections in 1994. In Uganda, the process was more gradual. The 1995 Constitution brought many changes to the political system that moved it in a democratic direction, but it established a restricted political system, with competition between individual candidates but political parties were barred from competing. The first multiparty elections in Uganda were held in February 2006.
5   See Gloppen and Kanyongolo (2006); Gloppen et al (2007).

2003, the High Court decided against the government in 54 per cent of the cases in which the government was a party. The judiciary was equally assertive in cases that were important to the government, unlike in Zambia, where the government was more likely to win where its interests were strong (VonDoepp 2006; 2009).

In the African context, Malawi's elections have been relatively open. Until 2004, the electoral outcomes displayed a regional pattern. The Malawi Congress Party (MCP), the pre-transition ruling party, controlled the central region; the United Democratic Front (UDF) dominated the populous southern region, while the Alliance for Democracy (AFORD) was the largest party in the sparsely populated northern region. The UDF won all elections up to and including the elections of May 2004, but never commanded a majority in Parliament and ruled in coalition with smaller parties, mainly AFORD. Since a party split in 2005, the UDF has been in opposition and, in May 2009, it lost the position of largest party to the Democratic Progressive Party (DPP), the new party formed by President Bingu wa Mutharika after he left the UDF in 2005. As shown in tables 4.1 and 4.2, the DPP dominated in all the three regions in the 2009 elections, changing the regional voting pattern and, for the first time, providing the President's party with a majority of parliamentary seats. Several factors contributed to this result: significant voter satisfaction with President Bingu wa Mutharika's achievements in his first term; an efficient campaign by the DPP helped by a dramatic incumbency advantage in terms of resources, media coverage, etc; and a poor campaign by the opposition, exacerbated by a last-minute alliance between two traditional enemies, the UDF and MCP.

In the first three elections since 1994, Malawian courts were called on to decide disputes related to the fairness of the electoral rules; as well as their

Table 4.1: Results of Malawi's presidential elections (in %), 1994–2009

	1994		1999		2004		2009	
DPP	-		-		-	-	Mutharika	66
UDF	Muluzi	47	Muluzi	52	Mutharika	36	-	-
MCP	Banda	33	-	-	Tembo	27	Tembo	31
AFORD	Chihana	19	-	-	-	-	Nyasulu	0.5
MCP/AFORD*	-	-	Chakuamba	45	Chakuamba	26	-	-
Other	Other	1	Other	3	Other	11	Other	2.5
Total		100		100		100		100

* In the 1999 elections, Chakuamba was the presidential candidate of both MCP and AFORD; in 2004, he contested the presidential elections for the Mgwirizano coalition.

Sources: African Elections Database, available at http://africanelections.tripod.com/mw.html and, for 2009 election results, Malawi Election Archive of the Electoral Institute for the Sustainability of Democracy in Africa (EISA). Available at http://www.eisa.org.za/WEP/malelectarchive.htm. Both accessed on 30 September 2010.

Table 4.2: Number of seats in Malawi's National Assembly per party, 1994–2009

	1994	1999	2004	2009
DPP	-	-	-	113
UDF	84	93	49	17
MCP	55	66	59	27
AFORD	36	29	6	1
Mgwirizano	-	-	27	-
Independent	-	4	38	32
Invalid	2	-	-	-
Other	-	-	14	3
TOTAL	177	192	193	193

Sources: African Elections Database. Available at http://africanelections.tripod.com/mw.html and, for 2009 election results, Malawi Election Archive of the Electoral Institute for the Sustainability of Democracy in Africa (EISA). Available at http://www.eisa.org.za/WEP/malelectarchive.htm. Both accessed 30 September 2010.

interpretation and application. Central concerns for the litigants have been to secure the space for participation and support in battles regarding political succession, including intra-party disputes — as well as the adjudication of the more directly election-related petitions.[6]

During Malawi's political transition, the courts displayed a new-found willingness to constrain the abuse of power by state institutions and to secure a democratic process. The High Court reversed a decision barring members of the army and police from voting in the 1993 referendum,[7] and found unconstitutional an order banning specific people from addressing public rallies[8] or performing in secondary schools.[9] These and other decisions enabled broader participation.[10] In the subsequent 1994 multiparty elections, the judiciary enforced the rules of the game relating to nominations, polling and the counting of votes[11] (Gloppen & Kanyongolo 2006; VonDoepp 2009).

---

6   Election petitions and complaints are handled by the MEC. Appeals are made to the High Court. Presidential election petitions must be received by the High Court within 48 hours of closing of polls.

7   *Nkhwazi v Referendum Commission* Civil Cause No 96 of 1993 (unreported).

8   *Aaron Longwe v Attorney General* Miscellaneous Civil Application No 11 of 1993 (unreported).

9   *Du Chisiza v Minister of Education* [1993] 16(1) MLR 81.

10   The judiciary also upheld laws hampering the democratisation process. For example, *Chakufwa Chihana v Republic* [1992] MLR 71 involved a sedition charge against the leader of a pro-multiparty pressure group; in *Muluzi & Thomson v Attorney General* Civil Cause No 66 of 1993 (unreported), opposition members were denied an injunction to prevent the police from stopping their publicity for a public meeting.

11   In *In Re Nomination of J.J. Chidule* Civil Cause No 5 of 1995 (unreported), the High Court held that parliamentary candidates must be registered, but not necessarily in the constituency in which they intend to contest. Election petitions include *Chikweza v The Electoral Commission* Civil Cause No 1061 of 1994 (unreported) and *Phoso v The Electoral Commission* Civil Cause No 1271 of 1996 (unreported).

The rules of the democratic game are often contested in the context of elections. In 1999, the Malawian judiciary ruled that presidential candidates could contest with a vice-presidential candidate from another party,[12] ordered the Malawi Electoral Commission (MEC) to register prisoners as voters,[13] instructed the MEC to ensure that the elections were free and fair,[14] and ordered the polling date to be set in accordance with the Constitution.[15] This enhanced voter participation and promoted constitutionalism.[16] A particularly significant case concerning the political space was *Kafumba v Electoral Commission & Malawi Broadcasting Corporation*, where the High Court ordered the Malawi Broadcasting Corporation (MBC) to give balanced campaign coverage.[17] On paper, the judgment was a victory for the opposition, but the MBC continued to defy the principle laid down by the court (Gloppen & Kanyongolo 2006).

The 2004 elections also saw court cases addressing the electoral rules and the restriction of the political space. Particularly significant was the Malawi Supreme Court of Appeal (MSCA)'s ruling postponing the election day to allow for a further inspection of the voters' roll.[18] It also underscored the MEC's obligation to prevent the use of state resources for partisan campaign purposes. Another case addressed bias in media coverage.[19] But instead of using the 1999 precedent on biased media coverage (*Kafumba* above), the Court dismissed the case on technical grounds (Gloppen & Kanyongolo 2006).

After Mutharika was elected President in 2004, the opposition increasingly turned to the courts to contest executive appointments, including appointments to bodies that are central to the electoral process. The courts (temporarily) blocked appointments to the MEC and the Malawi Communications Regulatory Authority (MACRA) on grounds of breach of procedure.[20] The case concerning MACRA is important to preserve the space for criticism. It should be seen in the context of attempts to limit press freedom by requiring private radio stations to obtain MACRA's permission before live broadcasts (CPJ 2007; MISA 2007; 2008).

---

12   *Chakuamba & Chihana v The Electoral Commission* Civil Cause No 25 of 1999 (unreported).

13   *Phambala v Chairman of the Electoral Commission* Civil Cause No 34 of 1999 (unreported).

14   *Khembo v Electoral Commission* Civil Cause No 70 of 1999 (unreported).

15   *Mungomo v Electoral Commission* Civil Application No 23 of 1999 (unreported).

16   Cases which upheld the decisions of the MEC include *Attorney General v Chakuamba & Others v Electoral Commission* Civil Cause No 30 of 1999 (unreported).

17   Civil Cause No 30 of 1999 (unreported).

18   *Republic v Chikhadwe & Chikhadwe* Criminal Case No LL/CR/60/1/2004 (Lilongwe First Grade Magistrate Court, unreported).

19   *National Democratic Alliance (NDA) v Electoral Commission & Others* Constitutional Cause No 3 of 2004 (unreported).

20   See *State v President of the Republic of Malawi, ex parte Muluzi & Tembo* Civil Cause No 99 of 2007 (unreported); *State v President of the Republic of Malawi & Malawi Communications Regulatory Authority, ex parte Joy Radio Ltd* Miscellaneous Civil Cause No 198 of 2006 (unreported).

In Malawi, as elsewhere, battles over political succession involve the highest political stakes and have thoroughly tested the accountability function of the judiciary. The first major succession case challenged the 1999 presidential election result, alleging irregularities and disputing the interpretation of the term 'majority of the votes'.[21] The MEC interpreted this term as a plurality of votes cast while the petitioners thought it meant an absolute majority of the registered voters. Malawian courts are notable for deciding election cases swiftly, but it took the MSCA almost a year to decide this petition. The judiciary faced criticism both for the delay and for upholding President Muluzi's re-election. When interviewed, the judges indicated that it would have been easier to decide against the incumbent in a quick decision just after the election (Gloppen & Kanyongolo 2006).

The 2004 election also produced court battles over political succession. President Muluzi sought to amend the Constitution to enable him to stand for a third term, but the courts made a decision which prevented Muluzi from mustering the required two-thirds parliamentary majority to effect the amendment. When seven Members of Parliament (MPs) critical of Muluzi were expelled from Parliament for crossing the floor, the High Court issued an injunction against the Speaker and asked the lawyers to file for judicial review (VonDoepp 2005).[22] A ban imposed on demonstrations relating to the proposed third term constitutional amendment was found unconstitutional,[23] which kept open the space for political contestation and added to the political momentum that eventually saw Muluzi bow down.

Reacting to some of these decisions, Parliament passed a motion to impeach three judges, alleging incompetence and misbehaviour. After an outcry from civil society; fact-finding missions from international organisations including the International Commission of Jurists, and reactions from the donor community, the President eventually pardoned the judges (Gloppen & Kanyongolo 2006).

Giving up changing the term limit, Muluzi threw his weight behind his hand-picked successor, Bingu wa Mutharika. The poorly organised 2004 elections gave rise to many court cases including a presidential petition,[24] which later collapsed, mainly for political reasons.[25]

---

21 *Chakuamba & Others v Attorney General* MSCA Civil Appeal No 20 of 2000 (unreported).
22 In the case of *Registered Trustees of the Public Affairs Committee v Attorney General & Another* Civil Cause No 1861 of 2003 (unreported), the High Court upheld the right of MPs to freely associate with civil society groups in political advocacy campaigns.
23 *Malawi Law Society v State* Civil Cause No 78 of 2002 (unreported).
24 *Tembo v Electoral Commission* Civil Cause No 282 of 2009 (unreported).
25 The first petitioner withdrew after being given a cabinet post. The second petitioner was ruled out of the case.

Once elected, President Mutharika initiated an anti-corruption campaign affecting prominent members of the previous government, including Muluzi himself, causing a fall-out with the party. Mutharika left the UDF in January 2005, establishing his own party, the DPP. The UDF, now finding itself in opposition, joined forces with other opposition parties and initiated a process to impeach the President. However, the High Court ordered Parliament to stop the proceedings until the courts subjected the procedural rules for impeachment to judicial review[26] — the slowness of the process working to the President's advantage. Haemorrhaging MPs to the DPP, the opposition asked the Speaker to enforce section 65 of the Constitution, holding that MPs elected on a party ticket lose their seat if they voluntarily leave and join another party. They argued that not only those who had formally resigned had lost their seats, but also MPs elected for another party who now consistently supported the President. The President replied by asking for a constitutional review of section 65, arguing that this section was inconsistent with the freedom of association of MPs.

When the parliamentary session ended, President Mutharika refused to call a new session for over half a year, by which time he had secured enough support to prevent the impeachment motion from succeeding.

Meanwhile, the *Section 65* case went through the court system. Both the High Court, sitting as a Constitutional Court, and the MSCA ruled against the President.[27] The MSCA's ruling authorised the Speaker of Parliament to declare vacant the seats of an estimated 80 MPs who had shifted their allegiance from other parties to the DPP. The affected MPs, fearing for their seats, obtained court injunctions barring the Speaker from executing the order, leading to a stand-off between the government and the opposition. The latter refused to pass the 2007–2008 budget unless section 65 was enforced and the defecting MPs removed, while the government refused to discuss the issue until the budget was passed. As public opinion turned against the opposition, perceived to jeopardise the welfare of the country for personal gain, the opposition gave in and passed the budget. The understanding was that section 65 would subsequently be implemented, but the President reversed his stance and prorogued Parliament for the remainder of the session (Gloppen et al 2007). Similar prorogues took place four times the following year, and by the time of the 2009 elections, the *Section 65* judgment had still not been implemented.

---

26 *In the Matter of a Presidential Reference of a Dispute of a Constitutional Nature Under s. 89(1) of the Constitution* Constitutional Cause No 13 of 2005 (unreported).

27 *In the Matter of a Presidential Reference of a Dispute of a Constitutional Nature Under s. 89(1) of the Constitution* Presidential Reference Appeal No 44 of 2006 (unreported). For critiques of the judgment, see Silungwe (2008); Matumbi (2008).

The *Section 65* case marks both a high and a low point for the judiciary's accountability function in Malawi. Knowing that their decision would enrage the government, the judges prevented the President's attempt to bolster his position through unconstitutional means. The judgment, with its potentially devastating consequences for the President, demonstrates the strength of the courts — but the effect was minimal in practice. The lengthy court process worked to the President's advantage, by affording a two-year respite. The *Section 65* case also had consequences for the judiciary. Political pressure related to the case led to the (slightly) early retirement of Chief Justice Unyolo in June 2007, and a more politicised appointment of the current Chief Justice.

The High Court was to be involved in a political case concerning the former president Bakili Muluzi in the run-up to the 2009 elections. Muluzi sought nomination as the UDF presidential candidate for the 2009 election, arguing that having been out of office, he was no longer affected by the constitutional stipulation that a person could serve as President for no more than 'a maximum of two consecutive terms'.[28]

The constitutionality of Muluzi's candidacy remained disputed. Two months before election day, the MEC found that Muluzi did not qualify as a candidate. Consequently, Muluzi applied to the High Court for judicial review. Three days before the election, the Court ruled that someone who had served two terms of office could not run for the state presidency again.[29] By then, the UDF had entered into an alliance with the MCP, supporting their presidential candidate, John Tembo.

The 2009 electoral process is notable for the court cases that did *not* come. Unlike in 1999 and 2004, no cases were filed to challenge the worse than ever and better documented bias in media coverage,[30] or the ruling party's use of state resources in the campaign. Neither was the presidential election itself challenged. It is difficult to tell whether this was due to disappointment with previous court attempts or the lack of confidence in the ability of the MEC to handle the electoral process and disputes arising from it independently and satisfactorily. We cannot firmly conclude that the absence of court cases has something to do with a decline in the political actors' trust in the political independence of the courts.

---

28 Section 83(3).

29 *Muluzi & United Democratic Front v Electoral Commission* Constitutional Cause No 1 of 2009 (unreported).

30 Documented in reports by the MEC's own media monitoring project as well as by election observers. According to the Electoral Institute of South Africa (EISA 2009), 'Malawi Television (TVM) and the Malawi Broadcasting Corporation (MBC) ... excessively favoured the DPP who, according to the Malawi Communications Regulatory Authority (MACRA), received on average over 90% coverage'.

3. Courts and elections in Uganda

The political significance of Uganda's judiciary has increased dramatically since the move towards multiparty elections in 2003. Parts of the formerly deferential judiciary have clashed with the political branches of government, producing remarkable decisions. However, the government's strategic use of the judicial process to get at political opponents and critics is also pronounced.

After the National Resistance Movement (NRM) came to power in Uganda in 1986, it initiated a widely consultative constitution-making process (Moehler 2006; Odoki 2005). The 1995 Constitution established the judiciary as an independent branch of government, granted the courts judicial review powers, gave prominence to the protection and enforcement of fundamental rights and freedoms, and established a Constitutional Court to interpret the Constitution.

Unlike in Malawi, the new Ugandan Constitution induced no immediate change in judicial behaviour and the courts continued to exercise judicial restraint. One explanation for this difference is that the 1995 Uganda Constitution came into force in a restrictive political environment, dominated by a military government and devoid of political parties that would initiate or sponsor court cases. In contrast, in Malawi, the Constitution that created a conducive environment for judicial activism was enacted in a political environment in which there were strong opposition parties and civil society organisations and a less dominant executive.

Half a decade later, more assertive constitutional interpretations started to come from the Ugandan courts, rendering them more attractive as an arena for the political opposition to contest legislative and executive actions. The courts' assertiveness coincided with the decline of the country's particular no-party democracy or 'movement system', which allowed competitive elections between individual candidates within the NRM, but barred political parties from competing. The process towards multiparty politics culminated in the 2005 referendum, which formally abolished the no-party system, paving the way for multiparty elections in February 2006.

The number of politically important cases increased during the transition to a multiparty system, resulting in judgments enforcing constitutional rules regarding referenda; opening the space for political parties to organise; and protecting freedom of the press, the independence of the Electoral Commission (UEC) and the jurisdiction of civil courts. This gave the opposition more faith in the courts as an arena in which to challenge the government. However, there have also been politically deferential decisions and an active use of the courts by the Ugandan government to repress the opposition (Ellet 2008; Gloppen et al 2008).

Table 4.3: Results of Uganda's presidential elections (in %), 1996–2006

	1996		2001		2006	
NRM*	Museveni	75.5	Museveni	69.3	Museveni	59.3
FDC*	-	-	Besigye	27.8	Besigye	37.4
DP*	-	-	-	-	Kizito	1.6
n.a	Ssemogerere	22.3	-	-	-	-
n.a	-	-	Awori	1.4	-	-
n.a	Manyanja	2.2	Manyanja	1.0	-	-
Other	-	-	Other	0.5	Other	1.7
Total		100		100		100

* In the 1996 and 2001 elections, no political parties were allowed. In a referendum held on 28 July 2005, Ugandans agreed to open up the political space and allow political parties to compete in elections.

Source: African Elections Database. Available at http://africanelections.tripod.com/ug.html. Accessed 15 November 2010.

Table 4.4: Number of seats in Uganda's Parliament per party, 1996–2006

	1996*	2006
NRM	156	191
FDC	-	37
UCP	-	9
DP	-	8
Independent	-	36
Others	120	3
TOTAL	276	284**

* In the 1996 and 2001 elections, no political parties were allowed. The opposition boycotted both elections. No election results available for 2001. In a referendum held on 28 July 2005, Ugandans agreed to open up the political space and allow political parties to compete in elections.

**284 seats were contested in the 2006 elections: 215 constituency seats and 69 district women representatives. In addition, the Parliament of Uganda counts 10 seats reserved for army MPs and 10 ex officio MPs.

Source: African Elections Database. Available at http://africanelections.tripod.com/ug.html. Accessed 15 November 2010.

As table 4.3 shows, the presidential elections of 2001 returned President Museveni with a comfortable margin. Kizza Besyge, the main opposition candidate, challenged the result, alleging widespread electoral malpractice and violence.[31] The Supreme Court, by a majority of three to two, dismissed the petition, finding

---

31   Documented by observers, including the NGO Election Monitoring Group — Uganda (Redfern 2001).

that there was no evidence that the irregularities had substantially affected the election outcome.[32]

After the 2006 elections, Kizza Besigye filed his second presidential election petition in the Supreme Court, ten days after Museveni's victory was announced,[33] as did a large number of candidates who had lost in parliamentary and local elections. Unlike elsewhere in the region, the Ugandan Constitution sets tight time frames for filing a challenge to elections (ten days), disposal of the petition by court (30 days) and holding of another election.[34]

In 2006, President Museveni's margin was narrower than in 2001, and based on the Court's ground for upholding the 2001 election result, the opposition sought to demonstrate that this time the *scale* of the irregularities was sufficient to affect the outcome. The Court agreed that the UEC had disenfranchised voters by deleting their names from the voters' register or denying them the right to vote; that there were irregularities in the counting and tallying of results; and that bribery, intimidation, violence, multiple voting, and vote stuffing had compromised the election in some parts of the country. Yet, a majority of four of the seven judges concluded that 'it was not proved to the satisfaction of the Court, that the failure to comply with the provisions and principles ... affected the results of the presidential election in a substantial manner'. Hence the Court set a very high threshold for overturning a presidential election (Gloppen et al 2008).

The 1995 Constitution left some fundamental questions to be decided through referenda, including the future form of government. In 2000, Parliament passed legislation approving a referendum, but the Constitutional Court struck it down on procedural grounds. While the case was heard, Parliament pre-emptively enacted the Referendum (Political Systems) Act,[35] which was identical to the legislation that the Constitutional Court had invalidated. The Act was passed into law within two hours and was made retroactive. The new law was also challenged, both on procedural grounds and on its retrospective character.[36] However, the petition was not heard until after the June 2000 referendum and was, eventually, dismissed (Gloppen et al 2008). A related case argued that the constitutional provision for a referendum contravened fundamental constitutional rights and freedoms, but the Constitutional Court found that it lacked jurisdiction to reconcile the conflicting provisions in the Constitution.[37]

---

32   *Rtd. Col. Kizza Besigye v Electoral Commission & Museveni* [2001] UGSC 3.
33   *Rtd. Col. Kizza Besigye v Electoral Commission & Museveni* [2007] UGSC 24.
34   Section 104.
35   Act 9 of 2000.
36   *Rwanyarare v Attorney General* [2000] UGCC 2.
37   *Olum v Attorney General* [1999] UGCC 3.

After the referendum, a constitutional amendment was enacted in 2000 which retroactively legalised the legislation under which the referendum was held. Three years later the Supreme Court reversed the decision, ruling that this amendment was unconstitutional on procedural grounds.[38] Consequently, the opposition challenged the legitimacy of the government formed on the basis of the invalidated legislation. The Constitutional Court ruled unanimously that since the Referendum (Political Systems) Act was invalid, so was the referendum, hence the government was illegal. The government appealed to the Supreme Court, which overturned the ruling. While agreeing that the Act setting up the vote was unconstitutional, it nevertheless upheld the referendum result.[39]

The Constitution required Parliament to pass legislation regulating the activities of political parties. In 2002, the Political Parties and Organizations Act[40] was passed into law. However, this Act prohibited political parties from holding public meetings, opening branches below national level or holding more than one national conference a year. The Constitutional Court found these sections to be incompatible with Article 75 of the Constitution, which provides that Parliament shall have no power to enact a law establishing a one-party state.[41] This allowed political organisations to participate more freely in public life (Gloppen et al 2008).

In June 2004, the Ugandan government announced that it would relax restrictions on political party activities and hold a new referendum to decide whether the country should return to multiparty politics. The opposition, considering this a delay tactic, claimed that the referendum was unconstitutional since the existing Constitution did not envisage the establishment of a one-party state.[42] A majority of the Constitutional Court judges dismissed this application and the appeal to the Supreme Court could not be heard due to lack of quorum following the retirement of one judge. The retired judge was replaced only after the referendum had been held, rendering the appeal moot. By keeping the Supreme Court non-operational, the executive effectively denied the opposition justice.

The media are crucial in the context of elections. Uganda has seen several cases against journalists. In *Charles Onyango Obbo & Andrew Mwenda v Attorney General,* two leading journalists, who were prosecuted for publication of false news, challenged the constitutionality of section 50 of the Penal Code, which creates this criminal offence.[43] The Supreme Court struck down the legislation

---

38   *Ssemogerere v Attorney General* [2004] UGSC 10.
39   *Attorney General v Ssemogerere* [2004] UGSC 35.
40   Act 18 of 2002.
41   *Ssemogerere v Attorney General* (note 38 above).
42   *Okello v Attorney General* [2005] UGCC 9.
43   [2004] UGSC 1.

as unconstitutional, emphasising the importance of freedom of speech to the democratic process, thus establishing a high threshold for limiting press freedom. But legal action against journalists continued. In August 2005, Mwenda[44] was again arrested and charged with sedition and 'promoting sectarianism'. In December 2005, two journalists were arrested on equally serious charges of inciting sectarianism after criticising President Museveni.[45] While convictions on such charges are rare, they serve to intimidate and hinder the press from developing their role in supporting democracy (Gloppen et al 2008).

Brigadier Henry Tumukunde v Attorney General & The Electoral Commission[46] is another case concerning political space, where the judiciary's performance was lacklustre. A quota of parliamentary seats was reserved for the army. An army MP, Brigadier Tumukunde, who had publicly criticised the government's position, was directed by the President to resign, arrested and charged with insubordination in a military court. He petitioned the Court to restrain the UEC from holding the by-election to fill his seat, but a divided Constitutional Court (three to two) dismissed the petition relying on 'the political question doctrine'.[47] Split rulings are increasingly common in political cases, both in the Constitutional Court and in the Supreme Court (Ellet 2008; Gloppen et al 2008).

In February 2005, an 'Omnibus' constitutional amendment Bill was tabled before Parliament seeking to amend a large number of constitutional provisions at once, including lifting the two-term limit for the President. While the Bill was under consideration, a petition was filed challenging its constitutionality.[48] The Constitutional Court (again three to two) dismissed the petition on the ground that the Bill had not yet been enacted.

In Uganda, it is noteworthy how criminal cases became part of the 2006 election campaign, mainly directed at Kizza Besigye, Museveni's main opponent, and his party, the Forum for Democratic Change (FDC). In the 2001 presidential campaign, Besigye was charged with 'seditious intent' and in the run-up to the February 2006 elections, this resurfaced as treason and terrorism charges, resulting in Besigye's arrest and frustrating his presidential campaign. He was also charged with rape in a case that proved weak and had clear links to the President.

The arrests of Besigye fall into a pattern of arresting political opponents on 'un-bailable' charges such as murder, treason and terrorism, so that they can be kept

---

44   Andrew Mwenda, political editor of *The Monitor* and KFM talk show host.
45   *Weekly Observer* editor James Tumusiime and reporter Semujju Ibrahim Nganda.
46   [2005] UGCC 1.
47   The judgment quoted Liberman (1987, 128), 'some questions are too political for the courts to give legal answers … over certain issues, the Constitution commits complete discretion to the other branches'.
48   *Matembe v Attorney General* [2005] UGCC 3.

in pre-trial remand for prolonged periods to frustrate their electoral campaigns (Gloppen et al 2006; 2008). It is highly significant that the High Court decided to release Besigye on bail, reaffirming that bail was a constitutional right and overriding the legislation classifying treason as an un-bailable offence during the first six months of detention. The international diplomatic corps closely followed the *Besigye* case and attended the court proceedings. While this may have strengthened the judges' resolve, it did not prevent the government from responding by posting paramilitaries in and around the High Court buildings. To keep Besigye and his co-accused in jail, they were re-charged with terrorism in the military court system. The conflict was exacerbated by the Court Martial's open defiance of the civilian judicial authorities. Despite a history of harsh criticism of anti-government rulings, the militant intimidation of the judiciary, reminiscent of Idi Amin, came as a shock. The threats against judicial independence elicited popular support for the judiciary, and unprecedentedly strong reactions from the legal community[49] (Ellet 2008; Gloppen et al 2006).

By detaining Besigye, the government sought to prevent his nomination as presidential candidate, but the UEC accepted his nomination *in absentia*. When this was challenged, the Constitutional Court upheld the nomination and underscored the UEC's independence.[50] Besigye remained incarcerated until six weeks before the elections, but while on 'interim bail', he was forced to divide his time between court hearings and campaigning. This affected his ability to campaign effectively throughout the country (Gloppen et al 2008).

4.   Do strategic models explain these patterns?

In the introduction, we explained how the development of independent judiciaries in a democratising context is commonly explained with reference to the strategic interests of the actors involved. One set of arguments emphasises how political and legal structures condition and constrain the operating space open to the courts, another stresses how contextual factors affect judges' incentives to act independently.

External strategic explanations assume that courts only exercise their accountability function if they believe that the government is willing to accept their authority, while governments are assumed to bow to judicial authority where this brings a benefit (or where undermining judicial independence carries a cost) exceeding the burden of judicial accountability. Fear of losing power in the next election is a key incentive for political power holders to respect the courts'

---

49   Similar paramilitary presence in court a year later caused very little reaction, nationally or internationally.

50   *Kabagambe v Electoral Commission* [2006] UGCC 7.

independence and authority (Englund 2000; Ross 2004; 2009; VonDoepp & Ellett 2008). Hence, courts are assumed to have more opportunities to develop accountability functions in the context of competitive elections. This fits well with the comparatively strong accountability function of the Malawian courts and the increasing significance of the Ugandan courts prior to competitive elections.

However, on a closer examination, these governments — contrary to the theoretical predictions — seem less interested in an independent judiciary when the chances of losing power in the next election increase. When the incumbent's position is weakened, courts are perceived as a potential threat to continued incumbency, leading to attempts to rein in the courts and undermine their independence. In Malawi, this is evident in relation to the impeachment processes put into motion after judicial actions helped derail President Muluzi's attempt to remove presidential term limits ahead of the 2004 election; and in the appointment of the current Chief Justice in breach of established seniority norms. In Uganda, attempts to rein in the judiciary were part of the constitutional reform package that accompanied the multiparty reforms, and blatant in the siege of the High Court to prevent Besigye's release. President Museveni has also actively used the appointment process to create a more agreeable judiciary.

Strategic defection arguments hold up better and seem to have considerable explanatory power. Particularly in Uganda, the unprecedented judicial assertiveness in the pre-election context fits the 'defection when there is uncertainty as to the continuity of the regime' prediction. However, there is a question as to whether the judges in fact saw the fall of the regime as a likely outcome and whether this was the driving force behind their actions.

As argued in Gloppen et al (2010), strategic models, while useful, are too limited to explain why the courts in Malawi and Uganda have developed stronger accountability functions. The same is true for structural approaches, focusing on how courts are embedded in civil and political society; institutional models, emphasising differences in structural independence; and attitudinal models, emphasising differences between the judges with regard to social, professional and political backgrounds. Each has insights to contribute, but single-factor explanations are incapable of explaining the patterns displayed by the judiciaries under study here.

5. Multifaceted explanations needed

To understand the accountability function of African judiciaries, it is crucial to understand how various factors interact and to look more holistically at the central actors' *opportunity situation*. The judges' opportunity situation — the incentives and constraints they face when deciding whether and how to hold political power to account — is influenced by an interplay of factors, including the social and political context and the institutional structure in which they function as well as certain of their individual characteristics.

5.1. Social and political context

To understand why competitive elections make people in positions of power more interested in an independent judiciary to safeguard their 'afterlife', it is important to take into account the centrality of political office to social and economic power. These are new polities where there is a fundamental uncertainty with regard to what awaits ex-Presidents personally, and whether there will be another chance for the party to bounce back. They are also neopatrimonial societies where positions and resources to a large extent follow ties of family and clan and where the loss of political power implies a fundamental loss of economic resources (VonDoepp 2009). So, while the government may have interests in an independent judiciary up to a point, the imperative of staying in power is much stronger than the strategic models seem to assume. This is not a fundamental criticism of the strategic approach but rather a suggestion as to what needs to go into the calculus.

For courts to perform their accountability function effectively, they need the support of political parties, the legal community, donors, business and the general public. Government officials are more likely to submit to judicial authority where there is a culture of legalism and where respect for the rule of law is central to the legitimacy of the regime. Similarly, where the legal community is strong, or where a strong business community requires a functioning legal system, it is more costly to ignore or overrule the courts (Widner 1999; 2001). Neither Malawi nor Uganda has particularly strong protective constituencies for the judiciary.[51]

It is also important to consider the nature of the political cases which come to the courts. Where there are no alternative channels of resolving political disputes and the government is unresponsive to significant social and political interests, such unresolved disputes are more likely to end up in the courts. In both countries, the lack of trust in electoral management bodies and political structures has contributed to the centrality of the courts in political dispute resolution. In Malawi, political accountability institutions are largely ineffectual and Parliament has been weak and ineffective. The lack of alternative institutions capable of solving

---

51   The 2001 impeachment of Malawian judges drew reactions from the international community, but not the 2007 resignation of the Chief Justice Leonard Unyolo. In Uganda, the international community reacted strongly to the military action in the Kampala High Court prior to the 2006 election, but not at all to a similar incident a year later.

political disputes, combined with the willingness of judges to take on political cases, helps explain why the courts have become an important player in Malawian politics. In Uganda, the NRM has considerable institutional capacity, but it has not been effective in addressing challenges from outside the movement.

History also helps to understand the relative strength of the judicial institution in Malawi. Unlike in many other one-party states, where the judiciary was 'captured from within' and subjected through politically appointed chief justices, President Banda marginalised the Malawian judiciary from political cases through establishing a parallel system of traditional courts. Ironically, this enabled the judiciary to emerge relatively untainted from the one-party regime (Kanyongolo 2004). Surviving the transition largely intact and aided by the 1994 Constitution, it established itself as a robust and politically significant institution in a context of dwindling trust in political institutions and processes (Ellett 2008; Gloppen & Kanyongolo 2006; 2007; VonDoepp 2009). Extensive use of injunctions to stop or delay government actions established the courts as a source of 'instant justice'.[52] As one interviewee phrased it, 'democracy in Malawi is to have a judge on call'.[53]

In Malawi, weak institutions appear to drive political cases to the courts. Court action is easier than collective mobilisation and provides a mechanism for conflict resolution when party structures and political bodies are incapable. While useful for politicians, the courts are less accessible to ordinary Malawians. Apart from faith communities, Malawi does not have a strong civil society or well-resourced non-governmental organisations (NGOs) who can provide legal aid, although some competent organisations have actively used the courts for 'accountability-litigation'.[54]

In Uganda, where the one-party (no-party) system gradually opened to political competition, the incumbent party retained its dominant position and control over the levers of political power and the process has stopped short of a fully democratic system. The ability of political and civil society to mobilise remains closely circumscribed and civil society is closely intertwined with 'the Movement'. This helps explain the importance of courts as an important mobilisation arena.

Competitive election processes increase the demand for the courts' intervention, providing new opportunities for exercising their accountability

---

52 An injunction requires someone to stop (or take) specific actions. Preliminary injunctions temporarily restrain actions until the court has made a final decision after a trial.

53 Interview with a Malawian judge, July 2004.

54 This includes the Public Affairs Committee (PAC), a civil society body comprising many of the country's faith communities. For the role of Malawi's civil society and faith communities see Englund (2000); Ross (2004); Svåsand and Patel (2007); VonDoepp (2002).

function. To be called on when democracy is at stake may generate a sense of urgency and compel judges to do what they see as normatively right. Interviews indicate such a dynamic, particularly at historical moments when 'all eyes' are on the judiciary—such as at election time, when major court decisions are scrutinised nationally and internationally. This normative urgency may account for the sudden rise in accountability performance by Ugandan courts before the 2006 elections. Interviews indicate that few judges expected President Museveni to leave, but had a strong sense that the democratic transition was in danger. Parts of the judiciary also seemed to act out of resentment against being used strategically to get rid of political opponents.[55]

Moral urgency explanations can be coupled with a broadened strategic defection argument. Judges may strategically defect from the government and strengthen their accountability function if they position themselves for alternative career opportunities, whether in national politics or international organisations. This may trigger a display of independence, particularly when cases receive international attention, which has been a factor in both countries.

Both Uganda and Malawi have experienced overt 'battles over the bench' in reaction to adverse judgments: impeachments, criticism and informal pressure in Malawi; and in Uganda, everything ranging from harsh rhetoric and a display of physical force on court premises, to political appointments and attempts to undercut the courts' powers and independence through constitutional reform. This has polarised the judiciary—timorous souls become more deferent, others emboldened. In Malawi, the 2001 impeachment incident appeared to strengthen the judiciary and demonstrated their protective constituency. The Ugandan government is less sensitive to external pressure, and donors are unstable as a protective constituency, themselves 'strategically defecting' once the elections are over and the power holders for the next five years have been identified.

Presidential election petitions (in Malawi in 1999 and 2004; in Uganda in 2001 and 2006) provide spectacular accountability cases and similar patterns. Despite acknowledging irregularities, the courts have eventually verified the elections. The reluctance to do so is more evident in Uganda. Both the 2001 and 2006 presidential petition judgments contained severe criticism of the election process and ended with split decisions. The Ugandan Chief Justice smiled when commenting that to nullify a presidential election would be suicidal,[56] nevertheless, to remove a sitting president from office, however justified and formally within their powers, seems in reality to be outside the realistic opportunity structure of these judiciaries.

---

55   Author interviews, Kampala February 2006.
56   Interview with author, April 2005.

5.2. Institutional design

Many explanations of judicial behaviour are based on variations in institutional design (Gloppen et al 2004, 2010; Gloppen & Kanyongolo 2007). They take as their point of departure assumptions about how institutional mechanisms preserve the authority of the judiciary and insulate judges from government interference (UN Basic Principles on the Independence of the Judiciary 1985; IFES). A limited role for the executive in the selection and disciplining of judges, and security of tenure and resources are expected to yield judiciaries which are better positioned to hold executives to account. The probability of a strong judiciary is also assumed to increase with stronger formal powers.

Findings from Malawi and Uganda suggest that political influence on appointments affects the courts' performance, despite institutional safeguards. Judicial appointments are comparatively well protected. In Uganda, all judicial appointments require nomination by the Judicial Service Commission and parliamentary approval. In Malawi, the appointment of a Chief Justice requires approval by two-thirds of MPs. Despite these formal procedures, political influence is (perceived as) a problem in Uganda, where parliamentary approval is ineffective due to a weak political opposition. In Malawi, the formal procedures did not prevent a politicised appointment of the current Chief Justice. This shows that institutional barriers have limited effect if executives have their minds set on 'appointing cadres to the bench'.

Ugandan judges have comparatively strong protection in terms of salaries and benefits. Also in Malawi, despite the 2001 impeachment incidence, the protection of judicial tenure is generally adequate. However, the fact that judges negotiate their conditions of employment with the government represents a potential vulnerability.

Court structure may also influence the accountability function of the judiciary. Both in Uganda and Malawi, the Supreme Court is the apex court in constitutional and other matters. The 'Constitutional Courts' in both countries are panels of High Court judges[57] hearing constitutional cases as courts of first instance. These panels provide an opportunity to the judges to build their competence in constitutional jurisprudence and awareness of constitutional principles and values, albeit to a lesser extent than specialised constitutional courts.

Another significant aspect of the court structure is the disciplining force of the judicial hierarchy. Where the Chief Justice is politicised and close to the executive this may affect courts' accountability functions. Lack of trust in the courts' political independence may discourage litigation, and judges may be

---

57   In Uganda judges of the Court of Appeal.

more cautious if they believe that the Chief Justice will punish independent-minded judgments. In Uganda, chief justices have historically changed with new presidents, contrary to formal norms and sometimes violently. Perceived close links between the Chief Justice and the executive may explain the lapse in time from the passing of the Constitution in 1995 to the strengthening of the judiciary's assertiveness. In Malawi, on the other hand, the now discontinued practice of appointing the Chief Justice on a seniority principle may have been conducive to the broad individual variation among Malawian judges, helping to explain why the courts have maintained legitimacy despite their increasingly central political role, and sometimes apparently partisan judges (VonDoepp 2006).

Court procedure is also relevant. Both Ugandan and Malawian courts do not have the power to initiate cases at their own instance, and the rules of procedure and standing (who can bring which cases) influence what cases are brought before them. Procedures and costs remain barriers, but access to the higher courts is easier in Uganda where public interest litigation is allowed, than in Malawi, where restrictions on standing hamper the ability of NGOs to litigate. However, once cases have been accepted (particularly cases related to elections), Malawian courts have been quick and have frequently used injunctions to stop government action.

There are significant differences in jurisdiction and review powers of the courts in the two countries. The jurisdiction of the courts in Uganda is threatened by the government's use of military courts for political purposes. In contrast, Malawi has constitutional provisions preserving the right of the highest courts to decide what falls under their jurisdiction, thus protecting the courts' jurisdiction from encroachment.

These differences in the institutional design can enhance our understanding of the opportunity structure facing judges, litigants and political power-holders.

5.3. Characteristics of individual judges

Does it matter who the judges are? A considerable amount of literature explains differences in courts' assertiveness with differences in the judges' background, or political and ideological orientation (Gloppen et al 2010).

There are few statistical analyses of ideological voting patterns among African judges, partly due to lack of systematic data. However, Von Doepp (2006; 2009), analysing how judges in Malawi and Zambia vote in political cases, finds that variables normally considered important — for example, who appointed the judge and the judge's previous record — are not significant. Looking at identities such as ethnicity, region of origin and religion which are politically significant in many African countries, he finds that in Malawi, a judge's regional identity appears to exert some influence. Judges from the President's region are more likely to decide for the government (Von Doepp 2006; 2009). Comparative studies suggest that judges from academic backgrounds exercise an activist democracy-enhancing accountability function more assertively and in our cases there also seems to be some support for this (Gloppen et al 2010).

Given the hierarchical structure of the judiciary, the Chief Justice's personality and the degree of politicisation of the office is central to the development of an independent judiciary. In the context of a new democracy, chief justices strongly influence the judicial corporate culture and the judges' conception of their own role vis-à-vis the executive and the political domain. In Malawi, we have suggested that the appointment of the Chief Justice according to seniority contributed to the depoliticisation of the office.

6. Conclusion

Courts in Malawi and Uganda play a significant role in promoting and facilitating governmental accountability. This is evident in relation to judicial interventions in electoral processes. Both in Malawi and Uganda, the courts display a turbulent pattern in election-related decisions, at times performing a strong accountability function, at other times bowing to executive pressure. The evidence from the two countries indicates that judicial independence is a key variable that affects the effectiveness of courts in performing their accountability function at all stages of the electoral cycle. In turn, judicial independence is a function of the interplay of the social and political context, the institutional design of the judiciary and the characteristics of individual judges.

In Malawi, the judiciary has played an active role in the electoral process since the formal establishment of a democratic political order in the mid-1990s. Through its intervention in electoral disputes, the judiciary has become involved in politics, both as arbiter and actor, especially in the context of post-2005 succession politics. Court intervention in the floor-crossing cases, which effectively prevented a change in the numerical power balance in the National Assembly which could have led to the impeachment of the President, increased judicial involvement in 'political' cases. In turn, this focused public attention on the actual and perceived political independence of the courts and their effectiveness in enforcing governmental accountability. However, the relative restraint of the judiciary with respect to the 2009 election cases suggests a movement towards insulating the judiciary and its independence from politics and thus enhancing its potential for performing its accountability function. At the same time, however, the development could be viewed as a self-imposed restriction of the accountability role of the courts introduced by a newly-appointed Chief Justice who is perceived in some quarters as an ally of the

President and who was appointed to the position from outside the judiciary in a departure from the practice of appointing the most senior judge to the position. It could also be that there is simply a fall in the number of electoral disputes referred to the courts due to a more credible electoral commission and a more competently run electoral process.

Uganda illustrates even more clearly how strengthening of the courts' accountability function has led to confrontation with the executive and has generated a political backlash in the form of the government's attempts to undermine judicial independence. The courts strengthened their accountability function in the process leading up to the 2006 elections, stimulating a growing number of political cases. The judiciary was further politicised by the government's use of the judicial process to suppress its political opponents and critics. The ongoing battle over the loyalty of the judiciary is evident in the appointments of party-loyal judges and the pattern of split decisions on the Constitutional and Supreme Courts, where judges seeking to hold the government to account for unconstitutional action lose out to a more deferential majority.

To see the courts' accountability role as a function of political space carries significant explanatory power. The concept of protective constituencies, combined with a broadened notion of strategic defection, highlights how courts rely on cracks in the political power structure and counterweights to executive power, rendering the executive politically sensible to tolerate judicial authority. When protective constituencies provide some assurance that to assert their authority is not professional suicide, the motivation of judges to stand up to the government increases. The specific constituencies playing this role vary between the countries and over time, ranging from political opposition parties using the courts, via the legal community and national and international civil society, to international donors.

Strategic defection explanations (Helmke 2002; 2003; 2005) assume that judges are primarily concerned with their future, individually and as an institution, and predict that in uncertain political contexts (typically before a competitive election), judges are likely to shift their allegiance away from the sitting regime and perform a stronger accountability function. While this superficially fits the pattern in Uganda and Malawi, interviews suggest that judges became more assertive, despite believing that the incumbent would not lose. In these cases, judicial independence seemed influenced by the judges' normative orientation, and how this was activated in the political context, creating a sense of urgency, a 'need to save democracy'. This is linked to the legal culture and professional norms within the judiciary, and is reinforced by being in the public eye and being part of a regional and international professional community of judges, where standing among peers — and sometimes attractive international appointments — depends on adherence to shared professional norms.

While modified strategic models seem able to capture important dynamics leading to increased judicial assertiveness in the context of competitive elections, they are less able to explain the efforts by executives in both countries to rein in the judiciary. They fail to capture the dynamics of African neopatrimonial politics, where 'the insurance' of an independent judiciary is insufficient to make the possibility of leaving office an acceptable option.

No single factor can explain the patterns of judicial independence displayed in the two countries and their impact on the accountability function of the courts. Multifaceted explanations are needed. By extension, explaining the effectiveness of the judiciary in facilitating accountability of governments requires an appreciation of the totality of factors that define the structure of the courts and the specific political contexts in which they operate.

References

Legislation

Constitution of the Republic of Malawi, 1994.
Constitution of the Republic of Uganda, 1995.
Penal Code, chapter 120 of the Laws of Uganda.
Political Parties and Organizations Act 18 of 2002.
Referendum (Political Systems) Act 9 of 2000.

Reports

Basic Principles on the Independence of the Judiciary. Seventh United Nations Congress on the Prevention of Crime and the Treatment of Offenders. 26 August–3 September 1985. Milan, Italy.

Cases

Aaron Longwe v Attorney General Miscellaneous Civil Application No 11 of 1993 (unreported).
Attorney General v Chakuamba & Others v Electoral Commission Civil Cause No 30 of 1999 (unreported).
Attorney General v Ssemogerere [2004] UGSC 35.
Brigadier Henry Tumukunde v Attorney General & The Electoral Commission [2005] UGCC 1.
Chakuamba & Chihana v The Electoral Commission Civil Cause No 25 of 1999 (unreported).
Chakuamba & Others v Attorney General MSCA Civil Appeal No 20 of 2000 (unreported).

Chakufwa Chihana v Republic [1992] MLR 71.

Charles Onyango Obbo & Andrew Mwenda v Attorney General [2004] UGSC 1.

Chikweza v The Electoral Commission Civil Cause No 1061 of 1994 (unreported).

Du Chisiza v Minister of Education [1993] 16(1) MLR 81.

In Re Nomination of J.J. Chidule Civil Cause No 5 of 1995 (unreported).

In the Matter of a Presidential Reference of a Dispute of a Constitutional Nature Under s. 89(1) of the Constitution Constitutional Cause No 13 of 2005 (unreported).

In the Matter of Presidential Reference of a Dispute of a Constitutional Nature under Section 89(1)(h) of the Constitution and In the Matter of Section 65 of the Constitution and In the Matter of the Question of the Crossing of the Floor by Members of the National Assembly MSCA Presidential Reference Appeal No 44 of 2006 (unreported).

Kabagambe v Electoral Commission [2006] UGCC 7.

Kafumba v Electoral Commission & Malawi Broadcasting Corporation Civil Cause No 30 of 1999 (unreported).

Khembo v Electoral Commission Civil Cause No 70 of 1999 (unreported).

Malawi Law Society v State Civil Cause No 78 of 2002 (unreported).

Matembe v Attorney General [2005] UGCC 3.

Muluzi & Thomson v Attorney General Civil Cause No 66 of 1993 (unreported).

Muluzi & United Democratic Front v Electoral Commission Constitutional Cause No 1 of 2009 (unreported).

Mungomo v Electoral Commission Civil Application No 23 of 1999 (unreported).

National Democratic Alliance (NDA) v Electoral Commission & Others Constitutional Cause No 3 of 2004 (unreported).

Nkhwazi v Referendum Commission Civil Cause No 96 of 1993 (unreported).

Okello v Attorney General [2005] UGCC 9.

Olum v Attorney General [1999] UGCC 3.

Phambala v Chairman of the Electoral Commission Civil Cause No 34 of 1999 (unreported).

Phoso v The Electoral Commission Civil Cause No 1271 of 1996 (unreported).

Registered Trustees of the Public Affairs Committee v Attorney General & Another Civil Cause No 1861 of 2003 (unreported).

Republic v Chikhadwe & Chikhadwe Criminal Case No LL/CR/60/1/2004 (Lilongwe First Grade Magistrate Court, unreported).

Rtd. Col. Kizza Besigye v Electoral Commission & Museveni [2001] UGSC 3.

Rtd. Col. Kizza Besigye v Electoral Commission & Museveni [2007] UGSC 24.

Rwanyarare v Attorney General [2000] UGCC 2.

Ssemogerere v Attorney General [2004] UGSC 10.

State v President of the Republic of Malawi, ex parte Muluzi & Tembo Civil Cause No 99 of 2007 (unreported).

State v President of the Republic of Malawi & Malawi Communications Regulatory Authority, ex parte Joy Radio Ltd Miscellaneous Civil Cause No 198 of 2006 (unreported).

Tembo v Electoral Commission Civil Cause No 282 of 2009 (unreported).

Articles, books, chapters in books and other works

AFP. 2009. Malawi court delays decision on ex-president's run. 15 May. Available at http://www.google.com/hostednews/afp/article/ALeqM5hVtZ2pZ4DhJMsQ1L hjDhRktyOjJ. Accessed 15 November 2010.

CPJ (Committee to Protect Journalists). 2007. Malawi: Private radio stations censored over political coverage. April 17. Available at http://allafrica.com/stories/200704 180033.html. Accessed 15 November 2010.

EISA (Electoral Institute of South Africa). 2009. Interim report from the EISA observer mission. 21 May. Available at http://www.eisa.org.za/EISA/pr20090521.htm. Accessed 15 November 2010.

Ellett, R.L. 2008. *Emerging Judicial Power in Transitional Democracies: Malawi, Tanzania and Uganda*. Ph.D. Dissertation, North-Eastern University, Boston, MA.

Englund, H. 2000. The dead hand of human rights: Contrasting Christianities in post-transition Malawi. *Journal of Modern African Studies*, 38(4): 579–603.

Gloppen, S., Gargarella R. & Skaar, E. (eds). 2004. *Democratization and the Judiciary: The Accountability Function of Courts in New Democracies*. London: Frank Cass.

Gloppen, S. & Kanyongolo, F.E. 2006. The role of the judiciary in the 2004 general elections in Malawi. *East African Journal of Peace and Human Rights*, 12(2): 279–317.

Gloppen, S. & Kanyongolo, F.E. 2007. The judiciary. In Patel, P. & Svåsand, L. (eds). *Government and Politics in Malawi*. Lilongwe: Kachere Publishers, 109–135.

Gloppen, S., Kasimbazi, E. & Kibandama, A. 2006. The evolving role of the courts in the political transition process. Chr Michelsen Institute and Makerere University: Legal and Institutional Context of the 2006 Elections in Uganda Research Notes. Available at www.cmi.no/pdf/?file=/uganda/doc/gloppen-kazimbazi-kibandama-courts-political%20transition-research-note-Jan-06.pdf. Accessed 15 June 2009.

Gloppen, S., Kasimbazi, E. & Kibandama, A. 2008. Elections in court: The judiciary and Uganda's 2006 election process. In Kiiza, J., Makara, S. & Rakner, L. (eds). *Electoral Democracy in Uganda: Understanding the Institutional Processes and Outcomes of the 2006 Multiparty Elections*. Kampala: Fountain Publishers, 53–89.

Gloppen, S., Rakner, L. & Svåsand, L. 2007. Political paralysis in Malawi: Repercussions of party splits in a weakly institutionalised democracy. Paper presented at the 2007 European Consortium for Political Research, Pisa (on file with author).

Gloppen, S., Wilson, B., Gargarella, R., Skaar, E. & Kinander, M. 2010. *Courts and Power in Latin America and Africa*. New York: Palgrave Macmillan.

Helmke, G. 2002. The logic of strategic defection: Court—executive relations in Argentina. *American Political Science Review*, 96(2): 291–303.

Helmke, G. 2003. Checks and balances by other means: Strategic defection and the 're-reelection' controversy in Argentina. *Comparative Politics*, 35(2): 213–228.

Helmke, G. 2005. *Courts under Constraints. Judges, Generals, and Presidents in Argentina*. Cambridge: Cambridge University Press.

IFES (International Foundation for Election Systems). N.d. Guidance for promoting judicial independence and impartiality. Available at www.ifes.org/publication/0e49c

032c28f9e60a181630f281eda5a/judicial_independence.pdf. Accessed 15 November 2010.

ICJ (International Commission of Jurists). 2002. Malawi: Final report of fact-finding mission and trial observation to Malawi. Available at http://www.icj.org/news. php3?id_article=2781&lang=en. Accessed 16 November 2010.

Kanyongolo, F.E. 2004. State of the judiciary report: Malawi 2003. Washington DC: IFES, State of the Judiciary Report Series.

Liberman, J.K. 1987. *The Enduring Constitution: A Bicentennial Perspective.* St. Paul: West Publishing Company.

Matumbi, B.P. 2007. The presumption of perfection and the Presidential Reference on Section 65. *Malawi Law Journal*, 1(2): 247–257.

MISA (Media Institute of Southern Africa). 2007. Malawi: High Court nullifies improperly-appointed Communications Regulatory Board. 20 July. Available at http://allafrica.com/stories/200707230869.html. Accessed 15 November 2010.

MISA (Media Institute of Southern Africa). 2008. Malawi: Joy Radio allowed resuming broadcasting. 17 December. Available at http://allafrica.com/stories/200812171066. html. Accessed 15 November 2010.

Moehler, D.C. 2006. Public participation and support for the Constitution in Uganda. *Journal of Modern African Studies*, 44(2): 275–308.

Odoki, B. 2005. *The Search for a National Consensus: The Making of the 1995 Uganda Constitution.* Kampala, Uganda: Fountain Publishers.

Redfern, P. 2001. Vote theft, intimidation, dent Museveni's image — UK media. *The Monitor,* 14 March.

Ross, K.R. 2004. Worrisome trends: The voice of the churches in Malawi's third term debate, *African Affairs,* 103: 91–107.

Silungwe, C.M. 2007. Courts' powers of review and the Presidential Reference on Section 65. *Malawi Law Journal*, 1(2): 235–246.

Svåsand, L. & Patel, N. (eds). 2007. *Government and Politics in Malawi.* Zomba: Kachere Books.

VonDoepp, P. 2002. Are Malawi's local clergy civil society activists: The limiting impact of creed, context and class. In Englund, H. (ed.) *A Democracy of Chameleons: Politics and Culture in the New Malawi.* Uppsala: Nordiska Afrikainstitutet, 123–139.

VonDoepp, P. 2005. The problem of judicial control in Africa's neopatrimonial democracies: Malawi and Zambia. *Political Science Quarterly*, 120(2): 275–301.

VonDoepp, P. 2006. Politics and judicial assertiveness in emerging democracies: High Court behaviour in Malawi and Zambia. *Political Research Quarterly*, 59(3): 389–399.

VonDoepp, P. 2009. *Judicial Politics in New Democracies: Cases from Southern Africa.* Boulder, CO: Lynne Rienner.

VonDoepp, P. & Ellet, R. 2008. Strategic models of executive–judicial relations: Insights from new African democracies. Paper presented at the annual meeting of the American Political Science Association, 27–31 August, Boston, MA.

Widner, J.A. 1999. Building judicial independence in common law Africa. In Schedler, A., Diamond, L. & Plattner, M.F. (eds). *The Self-Restraining State: Power and Accountability in New Democracies.* Boulder, CO: Lynne Rienner Publishers, 177–194.

Widner, J.A. 2001. *Building the Rule of Law.* New York: W.W. Norton & Company.

Chapter 5

From parliamentary supremacy to judicial review: Relations between Parliament and the judiciary in Tanzania

Jwani T. Mwaikusa

1. Introduction

In many countries, the judiciary, through its judicial review powers, is seen as a vital check on the executive and, increasingly, on Parliament. However, in Tanzania, relations between Parliament and the judiciary have traditionally been dominated by the principle that Parliament is the supreme law-making body and the judiciary administers justice according to the law as enacted by Parliament. Accordingly, courts have no mandate to review and question what Parliament has enacted. Curiously, constitutional developments in Tanzania and elsewhere on the African continent show a departure from this position. Several countries have adopted Constitutions which proclaim the supremacy of the Constitution, prescribe limits to the legislative powers of Parliament, and empower the judiciary to enforce those limits by way of judicial review of parliamentary action. This has brought into question the traditional claims of parliamentary supremacy and a new opening for holding Parliament to account (horizontal accountability), beyond the traditional, vertical accountability of Parliament and parliamentarians to the electorate.[1]

This chapter examines the role of judicial review as a means of holding the Tanzanian Parliament to account.[2] This issue is dealt with from historical and contemporary perspectives. Before the new Constitution was adopted, the doctrine of parliamentary supremacy meant that courts had limited powers of reviewing parliamentary action. In 1984, when the notion of constitutional supremacy was endorsed and a Bill of Rights was included in the Constitution, Tanzanian courts were entrusted with constitutional powers to inquire into

---

1   See chapter 1.
2   For a recent study on this subject, see Mwihambi (2009).

legislative acts. This chapter will underscore the significance of this development as far as enhancing the accountability of Parliament in Tanzania is concerned.

However, as will become clearer in this chapter, the power of the courts to review legislative action, important as it is, is yet to be understood fully by the general public, as well as the executive and Parliament. It is therefore not surprising that Parliament has on several occasions refused to cooperate with the courts, either by disobeying court orders or overturning court decisions. Although such recalcitrance has mainly been at the instance of the executive, whose dominance of the legislative process is well known, it has in some instances originated from Parliament itself. Many in Tanzania, especially parliamentarians, still believe that Parliament is supreme despite the fact that Tanzania no longer subscribes to the doctrine of parliamentary supremacy, having adopted the idea of constitutional supremacy in 1984. Clearly, the idea of checks and balances will not find full application in Tanzania unless the principle of constitutional supremacy is understood and respected by all organs of state, including Parliament.

2. Parliamentary supremacy in Tanzania

In determining the extent to which judicial review may be used to hold Parliament to account, courts are guided by the doctrine of the separation of powers.[3] As noted earlier, the principle of parliamentary supremacy in Tanzania meant that the courts could not question the legislative Acts of Parliament. The duty of the courts, in accordance with this principle, was regarded as being limited to that of administering justice according to the law. In the exercise of their mandate, courts did not have the legitimacy to make law, no matter what one may say about the effect and implications of judicial precedent in common-law systems. Effectively, the judiciary was subservient and subordinate to Parliament — which was the supreme law-maker.

Nevertheless, in interpreting the law, courts sometimes extended the application of the law to new situations that were not envisaged when the law was enacted. In applying what is described as a 'purposive approach' to statutory interpretation, courts went to the extent of 'reading words' into some statutory provisions so as to give them a reasonable meaning or to eliminate absurdities.[4] This technique has been accepted as part of the task of interpreting the law, and not law-making *per se*.

---

3   See, for example *Rev Christopher Mtikila v Attorney General* [1995] TLR 31; *Attorney General v Lohay Akonaay & Another* [1995] TLR 80, [1994] 2 LRC 399; *Mwalimu Paul John Mhozya v Attorney General* [1996] TLR 130; *Lujuna Shubi Ballonzi v Registered Trustees of Chama cha Mapinduzi* [1996] TLR 203.

4   *Kammins Ballrooms Co Ltd v Zenith Investments (Torquay) Ltd* [1970] 2 All ER 871; *Nothman v Barnet London Borough* [1978] 1 All ER 1243.

In Tanzania, the technique of reading of words into a statute was used for the first time by the Court of Appeal in *Joseph Warioba v Stephen Wassira & Another*.[5] Section 114 of the Elections Act 1 of 1985 provided that a person could be disqualified from registration as a voter or contestant in an election if that person was guilty of illegal practices. In this case, the court inserted the words 'corrupt or' immediately before the word 'illegal' in this section to make the provision read that 'corrupt or illegal practices' by any contestant in an election were punishable. The court did this to avoid the absurdity implicit in the Act which prescribed a severe penalty of disqualification from contesting in an election where a candidate committed an illegal practice, but not where a person committed the more serious offence of corruption. Subsequently, in *Registrar of Societies v Baraza la Wanawake Tanzania*,[6] the court read, in a similar fashion, the word 'or' into section 5 of the Basic Rights and Duties Enforcement Act 33 of 1994, thereby making it clear that an application for the enforcement of basic rights may be commenced either 'by petition or by originating summons'.

As can be deduced from the foregoing discussion, judges can serve as a check on Parliament even in the context of parliamentary supremacy through their normal task of interpreting and applying the law. Interpretative techniques can be used to remove absurdities and ambiguities in the laws and to whittle down unjust or unfair laws. However, the notion of parliamentary supremacy severely circumscribes the powers of the courts to review legislative action. Reading words into statutes or striking words from an Act of Parliament is often criticised as judicial law-making. This limits the extent to which the courts may hold Parliament accountable.

3. From parliamentary supremacy to judicial review

The doctrine of parliamentary supremacy, at least as it was applied in Tanzania, is derived from British constitutional history. The British Parliament was at one time said to be both omnipotent and omni-competent. It could, without any inhibition whatsoever, pass any law on any topic, affecting any person and anything anywhere. There was nothing in respect of which Parliament could not legislate. What is more, courts were enjoined to enforce all such laws without question. Evidently, this is not the case in Britain today where limitations on legislative powers have since been recognised.

Unlike in the British Parliament, the Parliament of Tanzania is a creature of a written Constitution. This means that the Tanzanian Parliament is subordinate to the Constitution. The judiciary has been given certain powers under the

---

5   [1997] TLR 272.
6   Civil Appeal No 82 of 1999 (unreported).

Constitution including the power to guard the limits on parliamentary powers prescribed in the Constitution. This is the current position in most African countries with written Constitutions. The fact that the Parliament of Tanzania is subject to the limits imposed by the Constitution introduces the concept of judicial review of parliamentary action, a concept which is unknown to British constitutional practice.

The power of judicial review of parliamentary action was introduced in Tanzania by the Constitution (Fifth Amendment) Act 15 of 1984 which came into force on 1 March 1985. This amendment was a landmark in the constitutional history of Tanzania mainly because it introduced the Bill of Rights into the Constitution. It also introduced a number of other significant provisions. For example, article 4 made a formal declaration of the doctrine of the separation of powers. Furthermore, articles 30(4) and (5) and 64(5) affirmed the supremacy of the Constitution. In entrenching these provisions, the Constitution (Fifth Amendment) Act replaced the rule by political fiat, which characterised Tanzanian government under the one-party state, with the rule of law.[7]

Particularly relevant to this chapter is the introduction of the power of the High Court to declare any Act of Parliament null and void for contravening the Constitution.[8] Thus, the High Court, for the first time, had the power to *undo* what Parliament had done. It marked the beginning of a new development in the relationship between Parliament and the judiciary; the beginning of a new era in which questions would be raised about Parliament's law-making power and about the extent to which, and the circumstances in which, the judiciary plays an oversight role.

4. An uneasy relationship

The sections that follow discuss some of the prominent cases in which the judiciary invoked its powers of review against Parliament and the reaction they provoked. The first of such cases is *Chumchua Marwa v Officer i/c Musoma Prison & Attorney General.*[9] In this case, the High Court held that the Deportation Ordinance[10] was unconstitutional and invalid. The issue concerning the constitutionality of this Ordinance was actually raised by the court *suo motu*, not by the parties to the case. On appeal by the Attorney

---

7   Before 1992, article 3 of the Constitution proclaimed the Revolutionary State Party (Chama Cha Mapinduzi) as the supreme organ of state with 'final authority in respect of all matters subject to this Constitution and the constitution of the Party'. The Constitution (Fifth Amendment) Act 15 of 1984 and the Constitution (Eighth Amendment) Act 4 of 1992 effectively introduced multiparty politics in Tanzania.

8   Articles 30(4) and (5) and 64(5) of the Constitution.

9   Miscellaneous Criminal Cause No 2 of 1988 (unreported).

10 Chapter 38 of the Laws of Tanzania.

General,[11] the Court of Appeal held that the lower court did not err in raising that issue *suo motu*. However, it faulted the lower court for proceeding to consider and determine the issue without first inviting the parties to address the court on it. As a result, it quashed the lower court's decision and remitted the case back to the High Court with a direction that the parties be allowed to make submissions on whether the Ordinance was constitutional or not, and that a fresh ruling on the issue be made after considering those submissions. The Court of Appeal also directed that the entire record be sent back to it for its final consideration. The High Court complied with these directions, invited the parties to address it on the issue and then delivered a fresh ruling, which once again declared the Ordinance to be unconstitutional and therefore null and void.

This was the first case in which legislation was struck down by a court for contravening the Constitution. A few more cases followed.[12] For example, section 148(4) and (5) of the Criminal Procedure Act 9 of 1985 relating to bail was held to be invalid,[13] and section 6 of the Government Proceedings Act 16 of 1967 requiring the consent of the Minister before one could sue the government was similarly struck down.[14] It was soon to be accepted that courts had the power to undo, so to speak, what Parliament had enacted if it offended against the Constitution. The claim of supremacy of Parliament would no longer be accepted.

The nullification of the Deportation Ordinance was not taken very kindly by the executive and the legislature. A Bill was immediately presented to Parliament to amend the Ordinance in an attempt to make it comply with the provisions of the Constitution. This move was quite absurd because the High Court had declared the entire Ordinance, not only parts of it, null and void and there was therefore nothing left to amend. While debating the Bill, the fact that the entire Ordinance had been nullified by the court puzzled some Members of Parliament (MPs). The Minister for Home Affairs, Edward Mwesiumo, made use of his experience as a former judge of the High Court in quoting judicial pronouncements from the British House of Lords to show that no court had any power or right to tamper with what Parliament had enacted. He argued that Parliament in Tanzania was supreme and that whatever it enacted could not be questioned by any court. This line of thinking persuaded Parliament to amend the nullified Ordinance.[15] Since Parliament was supreme, it was capable of doing anything — including amending a nullity!

11   *Officer i/c Musoma Prison & the Attorney General v Chumchua Marwa* Civil Appeal No 95 of 1988 (unreported).

12   Justice James L. Mwalusanya of the High Court did so in many cases between 1989 and 1994. Some of these were confirmed on appeal, others were reversed, but many more never got to the Court of Appeal.

13   See *Director of Public Prosecutions v Daudi Pete* [1993] TLR 22, [1991] LRC (Const) 553.

14   *Peter Ng'omango v Mwangwa* [1993] TLR 77; *Kukutia Ole Pumbun v Attorney General* [1993] TLR 159.

15   See the Deportation Ordinance (Amendment) Act 3 of 1991.

The nullified provisions of the Criminal Procedure Act also found their way back into the law. Parliament passed the Written Laws (Miscellaneous Amendments) Act 1 of 1977, which re-enacted the offending provisions by adding them to sections that had not been struck down. Although passed by Parliament, these amendments were driven by the executive which urged Parliament to exploit its alleged supremacy.

The reaction to the nullification of the requirement of ministerial consent before a litigant could sue the government was somewhat different. As a response to the relevant court decisions, the Government Proceedings Act was amended to replace the requirement of consent with that of giving 90 days' notice of an intended suit.[16]

The case of *Attorney General v Lohay Akonaay & Joseph Lohay*[17] is also of interest mainly because it sparked off a serious affront to the judiciary. In December 1992, Parliament passed the Regulation of Land Tenure (Established Villages) Act 22 of 1992, extinguishing all customary rights to land in the villages covered by *Operation Vijiji*.[18] The Act also prohibited the right to compensation for any loss resulting from the extinction of any customary rights; it ousted the jurisdiction of courts over any or all disputes relating to those rights; and it terminated all proceedings pending in courts and prohibited the enforcement of any court decision or decree concerning matters in respect of which jurisdiction was ousted. It established, instead, a tribunal with exclusive jurisdiction to deal with these matters. The respondents were aggrieved by this new law, because they had just won a case concerning customary land rights in a resident magistrates' court. This Act meant that they could not enforce that court decision. They thus petitioned the High Court for an order that the new law be declared unconstitutional. Succeed they did, but the Attorney General appealed to the Court of Appeal.

While the Court of Appeal upheld the decision of the High Court, it struck down only those sections of the Act which offended against the Constitution. In its decision, the Court of Appeal made a powerful statement on the principle of the separation of powers:

> It is the basic structure of a democratic constitution that state power is divided and distributed between three state pillars. These are the Executive, vested with executive power; the Legislature vested with legislative power, and the Judicature vested with

---

16 Government Proceedings (Amendment) Act 40 of 1974.

17 Note 3 above.

18 This was a massive operation carried out by the government in 1973–74 under which large numbers of people in rural areas were moved, some of them forcibly, from their respective areas of residence and re-settled in what were supposed to be planned villages. It is estimated that close to 6 million people were affected by that operation.

judicial powers. This is clearly so stated under article 4 of the Constitution. This basic structure is essential to any democratic constitution and cannot be changed or abridged while retaining the democratic nature of the constitution. It follows therefore that wherever the constitution establishes or permits the establishment of any other institution or body with executive or legislative or judicial power, such institution or body is meant to function not in lieu of or in derogation of these three central pillars of the state, but only in aid of and subordinate to those pillars. It follows therefore that since our Constitution is democratic; any purported ouster of jurisdiction of the ordinary courts to deal with any justiciable dispute is unconstitutional. What can properly be done wherever need arises to confer adjudicative jurisdiction on bodies other than the courts, is to provide for finality of adjudication, such as by appeal or review to a superior court, such as the High Court or Court of Appeal.[19]

Six years after this decision, an amendment was made to the Constitution,[20] introducing a new article 107A(1) which provided that the judiciary has final authority in matters relating to the administration of justice. It is difficult to say whether this amendment was a direct response to the judicial pronouncement cited above. However, it is certain that the decision of the Court of Appeal led to an amendment of the Regulation of Land Tenure (Established Villages) Act 18 of 1995, removing all the offensive provisions.

5. The Mtikila case: The judiciary and Parliament collide

The case of *Rev Christopher Mtikila v Attorney General*[21] set the judiciary and the legislature on a collision course. It involved a petition by Rev Mtikila asking the High Court to declare that independent candidates had the right to contest in Tanzania's general elections. In upholding the petition, the High Court held that the section 98(2)–(3) of the Elections Act (as amended by the Electoral Law (Miscellaneous Amendments) Act 4 of 2000 allowing only candidates who were members of and sponsored by political parties to contest in general elections was unconstitutional.

The political developments around this case present an interesting story. After the hearing was concluded, the High Court reserved its ruling. While the ruling was thus being awaited, the government tabled a Bill before Parliament to amend *the Constitution itself* so as to bar independent candidates from contesting elections. However, before Parliament passed the Bill, the High Court delivered its ruling, declaring that independent candidates had the right to contest

---

19 Note 3 above 92 (cited to TLR).
20 See section 17 of the Constitution (Thirteenth Amendment) Act 2 of 2000.
21 *Rev Christopher Mtikila v Attorney General* (note 3 above).

elections along with party-sponsored candidates. Although the government lodged an appeal against the decision, Parliament passed the Bill in December 1994 — before the appeal was heard by the Court of Appeal — thus amending the Constitution and prohibiting independent candidates from contesting elections.[22] Effectively, therefore, Parliament overruled the decision of the High Court while an appeal against it was still pending before the Court of Appeal. When the appeal was finally called up for hearing, the Attorney General applied for and was granted leave to withdraw the appeal because the constitutional amendment had rendered the appeal moot.

In granting leave to withdraw the appeal, Kisanga Ag CJ deeply lamented what had occurred:

> Thus the Government consciously and deliberately drew the Judiciary into direct clash with Parliament by asking the two organs to deal with the same matter simultaneously. For, as it turned out, that exercise ended up producing two conflicting results, the court upholding the right of private candidates to stand for Presidential, Parliamentary and Local Councils elections on the one hand, and Parliament barring such right on the other. Such a state of affairs was both regrettable and most undesirable. It was wholly incompatible with the smooth administration of justice in society, and every effort ought to be made to discourage it.[23]

About ten years after this lamentation, Rev Mtikila was back in the High Court seeking, once again, to vindicate the right of independent candidates to contest elections.[24] This time, he challenged the validity of the constitutional amendment of 1994 that prohibited independent candidates. The High Court, sitting as a panel of three judges, allowed the petition, declaring that it was 'lawful for private candidates to contest for the posts of President and Member of Parliament along with candidates nominated by political parties'. By holding so, the High Court allowed exactly what Parliament had prohibited.

In addition, the High Court went on to order as follows:

> Exercising our powers under any other relief as prayed in the petition and cognizant of the fact that a vacuum might give birth to chaos and political pandemonium, we shall proceed to order that the Respondent, in the true spirit of the original article 21(1) [of the Constitution] and guided by the Fundamental Objectives and Principles of State Policy contained in Part II of the Constitution, between now and the next general elections, put in place a legislative mechanism that will regulate the activities of private candidates.[25]

---

22   Constitution (Eleventh Amendment) Act 34 of 1994.
23   *Attorney General v Rev Christopher Mtikila* [1998] TLR 100, 104.
24   *Rev Christopher Mtikila v Attorney General* [2006] TLR 279.
25   Ibid 312.

The High Court handed down this ruling on 5 May 2006. Once again, the Attorney General appealed and the appeal was eventually set for hearing in April 2010. Considering that the general elections were due in October 2010 and that the High Court order had not yet been set aside, it was expected that legislative measures would be put in place to facilitate the participation of independent candidates in the October elections, in case the Court of Appeal upheld the lower court's decision. As it turned out, the Court of Appeal did not do so. It reversed the decision of the High Court on the grounds, among other things, that courts did not have the power to nullify a constitutional amendment duly enacted by Parliament and that the responsibility to decide whether independent candidates would be allowed to contest elections rested with Parliament, not the courts.[26]

6.   Further clashes between Parliament and the judiciary

So far this chapter has addressed issues concerning the relations between Parliament and the judiciary in which the executive was involved in one way or another. Indeed, the executive's influence on the conduct of Parliament is often overwhelmingly clear. However, there have been occasions when Parliament and the judiciary have clashed without any involvement of the executive. One such incident occurred in February 2002 in the wake of the decision of the Court of Appeal in the case of *Julius Ndyanabo v Attorney General*.[27] At issue in this case was the constitutionality of section 111(2) of the Elections Act, which required a petitioner to pay Shs 5 000 000 as security for costs before an election petition could be set for hearing by the High Court. The appellant successfully contended that this requirement effectively denied petitioners in electoral disputes access to justice and that it was discriminatory.

The decision came under severe criticism from the Speaker of the National Assembly, Mr Pius Msekwa. In particular, he was critical of the court's view that the legislative competence of Parliament was limited to making laws that were consistent with the Constitution. He published an article in the English daily with the widest circulation in Tanzania in which he argued that there were no limits on the general power of Parliament to legislate and that the court had no competence or legitimate authority to question and invalidate what Parliament had ordained.[28]

At the time, Mr Msekwa's knowledge of, and experience with, Parliament had no comparison in Tanzania. He served as Clerk to the National Assembly from

---

26   *Attorney General v Rev Christopher Mtikila* Civil Appeal No 45 of 2009 (unreported).
27   [2004] TLR 14.
28   *Daily News*, 26 February 2002; the article was later published in a special issue of the *Bunge News*, a publication of the National Assembly to which Mr Msekwa was the most regular and dominant contributor.

1963 to 1967, after which he held a series of senior positions in the public service before getting elected to Parliament in 1990. He was immediately elected Deputy Speaker and served in this capacity until 1994 when he became the Speaker. His criticism of the court's decision was thus taken seriously and was seen as representing the views of Parliament. Although, perhaps not surprisingly, the judiciary successfully resisted the temptation to respond to this attack and the Tanganyika Law Society issued a press release on 28 February 2002 strongly supporting the decision of the Court of Appeal. As argued in this chapter, the argument that the legislative competence of Parliament 'knows no limits' fails to take proper account of the provisions of article 64(5) of the Constitution.

Another incident relates to remarks the Chief Justice made at the Law Day held on 6 February 2009[29] in the presence of both the President and the Speaker of Parliament. In his speech, the Chief Justice praised the President, Mr Jakaya Kikwete, for the absence of executive interference with the judiciary over the three years of his administration, but made a critical remark about Parliament. He expressed some disquiet that the Speaker had on one occasion openly criticised the judiciary for passing a judgment that was unfavourable to Parliament. He also mentioned that Parliament had attempted to interfere with the independence of the judicary in various ways, including the creation of a committee with judicial powers to punish anyone who picked a quarrel with an MP.[30] The Speaker reacted to those remarks by issuing a statement under rule 33(2) of the Rules of the House, reiterating the powers and privileges of the House, including its right to adjudicate disputes between members and non-members arising from what transpires in the proceedings of Parliament.

This kind of confrontation between Parliament and the judiciary is regrettable and, in this case, it could be argued that some of the disputes which the committee in question is empowered to resolve may not successfully be resolved by courts. Article 100 of the Constitution provides for parliamentary immunity; it prohibits anyone to question or challenge anything said in the House. The Parliamentary Immunities, Powers and Privileges Act 3 of 1988, enacted pursuant to article 101 of the Constitution, casts the net of prohibition and immunity even wider to include anything said by persons who are not MPs. In light of these provisions, the Court of Appeal has held that even a mere officer or other person employed

---

29 This is an annual event held by the judiciary, usually in the first week of February, to mark the commencement of the judicial calendar.

30 This was probably a reference to the attempts by the Chair of the House Committee for Parliamentary Immunities, Powers and Privileges during the 2000–2005 Parliament to vest in this committee powers to summon, charge, convict and punish any individual who was deemed to have failed to treat the House or any of its members with the required dignity. The Chair actually summoned a number of individuals to answer allegations of that kind before this committee. It included the indictment before this committee of a media tycoon, Mr Reginald Mengi, who was not a Member of Parliament, in respect of comments he had made about what Mr Adam Malima, an MP, had said in Parliament.

to transcribe minutes of proceedings before Parliament or any of its committees cannot be called to give evidence in court regarding what he or she transcribes unless 'special leave' is obtained from Parliament.[31] However, when Parliament is exercising non-legislative functions, such immunity will not apply. This is particularly the case when Parliament is exercising powers which are judicial in nature — usually called quasi-judicial powers.

7.   The excercise of judical powers by Parliament

It is generally accepted that parliament has the power to make determinations in relation to matters or disputes arising from what transpires in the House. Parliament in Tanzania has sometimes used these powers to discipline its members. In 1998, an unsuccessful attempt was made to challenge Parliament's powers in this regard.[32]

It is relatively uncontroversial for Parliament to exercise quasi-judicial powers in respect of its members. The same cannot be said in respect of Parliament's power to discipline persons who are not MPs. In the Zambian case of *M'membe & Another v Speaker of the National Assembly & Others*,[33] the applicants were journalists, not members of the Zambian National Assembly. They were arrested and detained on grounds relating to newspaper articles they published after the Standing Orders Committee of the National Assembly had convicted them, *in absentia*, of gross contempt of the House. This case raised the question whether the National Assembly had the authority to commit the applicants to prison for contempt. The High Court held in the affirmative and then went on to explain why:

> The reason why Commonwealth Parliaments exercise the power of committal is simply that it is the only way they can deter those who deliberately plan to ridicule its members and officials, or lower its dignity through odious utterances and writings. The Zambian Parliament is a Commonwealth Parliament, which emulates a lot of its practice from Britain, and other Commonwealth countries. On the basis of this argument I find that our Parliament, even in the absence of express constitutional or other statutory provisions, has the power to commit to prison any person who it finds guilty of contempt of it, or of breach of any of its privileges.[34]

No precedent on this point exists in Tanzania, but it must be noted that the power to hold a person in contempt is judicial and not legislative in nature. Considering the reasoning in *Attorney General v Lohay Akonaay & Another*[35] and article 107A(1) of the Constitution referred to earlier, one could argue that

---

31   *Augustino Lyatonga Mrema v Republic* [2002] TLR 6.
32   *Augustino Lyatonga Mrema v Speaker of the National Assembly & Another* [1999] TLR 206.
33   [1996] 1 LRC 584.
34   Ibid 596.
35   Note 3 above 92.

Parliament in Tanzania cannot exercise adjudicative powers without the sanction of 'a superior court, such as the High Court or Court of Appeal'. Evidently, therefore, in the exercise of its judicial or quasi-judicial powers, the Tanzanian Parliament cannot be immune from judicial enquiry.

The High Court of Zambia did address this point in the case of *M'membe & Another v Speaker of the National Assembly & Others*:

> ... superior courts in this country, which include this court, do have power to inquire into the correctness and lawfulness of the legislative and administrative functions which affect the whole country and outsiders at large. And this power includes complaints by parliamentary officials or employees involving allegations of grave injustices done to them by the institution.[36]

The court then considered the meaning and implication of the statutory provision ousting the jurisdiction of the courts in matters concerning the exercise of any power conferred on or vested in the National Assembly, the Speaker or any officer of the Assembly by the Constitution or other law, and held:

> ... this purported ouster of courts' jurisdiction only refers to matters which belong purely to the internal arrangement of Parliament ... Even here, however, the courts may intervene to settle a dispute between Parliament and any aggrieved individual who claims to have suffered grave injustice caused to him by Parliament. In this sense, therefore, orders of certiorari, mandamus and prohibition may be issued against any of its committees which exercise a quasi-judicial function.[37]

This holding is similar to the observations by the High Court of Tanzania in *Augustino Lyatonga Mrema v Speaker of the National Assembly & Another*,[38] in which the applicant, an MP, sought to challenge the decision to suspend him from the House. The High Court reiterated the constitutional role of the courts to uphold the rights of individuals and to protect them from abuse by any organ of state however highly placed it may be, including Parliament. It also stated that any party or person aggrieved by any organ of state, including Parliament, had the right of access to court. Both cases demonstrate that the supreme authority in matters concerning adjudication or the administration of justice is vested in the judiciary. In other words, Parliament cannot insulate itself from judicial scrutiny when it exercises quasi-judicial powers.

8. Conclusion

The doctrine of the separation of powers assigns separate powers and functions to each organ of state so as to create a framework for the operation of a system

---

36 Note 33 above 593.
37 Ibid 593–4.
38 Note 32 above.

of checks and balances. The relationship between Parliament and the judiciary must be seen in this context. Of the three organs of state, Parliament is the only one in respect of which claims of supremacy are often made. Sometimes this supremacy is qualified as legislative supremacy. These claims usually derive from the fact that Parliament in a modern democracy is the only state organ which has democratic legitimacy. Parliament and its members often claim that they represent the will and the interests of the people. Unfortunately, this can also be, and sometimes is, used as a pretext for attempts by parliamentarians to avoid accountability.

In Tanzania, Parliament is yet to fully acknowledge that there are limits on its legislative power. As this chapter has shown, legislative competence and action in Tanzania is subject to constitutional limits and courts have shown willingness to exercise their authority to enforce those limits. Furthermore, Parliament cannot claim to be supreme when exercising quasi-judicial functions.

Two examples illustrate the dangers of parliamentary supremacy. After the Arusha Declaration of 5 February 1967, by which Tanzania decided to adopt socialist policies, a number of private firms, including banks, insurance companies and other financial institutions, were immediately nationalised without legal backing. Subsequently, Parliament convened a special session to pass a number of laws giving retrospective legal effect to these nationalisations. Then, too, in 1983 there was a massive campaign, popularly described as a war against economic sabotage. In this campaign, a large number of people were arrested and detained under orders that were made and enforced without any legal foundation. A couple of weeks after their arrest, a hurriedly prepared statute, the Economic Sabotage (Special Provisions) Act 9 of 1983, was passed to give retrospective legality to these arrests and detentions.

On both occasions, Parliament was moved to legalise, *ex post facto*, executive actions that had been taken in total disregard of the tenets of the rule of law. In the latter case, the law passed by Parliament criminalised, retrospectively, acts that were quite lawful when they were done, and established special tribunals to try the suspected offenders who had already been unlawfully arrested and detained. The Economic Sabotage (Special Provisions) Act denied them the right to legal counsel and discarded certain principles of evidence and procedure to make it easy to secure convictions. Subsequently, in response to political pressure, Parliament made amendments to the Act,[39] taking away the right to bail and the right of appeal of those charged, detained or convicted under this law.

The judiciary did not get involved in these cases as no court action was taken to challenge these Acts and actions. In the case of the nationalisations,

---

39   See Economic Sabotage (Special Provisions) (Amendment) Act 10 of 1983.

the government succeeded in preventing court action by paying compensation to those whose property and businesses had been expropriated. As to the 1983 events, Parliament prohibited all forms of court action outside the special tribunals. Although these special tribunals were chaired by judges of the High Court, they were certainly not courts. At least one judge, Justice KSK Lugakingira, is on record as having refused to serve on them. However, it is now publicly known that the events around the alleged war on economic sabotage prompted the Chief Justice, Francis Nyalali, to seek a private audience with President Julius Nyerere in order to raise concerns about the breakdown of the rule of law. It is widely believed that this meeting led to the repeal of the Economic Sabotage (Special Provisions) Act and the enactment of the Economic and Organized Crime Control Act 13 of 1984 in its place. The new law brought all cases of suspected economic sabotage within the jurisdiction of ordinary courts.

The alleged war on economic sabotage presented a serious threat to the rule of law in Tanzania. It gave new impetus to demands for constitutional reform that would strengthen the protection of human rights. While suspects of economic sabotage were languishing in custody with periodic appearances before the special tribunals, a nationwide debate on proposals to amend the Constitution was unfolding. The officially published proposals for constitutional reform did not include a Bill of Rights. In the ensuing debate, however, a Bill of Rights was demanded and incorporated in the Constitution with the enactment of the Constitution (Fifth Amendment) Act. This Act also changed relations between Parliament and the judiciary in Tanzania, moving from parliamentary supremacy to judicial review of parliamentary action.

References

Legislation and other legal documents

Arusha Declaration of 5 February 1967.
Basic Rights and Duties Enforcement Act 33 of 1994.
Constitution of the United Republic of Tanzania Act, 1977.
Constitution (Fifth Amendment) Act 15 of 1984.
Constitution (Eighth Amendment) Act 4 of 1992.
Constitution (Eleventh Amendment) Act 34 of 1994.
Constitution (Thirteenth Amendment) Act 2 of 2000.
Criminal Procedure Act 9 of 1985.
Deportation Ordinance, chapter 38 of the Laws of Tanzania.
Deportation Ordinance (Amendment) Act 3 of 1991.
Economic and Organized Crime Control Act 13 of 1984.
Economic Sabotage (Special Provisions) Act 9 of 1983.
Economic Sabotage (Special Provisions) (Amendment) Act 10 of 1983.
Elections Act 1 of 1985.

Electoral Law (Miscellaneous Amendments) Act 4 of 2000.
Government Proceedings Act 16 of 1967.
Government Proceedings (Amendment) Act 40 of 1974.
Parliamentary Immunities, Powers and Privileges Act 3 of 1988.
Regulation of Land Tenure (Established Villages) Act 22 of 1992.
Regulation of Land Tenure (Established Villages) Act 18 of 1995.
Written Laws (Miscellaneous Amendments) Act 1 of 1977.

Cases

Attorney General v Lohay Akonaay & Another [1995] TLR 80, [1994] 2 LRC 399.
Attorney General v Rev Christopher Mtikila [1998] TLR 100.
Attorney General v Rev Christopher Mtikila Civil Appeal No 45 of 2009 (unreported).
Augustino Lyatonga Mrema v Republic [2002] TLR 6.
Augustino Lyatonga Mrema v Speaker of the National Assembly & Another [1999] TLR 206.
Chumchua Marwa v Officer i/c Musoma Prison & the Attorney General Miscellaneous Criminal Cause No 2 of 1988 (unreported).
Director of Public Prosecutions v Daudi Pete [1993] TLR 22, [1991] LRC (Const) 553.
Joseph Warioba v Stephen Wassira & Another [1997] TLR 272.
Julius Ndyanabo v Attorney General [2004] TLR 14.
Kammins Ballrooms Co Ltd v Zenith Investments (Torquay) Ltd [1970] 2 All ER 871.
Kukutia Ole Pumbun v Attorney General [1993] TLR 159.
Lujuna Shubi Ballonzi v Registered Trustees of Chama cha Mapinduzi [1996] TLR 203.
M'membe & Another v Speaker of the National Assembly & Others [1996] 1 LRC 584.
Mwalimu Paul John Mhozya v Attorney General [1996] TLR 130.
Nothman v Barnet London Borough [1978] 1 All ER 1243.
Officer i/c Musoma Prison & the Attorney General v Chumchua Marwa Civil Appeal No 95 of 1988 (unreported).
Peter Ng'omango v Mwangwa [1993] TLR 77.
Registrar of Societies v Baraza la Wanawake Tanzania Civil Appeal No 82 of 1999 (unreported).
Rev Christopher Mtikila v Attorney General [1995] TLR 31.
Rev Christopher Mtikila v Attorney General [2006] TLR 279.

Articles, books, chapters in books and other works

Msekwa, P. 2002. *Daily News,* 26 February. Re-published in *Bunge News,* special issue and referred to in Shivji, I.G. 2009. Constitutional limits on parliamentary powers. In Shivji, I.G. & Murunga, G. (eds). *Where is Uhuru? Reflections on the Struggle for Democracy in Africa.* Oxford: Fahamu Books/Pambazuka Press, 108.
Mwihambi, N. 2009. *Parliament and the Judiciary: Partners in Law Making or Hostile Combatants?* University of Dar es Salaam: LLM Thesis.
Phillips, O.H. & Jackson, J. 1987. *Constitutional and Administrative Law.* London: Sweet & Maxwell.

Chapter 6

Judicial review of parliamentary actions in South Africa: A nuanced interpretation of the separation of powers

Hugh Corder

1. Introduction

This chapter describes the ways in which the judiciary in South Africa monitors and regulates parliamentary actions according to the prescripts of the Constitution. After briefly addressing the background and current constitutional provisions regulating this area of the law, the chapter discusses the cases which are paradigmatic of the current judicial approach to reviewing parliamentary conduct. It sketches the active yet careful role the judiciary has developed, addresses the limits of judicial intervention and highlights the nuanced interpretation of the doctrine of the separation of powers that characterises the case law on this matter.

No consideration of a topic within the broad field of constitutional law in South Africa should occur without taking into account the country's constitutional history. As Lord Steyn famously said in *R v Secretary of State for the Home Department, ex parte Daly*, '[i]n law, context is everything'.[1]

Parliamentary sovereignty of the Westminster model was the founding principle of South Africa's first Constitution, the South Africa Act of 1909. Parliamentary sovereignty was qualified as to 'manner and form' only by the two 'entrenched' clauses, which attached special significance to the non-racial franchise in the Cape Province, and the status of the two official languages, English and Dutch (the latter changed to Afrikaans in the 1920s). Amendments to these provisions required approval by at least a two-thirds majority of both Houses of Parliament in a joint session. This special procedure was duly followed in the 1930s in order to place 'native' voters on a separate voters' roll.[2]

---

1   [2001] 3 All ER 433 (HL) 447A.
2   *Ndlwana v Hofmeyr NO* 1937 AD 229.

It is notorious that the special procedure was not followed initially in the 1950s, when the same shift of 'coloured' voters was attempted. This led to a well-known constitutional crisis, the stand-off between Parliament and the highest court at the time, the Appellate Division of the Supreme Court of South Africa (AD), over the special requirements of the Constitution.

Building on the Australian case of *Attorney General, New South Wales v Trethowan*,[3] the Court insisted in *Harris v Minister of the Interior* (first *Harris* case)[4] that it had the authority to pronounce on whether Parliament had complied with the limits imposed on its 'manner and form' of making law. It found further that Parliament had failed to do so through non-compliance with the special requirements of a unicameral sitting and the two-thirds majority. Parliament then tried to circumvent the Court's judgment by constituting itself as a 'High Court' with the jurisdiction to hear appeals (but only from the state) from decisions of the Appellate Division, but this legislative attempt (in the form of the High Court of Parliament Act 35 of 1952) was also struck down by the Appellate Division in *Minister of the Interior v Harris* (second *Harris* case, also known as the High Court of Parliament case),[5] on the basis that Parliament in another guise could not possess the essential attributes of a court as commonly understood.

Licking its wounds, the governing party went to the polls, and was returned with a larger majority, but still not large enough to summon the two-thirds needed. It then by sleight of hand achieved that majority by doubling the size of the Upper House (the Senate) through the Senate Act 53 of 1955, and appointing its supporters to almost all the vacancies. Just to be safe, the number of appellate judges was also doubled by the Appellate Division Quorum Act 27 of 1955, and 'friendly' judges were elevated to these positions, so that when the South Africa Act Amendment Act 9 of 1956, which removed coloured voters from the common voters' roll, was duly passed by more than a 67 per cent majority in a joint sitting, all but one judge upheld the validity of the Acts concerned.[6] It was as if the Court had been beaten into submission over a seven-year period.

While the initial judicial stand against parliamentary perfidy earned it strong affirmation abroad and from government opponents in South Africa, these events scarred both the legal profession and the public perception about the manipulability of the law-making power. They may well have contributed to two key elements of the post-apartheid constitutional dispensation: the supremacy of the Constitution, to which even the legislature (Parliament) is subject, as well

---

3   [1932] AC 526 (PC).
4   1952 (2) SA 428 (AD).
5   1952 (4) SA 769 (AD).
6   *Collins v Minister of the Interior & Another* 1957 (1) SA 552 (AD).

as the inclusion of a far-reaching and sophisticated Bill of Rights, which in itself inhibits the scope of the law-making power.

The South African 'interim' Constitution of 1993[7] included a chapter of fundamental rights, but the legislative process contained no unusual requirements relating to manner and form. Section 67 provided that the public should have access to the sittings of Parliament, but fell far short of what was included in the 'final' Constitution of 1996[8] which came into force in early 1997. The 1996 Constitution contains several manifestations of the character of the constitutional democracy aimed for.

Section 1 expresses the foundational values of the Constitution and is amendable only with a 75 per cent majority of the National Assembly and the concurrence of six of the nine provincial legislatures. These values include the essence of many of the 34 Constitutional Principles which were agreed to during the long process of negotiation before 1994, and against which the constitutionality of the final constitutional text was assessed by the Constitutional Court of South Africa (CC) in its certification judgments.[9] Those parts of section 1 relevant for present purposes state that the Republic of South Africa 'is one, sovereign, democratic state' founded on the values of the supremacy of the Constitution, the rule of law, and 'a multi-party system of democratic government, to ensure *accountability, responsiveness and openness*' (emphasis added).

Section 59(1) takes the idea of public consultation, indeed participation, in the legislative process much further. It states that Parliament 'must facilitate public involvement in the legislative and other processes' of the Houses and their committees. It must also conduct its business in an open manner and sit in public. An almost identical provision is made for public participation in respect of the other House of Parliament, the National Council of Provinces, in section 72, and in respect of provincial legislatures, in section 118.[10]

The Constitutional Assembly[11] emphasised the importance of public consultation by including an extensive 'public participation programme' in the process of drafting the Constitution, which led to a high level of popular awareness of and commitment to the eventual text at the time of its adoption (Ebrahim 1998).

---

7   Constitution of the Republic of South Africa Act 200 of 1993.

8   Constitution of the Republic of South Africa, 1996 (Constitution).

9   See *In re Certification of the Constitution of the Republic of South Africa, 1996* 1996(4) SA 744 (CC), 1997 (10) BCLR 1253 (CC); *Certification of the Amended Text of the Constitution of the Republic of South Africa, 1996* 1997 (2) SA 713 (CC), (1) BCLR 1 (CC).

10   Curiously, there is no equivalent provision in respect of local government, perhaps because it may have been seen as too onerous, or perhaps because that level of government should, by definition, be close to the people it serves.

11   From 1994 to 1996 the two Houses of Parliament sat as the Constitutional Assembly to draft and pass the 1996 Constitution.

The first Parliament elected after the exercise of universal suffrage in 1994 was an exciting, open and vibrant place. The Members of Parliament (MPs) were typically of high quality, independent-minded, many of them veterans of the 'struggle', and determined to set up a Parliament which was in every way the antithesis of the apartheid regime. As a result, a system of multiparty portfolio committees was established, a welcoming atmosphere for the public was created, disclosure of assets in a Register of Members' Financial Interests was drafted, implemented and monitored, a method for scrutiny of delegated legislation was researched and a more effective means for carrying out Parliament's 'oversight' function was negotiated. This was in partial fulfilment of the requirements of section 55(2) of the Constitution:

> The National Assembly must provide for mechanisms —
> (a) to ensure that all executive organs of state in the national sphere of government are accountable to it; and
> (b) to maintain oversight of —
>   (i) the exercise of national executive authority, including the implementation of legislation; and
>   (ii) any organ of state.

Regrettably, during President Mbeki's almost two terms of office (1999–2008), Parliament became much less active in its monitoring roles, as the hold of the ruling African National Congress (ANC) over its MPs (elected according to the proportional representation party list system) tightened, and as the new generations of MPs were drawn increasingly from the ranks of less heroic figures.

After this brief sketch of the development of constitutional law and the context of the current legal framework for judicial review of parliamentary action, this chapter now turns to the question of how this constitutional regime has developed through case law. How have the courts in their judgments interpreted and enforced the legislative framework? What is the role of the judiciary in monitoring the law-making and other processes in Parliament and the provincial legislatures?

2. The judicial approach to reviewing parliamentary actions

Many factors, both historical and contemporary, influence the courts in their attitude to their authority to review parliamentary actions. In post-apartheid South Africa, although the constitutional demand was clear from the outset, the hold of the idea of Westminster parliamentary sovereignty on both judicial and political minds was tenacious. This necessarily influenced the general approach to the doctrine of the separation of powers under the Constitution, and has resulted in an interesting group of judgments in cases where litigants sought review of parliamentary conduct. There are at least four groups of cases which shed light on the relationship between the judicial and legislative branches of government. This chapter will consider them in increasing order of importance.

2.1. Scrutinising the internal workings of Parliament

The case of *De Lille & Another v Speaker of the National Assembly*[12] provides a clear illustration of the shift in judicial power in relation to the scrutiny of the internal workings of Parliament since the enactment of the 1996 Constitution. In late 1997, a particularly feisty opposition MP, Patricia de Lille, named a number of senior government figures as former spies of the apartheid regime during a debate in the National Assembly. When the Speaker ordered her to withdraw her remarks as they contravened the rules of Parliament she did so immediately and unconditionally. A little while later, the ANC, the majority party, moved and approved a resolution in the House to appoint an ad hoc committee to investigate and report on De Lille's conduct and to recommend any further steps to be taken against her. Although this was a multiparty committee, the ANC members on it had clearly made up their minds in advance of its deliberations that the outcome should be further punishment for De Lille. After three meetings characterised by improper process, the committee recommended that De Lille should apologise, in a letter to the Speaker, to those she had named, and that she should be suspended for 15 parliamentary working days. This recommendation was endorsed by the National Assembly forthwith.

De Lille approached the Cape High Court with a request to set aside the suspension order, alleging procedural unfairness on the part of the committee. The Speaker's response was effectively to rely on the Powers and Privileges of Parliament Act 91 of 1963 and section 57 of the interim Constitution which gave Parliament control over its internal operations. In a carefully argued and authoritative statement of the law, Hlophe J[13] considered the various aspects of the case, and found for De Lille. On the basis of both English and South African common-law rules on procedural fairness, he found that the ad hoc committee had breached rules of natural justice, as it had not given De Lille a fair hearing and it had been biased (paras 15–19). However, this did not dispose of the matter, as the court had to consider arguments from the Speaker based on Parliament's statute-based 'exclusive jurisdiction to enforce its privileges and to punish those who infringe them' (para 20). Hlophe J, while observing that it 'is undesirable for the Courts of law to get steeped in politics', noted that a fundamental shift in the review jurisdiction of the courts

---

12   1998 (3) SA 430 (C).
13   King DJP concurring.

in regard to the exercise of all public power had occurred with the adoption of the Constitution (para 24),[14] and that there was precedent both in South Africa and neighbouring countries for judicial intervention where Parliament had infringed constitutionally protected rights (para 23). As he stated in conclusion on this point: 'the nature and exercise of parliamentary privilege must be consonant with the Constitution. The exercise of parliamentary privilege ... is not immune from judicial review' (para 33). The court strengthened this conclusion by finding that the punishment of suspension was an unlawful limitation on De Lille's rights in the Bill of Rights, and it also found that section 5 of the Powers and Privileges of Parliament Act, which allowed the Speaker to issue a certificate which purported to stay the proceedings of a court, was unconstitutional and invalid (para 41).

The Speaker duly took the matter on appeal. The Supreme Court of Appeal (SCA) dismissed the appeal with costs,[15] although on a much narrower basis than that relied upon by the Cape High Court. Mahomed CJ, for the SCA, chose to limit his rejection of the arguments of the Speaker to an examination of the authority of Parliament to order the suspension of one of its members. After endorsing the necessity of a focus on the Constitution, he stated in typical fashion: 'No Parliament, however *bona fide* or eminent its membership, no President, however formidable be his reputation or scholarship, and no official, however, efficient or well-meaning, can make any law or perform any act which is not sanctioned by the Constitution' (para 14). After analysing the arguments of the appellant's counsel and considering comparative precedent, he concluded that the National Assembly 'was not entitled in law' to suspend De Lille as it had purported to do. While these decisions fit consistently with the emerging endorsement of constitutional supremacy which emanated from the CC at the time, they also serve as important landmarks limiting any historically authorised tendency on the part of Parliament to carve out for itself a sphere of internal operations immune from the overall scrutiny of the courts.

2.2. Remedying unconstitutionality: Requiring Parliament to act

The judicial approach in its scrutiny of the main activity of Parliament, the making of laws, has initially been one of respectful guidance rather than assertiveness. The courts' decisions naturally have an effect on their relationship with Parliament each time a legislative provision is found to be unconstitutional. In this respect, the CC has from the outset displayed keen sensitivity to the limitations inherent in a political leadership almost totally new to governing,

---

14   Relying on *President of the Republic of South Africa v Hugo* 1997 (4) SA 1 (CC).
15   *Speaker of the National Assembly v De Lille & Another* 1999 (4) SA 863 (SCA).

and served by a bureaucracy which might find itself in tension with political leadership.

Judicial concern has been most clearly manifest in the crafting of remedies consequent on findings of unconstitutionality of Acts of Parliament and subordinate legislation, the typical order being an injunction to the lawmaker to remedy the defects, within a realistic period of time, pending which the offending legal rule would remain formally in place. So we see Parliament being given 12 months to legislate for same-sex marriages[16] and to remedy the defects in the State Liability Act 20 of 1957,[17] while the Court has also been prepared to 'read words into' an Act, in order, for example, to give relief to the surviving partner of a Muslim 'marriage'[18] and to revise the African customary law of succession so as to remove its male-centredness.[19]

The Court has usually laid down guidelines for Parliament to assist with the drafting of the legislative amendments deemed necessary to render the law constitutional. Parliament has generally complied within the period stipulated, although on a few occasions it has had to come back to court to seek an extension,[20] to which the CC has agreed, mostly grudgingly.

Recently, however, in relation to the reforms needed in the area of enforcement of liability of civil damages against the state, the Court has been more assertive in its attitude.[21] Faced with Parliament's failure to comply with its earlier order expeditiously and satisfactorily, the CC agreed to an extension of time for legislative changes but, in the interim, it ordered that the relevant section of the Act be read in a manner which gives litigants against the state some effective means of executing the judgments which they have obtained in their favour.

2.3. Defining the limits of Parliament's legislative authority

The CC has from the outset shown a willingness to limit the legislative authority of Parliament to its constitutional bounds. This is most clearly seen in *Executive Council of the Western Cape Legislature v President of the Republic of South Africa*,[22] which was the first case to explore the status of delegated legislative power in the post-apartheid era. The factual background, in brief, concerned

---

16 *Minister of Home Affairs v Fourie* 2006 (1) SA 524 (CC).

17 *Nyathi v MEC for Department of Health, Gauteng* 2008 (5) SA 94 (CC).

18 *Daniels v Campbell NO* 2004 (5) SA 331 (CC).

19 *Bhe v Magistrate, Khayelitsha* 2005 (1) SA 580 (CC).

20 See, eg, *Zondi v MEC for Traditional and Local Government Affairs* 2006 (3) SA 1 (CC).

21 See *Minister for Justice and Constitutional Development v Nyathi* (Case No CCT 53/09), delivered on 9th October, 2009, as yet unreported; see also the Order of the Court in *Fourie*, note 16 above, and in *Bhe*, note 19 above.

22 1995 (4) SA 877 (CC).

the holding of the first local government elections in South Africa after the advent of democracy. Because of unresolved issues relating to the holding of such elections in the Western Cape province, and given the necessity for making last-minute changes to the law to reflect agreements reached between the contesting political parties, Parliament authorised the President to make such legislative changes as were required on its behalf. The appellants argued that, in divesting itself of this plenary legislative power, Parliament had acted unconstitutionally. Significantly, this challenge emanated from a provincial government, still dominated by the party which had governed under apartheid, and was directed at the national executive then led by President Mandela. The undesirable consequence of the decision would be the postponement of local government elections in that province. Despite these circumstances, the CC held that Parliament had exceeded the limits of its powers to delegate its plenary law-making function to the executive, and it has continued to hold it to such limits in subsequent cases.[23]

Also involving the relationship between Parliament and the President, the judgment in *Pharmaceutical Manufacturers Association*[24]sheds light on the limits of the legislative process in another way. Here Parliament had completed its work in respect of a new Act, the Medicines and Medical Devices Regulatory Authority Act 132 of 1998, and the President had signed it into law, but the final decision as to when it should enter into force was left to the President. On the basis of bad advice from senior public servants, President Mandela brought the Act into force by proclamation in the *Gazette*, which effectively created chaos in the pharmaceutical industry, as the Act was of little use without its accompanying regulations. Having realised the gravity of the error, the executive itself applied to the High Court to review the President's action, to no avail. When the matter reached the CC, Chaskalson P asserted the review authority of the judiciary, and relied on irrationality as an aspect of the principle of legality to set aside the President's action, attributing it to an error in good faith. While important for a number of other reasons,[25] this judgment shows that the Court will draw a line at the end of the law-making process once the President has assented to an Act: beyond that, one moves into the scope of executive conduct, where the Court is able to exercise its power of review. But what of judicial review of the legislative process itself, either in retrospect or while in progress?

---

23   Such as *Ynuico Ltd v Minister of Trade and Industry* 1996 (3) SA 989 (CC), and *Executive Council of the Western Cape v Minister for Provincial Affairs and Constitutional Development* 2000 (1) SA 661 (CC).

24   *Pharmaceutical Manufacturers Association of South Africa & Another: In re Ex Parte Application of the President of the Republic of South Africa & Others* 2000 (2) SA 674 (CC).

25   Such as the fact that it marked the Court's definitive ruling that there was only one system of judicial review of administrative action, with the Constitution as its foundation, and that the common law relating to judicial review did not continue to exist as a parallel system: see para 44.

2.4. The constitutional duty to facilitate public involvement in the legislative process

Perhaps most controversially in its relationship with the legislative arm of government, the CC has begun to explore the meaning of the concept of a democracy characterised by responsive, accountable and open government, as is described in the 'values statement' of the Constitution, and as the Constitution requires[26] of the two Houses of Parliament.

The series of cases relating to Parliament's constitutional duty to facilitate public involvement in the legislative process starts with *King & Others v Attorney' Fidelity Fund Board of Control & Another*.[27] The Attorneys Act 53 of 1979 provided for the functioning and extent of liability of the Attorneys' Fidelity Fund. It was amended by the Attorneys and Matters Relating to Rules of Court Amendment Act 115 of 1998 so as to preclude any claims in respect of monies deposited with an attorney to invest on behalf of a client. King and many others had lost money consequent on the insolvency of a firm of attorneys with which they had invested, and they claimed that the public consultation which had preceded the adoption of the amendment was insufficient to constitute a fulfilment of Parliament's duty 'to facilitate public involvement' in its legislative process. The issue was dealt with by the SCA largely as an exercise in deciding which court had jurisdiction to hear the matter, the CC or itself.[28] Cameron and Nugent JJA for the SCA ruled that matters of the 'manner and form' of Parliament at a crude level were for the decision of any superior court, whereas the extent of parliamentary compliance with the 'public involvement' obligation was for the CC alone to determine (paras 18, 21 and 22).[29] The SCA thus struck the appeal from the roll.

The case which set the benchmark in relation to Parliament's duty to facilitate public involvement was *Doctors for Life International v Speaker of the National Assembly*.[30] The applicant, a non-governmental organisation which opposes choice on the termination of pregnancy, challenged the constitutionality of the Choice on Termination of Pregnancy Amendment Act 38 of 2004; the Sterilisation Amendment Act 3 of 2005; the Traditional Health Practitioners Act 35 of 2004; and the Dental Technicians Amendment Act 24 of 2004. Although there had been some opportunities for the public to comment on the proposed amendments, such consultations had been insufficient in the view of the CC

---

26   See ss 59(1) and 72(1).

27   2006 (1) SA 474 (SCA) (*King*).

28   The answer to this turned on an interpretation of ss 167(4)(e) and 172(2)(a) of the Constitution, which defined the jurisdictions of the CC and all other superior courts, respectively.

29   The Court showed a keen appreciation of the political context in which such a power was to be exercised: see para 14, for example.

30   2006 (6) SA 416 (CC) (*Doctors for Life*).

when the relevant committee of the National Council of Provinces (NCOP) had dealt with the relevant Bills. The CC thus set aside the Traditional Health Practitioners Act and the Choice on Termination of Pregnancy Amendment Act on the ground of lack of public participation in their enactment, and Parliament had to go through the legislative process again. Although the Court was not unanimous in its judgment,[31] a sufficiently weighty majority was willing to hold Parliament to its constitutional mandate in this respect. This was not necessarily a popular stance, for the formal policy of the government was strongly in favour of choice on the termination of pregnancy, and Doctors for Life was not a mass-based organisation with a prominent public profile.

In reaching these conclusions, the majority judgment[32] shed helpful interpretive light on a number of issues of importance to the scope and intensity of judicial review of the legislative process. The chief points to be noted here are the CC's agreement with the jurisdictional approach of the SCA in *King* (paras 21 and 30); the Court's sensitivity to the separation of powers (paras 37–39); the judicial explication of the circumstances in which it would be appropriate to intervene (paras 56, 59, 64 and 71); and the Court's perception of the nature of the constitutional democracy of which it forms a vital part (paras 116 and 137).[33]

Key findings of the Court are best noted in the words of Ngcobo J, as follows:

> I conclude, therefore, that after Parliament has passed a bill and before the President has assented to and signed the bill, it is not competent for this Court to grant any relief in relation to the bill, save at the instance of the President and in the limited circumstances contemplated in section 79 (para 56). The fact that the statute may not have been brought into operation cannot deprive this Court of its jurisdiction (para 64). And if in the process of performing their constitutional duty, courts intrude into the domain of other branches of government, that is an intrusion mandated by the Constitution (para 70). That said, however, it is not necessary to reach any firm conclusion on whether it is competent for this Court to interfere in the deliberative process of Parliament to enforce the duty to facilitate public involvement (para 71).

This firm statement of the Court's view of its constitutional mandate in regard to the legislative process set the scene for the next and more controversial phase of development of judicial review of legislative activity. This is almost part two of

---

31   Ngcobo J spoke for the majority, while Van der Westhuizen J and Yacoob J wrote separate dissenting opinions.

32   Written by Ngcobo J, with which seven justices concurred.

33   At para 230 Sachs J remarked: 'Accountability, responsiveness and openness ... are by their very nature, ubiquitous and timeless. ... Thus it would be a travesty of our Constitution to treat democracy as going into a deep sleep after elections, only to be kissed back to short spells of life every five years.'

Doctors for Life,[34] but in a much more politically charged context: the changing of the physical boundaries of several provinces in an apparent attempt by the national government to eliminate 'cross-border municipalities'.

While changing provincial boundaries in order to avoid cross-border municipalities may seem a logical step, the disparate levels of wealth and substantially differing level of service delivery between the provinces concerned led most residents of the towns affected to object strongly to the proposed changes. In law, any such change required a constitutional amendment, which in turn necessitated the achievement of support of a two-thirds majority in the National Assembly, as well as support in the NCOP of at least six of the nine provinces.[35] Furthermore, the express support of the provincial legislatures of the provinces *directly* affected by the boundary changes was required.[36]

The first town to go to court to challenge the legality of its transfer from KwaZulu-Natal (KZN) to the Eastern Cape was Matatiele. After a preliminary skirmish,[37] the matter made its way again to the highest court.[38] The applicant residents argued that the provincial legislatures had to comply with the 'public involvement' requirement before signifying their consent to any such changes, and that the Eastern Cape Legislature had done so, whereas the KZN Legislature had done nothing in this respect. The majority of the CC agreed with this argument, holding that the Constitution Twelfth Amendment Act of 2005 was thus unconstitutional, based on a relatively simple and clear-cut set of facts.[39]

The next case involving the Court and the legislative process, however, took its jurisprudence to an altogether different level. This dispute kept the Court's focus on the alteration of provincial boundaries. The case of *Merafong Demarcation Forum v President of the Republic of South Africa*[40] was triggered by an attempt to excise a part of a town on the West Rand from Gauteng and incorporate it into the North West province. This translated into law in the form of the Constitution Twelfth Amendment Act of 2005 and the Cross-boundary Municipalities Laws Repeal and Related Matters Act 23 of 2005. As in *Matatiele*, the context was an apparently intransigent executive 'leaning on' its party colleagues in a provincial legislature to toe the party line imposed from above. This was a highly charged

---

34   The judgment in *Matatiele* was handed down the day after.

35   See section 74(3)(b) of the Constitution.

36   Ibid section 74(8).

37   See *Matatiele Municipality & Others v President of the Republic of South Africa & Others* 2006 (5) SA 47 (CC).

38   See *Matatiele Municipality & Others v President of the RSA & Others* (No 2) 2007 (6) SA 477 (CC) (*Matatiele*).

39   See the judgment of Ngcobo J, with which eight justices concurred. The dissenting judgment of Yacoob J was based on his view in *Doctors for Life*, which had been considered simultaneously, (see paras 124–127), and was concurred in by Skweyiya and Van der Westhuizen JJ, who in very brief judgments based their dissents on the same reasoning he employed.

40   2008 (5) SA 171 (CC) (*Merafong*).

political issue for people on the ground, as was shown by the extraordinary level and ferocity of public protest in Merafong. For these reasons, and because the CC proved on this occasion to be more divided in its response, the circumstances and judgments in the case will be set out in greater detail.

2.5. The Merafong case

The applicants in *Merafong* asked the CC to declare that the Gauteng Legislature had failed to comply with section 118 of the Constitution which imposed an obligation on it to facilitate public involvement in the process leading to the adoption by the NCOP of the constitutional amendment. Alternatively, they sought a declaration that the Gauteng Legislature had failed to act rationally when it supported the Constitution Twelfth Amendment Bill in the NCOP. The factual background was briefly as follows. In late 2005, both provincial legislatures affected called for and received representations on the location of Merafong. A well-attended public hearing was also held, and the majority view was that part of Merafong should stay within the Gauteng province. The relevant committee of the Gauteng Legislature thus formulated a 'negotiating mandate', which associated itself with the abolition of cross-border municipalities as a general principle and recorded its support for the Constitution Twelfth Amendment Bill, but on condition that the Bill be amended to incorporate Merafong into Gauteng. However, after being advised that such conditional support was not possible — that is, a province could not seek to amend but only to vote for or against a part or the whole of such a Bill, the committee changed its tune, and recommended to the full Gauteng Legislature that it give its unconditional support to the Bill, which duly happened. This was done without notice to, nor consultation with, the residents of Merafong.

The applicants were granted direct access to the CC as they were challenging the validity of a constitutional amendment which falls within the exclusive domain of that Court.[41] It was almost to be expected that the CC would respond in a number of ways, given the divisiveness of the issues and the complexity of the constitutional provisions which fell to be interpreted. The leading judgment for the majority, which held both that the Gauteng Legislature had complied with its duty to facilitate public involvement in the process and that it had acted rationally in changing its mandated view, thus dismissing the application, was delivered by Van der Westhuizen J.

As to the adequacy of the facilitation of public involvement, Van der Westhuizen J (with whom eight other justices concurred) found that the Gauteng Legislature had fulfilled its constitutional duty, as it had taken reasonable steps to solicit public comment and consider the submissions and comments made in

---

41 See section 167(4)(d) of the Constitution.

the process. Although the provincial legislative Committee had failed to report back to the community its change of position from its 'negotiating mandate', this could possibly be characterised as 'disrespectful', rather than unconstitutional, conduct.[42]

Only Sachs J disagreed with this finding. He reasoned that the Legislature's failure to communicate its change of view to the community amounted to a breach of its constitutional obligations. For him, the nature of the legislation under consideration, the extent of the impact of the change on the community and the strong public expectation that the Legislature had created that it would support the majority view in the community resulted cumulatively in a requirement that the community be appropriately involved in the entire decision-making process (paras 295–298). Sachs J expressed himself as follows:

> Arms-length democracy is not participatory democracy, and the consequent and predictable rupture in the relationship between the community and the Legislature tore at the heart of what participatory democracy aims to achieve ... after making a good start to fulfil its obligation to facilitate public involvement, the Legislature stumbled badly at the last hurdle. It ended up failing to exercise its responsibilities in a reasonable manner, with the result that it seriously violated the integrity of the process of participatory democracy. In choosing not to face the music (which, incidentally, it had itself composed) it breached the constitutional compact requiring mutuality of open and good-faith dealing between citizenry and government, and thereby rendered the legislative process invalid (paras 300–301).

The issue of the rationality of the Legislature's decision-making process proved much more divisive. The applicants had argued that the decision was irrational on its merits, and because the Gauteng Legislature had changed its mind. On the standard of rationality to be applied, Van der Westhuizen invoked the previous approach of the CC:

> The exercise of public power has to be rational. In a constitutional state arbitrariness or the exercise of public power on the basis of naked preferences cannot pass muster. Judgments of this court suggest that, objectively viewed, a link is required between the means adopted by the legislature and the end sought to be achieved (para 62).

After detailed examination of the question whether the Gauteng Legislature sufficiently well understood the nature and extent of its constitutional powers and obligations (paras 67–102), he concluded that it could not be said to have laboured under misconceptions in this regard. Furthermore, it was impossible to conclude that the Legislature's decision was irrational on its merits — that is,

---

42 This issue is resolved for the majority in paras 42–60. For the minority, see the remarks of Moseneke DCJ at para 123, who characterises the legislative conduct as reasonable, although taken in 'unseemly haste'.

that there was no link between the means adopted by the Legislature and the legitimate government end sought to be achieved (paras 114–115).

Ngcobo J agreed that the Legislature had not acted irrationally, as the negotiating mandate was by definition subject to change (para 252). The Legislature changed its position once it fully appreciated the legal framework within which it was operating. The Legislature's reasons for supporting the Twelfth Amendment Bill were rationally related to legitimate governmental objectives, and its action was thus constitutional (para 268). In a further concurring judgment which rejected the application, Skweyiya J stressed that it was not the function of the Court to determine the merits of the demarcation exercise (para 305). The Court was not a site for political struggle, and it was the role of the Constitution to provide a forum in which politicians could be held accountable through regular, free and fair elections (para 309). In his words: 'Courts deal with bad law; voters must deal with bad politics. The doctrine of separation of powers, to which our constitutional democracy subscribes, does not allow this Court, or any other court, to interfere in the lawful exercise of powers by the legislature' (para 308). Yacoob J concurred in all three judgments outlined on this issue thus far, while Langa CJ and Mpati AJ concurred in the judgments of both Van der Westhuizen J and Ngcobo J, thus constituting a majority of six justices in rejection of the application.

Moseneke DCJ spoke for the minority on this issue[43] and acknowledged that a judicial enquiry into rationality does not give the court licence to 'place its own preference above that of the public functionary properly charged with the power' (paras 169–170). He characterised the issue before the Court as one concerning not a general legislative power but a specific question about the approval or not of the alteration of provincial boundaries. The factual circumstances admitted of no speculation about the action taken and the legislative motivation, thus making judicial scrutiny entirely appropriate (para 171). He went on to find that the reversal without rational explanation of the clear negotiating stance of the legislative committee, arrived at after proper public participation and consultation, pointed to arbitrary and irrational conduct (para 175). He held further that the provincial legislature had misconceived its powers and obligations, in taking the view that only two courses of action (to support or reject the amendment Bill in its entirety) were open to it (paras 179–180). After discussing three possible implications of Gauteng's failure to support that part of the Bill referring to Merafong,[44] Moseneke DCJ reached the 'inescapable conclusion that the

---

43   He was joined by Madala, Nkabinde and Sachs JJ.
44   See paras 181–190.

provincial legislature had not only misconceived its constitutional obligations but also misconstrued the consequences of the exercise of its powers under the Constitution'. This led to the finding that the legislative conduct under scrutiny was both irrational and inconsistent with the Constitution (para 192).

Madala J pithily expressed his support for the minority view, casting the justification for the obligation to consult the public within the historical experience of black people under apartheid. He reminded the Court that 'during the apartheid era the views of the black population were never canvassed when legislation affecting them was being mooted', and that public involvement in the legislative process 'was also intended to salvage the dignity of black people which had been ravaged by apartheid' (paras 206–207).

What lessons are to be drawn from the judgments in the *Merafong* case? While the sudden and embarrassing about-face of the Gauteng Legislature and its representatives on the NCOP made a mockery of the process of consultation in good faith, it was certainly feasible for a court to have held that this was the prerogative of a representative and deliberative body, after due consideration. Perhaps the most striking aspect of all the judgments is that the six judges who spoke showed clearly that they were not unwilling to get involved, so to speak, to give content to the requirement of 'facilitating public involvement' in the legislative process.

A wide range of judicial views on the limits of legislative and judicial authority is exposed in the judgments. There is also frank discussion of the role of the courts in such circumstances, ranging from justified intervention to a hands-off stance. It is significant that the CC was unanimous in its disapproval of the discourteous and misleading conduct of the Gauteng Legislature, on occasion in quite strong language. The narrowness of the majority indicates that the difference of opinion is probably to be attributed to differing conceptions of the propriety of judicial intervention under the separation of powers, that is, where on a spectrum of legislative impropriety the point of judicial intervention is reached.

3. The limits of judicial intervention

The issue of the propriety of judicial intervention is taken further in *Glenister v President of the Republic of South Africa & Others*,[45] the attempt by a private party acting (and being given standing as such) in his own cause, as a member of a group or class of people, and in the public interest, to arrest the legislative process before it had run its course. Again here, the political profile of the matter could hardly have been higher, concerning as it did the discharge of a mandate given by the ruling party to its leadership during a highly contentious ANC party

---

45   2009 (1) SA 287 (CC).

congress at Polokwane in December 2007. This case was fought out at a more elevated level than *Merafong* in that there was no mass mobilisation of citizens which preceded it. However, media coverage was probably more pronounced, precisely because of the generality of the effects of the proposed legislation, and of the direct party-political interest in the objectives ostensibly sought to be achieved by the legislation.

The ANC had resolved at Polokwane to require the party leadership to disband the Directorate of Special Operations — commonly known as the Scorpions, an investigative arm of the National Prosecuting Authority which had achieved major successes in the fight against organised crime and corruption — and to absorb its activities and membership into the South African Police Services. Cabinet had duly decided to initiate legislation to achieve such goals, which had apparently led to a substantial number of resignations and a loss of morale amongst the staff of the Scorpions, thus directly affecting its ability to do its work effectively. Glenister, a businessman who argued that his vested interest in the survival and growth of the South African economy would be damaged by the reduced ability to fight crime which would flow from the adoption of the amending legislation, applied to the Pretoria High Court for an interdict to stop the legislative process at the stage of Cabinet's drafting of legislation to realise the ANC resolution. The Pretoria High Court found that it lacked jurisdiction to hear the application, and the matter was struck from the roll.[46] Glenister then applied for leave to appeal this decision to the CC, seeking an order compelling Cabinet to withdraw the relevant Bills from Parliament.[47]

The Chief Justice directed the parties to confine their arguments to a single issue: 'Whether, in the light of the doctrine of the separation of powers, it is appropriate for this court ... to make any order setting aside the decision of the national Executive that is challenged in this case' (para 9). Glenister answered this question by arguing that there are 'exceptional circumstances in which an aggrieved litigant cannot be expected to wait for Parliament to enact a statute before he or she challenges it in court', and that the underlying question should thus be 'whether effective redress could be given after the legislation had been enacted' (para 19). If not, then it was appropriate for the court to intervene in advance of the completion of the legislative process, which Glenister averred to be the case here. Government responded essentially that the separation of powers as provided for in the Constitution depended on a delicate balance of powers between the three arms of government, and that judicial intervention with the legislative process as sought by Glenister would unnecessarily and

---

46   Judgment of Van der Merwe J, 27 May 2008, unreported.
47   For the factual background and details of the parties involved, see paras 1–7 and 10–17 of the judgment.

unjustifiably upset that balance: the exceptional circumstances referred to by the applicant were not present in this case (paras 25–28).

Langa CJ delivered a relatively short judgment. He started with a review of the place of the doctrine of the separation of powers in the Constitution noting that, although not expressly mentioned in the text, it was 'axiomatic' that it was part of the constitutional design.[48] He summed up the situation in this respect as follows:

> It is a necessary component of the doctrine of the separation of powers that courts have a constitutional obligation to ensure that the exercise of power by other branches of government occurs within constitutional bounds. But even in these circumstances, courts must observe the limits of their powers (para 33).

After extensive reference to *Doctors for Life*,[49] he formulated the test for intervention by a court in the legislative process as follows:

> Intervention would only be appropriate if an applicant can show that there would be no effective remedy available ... once the legislative process is complete, as the unlawful conduct will have achieved its object in the course of the process. The applicant must show that the resultant harm is material and irreversible (para 43).

Having acknowledged that this cast a 'formidable burden' on any applicant in such cases and that circumstances which warranted intervention would be 'extremely rare', Langa CJ cautiously declined to speculate about what would in general amount to the 'exceptional circumstances' required to justify intervention; this would have to be decided on a case-by-case basis. Applying the test, he held that the circumstances did not justify judicial intervention (para 57), for two main reasons: it was possible that Parliament would amend the proposed legislation, so that its ultimate effect was not able to be determined; and the causal connection between the proposed legislation and the loss of staff by the Scorpions had not been clearly established: even if the connection were established, it would not necessarily amount to irreversible harm of the degree required by the test (paras 51–52).

All concerned were acutely aware of the forces at work behind the litigation. Indeed, the judgment refers to the applicant arguing with a 'great deal of passion, no doubt because of the important and emotive debates in the country about the unacceptable levels of crime, its prevention and the measures that ... should be employed to combat it' (para 48). The highly visible and contested context of the case may well account for the unanimous judgment of the Court, with weight being added by it being delivered by the Chief Justice. Of particular interest is the

---

48   See paras 29–32.
49   Note 31 above.

approach of the Court to the argument that Cabinet and Parliament were 'acting under dictation' from the ANC party congress reminiscent of an administrative-law ground of review (para 54). This judgment can fairly be described as ultimately but appropriately deferential, in the sense of being respectful to the limits of the Court's jurisdiction vis-à-vis the other branches of government. This is not to suggest that the Court should refrain from intervention in the legislative process, because of the risk of calamitous political fallout; it is rather to acknowledge the necessity of political consciousness and wisdom as guides to the judges in such circumstances.

In sum, *Merafong* and *Glenister* build on *Doctors for Life* and take appreciably further the willingness of the Court to insist upon measures to enhance the notion of a participative democracy in its legislative guise, as required by the Constitution. At the same time, they appear to keep the judicial branch on the correct side of the justifiable limits of authority prescribed for the courts, the executive and Parliament, according to the nuanced understanding of the doctrine of the separation of powers prescribed in the Constitution.

4. Conclusion

This chapter has described how judicial review of parliamentary action has served to hold the South African Parliament and provincial legislatures accountable. There has been some academic comment on the cases discussed here (Malan 2007; Malherbe 2007; Rautenbach 2007). Very tentatively, I would argue that the Court's interpretation of its role in securing parliamentary compliance with the Constitution has been formally if tardily accepted by both the executive and the legislature, if parliamentary responses are the guide.

The courts began with determining the scope of the parliamentary autonomy over its internal operations, powers and privileges. In *De Lille*, the SCA emphasised that Parliament was constrained by the concept of legality just as any other organ of the state. It could thus neither make any law nor perform any act which was inconsistent with the Constitution. In that case, it was specifically held that Parliament could not claim immunity in cases where its actions had an adverse effect on the rights of an individual or group of persons. Subsequently, the CC held in *Executive Council of the Western Cape Legislature v President of the RSA* that Parliament could not delegate its primary law-making powers to the executive. By policing the province of legislative action, courts have ensured that Parliament adheres to its constitutional mandate.

In a number of cases, provisions of several Acts of Parliament have been declared unconstitutional and invalid. As a show of respect for Parliament, the CC has on several occasions issued orders requiring Parliament to amend the relevant legislation within a prescribed period, instead of curing the defects itself. Although Parliament has in some cases asked for extensions, there has not been any recalcitrance on its part.

Arguably, the most important area in which the courts have reinforced the notion of accountable and responsive government is through giving content to the idea of 'participatory democracy'. The manner in which they have done this would certainly fit comfortably with the basic values and many other provisions of the Constitution, and are likely to elicit support and respect from most South Africans.

References

Legislation

Appellate Division Quorum Act 27 of 1955.
Attorneys Act 53 of 1979.
Attorneys and Matters Relating to Rules of Court Amendment Act 115 of 1998.
Choice on Termination of Pregnancy Act 38 of 2004.
Choice on Termination of Pregnancy Amendment Act 38 of 2004.
Constitution of the Republic of South Africa Act 200 of 1993.
Constitution of the Republic of South Africa, 1996.
Constitution Twelfth Amendment Act of 2005.
Cross-boundary Municipalities Laws Repeal and Related Matters Act 23 of 2005.
Dental Technicians Amendment Act 24 of 2004.
High Court of Parliament Act 35 of 1952.
Medicines and Medical Devices Regulatory Authority Act 132 of 1998.
Powers and Privileges of Parliament Act 91 of 1963.
Senate Act 53 of 1955.
South Africa Act, 1909.
South Africa Amendment Act 9 of 1956.
State Liability Act 20 of 1957.
Sterilisation Amendment Act 3 of 2005.
Traditional Health Practitioners Act 35 of 2005.

Cases

Attorney General, New South Wales v Trethowan [1932] AC 526 (PC).
Bhe v Magistrate, Khayelitsha 2005 (1) SA 580 (CC).
Certification of the Amended Text of the Constitution of the Republic of South Africa, 1996 1997 (2) SA 713 (CC), (1) BCLR 1 (CC).
Collins v Minister of the Interior & Another 1957 (1) SA 552 (AD).
Daniels v Campbell NO 2004 (5) SA 331 (CC).
De Lille & Another v Speaker of the National Assembly 1998 (3) SA 430 (C).
Doctors for Life International v Speaker of the National Assembly 2006 (6) SA 416 (CC).
Executive Council of the Western Cape v Minister for Provincial Affairs and Constitutional Development 2000 (1) SA 661 (CC).

Executive Council of the Western Cape Legislature v President of the Republic of South Africa 1995 (4) SA 877 (CC).

Glenister v President of the Republic of South Africa & Others 2009 (1) SA 287 (CC).

Harris v Minister of the Interior 1952 (2) SA 428 (AD).

In re Certification of the Constitution of the Republic of South Africa, 1996 1996 (4) SA 744 (CC), 1997 (10) BCLR 1253 (CC).

King & Others v Attorneys' Fidelity Fund Board of Control & Another 2006 (1) SA 474 (SCA).

Matatiele Municipality & Others v President of the Republic of South Africa & Others 2006 (5) SA 47 (CC).

Matatiele Municipality & Others v President of the Republic of South Africa & Others (No 2) 2007 (6) SA 477 (CC).

Merafong Demarcation Forum v President of the Republic of South Africa 2008 (5) SA 171 (CC).

Minister for Justice and Constitutional Development v Nyathi (Case No CCT 53/09), delivered on 9th October, 2009, as yet unreported.

Minister of Home Affairs v Fourie 2006 (1) SA 524 (CC).

Minister of the Interior v Harris 1952 (4) SA 769 (AD).

Ndlwana v Hofmeyr NO 1937 AD 229.

Nyathi v MEC for Department of Health, Gauteng 2008 (5) SA 94 (CC).

Pharmaceutical Manufacturers Association of South Africa & Another: In re Ex Parte Application of the President of the Republic of South Africa & Others 2000 (2) SA 674 (CC).

President of the Republic of South Africa v Hugo 1997 (4) SA 1 (CC).

R v Secretary of State for the Home Department, ex parte Daly [2001] 3 All ER 433 (HL).

Speaker of the National Assembly v De Lille & Another 1999 (4) SA 863 (SCA).

Ynuico Ltd v Minister of Trade and Industry 1996 (3) SA 989 (CC).

Zondi v MEC for Traditional and Local Government Affairs 2006 (3) SA 1 (CC).

Articles, books, chapters in books and other works

Ebrahim, H. 1998. *The Soul of a Nation: Constitution-Making in South Africa*. Cape Town: Oxford University Press.

Malan, J.J. 2007. Democratic legislation and administrative action in view of recent case law. *SA Public Law*, 22: 61–78.

Malherbe, R. 2007. Openbare betrokkenheid by die wetgewende proses kry oplaas tande: *Doctors for Life International v Speaker of the National Assembly and Chairperson of the National Council of Provinces* [2006] 12 BCLR 1399. *Tydskrif vir die Suid Afrikaanse Reg*, 3: 594–606.

Rautenbach, I.M. 2007. Die konstitutionele hof se uitsluitlike jurisdiksie oor die nienakoming van sekere pligte van parlement: *King v Attorneys Fidelity Fund Board of Control* [2006] 4 BCLR 462 (HHA); *Doctors for Life International v Speaker of the National Assembly and Chairperson of the National Council of Provinces* [2006] 12 BCLR 1399 (KH). *Tydskrif vir die Suid Afrikaanse Reg*, 3: 581–588.

Chapter 7

Prosecutions, politics and the law: The way things are

Philip C. Stenning

'It's politics, it's the law, it's the way things are'
Robert Wardle[1]
'It is the province of the statesman and not the lawyer to discuss, and of the legislature to determine, what is best for the public good, and to provide for it by proper enactments.'
Coleridge J in Egerton v Earl of Brownlow (1853) 4 HL Cas 1.

1. Introduction

In recent years, a lively debate has been revived in many countries, including South Africa, about what are, and what should be, the constitutional and institutional arrangements for the exercise of investigative and prosecutorial discretion. A host of different cases have fuelled these debates. Some involve investigations into the activities of high profile political or other powerful individuals or corporations, and others involve ordinary citizens with no particular public profile but who have often unwittingly attracted public attention. What these cases have in common is that they raise challenging questions about (i) who should have the ultimate authority to determine what 'the public interest'[2] requires in such cases, (ii) the conditions under which such decisions should be made, and (iii) how those who make them can effectively be held publicly accountable.

The fact that such decisions revolve around 'the public interest' arises from a long tradition, particularly in common law jurisdictions,[3] about how

---

1   Director of the UK Serious Fraud Office (SFO), referring to his decision to terminate the SFO's investigation into allegations of corruption against BAE Systems plc in December 2006. Interview on 'Panorama' programme, 'Princes, planes and pay-offs', BBC TV, 11 June 2007.

2   Or in some cases the national interest or even the international interest.

3   By contrast, in continental European 'civil law' systems, a principle of legality has traditionally been the underlying principle governing investigative and prosecutorial decision-making, according to which prosecutors and investigating magistrates, when faced with credible evidence of criminality, have a *duty* to prosecute, and may themselves be subject to sanctions if they fail to do so (Fionda 1995).

prosecutorial discretion should be exercised. This is commonly referred to as the two-step test, which is now recognised, almost without exception, in published prosecutorial policies, guidelines and codes of practice throughout the common-law world.[4] According to this test, the first consideration for a prosecutor must be whether there is sufficient credible and admissible evidence of a criminal offence which, if believed, could sustain a conviction — the evidential test. Although satisfaction of the evidential test is universally considered to be a necessary condition for a decision to prosecute, it is not by itself a sufficient one, as the English Attorney General, Sir John Simon, famously emphasised almost 85 years ago:

> ... there is no greater nonsense talked about the Attorney General's duty, than the suggestion that in all cases the Attorney General ought to decide to prosecute merely because he thinks there is what the lawyers call 'a case'. It is not true and no-one who has held that office supposes it is.[5]

And the House of Lords observed in the leading case of *Gouriet v Union of Post Office Workers*:

> Enforcement of the criminal law is of course a very important public interest, but it is not the only one, and may not always be the predominant one. There may be even more important reasons of public policy why such procedure should not be taken at a particular moment, and it must be proper for the Attorney General (acting of course not for political advantage) to have regard for them.[6]

So the second consideration, which only comes into play if the evidential test has been satisfied, is whether a prosecution is, under all circumstances, in the public interest. In most jurisdictions, once the evidential test has been satisfied, the default position is that 'a prosecution should follow, unless the public interest demands otherwise.'[7]

It is obvious that the evidential test essentially requires fine legal judgment and a solid understanding of the legal requirements of proof, the rules of evidence, etcetera. It also requires a good understanding of what factors are likely to affect the credibility of evidence and testimony; for example, whether a particular witness is likely to be regarded as credible. So while it does not only require straight legal expertise, it is nevertheless usually entrusted to experienced legal practitioners.

---

4   See, eg, part 4 of South Africa's Prosecution Policy, revised on 1 December 2005. Available at http://us-cdn.creamermedia.co.za/assets/articles/attachments/02475_npaprosecutionpolicy.pdf. Accessed 20 August 2010.
5   House of Commons, *Debates*, Vol 188, Col 2105, 1 December 1925.
6   [1978] AC 435, 523–4 (*per* Lord Fraser of Tullybelton).
7   South Africa's Prosecution Policy (note 3 above) para (c), A6.

By contrast, the public interest test clearly does not primarily require legal skills.[8] It is more accurately thought of as requiring essentially sound political judgment, in a non-partisan sense of the word. In cases with international ramifications, it may even require diplomatic judgment. The public interest test typically engages issues of *public policy* rather than law, and it is this characteristic which makes the allocation of responsibility for its determination a matter of controversy in some cases.

In liberal parliamentary democracies, the authority to make critical discretionary decisions, even with respect to dispositions in particular cases, is in practice, and sometimes by law, frequently shared between politicians, public servants and the courts, depending on the perceived implications of decisions (Stenning 2010a: 339–341). There is plenty of evidence that prosecutorial decision-making, despite some powerful rhetoric to the contrary, is no exception in this regard.

2. Prosecutorial authority: 'The way things are'

A wide variety of constitutional provisions and institutional arrangements for prosecutorial decision-making can be identified around the world, including among African jurisdictions. At the broadest level of analysis, there are models in which the ultimate responsibility for prosecutorial decisions is entrusted to politicians, public servants or judges. Within each of these broad categories, however, there are further variations.

In continental European civil-law jurisdictions and in countries which have inherited their legal traditions, prosecutorial decision-making in individual cases is typically entrusted to judicial officials — investigating magistrates or *juges d'instruction*, as they are called in France — usually with the advice and assistance of a public prosecutor who is a public servant, but who follows a similar career path to that of judges.[9] Even in common-law jurisdictions, exceptional circumstances can be found in which decisions to prosecute, although not initiated by judges, nevertheless require judicial consent or may be judicially authorised.[10] These are exceptions, however, and they will not be discussed further in this chapter.

---

8   For an argument for conceiving of 'the public interest' as a legal standard, see MacNair (2006) especially 184–196 with respect to prosecutorial discretion.

9   In France, for instance, prosecutors undergo similar training to that of judges, and once qualified, a person may alternate, over his or her career, in the roles of prosecutor and judge. Interestingly, the President of France recently announced that this system will soon be abandoned in favour of one more similar to that in common-law jurisdictions: 'Sarkozy on collision course with judges over investigating magistrates'. Available on guardian.co.uk, Wednesday 7 January 2009. More generally, see Hodgson (2005), and Delmas-Marty and Spencer (2002).

10   In Canada, and several other common-law jurisdictions, for instance, an indictment can only be preferred by someone other than the Attorney General with the consent of a judge: see subsection 574(3) of Canada's Criminal Code, RSC 1985, c C-46.

In England, from where former colonies have derived their own systems for the administration of criminal justice, a tradition has developed in which the ultimate prosecutorial authority is entrusted to a politician — nowadays a government minister and a member of one of the two Houses of Parliament — in the person of the Attorney General. As those who have studied the history of this unique office have demonstrated, a constitutional convention has evolved during the last two centuries according to which the Attorney General, in exercising his or her prosecutorial authority in individual cases, is expected to act independently (Edwards 1964; 1984). This concept of the independence of the Attorney General has been designed to ensure that, despite the fact that he or she is a politician and a government minister, his or her prosecutorial decisions will be based on broad legal and public interest considerations, rather than on narrow partisan political, private, personal or special interests. Since 1929, a further convention has developed, also designed to foster the actuality as well as the perception of the independence of the Attorney General, whereby although he or she is a senior government minister, he or she is not a member of the Cabinet.[11]

Since 1879, England has also had an official called the Director of Public Prosecutions (DPP) who serves under the 'superintendence' of the Attorney General. While originally this officer had limited powers over prosecutorial decision-making, in 1985 legislation was introduced to establish an independent Crown Prosecution Service[12] of which the DPP is now the head. Since then, two other specialised prosecution agencies have been established — the Serious Fraud Office (SFO) and the Revenue and Customs Prosecution Office (RCPO) — each headed by a Director who, like the DPP, serves under the 'superintendence' of the Attorney General. Although the intention behind the establishment of each of these prosecutorial agencies was to entrust day-to-day prosecutorial decision-making to independent public servants, the prevailing view is that the Attorney General's ultimate constitutional authority over prosecutorial decision-making has not been diminished by their creation, despite the fact that there has been some recent uncertainty as to the precise meaning and implications of the Attorney General's 'superintendence' of them.

---

11   Although not a member of the Cabinet, the Attorney General attended Cabinet meetings when matters arose with respect to which his advice as the chief legal adviser to the government was required. Throughout the Blair administration, from 1997 to 2007, however, the Attorney General routinely attended almost all Cabinet meetings. This practice was discontinued under the Brown administration, which reverted to the previous practice.

12   Prior to 1985, prosecutorial authority in England and Wales was primarily entrusted to Chief Constables. Scotland had long since adopted a public prosecutor office with the title of Procurator Fiscal (Edwards 1984).

The English model has been adopted, with some variations,[13] in many Commonwealth countries, although in many the convention that the Attorney General is not a member of the Cabinet has been rejected.

In other Commonwealth countries, including many in Africa, a different model has been adopted under which ultimate and exclusive prosecutorial authority with respect to decision-making in individual cases has been constitutionally or statutorily entrusted to an independent, non-political, appointed public servant, often holding the title of DPP.[14] While such officials are usually *accountable* to a greater or lesser degree to a government minister — for instance, an Attorney General or a Minister of Justice — what distinguishes this model from the current institutional arrangements in England, is that the minister concerned is not recognised as having any authority to give directions to the DPP with respect to decision-making in individual cases.[15] Nevertheless, the nature of the relationship between an independent DPP and his or her minister has been a source of disagreement and controversy in many of these jurisdictions.

3. The concept of prosecutorial independence

The idea of prosecutorial independence is recognised in almost all common-law jurisdictions, regardless of which institutional arrangements for the exercise of prosecutorial authority they have adopted, but it raises rather different questions when applied to different institutional arrangements. In those jurisdictions in which ultimate prosecutorial authority is vested in a government minister, such as an Attorney General, the main debate about the meaning of prosecutorial independence typically focuses on its implications for the relationship between that minister and his or her ministerial colleagues, including the Prime Minister.[16] The tradition which has developed whereby the Attorney General is not a member of the Cabinet reflects an attempt to reinforce the idea or at least the perception that the Attorney General acts independently in fulfilling his or her prosecutorial responsibilities. Despite this, debates about the proper relationship between an Attorney General and his or her ministerial colleagues have had a long and chequered history in England, and only in the latter half of the twentieth century did some cross-party consensus on this matter begin to emerge. This consensus was for a long time limited to the general proposition

---

13   In New Zealand, for instance, the Solicitor General is an appointed public servant who holds an office which is roughly equivalent to that of the DPP in England.

14   In several countries (eg, Israel, Botswana and Lesotho), a similar result has been achieved by converting the office of Attorney General into a non-political, appointed, public service office.

15   Thus recognising the important distinction between accountability, on the one hand, and control, on the other (Stenning 2008: 217–221).

16   Of course in countries having an executive President, such debates also include discussion of the implications of the concept for relations between the minister and the President.

that in making prosecutorial decisions an Attorney General must apply his or her own professional judgment as to what the public interest requires in the case at hand, and must not allow his or her decisions to be based on, or influenced by, partisan political, personal, private or special interests. Of course, discerning what the public interest requires is essentially a matter of political judgment and a politician's determination on this is frequently and inescapably liable to be considered inherently suspect and contestable. Thus, an Attorney General's claim of independence is often likely to be questioned or doubted in practice.

This problem of credibility has not been helped by the fact that three quite different positions emerged on the question of whether or not it is acceptable, or even required, that an Attorney General consult with his or her ministerial colleagues before making an independent decision in a case which could be regarded as potentially having significant political or public interest implications. The most extreme position emerged in 1924 when the first Labour Government of Ramsay MacDonald, with respect to the *Campbell* case, issued a Cabinet directive to the effect that: 'No prosecution of a political character should be undertaken without the prior sanction of the Cabinet being obtained'.[17] This position has since been rejected in the UK as an unlawful and unconstitutional negation of the Attorney General's constitutional independence.[18]

A second position on this matter is exemplified by the following statement to Parliament made by MacDonald's successor as Prime Minister, Stanley Baldwin, later in 1924, in which he explained why he rescinded his predecessor's instruction:

> ... it is the *duty* of the Attorney General, in the discharge of his responsibilities so entrusted to him, to inform himself of all relevant circumstances which might properly affect his decision: when the proposed prosecution is of such a character that matters of public policy are, or may be, involved, *it is the duty of the Attorney General to inform himself of the views of the government or of the appropriate Minister before coming to a decision.* It is because in the view of the government the instructions referred to in the question went beyond this that these instructions were rescinded by the Cabinet. (Emphasis added)

This position differs from the first in two important respects. In the first place, it replaces the requirement to obtain the 'prior sanction of the Cabinet' with a

---

17 The Campbell prosecution was discontinued at the very outset by the Attorney General of the day. For the full background to the issuance of this directive, see Edwards (1964).

18 In 1959, Prime Minister Harold Macmillan made the following statement in the House of Commons: 'It is an established principle of government in this country, and a tradition long supported by all political parties, that the decision as to whether any citizen should be prosecuted, or whether any prosecution should be discontinued, should be a matter, where a public as opposed to a private prosecution is concerned, for the prosecution authorities to decide on the merits of the case without political or other pressure. It would be a most dangerous deviation from this sound principle if a prosecution were instituted or abandoned as a result of political pressure or popular clamour'. House of Commons, *Debates*, 16 February 1959, Vol 600, Col 31.

'duty of the Attorney General to inform himself of the views of the government or of the appropriate Minister before coming to a decision'. Secondly, it refers to a seemingly broader category of cases, replacing the reference to prosecutions of a 'political character' with prosecutions which are 'of such a character that matters of public policy are, or may be, involved'.

This second position has, in turn, been supplanted by a third position enunciated by subsequent holders of the office of Attorney General. The most frequently cited is the following statement which Attorney General, Sir Hartley Shawcross, made to the House of Commons in 1951:

> I think the true doctrine is that it is the duty of an Attorney General, in deciding whether or not to authorise the prosecution, to acquaint himself with all the relevant facts, including, for instance, the effect which the prosecution, successful or unsuccessful as the case may be, would have upon public morale and order, and with any other consideration affecting public policy. *In order to so inform himself, he may, although I do not think he is obliged to, consult with any of his colleagues in the government*, and indeed, as Lord Simon once said, he would in some cases be a fool if he did not. On the other hand, the assistance of his colleagues is confined to informing him of particular considerations which might affect his own decision, and does not consist, and must not consist, in telling him what that decision ought to be. *The responsibility for the eventual decision rests with the Attorney General, and he is not to be put, and is not put, under pressure by his colleagues in the matter.* Nor, of course, can the Attorney General shift his responsibility for making the decision on to the shoulders of his colleagues. If political considerations which in the broad sense that I have indicated affect government in the abstract arise it is the Attorney General, applying his judicial mind, who has to be the sole judge of those considerations.[19] (Emphasis added)

This statement, which is now widely accepted as expressing the 'true doctrine' of the prosecutorial independence of the Attorney General in England and Wales, accepts Baldwin's earlier assertion of a *duty* of the Attorney General 'to acquaint himself with all the relevant facts', but rejects any *duty* to consult colleagues in the government or anyone else, indicating instead that any such consultation is a matter for the Attorney General's discretion.

These different positions are of course also relevant for a discussion of the independence of non-political, public service DPPs in countries in which they have been given exclusive prosecutorial authority. In such jurisdictions, questions inevitably arise as to what is the appropriate relationship between such independent public prosecutors and the governments under which they serve.

---

19   House of Commons, *Debates*, Vol 483, Cols 683–684.

4. Selected constitutional arrangements from Africa

Section 179 of the Constitution of the Republic of South Africa, 1996 vests the ultimate and exclusive prosecutorial authority with respect to decisions in individual cases in the National Prosecuting Authority (NPA). The NPA is headed by the National Director of Public Prosecutions (NDPP), a non-political public servant who is appointed by the President of the country. Section 179(4) of the South African Constitution states explicitly that national legislation 'must ensure that the prosecuting authority exercises its functions without fear, favour or prejudice.'[20] However, the Constitution also stipulates that: 'The Cabinet Minister responsible for the administration of justice must exercise *final responsibility over the prosecuting authority*' (section 179(6), emphasis added), and that the NDPP must determine prosecution *policy* 'with the concurrence of the Cabinet member responsible for the administration of justice' (section 179(5)(a)).

What does this mean for the independence of the NDPP and the NPA, vis-à-vis the Minister, the government and the President? The particular constitutional or legislative language used in formulating this relationship seems to be of considerable importance.[21] In the first place, South African courts have interpreted the phrase 'final responsibility over the prosecuting authority' as *not* implying any right of the Minister to give directions to the NDPP or the NPA with respect to what decision they should make in an individual case. In the words of Harms J: 'the Minister may not instruct the NPA to prosecute or to decline to prosecute or to terminate a pending prosecution.'[22] Secondly, the wording of section 179(5)(a) of the South African Constitution makes it clear

---

20 Some have argued that since the specific word 'independent' does not appear in this provision, it is not appropriate to refer to the NPA and its National Director as 'independent'. As noted below, however, South African courts have interpreted this provision as requiring that the NPA and the NDPP act independently in making prosecutorial decisions in individual cases, and that any attempt to direct or instruct them as to what decision should be made would be unconstitutional (see note 22 below).

21 In the UK, for instance, some disagreement has recently been expressed over the meaning and implications of the Attorney General's 'superintendence' over the directors of the prosecuting agencies there (in particular whether this imports a right to overrule a director's decision in a particular case). See Stenning 2007: 5–6.

22 *National Director of Public Prosecutions v Zuma* 2009 (4) BCLR 393 (SCA) para 32. In reaching this conclusion, Harms, DP, cited the judgment in *Ex parte Attorney General, Namibia: In Re the Constitutional Relationship between the Attorney-General and the Prosecutor-General* [1995] 3 LRC 507, 1995 (8) BCLR 1070 (SCNm). Available at http://www.saflii.org/na/cases/NASC/1995/1.pdf. Accessed 20 August 2010, in which the Supreme Court of Namibia interpreted a similar provision in the Constitution of Namibia. Section 32 (1) of the South African National Prosecuting Authority Act 32 of 1998 (NPA Act) provides: '(a) a member of the prosecuting authority shall serve impartially and exercise, carry out or perform his or her powers, duties and functions in good faith and without fear favour or prejudice and subject only to the Constitution and the law; (b) subject to the Constitution and this Act, no organ of state and no member or employee of an organ of state nor any other person shall improperly interfere with, hinder or obstruct the prosecuting authority or any member thereof in the exercise, carrying out or performance of its, his or her powers, duties and functions.'

that although prosecution policy requires the 'concurrence' of the Minister, the duty and authority to determine prosecution policy vests in the NDPP, not in the Minister. This may seem a rather fine point, but it is an important one.

Is the NDPP under a *duty* to consult with the Minister, or with any other member of the government, and seek their views or advice, before making a prosecutorial decision with respect to an individual case? Currently there is no consensus on this question in South Africa. In its decision in the *Zuma* case, the Supreme Court of Appeal observed that: 'the Minister *is entitled to be kept informed* in respect of all prosecutions initiated or to be initiated *which might arouse public interest or involve important aspects of legal or prosecutorial authority*'[23] (emphasis added). A number of things about this observation deserve to be noted. In the first place, this statement is what lawyers refer to as *obiter dicta* — a statement made in a case that was not essential for the determination of that case. It does not therefore constitute a binding legal precedent. Even accepting that it is an authoritative and persuasive statement by one of the highest courts in the country, it must be noted that a duty to keep the Minister informed is not the same thing as a duty to seek or pay any attention to the Minister's views or advice. The fact that the Court did not refer to the latter duty might suggest that it favours the Shawcross approach to the NDPP's responsibilities rather than the Baldwin approach. This interpretation is arguably reinforced by the fact that the duty set out in section 33 of the NPA Act[24] to provide the Minister with information about, and reasons for, decisions in individual cases only arises if the Minister has requested such information. There is thus no *a priori* requirement for consultation of any kind before decisions are made, and no requirement that the NDPP necessarily follow any advice he or she may receive from the Minister or the President.

Not all commentators agree on this point. In the report of her inquiry into the fitness of Adv Pikoli to hold the office of NDPP, Dr Frene Ginwala offered the following alternative interpretation, which, incidentally, seems to have been to some extent endorsed by the comment of the Supreme Court of Appeal in the *Zuma* case:

> The fact that the NDPP is obliged to furnish the Minister with a report, upon her request, is expressly provided for in the Act. The parties accepted, correctly so in my view, that the corollary must apply, namely, that the NDPP has the responsibility to inform the Minister in respect of any material case, matter or subject that is dealt with by the NPA in the exercise of its powers, duties or functions. Such an interpretation gives meaning to the intention of the legislature. A meaningful

---

23 *Zuma* case ibid.
24 Note 22 above.

reading of the Act necessitates a conclusion that where the NDPP has information that is of importance relating to any significant case, matter or subject pertaining to the work of the prosecuting authority, the NDPP would be obliged in law to bring such case, matter or subject to the attention of the Minister. It is more so pertaining to matters that may impact on national security.

It is not my understanding that the duty placed on the NDPP to inform the Minister with regard to any significant case, matter or subject in the performance of the functions of the prosecutorial authority is to be done purely for information-passing sake. The legislature must have intended that the Minister would bring to the consideration of the NDPP such matters as government may find to be relevant in respect of such case, matter or subject. It should not be understood to mean that the NDPP would be bound by any input made by the Minister with regard to the exercise of his or her powers, the carrying out of his or her duties and the performance of his or her functions. The powers, functions and duties are those of the NDPP and should be exercised without fear, favour or prejudice. The legislature must intend that the information exchanged between the NDPP and the Minister must serve to enhance the constitutional goal of enabling the prosecuting authority to achieve its mandate to institute criminal proceedings on behalf of the state and for the Minister to exercise final responsibility over the prosecuting authority within the policy guidelines.[25]

Whatever may be one's view as to the correct interpretation of these constitutional and statutory provisions, some consensus or a definitive ruling or legislative clarification on the matter would undoubtedly be beneficial. In this context, the following provision in article 56(7) of the Constitution of Zambia Act 1 of 1991 (as substantially amended by Constitution (Amendment) Act 18 of 1996) is of interest:

In the exercise of the powers conferred on him by this Article, the Director of Public Prosecutions shall not be subject to the direction or control of any other person or authority:

Provided that where the exercise of any such power in any case may, in the judgment of the Director of Public Prosecutions, involve general considerations of public policy, the Director of Public Prosecutions shall bring the case to the notice of the

---

25   *Report of the Enquiry into the Fitness of Advocate VP Pikoli to Hold the Office of National Director of Public Prosecutions* (Dr Frene Ginwala, Chair), November 2008, paras 65 and 66, pp. 49–50. In the Namibian case in which the relationship between the Attorney General and the Prosecutor General in that country was considered (see note 22 above), Leon AJA, having concluded that the Attorney General's 'final responsibility for the office of the Prosecutor-General' does not include any right to give directions to the Prosecutor-General with respect to decision-making in particular cases, concluded his judgment with the following recommendation: 'I would strongly recommend that, these issues having been settled, the Attorney-General and the Prosecutor-General adopt the English practice of ongoing consultations and discussions which would be in the best interests of the cause of justice and the well-being of all the citizens of Namibia.'

Attorney General and shall in the exercise of his powers in relation to that case, act in accordance with any directions of the Attorney General.

This provision appears to be unique in Africa. It is noteworthy, that despite the obvious intent that the judgment of the Attorney General, who in Zambia is an *ex officio* member of the Cabinet,[26] should prevail in cases which 'may ... involve general considerations of public policy', the Constitution nevertheless leaves it to the judgment of the DPP, rather than the Attorney General, to determine which cases fall into this category.[27] By contrast, subsection 162(7) of the Constitution of the Kingdom of Swaziland 2005, which has a constitutionally independent DPP, provides:

> Without derogating from the provisions of subsection (6),[28] the Director shall, in the exercise of the powers under this Chapter, consult the Attorney General[29] in relation to matters where national security may be at stake.

Which protocol for this relationship is preferred is a matter of considerable importance in defining and understanding the scope and nature of the DPP's prosecutorial independence. There is an implicit trade-off, in that the more the government has the opportunity to express its views about a case to the DPP, the greater the risk that the DPP may be unduly and inappropriately influenced or pressured by those views, thus diminishing the reality or at least the public perception of his or her independence. In this context, the fact that the South African NDPP can be dismissed on the basis of a simple majority vote in the National Assembly and the National Council of Provinces, as has recently occurred, is not inconsequential.

Many may feel that such a trade-off in favour of *a priori* consultation with government is wise, at least with respect to cases that raise matters of great public, national or international interest. Regardless of which position one takes, it is a policy choice which might best be made deliberately and explicitly rather than on the basis of competing interpretations of constitutional and statutory

---

26 Article 54 of the Constitution of the Republic of Zambia.

27 By contrast, article 120 of the Constitution of Uganda 1995 provides for a fully independent Director of Public Prosecutions who, in exercising his or her functions, 'shall not be subject to the direction or control of any person or authority', and that: 'In exercising his or her powers under this article, the Director of Public Prosecutions shall have regard to the public interest, the interest of the administration of justice and the need to prevent abuse of legal process.' Similar provisions can be found in the Constitutions of Nigeria and Swaziland.

28 Subsection 6 provides: 'In the exercise of the powers conferred under this Chapter, the Director shall — (a) have regard to the public interest, the interest of the administration of justice and the need to prevent abuse of the legal process; and (b) be independent and not subject to the direction or control of any other person or authority.'

29 The Attorney General in Swaziland is the holder of a public office (appointed by the King on the recommendation of the Minister responsible for justice after consultation with the Judicial Service Commission), who is an *ex officio* member of the Cabinet (section 77 of the 2005 Constitution).

provisions whose meaning and intent are not self-evident.[30] It might also be wise to provide more enhanced security of tenure for an NDPP as protection against possible low-visibility abuses.[31]

5. Accountability: The other side of the coin

So far this chapter has considered whether, to what extent and in what ways governments are permitted to exercise control or influence over prosecutorial decision-making with respect to individual cases under different constitutional and institutional arrangements for prosecutorial authority. The other, equally important, side of the coin is accountability — the obligation to give someone else an account of one's decisions and conduct.

Effective accountability is an essential element of democracy. Governments are given an electoral mandate to govern in the name of, and for the benefit of, the people and must be effectively accountable to them. A Canadian judge once observed that a prosecutor's function 'is a matter of public duty than which in civil life there can be none charged with greater personal responsibility'.[32] Effective accountability for prosecutorial decision-making is therefore critical to ensure that this responsibility is exercised in the public interest, and for the public good, and not for partisan advantage, personal or private gain or corrupt motives. The more independent a prosecutorial authority is the more robust must be the mechanisms for holding that authority accountable.

One critical mechanism for ensuring effective accountability is the duty of independent prosecutors to account for their decisions via Parliament, either directly, in the case where ultimate prosecutorial responsibility lies with a government minister, or indirectly via a responsible minister, in cases where prosecutorial authority is vested in an 'independent' public servant, such as a DPP.[33]

---

30   I recognise, however, that this has not been the case in the UK, where this matter has been dealt with instead by the more uncertain, and possibly ephemeral, medium of a constitutional convention. This uncertainty is further reflected in recent disagreements about the precise meaning and implications of the Attorney General's statutory 'superintendence' of the DPP and the Directors of the SFO and RCPO. It is noteworthy in this respect, that following controversies over prosecutorial decision-making in some high-profile, politically sensitive cases, the Attorney General recently announced that the role of the Attorney General was being reviewed and reformed in part to introduce a new protocol that would safeguard the independence of Attorney General and the Directors (of the three prosecuting agencies over which she has 'superintendence').

31   In some countries, such as Uganda, Sierra Leone and Zambia, the DPP has security of tenure comparable or similar to that of a superior court judge.

32   Rand J in *Boucher v The Queen* [1955] SCR 16, 24 (Supreme Court of Canada).

33   Unusually, article 101(2) of the Constitution of the Republic of Malawi specifically provides that while the DPP shall exercise his or her powers 'independent of the direction and control of any authority or person', nevertheless the DPP or the Attorney General 'may be summoned by the Legal Affairs Committee of Parliament to appear before it to give account for the exercise of those powers'. In the case of the powers to take over criminal proceedings instituted by others, and to discontinue proceedings instituted by anyone, article 99(3) of the Constitution requires the DPP to provide reasons for such actions to the Legal Affairs Committee of Parliament within 10 days.

In this context, I would argue, *contra* Dr Ginwala, that the duty of a DPP to provide information to his or her minister on request does not necessarily imply a duty to seek out the government's views about a case before a prosecutorial decision is made. The requirement to provide information about a case can be justified as an essential ingredient of effective accountability, independently of a policy preference for considering the government's views before making prosecutorial decisions. The conflation of two key elements of governance — control/influence and accountability — is conceptually unsound and unhelpful (Stenning 1986: 285–286). Independence from unwanted control, direction, instruction, influence or pressure — whatever form it may take and from whatever source it may come — need not imply or result in any diminution of effective accountability. Accountability is not simply for the purpose of facilitating immediate control or influence.[34]

The timing of accountability requirements is important. Obviously, the earlier accountability is required — for instance, before a decision is actually made — the greater the risk that the process of accountability may be exploited in an attempt to influence the decision. The *sub judice* convention, according to which cases before the courts cannot be discussed in Parliament until after their conclusion, is a well-known example of an attempt to guard against this risk (Kelly 2007), as are court-ordered publication bans (Jobb 2006). To protect the independence of decision-makers, therefore, accountability requirements commonly come into play only *after* decisions have been made. Even then, there may sometimes still be valid reasons for delaying or limiting *ex post facto* accountability[35] but these are quite different from the reasons typically advanced for limiting or prohibiting *a priori* accountability, which usually reflect a desire to prevent unwanted control or influence.

6. Achieving the right relationships

So what would be the most desirable relationship between prosecutors and their governments in liberal democracies committed to the rule of law? And how can this best be achieved in terms of constitutional provisions and institutional architecture?

An ideal relationship would satisfy three principal objectives:
1. Prosecutorial decisions in individual cases should be impartial, fair, in the broad public interest, and in accordance with constitutional and legal

---

34 Although in appropriate circumstances it may serve that purpose. As the Australian scholars (Goldring & Wettenhall 1980: 136) expressed it in another context several years ago: 'When we speak of the responsibility of statutory authorities, we are referring to two parallel and interlocking mechanisms. The first is the mechanism of control, which extends from the controlling person or institution to the controlled statutory authority. The second is the mechanism of answerability or accountability. The control mechanism provides a means for ensuring that the statutory authority acts, or refrains from acting, in certain ways. The answerability mechanism provides information to the controller, and may indicate the occasions in which the control mechanism is to be brought into play.'

35 See, eg, section 8(5) of the Australian Commonwealth Director of Public Prosecutions Act 113 of 1983.

requirements. They must not be a product of partisan political, personal, private or special influence or pressure or corruption

2. In cases in which prosecutorial decisions have potentially serious implications for the public interest, national security, or international relations, peace or security, those possible implications should be fully and adequately taken into account by someone with the necessary understanding and competence to do so, before a prosecutorial decision is made

3. Those who make or have any significant influence over prosecutorial decisions must eventually be fully and effectively accountable to the public for those decisions.

6.1. Impartial and fair decisions in the public interest

It is in pursuance of this objective that the concept of prosecutorial independence has developed. By providing prosecutors with some insulation from undesirable political, personal or special influences, it is hoped that their decisions in individual cases will reflect the public interest, even though it may often be difficult to achieve consensus as to how the public interest might best be served. There seems to be broad agreement that, at least with respect to the prosecution of routine cases with no special implications for the public interest, this objective is best achieved by leaving prosecutors to exercise their discretion independently, within the parameters of established prosecutorial policy[36] and without political interference from ministers or other government officials.

Prosecutorial decisions must not only be impartial, fair and in the public interest but also in accordance with constitutional and legal requirements. This means that they must be subject to challenge and judicial review in the courts. The right of courts to review the constitutionality and legality of prosecutorial decisions, however, does *not* include any right to substitute their opinion as to what the public interest requires in a particular case for that of the prosecutor. The right to determine what the public interest requires — a decision requiring sound political, rather than legal, judgment — is vested in the prosecutor, not in the courts.

6.2. Taking serious public interest considerations into account

The vast majority of prosecutorial decisions do not have potentially serious implications for the public interest. The tiny minority of cases that do, however, are the ones that pose difficult dilemmas. Their implications might be for such matters as national security, international relations, peace and security, public health or the integrity of the national economy. The problem in such cases is

---

36   Sometimes such policy is reflected in published prosecutorial guidelines.

twofold. The first is that prosecutors, no matter how well qualified they may be as legal professionals, may not always be best qualified to adequately appreciate the possible implications of a decision to prosecute or not. In a case involving sensitive issues of national security or international relations, for instance, a prosecutor will often, for understandable reasons, not have sufficient access to top secret information. He or she will inevitably have to rely on the judgment of others. When a prosecutor is in a position where he or she does not effectively have the capacity to make an informed assessment and is dependent on the judgment of others, the idea that the prosecutorial decision is really his or hers is arguably a pure fiction.[37]

The second problem in such cases arises from the difficulty of determining whether a decision that is based on secret information, which for legitimate reasons cannot be made public, is really in the public interest, or whether it is a decision that reflects certain partisan political interests (eg, of the governing party), but is being presented as a decision in the public interest in order to give it an air of legitimacy. It is not difficult, for instance, to think of cases in which claims of national security were no more than a convenient cover for the pursuit of much more venal interests.

Different jurisdictions have taken different approaches to this dilemma. In England, and other common law jurisdictions, the approach has been to entrust final decision-making to the Attorney General, along with a constitutional convention that in making such decisions the Attorney General exercises his or her discretion independently of the government of which he or she is a member.[38] The chief merit of this approach, from the point of view of this second objective, is that an Attorney General who is close to, and involved in, government policy, priorities and information sources, is probably in a better position than a non-political appointed prosecutor to access and assess relevant information pertaining to the public or national interest in a particular case.

---

37 In the recent BAE investigation in the UK, the Attorney General insisted throughout that the decision to terminate the investigation was taken by the Director of the Serious Fraud Office and not by the Attorney General himself or anyone else. Yet two weeks after the decision was announced, the Prime Minister, in a press conference, stated: 'I have got to take a judgment about the national interest [in the case] and that is my job' (Prime Minister's press conference on 16 January 2007. This exchange is reproduced in House of Lords, *Debates*, 1 February 2007, Cols 361–2). And in its judgment in a judicial review of the decision, the House of Lords observed (per Lord Bingham) that the Director of the Serious Fraud Office 'was *obliged* and entitled to rely on the expert assessments of others' (para 40, emphasis added) and thus seemed to agree with the conclusion of Moses J in the court below, that the Director 'could not exercise an independent judgment on these matters. ... He might lawfully accord appropriate weight to the judgment of those with responsibility for national security who had direct access to sources of intelligence unavailable to him' *R (on the application of Corner House Research and Others) v Director of the Serious Fraud Office* [2008] UKHL 60, para 23.

38 Note that in many jurisdictions (such as the UK, the Commonwealth and some state jurisdictions in Australia, and in the Federal, Quebec and Nova Scotia jurisdictions in Canada) in which a statutory office of the DPP has been established, the ultimate prosecutorial authority of the Attorney General nevertheless remains undiminished.

In other jurisdictions, however, such as South Africa, the approach has been to entrust final decision-making to a prosecutor who is a non-political, appointed, independent public servant. The chief merit of this approach seems to be that such a prosecutor is, or is perceived to be, less likely to succumb to undesirable partisan political pressures than an Attorney General, even allowing for the constitutional convention of the independence of the Attorney General.[39]

The Attorney General approach arguably accords as much importance to the second objective — adequately taking serious public interest considerations into account — as to the first — ensuring impartial, non-partisan decision-making. The model of the non-political, appointed, independent public prosecutor arguably prioritises the first objective over the second. Both approaches, however, encounter serious problems of credibility in practice. In those countries which have adopted the Attorney General model, serious doubts have arisen as to whether an Attorney General can be credibly expected and trusted to act independently of the government and the political party of which he or she is a member. Similarly, in those countries which have adopted the non-political public prosecutor model, serious doubts have been raised as to whether his or her decisions can be credibly regarded as more than nominally those of the prosecutor, rather than of others, usually politicians, on whose judgment he or she must often inevitably rely.

6.3. Effective accountability

Achieving this third objective gives rise to two different challenges. The first arises in jurisdictions that have adopted the non-political, independent public servant model. Such prosecutors are usually required to be accountable to Parliament through a responsible minister who nevertheless is constitutionally barred from giving them directions with respect to prosecutorial decisions in individual cases. It is difficult to achieve adequate and effective accountability under this arrangement. Ministers and governments who effectively have no control over decisions are understandably reluctant to be held accountable for them. As one former Attorney General of England and Wales rather colourfully put it:

---

39 Of course, the independent public prosecutor model may also be vulnerable to suspicions as to whether the prosecutor really is independent of the government which appoints, and can remove, him or her. Clearly the robustness of the prosecutor's security of tenure, and the non-partisan history of the office holder, are critical factors in allaying such suspicions. The practice, which can be observed in many countries, of appointing governing party supporters to supposedly 'independent' offices can only damage the credibility of their independence — a similar problem to that of the credibility of the independence of political attorneys general. Consider, for example, the recent dispute over the appointment of an 'independent' Attorney General for the new unity government in Zimbabwe. The Movement for Democratic Change (MDC) challenged the President's proposed appointment on the ground that the proposed appointee was a long-time Zimbabwe African National Union Patriotic Front supporter who had been responsible for prosecutions of members of the MDC: see 'Tsvangirai, Tomana sworn in as MPs'. Available at http://www.newzimbabwe.com/pages/parly62.19477.html. Accessed 20 August 2010.

If accountability to Parliament is essential, how can some official, however immaculately untainted by political interest, achieve it? To explain any controversial decision the presence of a Minister will always be demanded in the Chamber. If not the Attorney General, who should it be? If all the wretched Minister could say had to be prefaced with, 'I am informed that it was because of this, that or the other', he would be eaten alive. There would be talk of organ-grinders, monkeys and so forth.[40]

Nor does it seem reasonable to allow a government to be subjected to a motion of censure or a vote of no confidence with respect to a decision over which it had no control. In this respect, the Attorney General model appears to accord as much, perhaps even more, importance to the third objective of effective accountability as to the first. The non-political appointed prosecutor model on the other hand seems to prioritise the first — impartiality and (perceived) independence — over the third.

The second challenge for effective accountability applies equally to both models. This arises from the fact that prosecutorial decisions with serious potential implications either for national security or for international relations, peace and security, or for the reputation or privacy of individuals who have been investigated but not charged, are often made on the basis of information that can typically not, for obvious reasons, be made fully public until long after the decision has been made, if at all.[41] This challenge arises in all cases in which the reputation and privacy of persons who have been investigated but not prosecuted deserve protection. Trial by media is not an acceptable substitute for due process of law in a liberal democracy. Where cases involve significant considerations of national security or international relations, which for legitimate reasons cannot be publicly disclosed, this accountability challenge raises legitimate questions about who should be entrusted with ultimate decision-making authority. Unlike a government, a non-political, appointed prosecutor cannot be voted out of office on the basis of public doubts about the wisdom or integrity of his or her prosecutorial decisions.

---

40   House of Lords, *Debates*, 1 February 2007, Col 350. Imagine if the Director of the Serious Fraud Office in the BAE investigation in the UK, exercising his 'independent' discretion, had decided to prosecute, in the face of the advice he had received about the possible threat to national security, and as a result of the threatened cessation of anti-terrorist cooperation by the Saudi Arabian government, a major terrorist attack occurred in the UK, killing hundreds of people. How would the Director (or the government, for that matter) be effectively held accountable for the consequences of his decision?

41   In his short statement in the House of Lords explaining the decision to terminate the BAE investigation on the day on which it was made, the Attorney General commented: 'Noble Lords will understand that further public comment about the case must inevitably be limited in order to avoid causing unfairness to individuals who have been the subject of investigation or any damage to the wider public interest'. See House of Lords, *Debates*, 14 December 2006, Col 1713.

7. Is there a possible 'third way'?

There is general agreement about the principle that no minister or government can lawfully *direct* an independent Attorney General or DPP with respect to what prosecutorial decision should be taken in an individual case. There currently seem to be three different views as to the appropriate relationship between an independent Attorney General or DPP and the government under which he or she serves. The first, advocated by Baldwin's government in the UK, and the Ginwala Commission in South Africa, is that an Attorney General or DPP is under a *duty* to inform the government or the minister to whom he or she is accountable about any and every case which involves substantial political or public interest implications, either before, or at least at the time that, a prosecutorial decision is made.

The second position is that a DPP is under a *duty to respond to a request* for such information from the Minister, but is not otherwise under a duty to provide it, or consult with anyone in government about a case. This is the position that might be derived from a literal reading of the relevant provisions of the NPA in South Africa referred to earlier.

The third position is the so-called Shawcross doctrine in the UK: whether or not an independent Attorney General seeks information about a case from, or provides information about it to any of his or her ministerial colleagues, is entirely at the Attorney General's discretion. There is no *duty* to either provide information or to consult with ministerial colleagues, although, as Shawcross himself suggested 'he would in some cases be a fool if he did not'.

Despite these differences, all three positions require that *the decision that is ultimately taken in the case must always be within the sole discretion of the Attorney General or DPP.* Thus, as far as the political independence of a prosecutor is concerned, and regardless of any requirements to give information or seek advice, there are really only two positions: either a prosecutor is free from political direction *in all cases*[42], or he or she enjoys no guarantee of freedom from political direction *in any case.*

There might, however, be a third option that is worth considering, namely whether different rules or principles might be applied in a limited number of *highly exceptional* cases than in non-controversial, routine cases.[43] This appears

---

42 For an exposition of this position, see the video of a public lecture entitled 'Independent Prosecutors and Democratic Accountability', delivered at the London School of Economics on 4th March 2010 by Sir Ken Macdonald QC (a former DPP of England & Wales), which can be accessed at http://www2.lse.ac.uk/newsAndMedia/videoAndAudio/publicEventsVideos/publicEventsVideosPrevious.aspx.

43 I should acknowledge here that there is also a possible fourth option, namely that of appointing an independent 'special prosecutor' from outside government in such cases, as has been a common practice in the US (eg, in the Watergate and Monica Lewinsky cases involving Presidents Nixon and Clinton respectively). I do not dwell further on this option here, however, because in my view it presents similar difficulties with respect to effective accountability to those which arise when the prosecutor is, for instance, a fully 'independent' DPP. With respect to US-style special prosecutors, see Harriger (2000).

to be an accepted convention in other areas of governmental decision-making (Stenning 2010a: 339–341). Governments are generally only expected to assume responsibility for taking decisions in individual cases — as opposed to making more general policy decisions — in the most exceptional circumstances, for example when these decisions have significant potential implications for public welfare, the national interest, international relations, etc. If we accept, and even expect, that governments will assume responsibility for decisions in such individual cases in other areas of governance, is there any good reason why we should not adopt a similar approach to prosecutorial decisions?

The approach suggested here should, however, not apply to all aspects of a prosecutorial decision. As indicated above, prosecutorial decisions involve a two-step test: only if and when the evidential test is satisfied, the public interest test comes into play. Even though highly qualified lawyers may sometimes disagree about whether the evidential test has been satisfied in a particular case,[44] the ultimate decision on this should always rest with an independent prosecutor. If such an official, exercising his or her best professional legal judgment, concludes that there is insufficient evidence to warrant a prosecution, that should *always* be the end of the matter, and the official should never be pressured to decide otherwise.

The public interest test is of a different order — it involves wise political judgment. Thus, there may be a limited number of exceptional cases, having serious public interest implications, in which it is not appropriate to leave the decision solely in the hands of an independent prosecutor, however highly qualified and respected he or she may be. In such cases, a democratically elected and accountable government may be a more appropriate body in which to vest the responsibility for making decisions.

An interesting example is mentioned in a letter to *The Times* shortly after the controversy surrounding the *Campbell* case in 1924.[45] The letter writer reminded readers of the decision that had to be made in 1914 as to whether the leaders of the Ulster movement should be indicted for high treason. 'Is it really suggested', he wrote, 'that the Law Officers of the day should have assumed the undivided responsibility for instituting or withholding proceedings and that the Cabinet could have claimed no voice in a decision on which the whole political future of Ireland might have turned?'[46] Subsequent interpretations of the prosecutorial independence of Attorneys General in England and Wales clearly indicate that

---

44   In the recent BAE investigation in the UK, for instance, the Attorney General acknowledged that he and the DPP were not in agreement as to whether there was a 'winnable' case against BAE. See House of Commons, *Debates*, 1 February 2007, Col 380.

45   See note 17 above 8.

46   The letter appeared in *The Times* on 17 December, 1924, and is quoted in Edwards (1964: 213–4 fn 48).

this was exactly what was being suggested. The Shawcross doctrine, which has become the accepted orthodoxy in many countries, makes it clear that the Cabinet should never be entrusted with such a decision, in *any* case. Thus, the approach suggested here is a minority position. It argues that there is a possible alternative approach to prosecutorial independence which might be worthy of consideration, whereby the government rather than an independent prosecutor might be constitutionally entrusted with the ultimate authority to decide, *in a strictly limited range of highly exceptional cases*, whether a prosecution would be in the public or national interest, and be publicly accountable in the usual way for its decision.

This may of course be regarded as a controversial proposition which would depend on a high degree of transparency and public accountability for its legitimacy. We live, however, in an age of technological and democratic sophistication in which unprecedented levels of transparency and accountability have become possible. Controversial decisions in the BAE investigation in the UK, for example, were the subject of numerous extensive debates and committee reports in both Houses of Parliament, litigation that proceeded all the way to the highest court in the land, a detailed report by the Organisation for Economic Co-operation and Development, and a mountain of press coverage, editorial comment and expert opinion, during the course of which a mass of relevant documentation has been disclosed.[47] We have witnessed similar public and political scrutiny of certain controversial prosecutorial decisions and decisions about prosecutors in South Africa.

Apart from these general accountability trends, some specific accountability provisions are worthy of consideration, in particular, the provisions which were originally incorporated in the statutes establishing DPPs in some Australian jurisdictions. Section 10 of the Commonwealth Director of Public Prosecutions Act, for instance, provides that the prosecutorial authority conferred on the DPP does not detract from the Attorney General's traditional prosecutorial authority, and confers on the Attorney General the right to issue written directions or guidelines of a general or specific kind (including directions related to a particular case) to the DPP. However, section 8(3) of the Act requires such directives or guidelines to be published in the official *Government Gazette* and laid before each of the two Houses of Parliament, so that they are open to public scrutiny.[48] In the approach suggested here, similar publication and disclosure requirements could be statutorily required to ensure transparency and accountability, and to guard against abuse. The chief prosecutor, whether an Attorney General or a

---

47   For a fuller account of the BAE investigation, see note 36, 39, 42 above; Stenning (2010b).
48   Similar provisions can be found in section 6 of the Nova Scotia (Canada) Public Prosecutions Act, 1990.

non-political office holder, could also be required to report to Parliament any case in which such a decision process has been followed.

Perhaps we are approaching a level of democratic maturity and accountability in which the determination of the public interest in prosecutorial decision-making does not need to be quite as insulated from government or political influence as has been aspired to in the past.

References

Legislation

Commonwealth Director of Public Prosecutions Act 113 of 1983 (Australia).
Constitution of Namibia, 1990.
Constitution of the Federal Republic of Nigeria (Promulgation) Decree 24 of 1999.
Constitution of the Kingdom of Swaziland, 2005.
Constitution of the Republic of Malawi, 1994.
Constitution of the Republic of South Africa, 1996.
Constitution of Uganda, 1995.
Constitution of Zambia Act 1 of 1991.
Constitution (Amendment) Act 18 of 1996 (Zambia).
Criminal Code of Canada, RSC 1985, c C-46.
National Prosecuting Authority Act 32 of 1998 (South Africa).
Nova Scotia (Canada) Public Prosecutions Act, 1990.

Cases

Boucher v The Queen [1955] SCR 16 (Supreme Court of Canada).
Egerton v Earl of Brownlow (1853) 4 HL Cas 1.
Ex parte Attorney General, Namibia: In Re the Constitutional Relationship between the Attorney-General and the Prosecutor-General [1995] 3 LRC 507, 1995 (8) BCLR 1070 (SCNm).
Gouriet v Union of Post Office Workers [1978] AC 435.
National Director of Public Prosecutions v Zuma 2009 (4) BCLR 393 (SCA).
R (on the application of Corner House Research and Others) v Director of the Serious Fraud Office [2008] UHKL 60, 3.

Articles, books, chapters in books and other works

Delmas-Marty, M. & Spencer. J. 2002. European Criminal Procedures. Cambridge: Cambridge University Press.
Edwards, J. 1984. The Attorney General, Politics and the Public Interest. London: Sweet & Maxwell Ltd.
Edwards, J. 1964. The Law Officers of the Crown. London: Sweet & Maxwell Ltd.
Fionda, J. 1995. Public Prosecutors and Discretion: A Comparative Study. Oxford: Clarendon Press.

Goldring, J. & Wettenhall, R. 1980. Three perspectives on the responsibility of statutory authorities. In Weller, P. & Jaensch, D. (eds). *Responsible Government in Australia.* Richmond: Drummond, 136–150.

Harriger, K. 2000. *The Special Prosecutor in American Politics* (2 ed). Lawrence, KS: University Press of Kansas.

Jobb, D. 2006. *Media Law for Canadian Journalists.* Toronto: Emond Montgomery Publications Ltd.

Kelly, R. 2007. The *sub judice* rule. London: House of Commons Library, Parliament and Constitution Centre. Available at http://www.parliament.uk/commons/lib/research/briefings/snpc-01141.pdf. Accessed 15 November 2010.

MacNair, M. 2006. In the name of the public good: Public interest as a legal standard. *Canadian Criminal Law Review,* 10(2): 175–204.

Stenning, P. 1986. *Appearing for The Crown: A Legal and Historical Review of Criminal Prosecutorial Authority in Canada.* Cowansville, Quebec: Brown Legal Publications Inc.

Stenning, P. 2007. A response to 'The governance of Britain: A consultation on the role of the Attorney General' (Cm 7192, July 2007). Submitted 26 November, 2007, electronic copy on file with the author.

Stenning, P. 2008. *The Modern Prosecution Process in New Zealand.* Wellington: Victoria University Press.

Stenning, P. 2010a. Discretion, politics and the 'public interest' in high-profile criminal investigations and prosecutions. *Canadian Journal of Law and Society/Revue Canadienne Droit et Société,* 24(3): 337–366.

Stenning, P. 2010b. Prosecutions, politics and the public interest: Some recent developments in the United Kingdom, Canada and elsewhere. *Criminal Law Quarterly,* 55(4): 449–478.

Chapter 8

The civilianisation of prosecutorial services in Tanzania

Sifuni Ernest Mchome

1. Introduction

Prosecutorial authorities perform an important watchdog role in a democracy. Not only are they central to ensuring law and order, they are also an important means of ensuring that holders of public power do not abuse their powers through corruption, mismanagement of state resources and other forms of abuse of the state machinery. For a prosecutorial authority to exercise its functions effectively, it must itself be accountable and operate independently and efficiently.

It is in this context that the government of Tanzania recently embarked on an ambitious process of civilianising and streamlining prosecutorial services in the country. Until 2008, many criminal cases were prosecuted by public prosecutors who were either police officers or employed in various investigatory agencies such as the Prevention and Combating of Corruption Bureau and the Tanzania Revenue Authority. In some cases, these public prosecutors did not have law degrees or any recognisable professional training in prosecutions.

In the 1960s, there were simply not enough trained lawyers in Tanzania to justify the creation of a fully-fledged office of the Director of Public Prosecutions (DPP). Hence, the government decided that police officers and officers in other investigatory agencies, who already had some experience in dealing with criminal matters, would assist in conducting prosecutions. Since then, over 30 agencies have been created to exercise both investigatory and prosecutorial functions.

This chapter examines recent developments towards an independent and accountable system of public prosecutions in Tanzania. As noted above, an effective prosecutorial system is essential in any democratic system but more so in emerging democracies where corruption and abuse of state resources continue to pose serious threats to development. It is therefore important that a prosecution system is credible, efficient and fair.

The development of an independent prosecution system in Tanzania has followed the international trend of creating a clear demarcation between investigatory and prosecutorial functions. The purpose of this demarcation is to maintain the independence, fairness and effectiveness of the prosecution service. This chapter shows that many challenges still have to be overcome before the new system can function effectively in Tanzania.

2. The concept of civilianisation

The notion of the civilianisation of public prosecutions is fairly recent. It refers to a process whereby the power to prosecute is vested in institutions which are independent and separate from investigatory units or agencies. Its development can be attributed to the human rights movement which has brought principles of accountability, integrity and professionalism to the fore in prosecutorial matters. Essentially, the argument is that police officers and members of other state agencies should not perform functions of both investigation and prosecution.

In modern societies it is the state's responsibility to investigate and prosecute crimes. This is based on the principle that a crime committed by an individual is a crime against the state. The investigation, prosecution and eventual punishment of a crime are the responsibility of the state, and not of the victim of the crime. Although criminal law entails retribution, the fact that the state acts on behalf of the victim limits the scope for vengeance and revenge. A criminal justice system that is just, fair and consistent with human rights displays a higher degree of impartiality.

Thus, the overall objective of civilianising and streamlining the prosecution system in Tanzania is to ensure that those who are accused of crimes are treated fairly and tried within a reasonable time, that those who deserve punishment are duly punished and that those who are innocent are released. To achieve these objectives, an effective and independent prosecution system is needed.

Before 2008, the police would receive reports on crimes and decide whether to investigate, whether to arrest suspects and whether to charge them or not, and whether to prosecute or not. The police would also decide who would be called as witnesses and how to conduct the prosecution. Both the Judicial System Review Commission of 1977 (commonly referred to as Msekwa Commission) and the Legal Sector Task Force of 1996 (Bomani Committee) concluded that this system was ineffective and posed a threat to human rights.

In contrast, civilianising and streamlining the prosecution system means that each department concentrates on its core functions: investigators focus on investigations, prosecutors on prosecutions and judges on adjudication. Such division of tasks could enhance their independence, facilitate a clear definition of their respective responsibilities and assist with the performance evaluation of the respective departments and agencies. Civilianisation will, however, not solve all the problems concerning prosecutions in Tanzania. Regardless of a separation of investigators and prosecutors, it will remain a challenge to ensure that crime is dealt with in a manner that is timely, fair and just. It might also prove difficult to ensure the independence of prosecutors in practice.

Independence in prosecutorial decision-making is of crucial importance in any legal system. In order to guarantee the independence of prosecutors, it is essential that they are properly trained and qualified, that they have sufficient resources to perform their functions effectively and efficiently, and that their tenure is guaranteed. Furthermore, the functions and accountability relations of prosecutors must be clearly prescribed by legislation. Moreover, publicly available guidelines must be promulgated to serve as a benchmark against which the performance of prosecutors can be assessed.

3. The legal framework for civilianisation

One of the changes brought about by the Constitution of the United Republic of Tanzania Fourteenth Amendment Act 1 of 2005 was the creation of the office of the DPP. The new article 59B of the Constitution declares that the DPP is in control of the entire prosecution system, initiates and manages criminal proceedings, and oversees proceedings initiated by other people with residual powers to intervene in — that is, take over or discontinue — prosecutions.

This development was followed by the enactment of the Office of the Attorney General (Discharge of Duties) Act 4 of 2005 (OAGDDA). Section 11 of the OAGDDA states that the DPP will supervise all officers discharging prosecution duties in his or her office and those who conduct prosecutions on his or her behalf by delegated authority or specific appointment; coordinate investigation duties conducted by investigative organs; enforce discipline among officers conducting prosecutions in the country; and do anything that is incidental to the conduct of prosecutions. The OAGDDA is premised on the assumption that the DPP is independent; that he or she will discharge his or her functions with the assistance of many other prosecutors; that the DPP will have offices across the country to manage and carry out prosecutions; and that a system will be put in place to ensure that prosecutions are conducted efficiently and professionally.

To give practical effect to these legal measures, the National Assembly enacted the National Prosecutions Service Act 1 of 2008 (NPSA) on 29 January 2008. The NPSA was necessary to give effect to the idea of the civilianisation and streamlining of the prosecutorial services and is now operational. It confirmed the coordinating role of the DPP in the investigative process and its control over prosecutions (sections 9, 16 & 17) and has laid a firm foundation for an investigative process that is led by the needs of the prosecution (prosecution-led investigation). The DPP now heads all operations concerning prosecutions. He or she has the power to determine the strategic direction of the National

Prosecution Service (NPS) and to set policies and guidelines relating to the exercise of prosecutorial discretion and powers.

The NPS is meant to be a nationwide institution, which means that it has to establish offices in the various regions and districts in the country. However, because the NPS is now responsible for all prosecutions in the country, it is unlikely in the short term that it will have sufficient capacity to fulfil its responsibility. At the moment, for example, the NPS operates mainly at regional level leaving all districts where district courts are located with limited NPS operations. Thus, the NPS will continue, for the time being, to rely on public prosecutors in the police and other state agencies to exercise the powers of the DPP in relation to prosecutions.

4.   The independence of the DPP and NPS

Article 59B of the Constitution provides that the DPP shall discharge his or her duties independently. Sections 10 and 11 of the OAGDDA and section 19 of NPSA seek to bolster this independence by guaranteeing the security of tenure for the DPP. In addition, sections 19(2) of the NPSA provides that the eligibility requirements for appointment to the office of the DPP are similar to those for judges of the High Court. The eligibility requirements for judges are contained in section 109 of the Constitution. They include the requirement that the candidate must be eligible to be enrolled as an advocate and must have acted in that capacity for at least five years. According to section 21 of the NPSA, the DPP's retirement age is 60 years. The DPP may not be removed from office unless he or she is unable to perform his or her functions due to illness or any other reason, or has committed an unethical offence, and unless an inquiry by a Special Tribunal appointed by the President has been conducted (section 19(4)–(5) of NPSA). In general, this means the DPP holds office *quamdiu se bene gesserint* (during good behaviour) and not at the pleasure of the executive. He or she also holds office *ad vitam aut culpam* (he or she cannot be removed except on grounds of misconduct or inability to perform his or her duties).

However, the independence of the DPP is weakened by the fact that he or she is appointed by the President and that there is no clear legislative framework prescribing how the President must go about the appointment process. This speaks to the need to devise a procedure that is informed by the constitutional values of transparency, inclusiveness and participatory governance, and that provides for proper checks and balances in the appointment of the DPP. For example, in the case of judges, the Judicial Service Commission scrutinises potential candidates before submitting eligible names to the President for appointment. A similar legislative framework would be ideal for the position of the DPP. Furthermore, officers in the prosecutorial service do not enjoy more security of tenure than other officers in public service. Also, although the DPP is empowered to supervise all officers discharging prosecutorial functions and to enforce discipline among all prosecutorial staff in the country, he or she has no power to hire and fire his or her staff. That right resides with the Attorney General in respect of state attorneys (section 5 of NPSA), the Deputy Attorney General in respect of other law officers (section 7 of the NPSA) and the Permanent Secretary in respect of support staff. Effectively, therefore, the DPP does not have his or her own staff. Furthermore, the DPP does not have financial autonomy since financial matters in the Office of the Attorney General where the NPS is placed are wholly handled by the Deputy Attorney General as the accounting officer. All these factors seriously limit the possibilities for holding the DPP properly accountable for his own performance and that of the NPS and its staff. Of particular concern is also section 11 of the NPSA, which provides that the DPP shall have regard to directions of a general and specific nature as may be given by the Attorney General or Deputy Attorney General in relation to the implementation of government policy and the supervision of officers in the NPS. These provisions are likely to pose serious challenges to the independence and accountability of the NPS, unless a clear framework is set out as to how, on what and when such directions may be issued to the DPP.

5. The current lack of capacity and resources in the NPS

A serious challenge to the civilianisation process in Tanzania is the lack of capacity within the NPS to discharge its prosecutorial functions. This means that the status quo whereby the DPP relies on prosecutors in the police and other investigative agencies will subsist unless sufficient resources are channelled towards enhancing the capacity of the NPS.

As noted earlier, the NPS is responsible for prosecuting all criminal offences committed in the country. The Penal Code alone recognises 271 offences. There are about 400 more Acts of Parliament which create additional offences for the prosecution of which the NPS is now responsible. Apart from this magnitude of offences, the jurisdiction of NPS spans the whole of mainland Tanzania, including 21 regions and 123 districts. Therefore, in order for the NPS to function effectively and efficiently, appropriate resources (financial, logistical, physical and personnel) need to be allocated. Indeed, a needs assessment survey in the six pilot regions of the NPS revealed that the new organisation is grossly under-resourced.

Although it would be unrealistic to expect a new institution like the NPS to start operating at full capacity within a short period of time, there must be a clear plan which shows how it will progressively expand its activities and capacity throughout the country. To its credit, the NPS has designed a short-term plan for improving the capacity of its head office and its offices in the six pilot regions. These regions comprise a total of 33 districts: 3 districts in Dar es Salaam, 6 districts in Tanga, 6 districts in Arusha, 7 districts in Mwanza, 4 districts in Ruvuma and 7 districts in Shinyanga. The medium-term goal to be reached in the next 2 to 3 years is to expand to at least half of the country's regions, followed by a roll-out throughout the whole country in the next 5 years.

While this plan is commendable, it is unlikely that the NPS will be in a position to attract many qualified lawyers partly because of the low salaries in the civil service and partly because the country does not have enough lawyers. Even if it did, the recruits would need further training in matters related to prosecutions. Justice Chipeta (1982: xiii) remarked:

> Like many occupations the job of a public prosecutor demands intelligence, training, courage, common sense, tact, patience, capacity for hard work and an interest in the job. A public prosecutor with these qualities is certain to derive pleasure and satisfaction from the work, and is an asset to the administration of criminal justice.

These attributes cannot be acquired unless there is strategic leadership and a system of training and support for public prosecutors. For example, adequate investment in information and communication technology is needed to enhance the effectiveness of prosecution services. By reducing the amount of time prosecutors spend on administration, correctly implemented information management systems can significantly improve the speed at which prosecutors dispose of cases.

Unless these issues are addressed over the next few years, they will adversely affect the effectiveness of the NPS. At present, the NPS has no offices or employees of its own. Its offices in the six pilot zones are the Attorney General's offices, and all officers are employed by the Attorney General. They do not only perform prosecutorial functions but also functions which state attorneys normally perform. Notwithstanding the fact that the new legislation designates the DPP as the overall responsible office in prosecutorial matters, the leaders in the six pilot zones are accountable to the Attorney General. Thus, despite its statutory independence, in practice, the NPS enjoys no independence on matters of staffing and resources.

6. Prosecutorial guidelines

Prosecution is guided by norms and standards. These can be used to determine whether the prosecutors are acting independently, consistently, in good faith and in the national interest. Both article 59B the Constitution and section 8 of the NPSA require the NPS to be guided by the public interest, the interest to do justice and the need to prevent abuse of process in carrying out its functions. These principles need to be further defined and implemented in operational rules, regulations, instructions and policies, generally referred to as prosecutorial guidelines.

Indeed, determining what is in the public interest or the interest to do justice is not always easy (Hetherington 1989). What is 'in the public interest' might be different from what is in the interest of the affected parties. In general, the 'public interest' requires the consideration of the present requirements for action, an appreciation of how such matters have been addressed in the past and a prediction of the consequences of a particular course of action for the future. In short, there is a time continuum to be considered, which in some cases makes it difficult to decide whether a given decision is both in the public interest and immediately acceptable to the affected parties. Indeed, in many situations, prosecutorial decisions are controversial (Cowdery 2004). For this reason, the DPP and the NPS need to develop guidelines that are accessible to the public. Such guidelines will enable the public to determine whether a prosecutorial decision in a particular case is in accordance with the principles set out in the relevant legislation.

The NPS is currently developing the Prosecution General Instructions (PGIs) in order to provide comprehensive and user-friendly prosecution guidelines for state attorneys and prosecutors in mainland Tanzania. In the words of the Draft Prosecution General Instructions for Tanzania Mainland State Attorneys and Prosecutors 2007:

> [P]rosecuting an individual who is alleged to have committed a crime is a serious step that requires seriousness and rational decisions in order to uphold a fair criminal justice system. As such, fairness, effectiveness and aptness should always guide those who play decisive roles in the prosecution process. This is essential in order to ensure justice to all who may be involved in the process — victims, witnesses or the accused — no matter how small or big a case may be. With this in mind, [the] existence of proper guidelines underlying the basic principles and procedural techniques in conduct of criminal matters is crucial. It helps to attain fair and consistent decisions about prosecutions.

7. The accountability of the DPP and NPS

According to Cowdery (2004), the accountability of a prosecutor means the following:

> ... the prosecutor must not have a completely free rein to do as he or she feels like doing. Unless the function is properly accountable to the people, then the people will not know what is being done and how it is being done and they will then not be

able to respect and support its execution. Disorder and vigilantism will gain a hold. [...] Transparency of decision making is a vexed issue, however. The most obvious way in which it is achieved is by the giving of reasons for decisions; but there may be sound arguments against such a course in a particular case (or for giving only the briefest of indications) based on privacy considerations, operational concerns, legal professional privilege, public interest immunity or the personal situation of those directly involved in matters. Nevertheless, the right balance must be struck. Accountability may be otherwise ensured by proper reporting relationships to the Attorney General or Minister of Justice and to the legislature. Prosecutors should also be factual, clear and direct in responding to criticism and if they are wrong, then they should admit it and do everything reasonable to avoid error in the future.

In Tanzania, the NPS is accountable for its actions through several channels. One of them is section 25 of the NPSA which provides:

(1) The Attorney General shall appoint a team of inspectors comprising persons with experience in prosecution and investigation matters.

(2) The team shall visit and inspect any specified public prosecution office, or zonal, regional or district in which the Service has [an] office as the Attorney General may instruct and shall—

   (a) inspect the available facilities and records to satisfy itself that they are being kept and utilised in accordance with the applicable guidelines or instructions;

   (b) assess the public perception on the performance of the Service in terms of care rendered to victim and witness, handling of complaints and its community links;

   (c) make recommendations aimed at enhancing the efficiency and effectiveness of the Service; and

   (d) report on any matter connected with the Service which the Attorney General has referred to the team.

(3) At the conclusion of every visit of inspection the team shall prepare a report and submit that report to the Attorney General and a copy to the Director.

While this mechanism may serve to hold the DPP and NPS accountable, it can easily be abused by the Attorney General, especially if there are differing views on how a particular issue, operational or otherwise, should be handled by the DPP and NPS. The powers given to the Attorney General in this context are too broad and may be used to undermine the work of the DPP and NPS, especially without any further procedures or protocol to guide the inspection process.

A second channel for accountability is section 10(2) of the NPSA, which requires the DPP to give reasons to the applicant, respondent or victim where the DPP takes over an appeal, revision or application pursuant to subsection (1)(b) of the NPSA and subsequently decides to withdraw the appeal, revision or application. The requirement to give reasons is important for the accountability of the DPP in that the affected person has an opportunity to scrutinise the reasons given and to decide whether justice has been served in a particular case or whether the reasons should be challenged. The duty to give reasons could also be attached to other decisions of the DPP, such as the decision to not commence or to discontinue a prosecution.

A third mechanism for accountability is the traditional procedure of judicial review. Administrative measures taken by the NPS that affect the rights and obligations of individuals are subject to judicial review. It must be conceded however that judicial review mechanisms in Tanzania are weak and would require significant improvement if they are to be effective in making state institutions such as the NPS accountable for their actions or omissions.

8. The practical implications of civilianisation

Although civilianisation means that the police and other investigators will retain the responsibility to investigate while civilian law officers will assume the role of prosecutors, the two will work hand-in-hand in many respects. The primary function of the NPS is to diligently and vigilantly pursue those who are suspected of violating the criminal law of the country. The law presumes every suspect and accused person to be innocent until proven guilty by a court of law. It is the role of the investigators to conduct credible investigations to reveal what occurred and then to determine whether the conduct of any person amounts to a crime as defined in the law. It is for the prosecution to determine whether there is sufficient evidence to warrant a prosecution on a chosen charge.

The new system in Tanzania requires investigative agents such as the police to investigate allegations of criminal conduct or actions. If the police fail to investigate or do so badly, there is hardly anything that the NPS can do except to conclude that there is not sufficient evidence to prosecute. Thus, mounting an effective prosecution for a crime depends on the competence and effectiveness of the investigatory agencies. Consequently, to ensure that prosecutors have sufficient and reliable evidence to ground a prosecution, it is necessary to build a link between the prosecutors and the investigators from the very inception of a case. This would mean that from the receipt of a complaint to the finalisation of investigations, the prosecutors must be informed of the investigations and where necessary provide advice on its progress.

In order to present a case for prosecution in a court, the prosecutor needs to have a file containing the evidence and other relevant information, including any criminal record the accused may have. While it is for the investigators to obtain the evidence as part of the process of investigation, assembling the file or docket is a task that should involve both the investigators and the prosecutors. Up to now, investigators compile prosecution files. Hopefully, once the civilianisation and streamlining of the prosecutorial system is completed, a coherent system of file management will be created that involves both investigators and prosecutors.

One of the most important tasks of a prosecutor is to review the evidence in the file in order to decide whether it justifies a prosecution, applying the evidential and public interest tests (see Stenning, chapter 7 in this volume). If the evidence is not sufficient, the prosecutor may either prosecute the accused on a lesser charge or discontinue the prosecution. Sometimes, the evidence may support a more serious offence than what the investigators originally pursued. In this situation, the NPS may require further investigation so that the accused can be prosecuted for the more serious offence. Much as some investigating officers may resent this power of the prosecutor, it is essential to ensure that only those prosecutions which are well investigated and backed up by the evidence proceed to court. Not only is it unwise and a waste of public resources to prosecute cases that stand no chance of success in court, it also serves the ends of justice to only charge suspects with offences they most likely have committed. Furthermore, prosecutors have the responsibility of checking whether the investigation process is in accordance with human rights. This can be a cause of discord between investigators and prosecutors.

To ensure a cordial relationship between prosecutors and investigators, both sides must make efforts to understand and respect each other's responsibility in criminal matters. On the one hand, the investigators must as far as possible respect the prosecutors' advice in order to ensure successful prosecution, and try their best to protect the due process of law in the course of their investigations. On the other hand, prosecutors must understand the difficulties investigators face in the course of their work and defer as much as possible, within the existing legal framework, to their discretion in investigations. Both the prosecutorial and investigatory agencies need to be guided by common goals and values and must cooperate with each other in order for the new system to succeed.

Figure 8.1 shows a summary of the roles of investigators at various stages of the process, and the possible areas of collaboration with prosecutors in the context of the new system.

Indeed, the separation of the prosecution function from that of investigation is not without challenges. Some of these challenges have already been highlighted in the course of this chapter. One of them relates to the tension that may occur especially when deciding whether to prosecute or not. From time to time the decision to prosecute or not will be controversial. In the case of Tanzania, the investigators have shown an inclination to prosecute in cases where the prosecutors would not recommend such a decision. All legal systems experience this kind of

During investigation

Investigators have the responsibility to:

- Receive reports on or detect crimes and investigate them in accordance with established procedures and protocols
- Coordinate with the NPS to ensure that the investigation is prosecution-led and in accordance with the law
- Comply with the instructions of prosecutors, eg requests for further investigation or clarifications
- Compile records, eg case files and dockets, in accordance with agreed format and
- Comply with prescribed time limits and other statutory safeguards for the legality of the investigation.

During charging

The investigators have a duty to:

- Study and evaluate the evidence collected during investigation and decide whether to charge any person
- In the case of a decision to charge, prepare the charge sheet or information and submit it to prosecutors together with the case file or docket
- Secure the availability of witnesses — their names, contact addresses — and their attendance at trial
- Follow up on all questions and queries raised by prosecutors in relation to the charge or investigation and provide regular feedback and
- In the case of a decision not to charge, compile the file and reasons for not charging and submit them to the appropriate authority.

During prosecution

Investigators have the responsibility to:

- Liaise with prosecutors regularly to secure witnesses
- Testify and tender exhibits in court as and when required
- Tender forensic evidence as and when required and
- Produce previous criminal records as and when required.

At post-trial stage

Investigators have the responsibility to:

- Liaise with the prosecutor to decide whether to appeal against an acquittal, sentence or any other order, or where the defendant appeals, whether to defend such an appeal and
- Collect the investigation file and complete the formalities to close the file and submit returns as required by the investigation system.

Figure 8.1: Areas of collaboration between investigators and prosecutors

tension between prosecutors and investigators, and Tanzania is not an exception. What is important is for both the prosecutors and investigators to subscribe to the principle that they are together acting as a check and balance on the exercise of power by each other. In this regard, the need for more communication, collaboration and coordination on their activities cannot be overemphasised.

9. Conclusion

The establishment of the NPS is an important step towards achieving the objective of civilianising the prosecutorial system in Tanzania and bolstering the capacity of prosecutorial authorities to hold public functionaries to account. The law has now clearly vested the responsibility to prosecute in the NPS and the DPP has overall control over the management and conduct of prosecutions. This legal development is pivotal to creating a division of labour between investigatory agencies and prosecutorial agencies. However, this chapter has shown that the journey towards civilianisation is not without challenges. There are many challenges of approach, attitude, working environment, staffing, staff retention and the magnitude of the prosecutorial work.

While all of these challenges need to be tackled, the lack of full independence of the DPP stands out as a major challenge which might derail the civilianisation process. Without a full complement of staff or the power to recruit and fire, manage or maintain its own staff, the establishment of an independent, specialised and effective prosecutorial system is still in limbo. The Attorney General's powers of oversight over the DPP and the NPS will most likely undermine their independence and effectiveness, especially if no guidelines are put in place to direct the oversight process.

For the new prosecution system to be successful, it must have the capacity to perform better and more efficiently than the old system, in terms of quality of work and increased speed in the disposal of cases, in terms of a higher degree of fairness and impartiality in decision-making, and in terms of upholding the rule of law and human rights. To achieve this goal, the DPP and NPS must be accountable to the public. The NPS must be staffed by personnel who are qualified and have integrity, and given additional training and adequate resources to do their job.

In as much as the separation of the prosecutorial and investigative functions is necessary to improve the efficiency of the prosecutorial system, all the relevant agencies need to hone their respective skills in order for the new system to make a difference. They also need to cooperate in crucial areas throughout the investigation, charging, prosecution and post-trial stages of the criminal justice process. Thus, civilianisation must not be regarded as a total separation of investigation and prosecution.

References
Legislation and other legal documents
Constitution of the United Republic of Tanzania (Fourteenth Amendment) Act 1 of 2005.

National Prosecution Service. 2007. *Draft Prosecution General Instructions for Tanzania Mainland State Attorneys and Prosecutors*. Dar es Salaam: NPS.

National Prosecutions Service Act 1 of 2008.

Office of the Attorney General (Discharge of Duties) Act 4 of 2005.

Reports
United Republic of Tanzania. 1977 *The Report of the Judicial System Review Commission*. Dar es Salaam: Government Printer.

United Republic of Tanzania. 1996. *The Report of the Legal Sector Task Force*. Dar es Salaam: Government Printer.

Articles, books, chapters in books and other works
Chipeta, B.D. 1982. *The Public Prosecutor and the Law of Criminal Procedure: A Handbook for Public Prosecutors*. Dar es Salaam: Eastern Africa Publications Limited.

Cowdery, N. 2004. The independence of the prosecutor and the general public interest. Paper presented at the 23rd Pacific Islands Law Officers Meeting at Tonga on 27–29 September 2004. Available at http://www.odpp.nsw.gov.au/speeches/A250953.htm. Accessed 30 October 2010.

Hetherington, T. 1989. *Prosecution and the Public Interest*. London: Waterloo Publishers.

Krone, T. 1999. Police and prosecution. Paper presented at the 3rd National Outlook Symposium on Crime in Australia entitled: 'Mapping the Boundaries of Australia's Criminal Justice System', convened by the Australian Institute of Criminology and held in Canberra, 22 — 23 March 1999. Available at http://www.aic.gov.au/en/events/aic%20upcoming%20events/1999/~/media/conferences/outlook99/krone.ashx. Accessed 30 October 2010.

Chapter 9

Accountable governance and the role of national human rights institutions: The experience of the Malawi Human Rights Commission

Danwood M. Chirwa and Redson E. Kapindu

1. Introduction

One of the novel features of the Constitutions adopted by African countries in the 1990s, in a flurry of democratic transitions, was the establishment of national human rights institutions (NHRIs) as a new and key mechanism for holding those in power accountable. Following this general trend, section 129 of the Constitution of the Republic of Malawi (Constitution) created the Malawi Human Rights Commission (MHRC). The modalities for the operation of this body were subsequently set out in the Human Rights Commission Act (HRC Act).[1]

In this chapter, we briefly consider the value of institutions such as the MHRC for constitutional democracy and identify a number of factors that are necessary to make them effective in discharging their mandate. We then use this framework to analyse the contribution the MHRC has made to accountable governance and the protection and promotion of human rights in Malawi. We hope that this exercise will lead to an understanding of the place of human rights institutions, especially in new democracies and how they can be made more effective and useful in curbing abuses of power and promoting accountability.

2. Brief constitutional history

The MHRC was established when the despotic regime of Dr Hastings Kamuzu Banda and his Malawi Congress Party (MCP) came to an end. Thirty years earlier, Dr Banda and the MCP came to power, replacing a colonial regime which showed no concern for, and considered itself unaccountable to, African citizens. However,

---

1   Act 27 of 1998.

the constitutional framework within which Banda's one-party dictatorship subsequently functioned was naively vague about, if not openly defiant of, the ideals of accountability and responsiveness. The independence Constitution adopted in 1964 entrenched a separation of powers and a Bill of Rights consisting of basic freedoms and civil liberties, but it did not take long for Banda and his MCP to begin retreating from their pre-independence commitments. Under the guise of wanting to transform the country into a republic, the new Constitution of 1966 enshrined the principles of unity, obedience, loyalty and discipline as the cornerstones of government. These new constitutional principles were intrinsically incongruent with the ethos of accountability, transparency and openness. Significantly, the 1966 Constitution also had the effect of concentrating power in the President, who was declared President for life with 'supreme executive authority of the Republic.'[2] The Bill of Rights was removed from the Constitution in favour of a vague and general commitment to the human rights recognised by the law of nations and the Universal Declaration of Human Rights.[3]

Although the 1966 Constitution recognised the concept of separation of powers, the hallmarks of this doctrine were severely truncated. The President had the power to appoint the Speaker of Parliament[4] and to dismiss him or her for any reason.[5] Moreover, the President had the power to appoint 15 Members of Parliament (MPs) in addition to the 50 elected ones.[6] The President could dissolve Parliament at any time[7] and multiparty politics was banned.[8] This constitutional framework and intolerant political atmosphere paralysed the National Assembly which became a chamber for hero-worshipping the person of Dr Banda and for rubber-stamping the MCP's political agenda and policies (Phiri & Ross 1998: 910).

Although theoretically independent, the judiciary was not expected to 'question or obstruct the policies of the executive government' (Ng'ong'ola 2002: 64). The power of the judiciary was severely circumscribed by the creation of a parallel system of traditional courts (Foster 2001: 278–284). The judiciary was also rendered sterile through a lack of qualified personnel. The atmosphere of oppression and intimidation meant that people could not challenge decisions of the executive in court.[9] The Banda era gave birth to a culture of silence, which formed a curtain behind which gross violations of human rights were committed by the state and the ruling MCP (Human Rights Watch 1990).

---

2   Section 1 of the 1966 Constitution.
3   Section 2(1)(iii) of the 1996 Constitution.
4   Section 25(1) of the 1966 Constitution.
5   Section 25(3)(c) of the 1966 Constitution.
6   Section 20 of the 1966 Constitution.
7   Section 45 of the 1966 Constitution.
8   Sections 4 and 23(d) of the 1966 Constitution.
9   For a detailed analysis of the role the judiciary has played since the dawn of democracy, see chapter 4 in this volume.

The new Constitution adopted in 1994 heralded a new beginning for Malawi. Unlike its predecessor, it contains a Bill of Rights and provides for regular and periodic elections,[10] universal adult suffrage,[11] multiparty politics[12] and judicial independence.[13] Due in part to the history of executive dominance over the judiciary and the National Assembly, the new Constitution enshrines the idea of constitutional supremacy[14] and makes provision for a wide range of new institutions to ensure the accountability of government. These include the Ombudsman,[15] the Auditor General,[16] the MHRC,[17] the Inspectorate of Prisons,[18] the Law Commission[19] and the National Compensation Tribunal[20].

3. The role of national human rights institutions

NHRIs are bodies, authorities or organisations whose main responsibility is to promote and protect human rights. They differ from non-governmental organisations (NGOs) in that they are established by and largely funded by the state, and derive their competence to promote and protect human rights from the law of the state concerned.

In 1946, the United Nations (UN) Economic and Social Council (ECOSOC) urged states to consider establishing local human rights committees to assist in furthering the work of the UN Commission on Human Rights at the national level.[21] The adoption of the Principles Relating to the Status and Functioning of National Institutions for Protection and the Promotion of Human Rights (Paris Principles) by the UN Commission on Human Rights[22] and the UN General Assembly[23] was an important milestone in the development of NHRIs. In the African context, establishing NHRIs is not a matter of choice but obligation. Article 26 of the African Charter on Human and Peoples' Rights specifically obligates states to 'allow the establishment and improvement of appropriate national institutions entrusted with the promotion and protection of the rights and freedoms guaranteed' by the Charter.

---

10   Section 40 of the 1994 Constitution.
11   Section 77 of the 1994 Constitution.
12   Section 40 of the 1994 Constitution.
13   Section 103 of the 1994 Constitution.
14   Section 5 of the 1994 Constitution.
15   Section 120 of the 1994 Constitution.
16   Section 184 of the 1994 Constitution.
17   Section 129 of the 1994 Constitution.
18   Section 169 of the 1994 Constitution.
19   Section 132 of the 1994 Constitution.
20   Section 137 of the 1994 Constitution.
21   See 'National human rights institutions for the promotion and protection of human rights in Africa' AU/ OAU Ministerial Conference MN/CONF/HRA/6(1). Available at http://www.achpr.org. Accessed 11 July 2009. Reprinted in Heyns (2004: 380, 381). See also UN Centre for Human Rights (1995: 4).
22   See Resolution 1992/54, March 1992.
23   UN GAOR, 48th Session, 85th Meeting, UN Doc A/RES/48/134, 20 December 1993.

NHRIs have become an important part of the accountability machinery (Ayeni 1997; Kanzira 2002; Murray 2007). The significance of NHRIs should be understood in the light of the limits of the traditional mechanisms of controlling the exercise of public power, such as judicial review, parliamentary oversight and periodic elections. Murray (2006: 9), for example, has argued that the traditional system of checks and balances has not always been effective in controlling the exercise of public power due principally to the predominance of party politics in Parliaments.

NHRIs have the advantage of speed, lack of formality, accessibility and flexibility over the courts. In new democracies, such as Malawi where the majority of the people do not have access to courts, NHRIs serve as an important means of obtaining timely redress for and preventing violations of human rights or government abuses. The fact that the methodologies of NHRIs are flexible and not limited to remedial or corrective action means that these bodies may proactively and effectively strike at the source of violations in a comprehensive manner. By the time the new Constitution was adopted in Malawi, for example, the country had just emerged from an oppressive era in which violence and lack of accountability had become institutionalised, and citizens had become accustomed to not challenging public authorities. Although the courts suddenly became an important means of holding the state accountable during the transition to democracy (1992–1994), it was deemed necessary to create additional mechanisms of accountability which would be able to deal with systemic problems in a proactive, non-adversarial manner.

NHRIs may not have the powers of coercion which the courts or Parliaments have. However, through research, investigation, persuasion, negotiation and education, NHRIs can play a pivotal role in the development of a culture of fairness, justice, transparency and good governance in public administration. Unlike courts, which are constrained by the tenets of the separation of powers, NHRIs have the latitude to advise the state on substantive policies, administrative arrangements and practices concerning human rights. Consequently, their influence may transcend justiciable issues (Reif 2000: 2). Not only can NHRIs influence policies, they can also actively push for or participate in law reform. Moreover, although NHRIs are not organs of state, strictly speaking, the fact that they are established by the state gives them the status of 'internal mechanisms' for correcting and preventing state maladministration and abuses. They are sufficiently autonomous from the government and the entities which implement human rights on a daily basis, yet their status as institutions established by the state puts them in a position in which it is easier for them to work with state organs to advance human rights.

NHRIs have also been noted for the vital role they play in facilitating the participation of the public in a de-politicised manner. Murray (2006: 7) has crisply observed:

> Located between citizens and the government, [NHRIs] provide a way in which the needs of citizens can be articulated outside the loaded environment of party politics. If [NHRIs] are truly independent they can provide a reliable voice for people, unburdened by the political exigencies of the day or vested interests.

In Malawi, for example, the majority of the people are poor and illiterate, with limited means of ensuring that their views are considered in state policies, judicial proceedings, legislative activities and other public decisions. NHRIs have the resources and mandate to assist such people so that their democratic right to participate is realised. Connected to public participation is the issue of human rights education. States have an international obligation to raise awareness about human rights. NHRIs play a critical role in fulfilling this obligation. The advantage that NHRIs have in performing this educational function lies in the fact that they are sufficiently autonomous from the state, which is viewed as a primary violator of human rights and therefore not in a good position to educate people about human rights.

4.   The effectiveness of NHRIs

There is a growing consensus that the key prerequisites for the effective operation of NHRIs are independence, adequacy of jurisdiction, accessibility and accountability (Paris Principles; Reif 2000; Amnesty International 2001). Independence is of great importance for the effectiveness of a NHRI because without it, the NHRI would lack credibility and public legitimacy. The principle of independence requires the NHRI to operate freely without any fear or favour. Its decisions and methodologies may need to be politically sensitive but the NHRI must not serve the needs of a particular political party, institution or person. 'Independence', in the context of NHRIs, means legal and operational autonomy, financial autonomy, independent appointment and dismissal procedures, and representative composition. Legal and operational autonomy is impossible unless an NHRI is established by law as a separate and autonomous entity. It is important that the enabling law establishes an accountability mechanism for the NHRI which is democratically legitimate, such as reporting to Parliament as opposed to direct accountability to the head of state. Commissioners must be appointed following a pre-determined transparent, legitimate and participatory procedure, and their tenure must be secured by enabling legislation. The law must clearly specify the attributes and qualifications of commissioners. At a minimum, commissioners must be credible and highly respected individuals with the requisite expertise and experience in human rights (Amnesty International 2001: 5). Demographic representation (of vulnerable, minority or historically disadvantaged groups) is an important aspect of independence in polarised, divided or unequal societies. The principle of independence does not only require the commissioners to act autonomously and competently; an NHRI must also have the independence to hire and fire its own staff. Apart from having the freedom to recruit and dismiss its own staff, an NHRI must be allowed to choose its own working methods. Financial autonomy means that an NHRI must be responsible for drawing up its own budget based on its needs and priorities, and that the government must not deviate from the budget proposals made unless there is justification for doing so.

A second factor that influences the effectiveness of NHRIs is adequate jurisdiction. An NHRI must have clearly defined personal and subject matter jurisdiction, specifying its powers and functions. The jurisdiction must be comprehensive enough to allow the NHRI to perform its human rights functions fully and effectively (Amnesty International 2001: 7). Clarity of jurisdiction is important to secure the authenticity and authority of its actions, decisions and recommendations. It is also necessary to avoid conflicts of jurisdiction with other organisations and state organs.

Accessibility is also crucial to the success of an NHRI. As noted earlier, the whole point of creating NHRIs is to ensure cheap and easy access to justice by the poor. It is therefore important that an NHRI is both physically and economically accessible (UN Centre for Human Rights 1995: 13). This also means that it must adopt procedures which are simple and short.

Lastly, in order for an NHRI effectively to hold the state accountable, it must itself demonstrate a commitment to good governance, accountability and transparency. For this reason, NHRIs must, in addition to the requirements of the enabling law, establish practices and measures of accountability to the public, including frequent reporting, publications, regular contact with victims of human rights violations and civil society, and providing access to information.

Following our observations about the role and effectiveness of NHRIs in general, we will now turn to the legal foundation and architecture of the MHRC and the role it has played thus far.

5. The legal framework of the MHRC

5.1. Establishment

Although the new Constitution came into force in mid-1994, the MHRC became operational only in January 1996 when the *ex officio* members — the Law

Commissioner and the Ombudsman[24] — were appointed and, as co-chairpersons of the MHRC, decided to take the work of the MHRC forward. This was a pragmatic move although it remains debatable whether the two *ex officio* members had the mandate to operate as the MHRC. It was only in December 1998, after the HRC Act was enacted, that five additional commissioners were appointed and the MHRC became fully operational.

Pursuant to section 8 of the HRC Act, the MHRC has established seven thematic committees, each of which is headed by a commissioner: the Economic, Social and Cultural Rights Committee; the Child Rights Committee; the Civil and Political Rights Committee; the Gender Balance and Women's Rights Committee; the Prisoners' Rights Committee; the Committee on Rights of Persons with Disabilities; and the Civic Education and Information Committee. The MHRC has also set up four regional committees with the aim of extending its reach to all parts of the country. Its secretariat is based in Lilongwe and headed by the Executive Secretary. The secretariat is administratively divided into five departments: Legal Services; Research and Documentation; Investigations; Education, Information and Training; and Administration and Finance. Recently, the MHRC submitted a proposal to government to restructure its secretariat, which included the scrapping of the Departments of Research and Documentation, and Education, Information and Training and replacing them with various thematic directorates along the lines of the thematic committees. This proposal has apparently been approved by government.

It is clear from the above that the MHRC has made laudable efforts to establish the framework for an effective institution. However, a balance between the need to make an impact on the most pressing human rights issues in the country and the need for accessibility of the MHRC for all Malawians has not yet been found. So far, the focus seems to have been on thematic areas, which raises the danger that human rights issues outside these areas might be neglected.

5.2. Powers

Section 129 of the Constitution states that the primary functions of the MHRC are 'the protection and investigation of violations of the rights accorded by this Constitution and any other law'. The promotion of human rights is not expressly mentioned as a primary function of the MHRC. This oversight is mitigated to some extent by section 130 of the Constitution, which provides the MHRC with the 'powers of investigation and recommendation' that are 'reasonably necessary for the effective promotion of the rights conferred by or under this Constitution'.

---

24   Section 131(1)(a) and (b) of the Constitution provides that the Law Commissioner and the Ombudsman are *ex officio* members of the MHRC.

From this provision, one may derive the promotional mandate of the MHRC. Thus, the MHRC has both protective and promotional mandates. However, its protective mandate does not entrust it with the remedial powers of a court of law.[25]

Curiously, the competence given to the MHRC by the HRC Act is seemingly broader than that accorded to it by the Constitution. Section 12 of the HRC Act states:

> The Commission shall be competent in every respect to protect and promote human rights in Malawi in the broadest sense possible and to investigate violations of human rights on its own motion or upon complaints received from any person, class of persons or body.

Unlike the Constitution, the HRC Act requires the MHRC to protect and promote human rights 'in the broadest sense possible'. Furthermore, sections 13 and 14 of the HRC Act enumerate the specific powers and responsibilities of the MHRC. In *Malawi Human Rights Commission v Attorney General*,[26] the issue arose as to whether the MHRC had the power to litigate before the courts on its own motion or only upon receiving a complaint. The MHRC relied on sections 10–15 and 22 of the HRC Act in arguing that it had such a power. The Attorney General argued that the ultimate powers of the MHRC were those specified under sections 129 and 130 of the Constitution and that sections 10–15 and 22 of the HRC Act were *ultra vires* because they conferred more powers on the MHRC than envisaged by the Constitution. However, the High Court held that the provisions of sections 129 and 130 of the Constitution were drafted in broad terms and, as such, needed to be fleshed out in the enabling Act. What was contained in the HRC Act was therefore an elaboration of those broad powers. In conclusion, the court held that the MHRC had the power and capacity to take up court action at its own instance or in pursuance of a complaint or generally to sue in its own name.

In view of this decision, the Constitution and HRC Act must be read together as conferring a broad mandate on the MHRC to execute a broad range of functions related to the protection and promotion of human rights. The Act has defined the functions of the MHRC in a way that leaves little doubt as to the nature of the MHRC's mandate and powers.

---

25 Section 22 of the HRC Act states that the MHRC shall seek an amicable settlement through conciliation, inform the complainant and respondent of their respective rights, render assistance to the complainant, transmit the complaint to any competent authority or make relevant recommendations to the relevant authority.

26 Miscellaneous Cause No 1119 of 2000 (unreported).

5.3. Appointment of commissioners

The MHRC is composed of seven commissioners, appointed in terms of section 131(1)(c) of the Constitution and sections 3 and 4 of the HRC Act, and two *ex officio* members — the Ombudsman and the Law Commissioner. The appointment procedure allows for some level of public participation in that organisations may nominate prospective commissioners. However, public participation is limited to organisations considered by the Law Commissioner and the Ombudsman 'in their absolute discretion' to be 'reputable organisations representative of Malawian society' and to be concerned with the promotion of human rights.[27] Section 4(2) of the HRC Act requires that the nominees should be independent, non-partisan and of high integrity and standing, but it is silent on the requirements of experience and expertise in the promotion and protection of human rights. Bizarrely, the Act requires the nominating organisations, not the nominees or appointees, to be representative of the Malawian society. Moreover, the nomination and appointment process is opaque and lacks the transparency necessary to ensure the credibility of the commissioners. It is only after the President has made the appointments that the full list of nominating organisations, the names of the nominees and the names of the appointed commissioners are published in the *Government Gazette*.[28] Thus, it is fair to say that the appointment process lacks the prerequisites for an independent and competent NHRI.

Once appointed, the commissioners elect a chairperson.[29] The position of chairperson is normally full time, which is important for the independence of the MHRC. Thus far, the MHRC has had four chairpersons. The first chair was a catholic priest; the second a professor in agricultural science; the third a professional nurse; and the current one an expert in public administration, political science and consumer protection. The fact that the chairperson has never been someone with human rights or legal expertise is an indication of the shortcomings of the appointment process of the commissioners.

In general, commissioners have come from a wide range of professional backgrounds. Prominent religious leaders from dominant faiths have consistently been appointed, but no attention has been given to minority religious groups. Around 30 per cent of all appointees have been women, but the picture is less

---

27 See section 131(1)(c) of the Constitution. The idea of absolute discretion has no place in a constitutional framework underpinned by the ideals of accountability and transparency. Malawian courts have held that wide discretionary powers are inimical to these ideals. See *Malawi Law Society & Others v State & Others* Miscellaneous Civil Cause No 78 of 2002 (unreported); *Mkandawire & Others v Attorney General* [1997] 20(2) MLR 1, 11. See also the South African case of *Dawood & Another v Minister of Home Affairs & Others* 2000 (3) SA 936 (CC).

28 Section 4(4) of the HRC Act.

29 Section 6(1) of the HRC Act.

positive when it comes to the representation of minority groups, such as Asians and persons living with disabilities. The proportion of members of the MHRC with legal qualifications or experience in human rights has been very small, especially in the light of the Commission's broad human rights mandate. The current commission has the largest number of commissioners with legal qualifications and experience in human rights. Of the seven current commissioners, three are lawyers, two of whom are human rights experts. Together with the two *ex officio* members, five members of the current MHRC have legal qualifications. Nevertheless, the commissioners with a legal background have generally been junior compared to those who have been appointed to the positions of Law Commissioner and Ombudsperson.

5.4.   Independence

The MHRC was established by the Constitution and the HRC Act as an autonomous legal entity. However, the Constitution does not expressly guarantee the independence of the MHRC as is the case with the Ombudsman. This oversight was rectified by sections 11 and 34 of the HRC Act which declare the independence of the MHRC.

What is of concern, however, is that section 13(2) of the HRC Act requires the MHRC 'to keep the President *fully informed* on matters concerning the *general conduct of the affairs* of the Commission'.[30] This provision could be misinterpreted to mean that the MHRC is accountable to the President. A clear manifestation of this danger arose in 2002 when President Bakili Muluzi directed the MHRC to withhold the release of its investigative report into the death of music star Evison Matafale until the President's own commission of inquiry released its report. Inexplicably, the MHRC acceded to this request, thus compromising its independence.

Interference with the MHRC's investigation also occurred in the case of Robert Manjena Phiri who was arrested by police on allegations of theft of rice valued at MK 50 (less than a US$). The police alleged that, whilst being questioned at a police station, Phiri assaulted a station officer. As he attempted to escape from lawful custody, he was beaten and stoned by a mob. While the police alleged that Phiri died at Kamuzu Central Hospital, two pathologists and a firearms and ballistics expert retained by the MHRC confirmed that there was evidence of gunshot wounds on the deceased's body consistent with shooting from 'point blank range'. Subsequently, when the MHRC obtained a court order to access all relevant documents, including the police's own internal investigative reports, and commanding all officers implicated including the officer-in-charge,

---

30   Emphasis added.

to appear before the MHRC, the Inspector General of the Police refused to cooperate. He went as far as seeking the intervention of the Attorney General to frustrate the inquiry. The investigation was allowed to continue only after protracted discussions between the MHRC and the Attorney General. It remains uncompleted to date. These incidences demonstrate that guaranteeing the independence of the MHRC in the law is an important step, but not enough. In practice, its independence will depend on the integrity of the commissioners and the willingness of the MHRC itself to defend its own space, mandate and decisions.

The MHRC appears to have used section 13(2) referred to above as an opportunity to engage directly with the President on various human rights issues. Such direct engagement is probably necessary to facilitate constructive dialogue on the promotion and protection of human rights. The challenge, however, lies in the fact that the engagement with the President is generally confidential. Consequently, it is difficult for the public to measure its success and effectiveness.

Section 32 of the HRC Act seeks to guarantee the financial autonomy of the MHRC by specifically requiring the government to 'adequately fund the Commission'. However, the MHRC has perennially complained of lack of adequate government funding (MHRC 2004: 41; 2005: 29; 2008: 35). As a result, the MHRC faces an acute shortage of office furniture, equipment and staff. Despite the fact that the government approved a request to establish regional offices in 2007, the government has consistently failed to provide funds for these offices to become operational (MHRC 2008: 36). This has affected the accessibility of the MHRC to the rural poor.

6. Holding the government to account: The experience of the MHRC

6.1. Brief overview of activities

The MHRC has been fully functional for over 10 years. During its first five years, the Commission established its offices, recruited staff, developed an understanding of its own mandate, formulated working methodologies and identified focus areas. The most notable achievements in its early days were the public interest litigation it engaged in and its monitoring of the presidential and parliamentary elections in 1999 (MHRC 1999). Over time, its broad powers to promote and protect human rights have enabled it to employ various techniques and strategies, including investigations, public hearings, research, conciliation, lobbying, public lectures and regular reporting, to highlight human rights abuses and accountability concerns. The Commission has lobbied for the ratification of international human rights instruments and repeatedly reminded the government of its reporting obligations to international human rights monitoring bodies. The MHRC played a crucial role in the preparation of country reports to the Committee on the Elimination of all Forms of Discrimination against Women and the Committee on the Rights of the Child in 2008 and 2009 respectively.

Through annual reports, the MHRC highlights the activities of the MHRC and makes useful recommendations concerning human rights to various organs of state. To the extent that these reports provide an overview of the status of human rights in the country, they could become more useful if more rigorous information-gathering techniques were used and mechanisms were put in place to follow up on compliance with the MHRC's recommendations.

In addition to its annual reports, the MHRC has published in-depth studies on specific themes, such as the human rights accountability of the three arms of government (MHRC 2007a); cultural practices and human rights (MHRC 2006a); law, policies and regulations in education and how they affect the girl child (MHRC 2007b); support services for child victims of sexual abuse (MHRC 2008); labour-related human rights violations (MHRC 2007c); and gender-based violence at the work place and maternity leave (MHRC 2006b). Through such studies, the MHRC can influence change in a wide range of fields and curb systemic violations of human rights or abuses of power.

The MHRC has regularly issued press statements on human rights and accountability issues. These press statements either commend the government for positive efforts made to advance human rights or condemn the state for violating human rights or abusing power. In general, they show that the MHRC is relatively free to criticise the government.

Interestingly, the MHRC has also played the role of conciliator in a number of bitter political standoffs, particularly during President Mutharika's first term of office (2004–2009). After taking office, Mutharika fell out with the party for which he had been the presidential candidate, the United Democratic Front (UDF), and left to form his own party. This resulted in huge tensions and a political and administrative gridlock (see further chapters 4, 11 and 13). The MHRC made various attempts, with different degrees of success, to bring the President and the opposition to the negotiating table. It also campaigned for Parliament to convene and function normally and to pass the annual budget — a process that was repeatedly derailed by the escalating political tensions.[31] To the extent that this political crisis had some implications for human rights, the MHRC was probably acting within its powers to step in as a mediator. The fact that there are no effective and trusted alternative avenues for resolving political

---

31   This also included litigation which was subsequently withdrawn when Parliament was finally convened. See *State v Attorney General & Others* Miscellaneous Civil Cause No 41 of 2005 (unreported).

disputes in Malawi (see chapter 4) also explains why the MHRC thought it necessary to intervene in the way it did. Nevertheless, the MHRC took a huge risk in throwing itself at the centre of the political war zone. That it emerged unscathed is commendable, but there is a great danger for a human rights institution to submerge itself into political battle fields. The damage sustained from such involvement may tarnish the institution irreparably and jeopardise its effectiveness in performing its core function, which is the promotion and protection of human rights, not political mediation.

6.2. Investigations and public hearings

A powerful tool the MHRC has at its disposal is that of conducting public investigations into human rights abuses and violations. The MHRC can launch an investigation of its own accord or upon request by an individual or a group. It can investigate a single violation or a series of systematic abuses. The power to investigate puts the MHRC in a unique position. Unlike the courts, the Commission can employ both reactive and preventative mechanisms to deal with individual or systemic violations of human rights.

The annual reports of the MHRC show that it has investigated thousands of individual complaints alleging violations or threats of violations of human rights. Most of the findings of these investigations have been relatively uncontroversial and have been respected by the parties involved. However, the emphasis on investigating individual cases, where court remedies are possible, seems to be misplaced. Given that it does not have the remedial powers of the courts, the MHRC's impact could be stronger if it focused on investigating systemic violations of human rights, violations which affect large numbers of people, or human rights issues of significant public interest. The findings of the Commission on such issues could also be vital for law and policy reform and administrative practices.

6.3. Litigation

In addition to investigations, the MHRC has discharged its protective mandate through litigation. Since the MHRC does not have binding remedial powers, it needs to rely on the courts in cases in which it has not succeeded in reaching an amicable resolution or where its recommendations have not been respected. The MHRC has intervened in court cases as a party to the proceedings but also as *amicus curiae* (friend of the court). Through these court interventions, the Commission has contributed to the development of human rights jurisprudence in Malawi.

A most prominent *amicus* intervention was in the so-called Madonna cases, which concerned the issue of inter-country adoptions. Celebrity icon Madonna jetted into Malawi in 2006 to adopt a Malawian infant. After a successful adoption, she came back in 2008 to adopt a second Malawian child. At issue in both cases was whether Madonna met the legal requirement of ordinary residence. In *In Re Adoption of David Banda*,[32] the High Court by-passed this requirement by holding that it had to be read in the light of the Constitution, international law and Malawi's current social context. It held that, although the residency requirement was an important protective device for children, it could not be applied rigidly to bar inter-country adoptions in cases where an applicant duly satisfied all other requirements. Two years later, the High Court reached a different decision concerning the adoption of the second child. In *In Re Adoption of CJ (A Female Infant)*,[33] it held that the residence requirement could not be circumvented. However, on appeal, the Malawi Supreme Court of Appeal (MSCA) endorsed the earlier decision, holding that residence had to be interpreted generously.[34] The court found that Madonna had established enough contacts with Malawi even though she was not physically living in the country, thereby satisfying the residence requirement. In both cases, the MHRC urged the court to prioritise the child's best interests, pay attention to the child's dignity and avoid resolving the issue based on mere legal technicalities.[35] Furthermore, the MHRC argued that in assessing the child's best interests, family-based solutions had to be given preference over institutional placement just as permanent solutions and domestic solutions had to be preferred to inherently temporary solutions and to inter-country solutions respectively. These considerations were expressly affirmed by the High Court in *In Re Adoption of David Banda* and by the MSCA.

The MHRC also intervened in the case of *Registered Trustees of the Public Affairs Committee v Attorney General & Another*,[36] which considered the constitutionality of an amendment to section 65 of the Malawian Constitution dealing with MPs who change their party affiliation, that is, cross the floor.[37] The amendment extended the reach of the floor-crossing provisions to organisations or associations whose objectives or activities are political in nature even though not represented in the National Assembly. The question before the court was whether the amendment was consistent with various constitutional provisions, including sections 32 and 40 on the freedom of association and political rights

---

32   Adoption Cause No 2 of 2006 (unreported).
33   Adoption Case No 1 of 2009 (unreported).
34   *In Re CJ (A Female Infant)* MSCA Adoption Appeal No 28 of 2009 (unreported).
35   It must be noted that the MHRC did not participate in the High Court proceedings of the case of *In Re Adoption of CJ (A Female Infant)* believing that the case would be decided in the same way as in *In Re Adoption of David Banda*.
36   Civil Cause No 1861 of 2003 (unreported).
37   Act 8 of 2001.

respectively. The MHRC argued that the extension confused the meaning of crossing the floor and unduly restricted the freedom of association and political rights of MPs. The High Court agreed with this contention.[38]

The case of *Kafantayeni v Attorney General*[39] is another landmark case in which the MHRC participated as *amicus curiae*. This case dealt with the constitutionality of the death penalty in Malawi. The Malawian Penal Code[40] allows for the use of this penalty as mandatory punishment in murder and treason offences[41] and as a discretionary sentence in rape and armed robbery offences.[42] The Constitution recognises the right to life, but subjects it to the caveat that the death penalty may be imposed by a competent court in accordance with the criminal laws of Malawi.[43] The MHRC urged the High Court, sitting as a Constitutional Court, to hold that the death penalty was unconstitutional at least to the extent that it was mandatory. The Court was unwilling to hold that capital punishment *per se* was unconstitutional. It did however rule that mandatory capital punishment was unconstitutional because it restricted the discretion of the courts in sentencing, abridged the prisoner's right to an appeal, and was inconsistent with the principle of proportionality in sentencing. In this case and through this decision, the MHRC contributed to the end of a long era of the mandatory death penalty.

In addition to instances where the MHRC has participated in litigation as *amicus curiae*, the Commission has also brought applications in its own name and on behalf of or jointly with complainants. For example, in *Ian Ngwira & Malawi Human Rights Commission v Republic*,[44] the MHRC came to the aid of the first applicant who, on 30 August 2000, was convicted of theft by public servant by the First Grade Magistrates Court at Dowa and sentenced to a mandatory custodial sentence of 14 years. His property was also confiscated as restitution. Although he appealed against his conviction and sentence within a month, the appeal was never heard, despite his relentless attempts to seek assistance from the MHRC, the Department of Legal Aid, the Ombudsman and the Chief Justice. In 2006, the MHRC decided to assist Ngwira with an application before the High Court for his unconditional release, alleging a violation of his right to a fair trial, especially the right to a speedy trial and the right to appeal. In its

---

38   However, the MSCA overturned this decision in a later case in which it held that courts have no power to nullify a constitutional amendment duly passed by Parliament. See *In the Matter of Presidential Reference of a Dispute of a Constitutional Nature under Section 89(1)(h) of the Constitution and In the Matter of Section 65 of the Constitution and In the Matter of the Question of the Crossing of the Floor by Members of the National Assembly* MSCA Presidential Reference Appeal No 44 of 2006 (unreported).

39   Constitutional Cause No 12 of 2005 (unreported).

40   Chapter 7:01 of the Laws of Malawi.

41   See sections 210 and 38 respectively.

42   See sections 132 and 301 respectively.

43   Section 16 of the Constitution.

44   Miscellaneous Criminal Application No 189 of 2006 (unreported).

judgment, the court refused to find any violation of these rights, but decided, on 'humanitarian grounds', to release the applicant indefinitely on bail pending hearing of his appeal.

Another case revolved around sexual harassment in the military. In *State v Attorney General & Director of Public Prosecutions, ex parte Captain Chanju Mwale & Malawi Human Rights Commission*,[45] Captain Mwale, the most senior female officer in the Malawi Army at the time, was violently assaulted by a fellow army officer at the army barracks in Lilongwe. She suffered extensive injuries and was referred to foreign hospitals for specialist treatment. Her complaint to army authorities was dealt with as a simple administrative case which ended in the assaulting officer being merely admonished. Dissatisfied with the manner in which the issue was resolved, she made a complaint to the police. When the police instituted criminal proceedings against the assaulting officer, the Director of Public Prosecutions (DPP), upon receiving specific directions from the Attorney General, discontinued the case on the putative ground that the case had already been dealt with by military authorities. Following Mwale's request for assistance, the MHRC commenced proceedings in the High Court to review the decision of the DPP. However, just before the full judicial review was heard, the DPP offered to settle the matter out of court, withdrawing the discontinuation of the criminal proceedings.

As is clear from this overview, the Commission has mostly intervened in or commenced individual cases involving one or a small number of victims of human rights. While such interventions may be worthwhile especially to the individuals concerned, the MHRC could make a more significant and lasting impact if it focused on cases which disclose a pattern of flagrant or systemic violations of human rights; have far-reaching consequences on law, policy and administrative practices; or raise issues of significant public interest. The case log of the MHRC also shows that it has dealt with cases dealing predominantly with civil and political rights, ignoring economic, social and cultural rights. Given that violation of the latter set of rights is more difficult to be instituted by individual claimants than violations of civil and political rights (because they tend to affect the general public similarly, require in-depth knowledge of state policies and legislation, and concern the less developed notion of positive obligations), the investigative powers of the MHRC are suited to exposing and remedying such violations.

6.4. Law reform

The fact that the Law Commissioner is an *ex officio* member of the MHRC provides a good starting point for cooperation between the MHRC and the

---

45 Miscellaneous Civil Cause No 40 of 2006 (unreported).

Law Commission. According to sections 13(1)(e) and 14(b)–(c) of the HRC Act, the MHRC has the responsibility to study and comment on the human rights implications of Bills, legislation and administrative practices, and to make appropriate recommendations.

Pursuant to this responsibility, the MHRC has regularly made submissions on Bills and legislation to the Law Commission as well as to the Legal Affairs Committee and Parliament. Some of the specific Acts and Bills that have benefited from the MHRC's submissions include the Penal Code, the Criminal Procedure and Evidence Code;[46] the Prevention of Domestic Violence Act;[47] the Police Act;[48] the National Registration Bill, 2005; and the Money Laundering and Prevention of Terrorist Financing Act.[49] The staff and commissioners of the MHRC have from time to time also been appointed to serve on specific law reform or review commissions. For example, the former Chairperson of the MHRC, Dorothy Nyasulu, served on the special commission on the review of the Constitution, whilst the former Director of Legal Services, Redson Kapindu, served on the special commission on the review of child rights legislation. Through submissions as well as participation in law reform commissions, the experience and insights gained through the work of the MHRC have shaped law reform and review efforts.

7. Conclusion

In 1994, Malawi emerged from 30 years of one-party rule to embrace new values of transparency, accountability, freedom and human rights. The MHRC was one of the new institutions created to complement the courts in ensuring that these new values are entrenched in the new political and legal dispensation. After a slow start, the MHRC has grown into a key human rights monitoring mechanism. It has played a particularly crucial role in monitoring the implementation of constitutional rights, in law reform and revision, in election monitoring, and by encouraging and assisting the state to comply with its international human rights obligations. The MHRC's contribution transcends the traditional divide between justiciable and non-justiciable issues. Through litigation, as *amicus* or a party, the MHRC has upheld rights, stopped and prevented abuses of power, and influenced the development of human rights and constitutional jurisprudence in Malawi. Through its investigative and educational mandate, it has tackled both systemic and individual violations of human rights. While we doubt whether it is wise and indeed lawful for the MHRC to be involved in political dispute

---

46   Chapter 8:01 of the Laws of Malawi.
47   Act 5 of 2006.
48   Chapter 13:01 of the Laws of Malawi.
49   Act 11 of 2006.

resolution, the MHRC has helped to placate bitter political tensions which at times threatened public order, peace and development efforts.

This chapter has also demonstrated that the contribution has been made under considerable constraints. The MHRC is financially dependent on the state, and has perennially been intermittently and inadequately funded. The appointment process of the commissioners lacks the transparency needed to guarantee the independence of the Commission. It is therefore not surprising that the integrity, competence and calibre of the commissioners have varied and, at times, been unsatisfactory.

Overall, government institutions respect the MHRC, but government recalcitrance and interference with the MHRC's activities, as this chapter has shown, have been more than occasional. The MHRC is making laudable efforts to sharpen its working methodologies and improve its effectiveness. The decade that has passed clearly gives us a basis for appreciating what this institution can do and how its contribution can be harnessed and maximised. As Malawi reviews its Constitution more than 15 years since it was adopted, a systematic review of the role of MHRC would also be worthwhile.

References

Legislation and other legal documents

Criminal Procedure and Evidence Code, chapter 8:01 of the Laws of Malawi.

Human Rights Commission Act, chapter 3:08 of the Laws of Malawi.

Money Laundering, Proceeds of Serious Crime and Terrorist Financing Act 11 of 2006.

National Registration Bill, 2005.

Parliamentary and Presidential Elections Act, chapter 2:01 of the Laws of Malawi.

Penal Code, chapter 7:01 of the Laws of Malawi.

Police Act, chapter 13:01 of the Laws of Malawi.

Political Parties Registration and Regulation Act 15 of 1993.

Prevention of Domestic Violence Act 5 of 2006.

Principles Relating to the Status and Functioning of National Institutions for Protection and the Promotion of Human Rights, UN GAOR, 48th Session, 85th Meeting, UN Doc A/RES/48/134, 20 December 1993.

Republic of Malawi Constitution, 1994.

United Nations Economic and Social Council Resolution 1992/54, March 1992.

Cases

Dawood & Another v Minister of Home Affairs & Others 2000 (3) SA 936 (CC).

Ian Ngwira & Malawi Human Rights Commission v Republic Miscellaneous Criminal Application No 189 of 2006 (unreported).

In Re Adoption of CJ (A Female Infant) Adoption Case No 1 of 2009 (unreported).

In Re Adoption of David Banda Adoption Cause No 2 of 2006 (unreported).

In Re CJ (A Female Infant) MSCA Adoption Appeal No 28 of 2009 (unreported).

In the Matter of Presidential Reference of a Dispute of a Constitutional Nature under Section 89(1)(h) of the Constitution and In the Matter of Section 65 of the Constitution and In the Matter of the Question of the Crossing of the Floor by Members of the National Assembly MSCA Presidential Reference Appeal No 44 of 2006 (unreported).

Kafantayeni v Attorney General Constitutional Cause No 12 of 2005 (unreported).

Malawi Human Rights Commission v Attorney General Miscellaneous Cause No 1119 of 2000 (unreported).

Malawi Law Society & Others v State & Others Miscellaneous Civil Cause No 78 of 2002 (unreported).

Mkandawire & Others v Attorney General [1997] 20(2) MLR 1.

Registered Trustees of the Public Affairs Committee v Attorney General and Another Civil Cause No 1861 of 2003 (unreported).

State v Attorney General & Director of Public Prosecutions, ex parte Captain Chanju Mwale & Malawi Human Rights Commission Miscellaneous Civil Cause No 40 of 2006 (unreported).

State v Attorney General & Others Miscellaneous Civil Cause No 41 of 2005 (unreported).

Articles, books, chapters in books and other works

Amnesty International. 2001. *National Human Rights Institutions: Amnesty International's Recommendation for Effective Protection and Promotion of Human Rights.* AI Index IOR 40/007/2001.

Ayeni, V.O. 1997. Evolution of and prospects for the Ombudsman in Southern Africa. *International Review of Administrative Sciences,* 63(4): 543–563.

Foster, P. 2001. Law and society under a democratic dictatorship: Dr Banda and Malawi. *Journal of Asian and African Studies,* 36: 275–293.

Heyns, C. (ed.). 2004. *Human Rights in Africa.* Vol 1. Leiden/Boston: Martinus Nijhoff.

Human Rights Watch. 1990. *Where Silence Rules: The Suppression of Dissent in Malawi.* New York: Human Rights Watch.

Kanzira, H.S. 2002. The independence of national human rights bodies in Africa: A comparative study of the CHRAJ, UHRC and SAHRC. *East African Journal of Peace and Human Rights,* 8(2): 174–210.

Malawi Government. 1965. White paper on the Republican Constitution of Malawi No. 002 of 1965.

Malawi Human Rights Commission. 2004. *2003 Annual Report.* Lilongwe.

Malawi Human Rights Commission. 2005. *2004 Annual Report.* Lilongwe.

Malawi Human Rights Commission. 2006a. *Cultural Practices and Their Impact on the Enjoyment of Human Rights, Particularly the Rights of Women and Children in Malawi.* Lilongwe.

Malawi Human Rights Commission. 2006b. *Gender-based Violence at the Workplace with a Focus on Maternity Leave*. Lilongwe.

Malawi Human Rights Commission. 2007a. *2006 Executive Report on Human Rights Accountability in Malawi by the Three Arms of Government*. Lilongwe.

Malawi Human Rights Commission. 2007b. *The Existence and Implementation of Laws, Policies, and Regulations in Education and How They Affect the Girl-child in Malawi*. Lilongwe.

Malawi Human Rights Commission. 2007c. *Labour Related Human Rights Violations: Practices and Policies that Negatively Affect Employees in the Formal Private Sector*. Lilongwe.

Malawi Human Rights Commission. 2008. *Support Services Accessible to Child Victims of Sexual Abuse in Malawi: A Baseline Survey*. Lilongwe.

Malawi Human Rights Commission. 2009. *2008 Annual Report*. Lilongwe.

Murray, C. 2006. The Human Rights Commission et al: What is the role of South Africa's chapter 9 institutions. *Potchefstroom Electronic Law Journal*, 2: 1–26.

Murray, R.H. 2007. *The Role of National Human Rights Institutions at the International and Regional Levels: The Experience of Africa*. Oxford & Portland, Oregon: Hart Publishing.

Ng'ong'ola, C. 2002. Judicial mediation in electoral politics in Malawi. In Englund, H. (ed.). *A Democracy of Chameleons: Politics and Culture in the New Malawi*. Uppsala: Nordic Africa Institute, 62–86.

Phiri, K.M. & Ross, K.R. 1998. Introduction: From totalitarianism to democracy in Malawi. In Phiri, K.M. & Ross, K.R. (eds.) *Democratisation in Malawi: A stocktaking*. Blantyre: CLAIM, 9–16.

Reif, L.C. 2000. Building democratic institutions: The role of national human rights institutions in good governance and human rights protection. *Harvard Human Rights Journal*, 13: 1–69.

Chapter 10

Balancing independence and accountability: The role of Chapter 9 institutions in South Africa's constitutional democracy[1]

Pierre de Vos

1. Introduction

In 1994 South Africa emerged from a racially divided and oppressive past which disrespected human rights and the most basic tenets of the rule of law. The new democratically elected government inherited a state which was 'farcically bureaucratic, secretive and unresponsive to the basic needs of the majority of its citizens' (Ad Hoc Committee 2007: 3). Most state institutions had little or no credibility, were profoundly distrusted by the majority of the people and were not accountable in any credible manner, either to courts or to one another. For some constitutional negotiators, it was therefore clear that transforming the South African society from an intensely oppressive into an open and democratic society would require more than a change in the system of government. It was necessary to create a set of credible independent institutions to strengthen constitutional democracy and to promote an open and accountable government, steeped in the disciplining paradigm of human rights.

It was envisaged that the new independent institutions, which included the Human Rights Commission, the Commission for Gender Equality, the Public Protector, the Commission for the Promotion and Protection of the Rights of Cultural, Religious and Linguistic Communities, the Auditor-General and the Electoral Commission, would support constitutional democracy in several ways. They would help to restore the credibility of the state and its institutions in the eyes of citizens; ensure that democracy and human rights and the values associated with them flourished in the new dispensation; ensure the

---

[1]   This chapter is partly based on the advisory work the author performed for the Ad Hoc Committee of the South African National Assembly which reviewed Chapter 9 and related institutions.

successful re-establishment of and respect for the rule of law; and contribute to an open, accountable and transparent government. The constitution-makers deemed it necessary to guarantee the independence of these so-called Chapter 9 institutions to protect them from undue influence and interference and to ensure that they would be able to fulfil the tasks set out above.

Section 181(2) of the Constitution[2] states that 'these institutions are independent, and subject only to the Constitution and the law, and they must be impartial and must exercise their powers and perform their functions without fear, favour or prejudice'. To underscore the need for their independence, section 181(3) requires all other organs of state to assist and protect these institutions and to ensure their independence, impartiality, dignity and effectiveness. Furthermore, section 181(4) prohibits any person or organ of state from interfering with the functioning of these institutions. However, section 181(5) states that these institutions are accountable to the National Assembly and requires them to report on their activities and the performance of their functions at least once a year.

Thus, South Africa's Chapter 9 institutions were established as independent watchdogs to support the consolidation of constitutional democracy. However, not all of them have been successful in fulfilling their constitutional mandates (Murray 2006), and some of them have been beset by persistent internal problems and conflicts (Da Costa 2006). There has also been confusion about the nature of their independence and how it should be balanced against both their own accountability to the National Assembly and their role of holding the executive and legislature to account.

Because of these problems, the South African National Assembly appointed an ad hoc committee to review Chapter 9 and associated institutions.[3] The committee produced a bulky report, which contains comprehensive recommendations to improve the effectiveness of the institutions. Most of these recommendations have not yet been implemented.

This chapter argues that Chapter 9 institutions can only be effective in holding the legislature and executive to account if their independence is safeguarded and if they are not 'captured' by the ruling party or other interest groups. This remains a challenge in the current political landscape where the ruling African National Congress (ANC) continues to hold the position of dominant party.

---

2   Constitution of the Republic of South Africa, 1996.
3   Members (five from the ruling party; five from opposition parties): Hon Prof Kader Asmal (Chairperson), Hon Mr SL Dithebe, Hon Ms C Johnson, Hon Adv TM Masutha later replaced by Hon Mr CV Burgess, Hon Mrs MJJ Matsomela, Hon Dr JT Delport, Hon Ms M Smuts, Hon Mr JH van der Merwe, Hon Mrs S Rajbally, Hon Mr S Simmons. Parliamentary support staff: Dr L Gabriel, Mr M Philander, Ms C Silkstone, Mr T Molukanele, Adv A Gordon (Adv M Vassen as alternate), Ms T Sepanya, Ms L Monethi, Ms J Adriaans, Mr T Schumann, and Mr E Nevondo.

The confusion about the independence of Chapter 9 institutions and their role as watchdogs might also be, at least partially, attributed to a tension in the Constitution itself. While it guarantees the independence of Chapter 9 institutions, it also states that they are accountable to the National Assembly. Nevertheless, the courts in South Africa have provided sufficient clarity on the role of Chapter 9 institutions vis-à-vis the legislature and the executive. This chapter will show that the Ad Hoc Committee drew on the courts' interpretation and adopted a robust view of the independence of Chapter 9 institutions.

Two fundamental questions are the central concern of this chapter. First, can Chapter 9 institutions be truly effective in promoting human rights and democracy and holding the legislature and the executive to account without being guaranteed the kind of institutional independence afforded to the judiciary? Second, if the nature of the independence of these institutions is different from that of the judiciary, what kind of independence would be needed for Chapter 9 institutions to effectively perform their mandates?

2. The independence of Chapter 9 institutions

The Ad Hoc Committee established to review the Chapter 9 institutions was mandated to investigate two interrelated aspects of accountability. First, it had to review the legal mandates of the institutions, their appointment and institutional governance arrangements and the role of Parliament in providing oversight over them. Second, it set out to review the relationship between Chapter 9 institutions and various branches of government; more particularly, the funding arrangements of the institutions in order to establish whether they were sufficiently independent to hold the legislature and the executive to account.[4]

The Committee set out broad principles according to which it would evaluate the various institutions.[5] In this context, it took the decision to focus on the independence of the institutions under review. This decision was of great importance as it directed the review to the manner in which the institutions related to the legislature and the executive and the concomitant question of whether they enjoyed sufficient independence from these branches of

---

4   The Ad Hoc Committee's terms of reference were adopted by the National Assembly on 21 September 2006, see http://www.pmg.org.za/docs/2006/061020terms.pdf. Accessed 10 September 2010.

5   The Ad Hoc Committee was also authorised to conduct its review with reference to other organs of state of a similar nature and whose work was closely related to the work of the institutions specifically mentioned in the resolution. At its first meeting of 10 October 2006, the Committee decided to include in its review, in addition to the Public Protector, the South African Human Rights Commission, the Commission for the Promotion and Protection of the Rights of Cultural, Religious and Linguistic Communities, the Commission for Gender Equality, the Auditor-General, the Electoral Commission and the Public Service Commission, the following institutions: the Pan South African Language Board, the Financial and Fiscal Commission, the Independent Communications Authority of South Africa and the National Youth Commission.

government. Thus, this chapter begins with a discussion of the independence of Chapter 9 institutions because, as was implicitly acknowledged by the Committee, without a considerable degree of independence, these institutions can neither hold the legislature and the executive accountable nor contribute to an open and transparent government.

Chapter 9 institutions find themselves in a precarious position because they are not judicial in nature and not all of them enjoy the same independence as the judiciary does. On the one hand, Chapter 9 institutions have to act as watchdogs holding the legislative and executive branches of government to account. On the other hand, they are required to cooperate with the legislature and the executive and account to the former. Thus, Chapter 9 institutions are caught between Scylla and Charybdis. They have to tread carefully to ensure the cooperation of the legislature and the executive while at the same time safeguarding their independence and, where necessary, criticising and even challenging executive or legislative actions. As pointed out above, this contradiction is apparent in the Constitution itself.

2.1. General test of independence

The Constitutional Court (CC) set out a general test for judging the independence of an institution in *Van Rooyen and Others v S & Others (Van Rooyen)*.[6] The case dealt with a challenge by Mr Van Rooyen, who had been convicted by a magistrate in the regional court on various counts of theft and sentenced to six years in prison, to the independence of the lower courts in South Africa. He had argued that magistrates in South Africa's lower courts are appointed by the Magistrates Commission which is dominated by politicians or political appointees and thus that magistrates lacked institutional independence as required by the Constitution. Consequently, he argued that his conviction and sentence by a magistrate's court was invalid. The South African Constitution guarantees the independence of the courts and states that courts must apply the law impartially and without fear, favour or prejudice (s 165(2)). Judicial independence and impartiality is also implicit in the rule of law which is foundational to the Constitution. At the same time, the Constitution distinguishes between the appointment processes of magistrates and judges (*Van Rooyen* paras 16–18).

In this context, the CC found that judicial independence at its core requires that individual judges must be able to hear and decide cases that come before them and that no outsider should be able to interfere with the way a judge or

---

6   2002 (8) BCLR 810 (CC). Although this judgment dealt more specifically with the independence of the judicial branch of government, the Ad Hoc Committee was of the opinion that the general principles set out by the CC in this case were relevant to understanding the independence of Chapter 9 and associated institutions.

magistrate conducts his or her case and makes his or her decision. This requires at a personal level that judges or magistrates should act impartially and, at an institutional level, that structures must be put in place to protect the courts and judicial officers against external interference (*Van Rooyen* para 31). At the same time, it is important to note that there are hierarchical differences between higher courts and lower courts and that the requirements for independence could be different for the two types of courts. Just because they are treated differently does not mean that magistrates' courts lack independence. As lower courts are entitled to protection by higher courts if a threat is made to their independence, the greater the protection of judicial independence of higher courts, the greater the protection of the independence of lower courts. Moreover, lower courts do not have the power to deal with constitutional matters and the jurisdiction of the lower courts set out in the Constitution is much more restricted than for higher courts. All this means that lower courts do not need the same kind of safeguards as higher courts do (*Van Rooyen* para 28).

The test for independence is whether the court or tribunal 'from the objective standpoint of a reasonable and informed person, will be perceived as enjoying the essential conditions of independence'. It is important that there must be public confidence in the administration of justice. The CC endorsed the following dictum from the Canadian case of *Valente v The Queen*:[7] 'Without that confidence, the system cannot command the respect and acceptance that are essential to its effective operation. It is, therefore, important that a tribunal should be perceived as independent, as well as impartial, and that the test for independence should include that perception' (*Van Rooyen* para 32). This test is an objective one. The apprehension of bias must be a reasonable one, held by reasonable and right-minded persons, applying themselves to the question and obtaining thereon the required information. One must ask what would an informed person, viewing the matter realistically and practically — and having thought the matter through — conclude. The question is whether a reasonable, objective and informed person would on the correct facts reasonably apprehend that the judge or magistrate has not or will not bring an impartial mind to bear on the adjudication of the case, that his or her mind is open to persuasion by the evidence and the submissions of counsel.[8] But it is important to note that this objective test must be properly contextualised. The perception that is relevant for such purposes is, however, a perception based on a balanced view of all

---

7   [1985] 2 SCR 273 (SCC) para 22.

8   On this point, the Constitutional Court relied on *President of the Republic of South Africa & Others v South African Rugby Football Union & Others* 1999 (4) SA 147 (CC); 1999 (7) BCLR 725 (CC) para 48 and the Canadian case of *Committee for Justice and Liberty & Others v National Energy Board* (1976) 68 DLR (3d) 716, 735.

the material information. '[W]e ask how things appear to the well-informed, thoughtful and objective observer, rather than the hypersensitive, cynical, and suspicious person.'[9] The CC continued:

> Bearing in mind the diversity of our society this cautionary injunction is of particular importance in assessing institutional independence. The well-informed, thoughtful and objective observer must be sensitive to the country's complex social realities, in touch with its evolving patterns of constitutional development, and guided by the Constitution, its values and the differentiation it makes between different levels of courts (*Van Rooyen* para 34).

The Ad Hoc Committee drew on *Van Rooyen* and accepted the view that not all Chapter 9 institutions require the degree of independence which the judiciary enjoys. It accepted that the stringency of the requirements for independence would differ depending on the nature of the institution at hand and the nature of the tasks performed by it. For example, an institution dealing with complaints against the legislature and the executive, such as the Public Protector, would require strong independence in order to safeguard its impartiality and ensure its legitimacy in the eyes of the public. Likewise, the Electoral Commission, whose task it is to guarantee free and fair elections, needs strong protection of its independence. However, not all Chapter 9 institutions require the degree of independence afforded to the judiciary to fulfil their mandates.

The independence of Chapter 9 institutions must be understood against the countervailing constitutional imperatives requiring cooperation between these institutions and other state organs and establishing the National Assembly as the body to whom these institutions account. As Corder et al (1999: para 7.1.2) made clear, some Chapter 9 institutions must be seen as complementary to Parliament's own oversight function and thus require a lesser degree of independence:

> Together with Parliament they act as watch-dog bodies over the government and organs of state [...] they support and aid Parliament in its oversight function by providing it with information that is not derived from the executive. [...] With the complex nature of modern government, Members of Parliament often do not have the time and resources to investigate in depth, or because of party discipline do not have the political independence that is required to arrive at an impartial decision on the complaint. Hence, state institutions supporting constitutional democracy have been created to assist Parliament in its traditional functions.

While Corder et al are correct in suggesting that some Chapter 9 institutions augment the accountability function of the legislature, certain commentators

---

9   On this point, the Constitutional Court was quoting the American case of *US v Jordan* 49 F3d 152 (5th Cir 1995) 156.

and politicians[10] have gone further to argue that Chapter 9 institutions are indeed part of government. This argument takes too narrow a view of the independence of the institutions under discussion (Murray 2006: 4). Were the Human Rights Commission or the Electoral Commission regarded as part of the government, these institutions would be under pressure to cooperate with the government of the day at all costs. This, in turn, would make it difficult for them to act without fear, favour or prejudice and to fulfil their functions effectively. Institutions mandated to make findings against those in power or to act against their interests will only be able to do so if they are given the freedom to exercise their powers impartially and independently.

In *Independent Electoral Commission v Langeberg Municipality*,[11] the CC endorsed the view that, although Chapter 9 institutions are organs of state as defined in section 239 of the Constitution, they cannot be said to be government departments over which Cabinet exercises authority. Although they are state institutions, they are not part of the government. Their independence refers to independence *from* the government. Chapter 9 institutions cannot be independent from the national government, yet be part of it (paras 28–29). The logic of this view dictates that Chapter 9 institutions are *not* subject to the cooperative government provisions set out in Chapter 3 of the Constitution. The CC held that Chapter 9 institutions perform their functions in terms of national legislation, but 'are not subject to national executive control' (para 31). They must 'manifestly be seen to be outside government' (Ad Hoc Committee 2007: 9). A legislative provision or executive action that creates the impression that a Chapter 9 institution is not manifestly outside government, would be constitutionally unacceptable (Govender 2007: 203).

2.2. Financial independence

In *Independent Electoral Commission v Langeberg Municipality*,[12] the CC affirmed the basic principle that Chapter 9 institutions must have some degree of financial independence. Were the executive to have absolute control over the funding of Chapter 9 institutions, the institutions would not be able to function and exercise their duties without fear, favour or prejudice. At the same time, the CC made it clear that financial independence does not mean that Chapter 9 institutions have the right to set their own budgets. Rather, it means that Parliament, as opposed

---

10 See, for instance, Anon *Sunday Times* http://www.sundaytimes.co.za/ 14 Nov: 'Not surprisingly, my media colleagues staged a synchronised volcanic eruption calling Mushwana's findings, among other things, a whitewash. The real question, though, is whether we should be in the least bit surprised that an office set up by government to investigate the affairs of government should fall so short of expectations.' Quoted in Murray 2006: 12–13.

11 2001 (9) BCLR 883 (CC).

12 Ibid.

to the executive, has the obligation to provide 'reasonably sufficient' funding to enable the Chapter 9 institutions to carry out their constitutional mandates (para 29).

The CC accepted that it is difficult to determine what would constitute reasonably sufficient funding. It stated that it is incumbent upon the parties (Parliament and the relevant Chapter 9 institution) to make every effort to reach an agreement by negotiation in good faith. The CC acknowledged that, when Parliament engages in this process of negotiation, it is obligated to consider the requests for funding in the light of competing national interests. Therefore, it must afford the Chapter 9 institutions an adequate opportunity to defend their budgetary requirements. In addition, 'no member of the executive or the administration should have the power to stop transfers of money to any independent constitutional body without the existence of appropriate safeguards for the independence of that institution' (Ad Hoc Committee 1997: 11).

Surprisingly, the Ad Hoc Committee's review revealed that not all Chapter 9 institutions enjoyed the degree of financial independence required by the CC. None of the institutions under review were able clearly to identify the various steps in their budget process. It appeared that the institutions followed different processes with some enjoying more autonomy than others. A common feature was that their budgets were located within the budgets of specific national government departments (Ad Hoc Committee 2007: 19). The Deputy Minister of Justice and Constitutional Development stated that his department did not have any authority to adjust the allocations to Chapter 9 institutions and that the allocated amount was transferred directly to the relevant Chapter 9 institution. Most of the institutions, however, stated that, although they submitted their budget proposals directly to the National Treasury, they were not given an opportunity to defend their proposals and seldom received the allocations they proposed. This situation is not ideal and appears to be in conflict with the CC's interpretation of financial independence.

The location of the budgets of Chapter 9 institutions within government departments impacts negatively on the perceived independence of the institutions. Their proximity to government departments creates the impression that they are accountable to those government departments for the use of their finances. Given these concerns, the Ad Hoc Committee (2007: 20) proposed that the budget processes of Chapter 9 institutions be revised to bring about uniformity and to promote and protect the independence of these institutions. Since most of the Chapter 9 institutions are accountable to the National Assembly, the Ad Hoc Committee recommended that funding for these institutions be located within Parliament's budget. It also highlighted the need for Parliament to establish or identify appropriate structures and mechanisms to ensure an effective and efficient budget process. The Committee proposed that budgets be negotiated with the National Treasury and that Chapter 9 institutions be given an adequate opportunity to motivate their budget proposals before final budget allocations are made (Ad Hoc Committee 2007: 20).

2.3. Administrative independence

In *New National Party of South Africa v Government of the RSA*,[13] the CC stated that Chapter 9 institutions require more than financial independence. For these institutions to operate and fulfil their respective tasks without fear, favour or prejudice, their administrative independence must be safeguarded (para 97). The CC made it clear that section 181(3) of the Constitution requires the executive to engage with these constitutional bodies in a manner that would ensure that their efficient functioning is not hampered (para 99). This implies that Chapter 9 institutions must have control over those matters directly connected with their constitutional functions. No matter what administrative arrangements Parliament or the executive might make, it is important that Chapter 9 institutions maintain operational control over their core business. Administrative arrangements must not interfere with the ability of these bodies to perform their constitutional duties impartially. Neither Parliament nor the executive may interfere with the day-to-day running of these institutions, or be directly involved in the employment or management of staff.

At the same time, Parliament and the executive have a duty to support Chapter 9 institutions. If institutional problems are of such magnitude or seriousness that they make it difficult or impossible for a Chapter 9 institution to fulfil its constitutional and legislative tasks, Parliament can, and indeed must, assist the relevant institution to resolve those problems. However, Parliament or the executive cannot do so in a way that removes final control over the administration from the Chapter 9 institution or that interferes with its effective functioning.

Consequently, it was held in the above-mentioned case of *New National Party of South Africa v Government of the RSA*[14] that the Department of Home Affairs could not tell the Electoral Commission how to conduct voter registration or whom to employ. However, if the Commission asked the government to provide personnel to assist in the registration process, the government would be obliged to provide such assistance if it was able to do so (para 99). Thus, the CC provided useful guidance on the nature of the administrative independence of Chapter 9 institutions. Whether these guidelines are adhered to in practice is another question which will be discussed in section 3 below.

---

13   1999 (5) BCLR 489 (CC).
14   Ibid.

2.4. Independence and appointment procedures

Independence means very little if Chapter 9 institutions, while formally independent, are staffed with individuals who are unwilling or incapable of holding the executive to account. While the Constitution provides safeguards to ensure the appointment of suitable and qualified individuals, in practice the appointment process has been the Achilles' heel of Chapter 9 institutions.

Section 193 of the Constitution states that the Public Protector, the Auditor-General and the members of all Commissions established under Chapter 9 must be South African citizens, persons who are fit and proper to hold the particular office and comply with any other requirements prescribed by national legislation. Furthermore, appointments must broadly reflect the race and gender composition of South Africa.[15] The President must appoint the Public Protector, the Auditor-General and members of the Human Rights Commission, the Commission for Gender Equality, and the Electoral Commission, upon the recommendation of the National Assembly. Nominations by the National Assembly emanate from a committee of the Assembly proportionally composed of members of all parties represented in the Assembly. These nominations must be approved by the Assembly by a resolution adopted by at least 60 per cent of the Members in the case of the Public Protector and the Auditor-General, and a simple majority in the case of members of Commissions. The Constitution also states that the involvement of civil society in the recommendation process may be provided for, in line with the requirement that the National Assembly must facilitate public involvement in the legislative and other processes of the Assembly and its committees.

The Auditor-General, the Public Protector and members of Commissions may be removed from office only on the grounds stipulated in section 194(1) of the Constitution, namely, misconduct, incapacity or incompetence. To further safeguard their tenure, they may only be removed if a committee of the National Assembly has made a factual finding regarding the existence of at least one of these grounds and after a necessary resolution is adopted by the Assembly calling for that person's removal from office. Such a resolution must be adopted by at least two thirds of the Members of the Assembly when dealing with the removal of the Public Protector or the Auditor-General and a majority of Members of the Assembly when any member of a Commission is to be removed (section 194(2)).

The review by the Ad Hoc Committee revealed that the appointment process of members of Chapter 9 institutions was more politicised than was envisaged

---

15   The Auditor-General must be a woman or a man who is a South African citizen and a fit and proper person to hold that office. Specialised knowledge of, or experience in, auditing, state finances and public administration is a prerequisite.

by the Constitution. It also became clear that there was insufficient involvement of civil society in the appointment process (Ad Hoc Committee 2007: 13). This was seen as a major weakness of the Chapter 9 architecture. First, the procedures for the appointment of members of the various Commissions are fleshed out in detail in legislation establishing each institution. This has brought about significant variations in the appointment processes of office bearers of Chapter 9 institutions (Ad Hoc Committee 2007: 21). Although the different mandates, powers and functions of the institutions mean that their composition and appointment procedures cannot be identical, a reasonable degree of consistency is required.

Second, the role played by the relevant Minister in the appointment processes of members of the Commission for Gender Equality, the Commission for the Promotion and Protection of the Rights of Cultural, Religious and Linguistic Communities, and the Independent Communications Authority of South Africa, is incompatible with the independence of these institutions and therefore inappropriate. In particular, the procedure of appointing members of the Commission for the Promotion and Protection of the Rights of Cultural, Religious and Linguistic Communities is highly problematic. The relevant legislation provides that, whenever vacancies need to be filled, the Minister for Provincial and Local Government must invite individuals and organisations to nominate suitably qualified individuals to serve on the Commission. The Minister must appoint a selection panel consisting of persons who command public respect for their fair-mindedness, wisdom and understanding of issues concerning South African cultural, religious and linguistic communities. This panel must subsequently submit a list of names to the President. Thus, the National Assembly is not involved in the appointment process. Because of this omission and the prescribed involvement of the Minister this legislation is clearly in tension with the relevant provisions of the Constitution.

One of the key recommendations of the Ad Hoc Committee concerned the involvement of civil society in the appointment process. Public involvement in parliamentary procedures is at the discretion of the National Assembly, but in the case of *Doctors for Life International v Speaker of the National Assembly*,[16] the CC stated:

> ... the general right to participate in the conduct of public affairs includes engaging in public debate and dialogue with elected representatives at public hearings. But that is not all; it includes the duty to facilitate public participation in the conduct of public affairs by ensuring that citizens have the necessary information and effective opportunity to exercise the right to political participation (para 105).

---

16   2006 (12) BCLR 1399 (CC).

Although the legislature has considerable leeway in deciding how to facilitate public involvement, this does not mean that it can leave it to others to ensure that public involvement is actually facilitated. Parliament has a responsibility to keep members of the public and interested parties informed of the pertinent issues and give them a reasonable opportunity to make their views known. What amounts to a reasonable opportunity will depend on the circumstances of each case. In view of this jurisprudence, the National Assembly has a duty to act reasonably to ensure that civil society is involved in the appointment of Commissioners and other office bearers of Chapter 9 institutions.

At present, the involvement of civil society in the appointment process is limited to the nomination of candidates. A committee of Parliament shortlists the nominees, conducts the interviews and presents a list of recommended candidates to the National Assembly for adoption. The recommendations of the National Assembly are then sent to the President for appointment. Civil society is not involved beyond the nominations stage.

The quality of the work of Chapter 9 institutions depends very much on the quality of the individuals appointed to these bodies. Active and meaningful participation of civil society in the appointment processes may result in the appointment of more suitable and qualified candidates. It is for this reason that the Ad Hoc Committee (2007: 25–26) proposed that the names of short-listed candidates should be published for public comment before the relevant committees of the National Assembly deliberate on the shortlist and send nominations to the National Assembly for adoption. Sadly, this recommendation has not (yet) been implemented.

3. The accountability of Chapter 9 institutions

The South African Constitution attempts to strike a balance between the independence of Chapter 9 institutions on the one hand and their accountability to the legislature on the other hand. As noted earlier, section 181(5) of the Constitution provides that state institutions supporting constitutional democracy 'are accountable to the National Assembly and must report on their activities and the performance of their functions to the Assembly at least once a year'. They are required to report to Parliament on the implementation of their mandates and their expenditure of public funds. Parliament has the duty to provide for mechanisms to ensure such accountability. It is crucial that these accountability mechanisms enable Parliament to engage effectively with the reports it receives from these institutions without interfering in their day-to-day running. This is a difficult balance to strike, more so because the institutions that are accountable to Parliament also have a mandate to hold Parliament itself accountable. The dominance of Parliament by one political party and other political factors which make it difficult for Chapter 9 institutions to act in a robust and truly independent manner exacerbate this problem (Govender 2007: 207–208)).

At present, there are two interrelated but distinct ways in which Chapter 9 institutions engage with the National Assembly. Firstly, their annual reports are tabled in the National Assembly. The Assembly refers annual reports to the relevant portfolio committee, which then engages with the Chapter 9 institution on the contents thereof. Second, some Chapter 9 institutions, particularly those concerned with human rights, submit substantive reports to the National Assembly for consideration and action. For example, the Human Rights Commission regularly submits reports on measures taken by government departments to realise the rights to housing, health care, food, water, social security, education and a healthy environment to the National Assembly pursuant to section 184(3) of the Constitution. Such substantive reports can serve as important sources of information for Parliament's oversight over government departments. The Speaker refers these reports to the relevant portfolio committee for consideration. Usually, these referrals are made without instructions to report back or to take specific action unless there is a legal requirement or a special request to do so. The lack of report back often results in parliamentary committees not adequately responding to substantive reports. Moreover, there appears to be some confusion over the precise nature of the responsibility of Parliament in relation to these reports. It is unclear whether it is Parliament or Chapter 9 institutions which should follow up on recommendations made in substantive reports (Ad Hoc Committee 2007: 28–29).

How to deal with these seemingly intractable problems is a difficult question. The solution does not lie in constitutional tinkering to further enhance the independence of Chapter 9 institutions. This chapter argues that Chapter 9 institutions are not courts and fulfil a different function from that performed by the judiciary. Thus, they should not be treated in the same manner. Corder et al (1999) recommended the adoption of the Accountability and Independence of Constitutional Institutions Act to recognise and regulate the relationship between Chapter 9 institutions and Parliament. It was an ambitious proposal that was never adopted by Parliament. The Ad Hoc Committee (2007: 31) has proposed a scaled-down version of such legislation which would assist in providing structure to the accountability of Chapter 9 institutions and the oversight work done by Parliament. However, it is far from clear that these proposals, if adopted, will solve the problems since they relate more to one-party dominance in Parliament and the nature and culture of South African politics than to particular legal structures or the lack thereof.

4. The effectiveness of Chapter 9 institutions

None of the Chapter 9 institutions performs the same function as the judiciary. Although many of them have extensive investigative powers, their findings and recommendations are not binding, unlike court judgments. Chapter 9 institutions are mandated to assist the legislature in holding the executive to account. They do not and cannot be expected to enjoy the same independence as the judiciary. As we have seen, the National Assembly plays an important role in the appointment of Commissioners and other office bearers. Members of Chapter 9 institutions can be removed from office more easily than judicial officers. The nature of the work of Chapter 9 institutions requires them to work with the legislature and, to some degree, with the executive. This places limits on their degree of independence. It might therefore be argued that Chapter 9 institutions are not well placed to play an effective role in holding the executive and legislature to account.

However, it is important to take a holistic view of the role of Chapter 9 institutions. First, Chapter 9 institutions are well placed to expose unlawful and corrupt practices and to uncover failures of the executive, the legislature or government officials (Murray 2006: 9). Secrecy is the enemy of accountability and Chapter 9 institutions are designed to ensure that public power is exercised in an open and transparent manner. They have a duty to reveal weaknesses and problems by collating and publishing information. They have powers to require answers or explanations from government and other actors (Murray 2006: 11). Ordinary citizens, in turn, can rely on this information to play their own role in holding the executive and legislative branches of government to account, to make decisions about their political preferences and, hence, to influence the policies and priorities of the government.

Second, Chapter 9 institutions play an educational role. They promote a culture of openness, transparency and respect for human rights in government and amongst ordinary citizens. These institutions actively promote constitutional values — something the judiciary cannot do as judges speak only through their judgments and are generally required to refrain from making general statements that have no relevance to the cases before them.

Third, as Murray (2006: 7) has pointed out, because Chapter 9 institutions are located between citizens and the government, they provide a politically neutral medium through which citizens can communicate their views, needs and concerns. If Chapter 9 institutions are truly independent, they can provide a reliable forum, unburdened by the political exigencies of the day or vested interests, for people to articulate their views. In this sense, the role of these constitutional bodies differs from that of the judiciary. They have an important but limited function of ensuring an open, transparent and accountable government. Hence, it is understandable that they do not enjoy the same degree of independence as the judiciary.

In theory, Chapter 9 institutions enjoy sufficient independence to play their watchdog role effectively. This does not mean that all of them have acted vigorously and effectively in holding members of the executive and the legislature to account. However, these failures cannot all be ascribed to a lack of independence in terms of their constitutional and legal architecture. Why then have these bodies not always lived up to their promise?

South Africa is the only country in the world where the Constitution established such a large number of different institutions to support constitutional democracy and to monitor, protect and promote human rights. This proliferation of bodies has definitely played a role in diminishing their effectiveness in holding the legislature and the executive to account. First, operating as separate bodies, Chapter 9 institutions are under-resourced. Budgets are not sufficient to fulfil their core mandates. Second, human rights are interdependent and indivisible and cannot be easily compartmentalised. Individuals often experience human rights violations in multiple ways and may not know which of the institutions to approach or may approach the wrong one. Third, one of the most important tasks of the human rights bodies is to assist those who would otherwise not be able to enforce their rights. Currently, with the exception of the Human Rights Commission, none of the Chapter 9 institutions is effectively fulfilling this task. Many vulnerable people, especially women and children and those living in rural areas, have no recourse when their rights are infringed.

The Ad Hoc Committee (2007: 37) therefore proposed to merge all human rights related bodies into one strengthened, well organised 'super commission', called the South African Commission on Human Rights and Equality. This body would be better equipped to deal with the many existing challenges to the promotion and protection of human rights in South Africa. The Committee recommended that the new commission be well funded and that it should be given the necessary legal power not only to promote human rights and address systemic violations of rights, but also to operate as an advice centre for the millions of people in South Africa who do not have access to justice (Ad Hoc Committee 2007: 39). It was envisaged that the new body would be more than the sum of its parts and would become a centre of excellence in research and knowledge creation across the full breadth of the equality and human rights spectrum. As such, it would be able to monitor, protect and enforce all human rights and promote cross-sectoral learning and information-sharing in a coherent and integrated way. It was also envisaged that the new human rights body would become the focus of a more informal non-court driven process to realise and protect human rights. Sadly, this proposal has not yet been implemented or widely discussed.

Would such a 'super commission' be able to avoid the problems faced by current Chapter 9 bodies? It must be conceded that in a one-party dominant democracy, the danger of 'state capture' will remain and that there are no guarantees that a 'super commission' will be more effective in playing its accountability role. However, it will at least have a better chance of doing so because it will have more institutional muscle and administrative capacity. Such a body may be better able to use its 'bully-pulpit' to promote and advance respect for human rights and hold the powerful to account by exposing wrongdoing. Even if it failed to deal decisively with the more politically sensitive cases, its broader reach would enable it to deal more effectively with the complaints of ordinary citizens and to hold at least low- and mid-level functionaries to account.

As alluded to earlier, the nature of the political landscape in South Africa has contributed to the failure of some Chapter 9 institutions to discharge their mandates effectively. The governing party in South Africa has garnered overwhelming support from the electorate in four consecutive elections. The opposition remains relatively weak and fragmented. Thus, a one-party dominant democracy has established itself (Giliomee 1998: 127; Brooks 2004). In this context, the National Assembly, dominated by the ruling party, has not always appointed Commissioners who have had the political will or the necessary skills to strike the correct balance between their need to cooperate with the legislature and the executive on the one hand, and their duty to hold these branches of government to account on the other. For example, the appointment, in 2002, of Lawrence Mushwana, who was previously an ANC Member of Parliament, as the Public Protector raised eyebrows (Govender 2007: 202). He was rightly criticised for his lack of independence when he controversially refused to investigate the Oilgate affair which involved allegations that a state-owned enterprise had paid money to a businessman who subsequently passed it on to the governing party. His decision not to investigate was subsequently set aside by the High Court (Murray 2006: 3). The fact that, in 2009, the same individual was appointed as the Chairperson of the Human Rights Commission further underlines the recurring problem of appointing unsuitable individuals to lead some of these institutions. South Africa's history of apartheid, the history of the ruling party as the former liberation movement, and the country's limited experience with democracy have all contributed to an atmosphere in which robust and vigorous engagement with members of the legislature, the executive and other ruling party officials is not always possible. Perhaps, over time, as South Africa's democracy matures, Chapter 9 institutions will become stronger and fulfil their promise as envisaged by the Constitution.

5. Conclusion

The South African Constitution created an array of Chapter 9 institutions to safeguard democracy and to promote human rights. Fifteen years after the advent of democracy, it is clear that, while some of these institutions — the Auditor-General, the Electoral Commission and, to some degree, the Human Rights Commission — have performed their role relatively well, others have not. Chapter 9 institutions find themselves precariously positioned between implementing their mandates and possibly angering government officials and institutions whose cooperation they need. They often rely on government and its officials for information, resources and goodwill in order to fulfil their tasks. At the same time, they have to act as watchdogs over these individuals and institutions.

While the ineffectiveness of some of the Chapter 9 institutions might be related to their constitutional positioning, other factors have contributed more to this problem. South Africa's one-party dominant system of democracy and its prevalent political culture seem to have exacerbated the ambivalence about the independence of Chapter 9 institutions. These political factors are also the reason why the need to appoint credible and brave individuals who will act without fear, favour or prejudice against the powerful and well-connected in society has not been fully acknowledged. Given the dominance of the ruling party in the National Assembly and the limited public involvement in the appointment processes, not all office bearers of Chapter 9 institutions are fearless and independent-minded individuals prepared to take on powerful institutions or individuals. In addition, there seems to be confusion among the Commissioners about their role vis-à-vis the legislature and the executive.

The report by the Ad Hoc Committee on the Review of Chapter 9 and Associated Institutions clarified many of these issues and made several useful proposals to bolster the work of Chapter 9 institutions. The Committee reaffirmed the need for the independence of Chapter 9 institutions. It countenanced a limited role for the legislature and the executive regarding oversight over and involvement in the day-to-day running of these institutions. Unfortunately, the report has not (as yet) found favour with these two branches of government and most of its recommendations have not been debated or implemented.

References

Legislation
Constitution of the Republic of South Africa, 1996.

Cases
Committee for Justice and Liberty & Others v National Energy Board (1976) 68 DLR (3d) 716.

Doctors for Life International v Speaker of the National Assembly 2006 (12) BCLR 1399 (CC).

Independent Electoral Commission v Langeberg Municipality 2001 (9) BCLR 883 (CC).

New National Party of South Africa v Government of the RSA 1999 (5) BCLR 489 (CC).

President of the Republic of South Africa & Others v South African Rugby Football Union & Others 1999 (4) SA 147 (CC); 1999 (7) BCLR 725 (CC).

US v Jordan 49 F3d 152 (5th Cir 1995).

Valente v The Queen [1985] 2 SCR 273 (SCC).

Van Rooyen & Others v S & Others 2002 (8) BCLR 810 (CC).

Articles, books, chapters in books and other works

Brooks, H. 2004. The dominant party system: Challenges for South Africa's second decade of democracy. EISA Occasional Paper No 25.

Corder, H., Jagwanth, S. & Soltau, F. 1999. Report on parliamentary oversight and accountability.

Da Costa, W.J. 2006. Public Protector stand-off set to go to court. *The Star*, 7 August. Available at http://www.iol.co.za/index.php?set_id=1&click_id=13&art_id=vn20 060807000151289C430422&newslett=1&em=26506a6a20060807ah. Accessed 30 September 2010.

Giliomee, H. 1998. South Africa's emerging dominant-party regime. *Journal of Democracy*, 9(4): 128–142.

Govender, K. 2007. The reappraisal and restructuring of chapter 9 institutions. *South African Public Law*, 22: 190–209.

Murray, C. 2006. The Human Rights Commission et al: What is the role of South Africa's chapter 9 institutions? *Potchefstroom Electronic Review*, 1–26.

Parliament of the Republic of South Africa. 2007. *Report of the Ad Hoc Committee on the Review of Chapter 9 and Associated Institutions*. A report to the National Assembly of the Parliament of South Africa, Cape Town, South Africa. Available at http://www. parliament.gov.za/content/chapter_9_report.pdf. Accessed 30 September 2010.

Chapter 11

Accountability compromised: Floor crossing in Malawi and South Africa

Lia Nijzink

1. Introduction

Since the 1999 elections, Malawi has witnessed a process of party fragmentation. The relatively stable three-party system, which reflected regional patterns of electoral support, has given way to a period of turbulence in Malawian party politics. In this context, floor crossing has become a hotly contested issue both in the political arena and in Malawian constitutional law. In 2005, President Mutharika, using his power to refer disputes of a constitutional nature to the High Court, brought the matter before the High Court and subsequently appealed to the Malawi Supreme Court of Appeal (MSCA). However, the MSCA's 2007 judgment did not signal the end of the controversy. Floor crossing remained at the core of a political impasse between the executive and the legislature that lasted until President Mutharika and his new party, the Democratic Progressive Party (DPP), won the 2009 elections.

In South Africa, where the ruling African National Congress (ANC) continues to hold a dominant position and occupies two-thirds of the seats in the National Assembly, floor crossing has also been a topic of constitutional controversy. In 2002, when it became possible for elected representatives to defect from their respective parties without losing their seats, several opposition parties decided to bring the matter before the Constitutional Court (CC). In 2009, merely seven years after floor crossing was legalised, the relevant provisions in the South African Constitution were changed again when the National Assembly decided that floor crossing had no place in the South African political system.

Constitutional issues around floor crossing cannot be fully understood without taking into account the broader political context in which defections take place. This chapter seeks to investigate how the floor-crossing phenomenon affects vertical accountability between voters and their elected representatives. The first section will set out the comparative approach of this chapter. The second section will discuss how the concept of floor crossing can best be defined and identify some of the legal issues it raises. The third section will describe and systematically compare the legal framework and political context of floor crossing in South Africa and Malawi. It will then turn to a discussion of the consequences of floor crossing for accountability and note a number of interesting similarities in the practice of floor crossing in both countries. Finally, this chapter will comment on the best way to regulate floor crossing and the interplay between politics and constitutional law.

2. Floor crossing in comparative perspective

Floor crossing is a controversial and highly topical issue not only in Malawi and South Africa, but also in many other young democracies on the continent. Because African politics tends to be leadership-centred and patronage-based (Bratton & Van der Walle 1997; Chabal & Daloz 1999; Burnell 2007; Gyimah-Boadi 2007) rather than ideologically orientated and because party organisations are generally weak (Salih 2003; Salih & Nordlund 2007; chapter 12 in this volume), the primary loyalty of Members of Parliament (MPs) does not necessarily lie with the party under whose flag they got elected. Because MPs often finance their own election campaigns and are under pressure to regard service delivery to their constituency as their main task (Lindberg 2010), loyalty to their party is not necessarily their top priority. This is not to say that MPs in African democracies are defecting from their political parties *en masse*. In fact, many countries in sub-Saharan Africa have explicitly prohibited floor crossing in their Constitutions.[1] However, these floor-crossing provisions often have to be implemented in situations where party boundaries are blurred and fluid, where politicians face incentives that encourage defections, or where a culture of respect for constitutional rules is not strong. Thus, the issue of floor crossing raises an interesting question of constitutional implementation.

This chapter looks at two countries in which the constitutional provisions regarding floor crossing and their implementation have been brought before the highest court: Malawi and South Africa. This comparison is interesting for a number of reasons. First, in Malawi, floor crossing is constitutionally prohibited, while the South African Constitution explicitly allowed elected representatives to cross the floor. Second, Malawi has a first-past-the-post electoral system (FPTP), while South Africa uses a system of proportional representation (PR) based on party lists. Lastly, in Malawi, floor crossing occurs in the context of a fragmented party system and weakly institutionalised parties. By contrast, in South Africa, floor crossing occurred in a context of a one-party dominant system in which

---

1   For example, Namibia, Zambia, Zimbabwe. In Kenya, like in Malawi, defections are permitted but trigger by-elections.

the ruling party is not only dominant in terms of electoral support but is also relatively well organised. This comparison gives us an opportunity to address a number of assumptions and misunderstandings about floor crossing and how it relates to vertical accountability — the relationship between the electorate and elected representatives.

3.   What is floor crossing?

'Floor crossing' refers to a situation in which an MP changes his or her party affiliation during his or her term in office. The term 'floor crossing' has its roots in the Westminster system, where the seating arrangements in the House of Commons reflected what used to be a two-party system. Members of the governing party sat on one side of the Chamber, while MPs of the party in opposition took their seats on the opposite side. In this context, crossing the floor referred to a situation in which an MP changed his or her party affiliation by physically taking a seat on the opposite side of the Chamber. Simply voting with the opposite side did not constitute an instance of floor crossing. Floor crossing was seen as a more permanent change, a change in party membership (Erskine May 2004).

Nowadays, 'floor crossing' does not just denote a situation in which a member changes sides in a two-party system, thus crossing the divide between the government and the opposition. It also applies in systems with more than two parties and, more broadly, refers to any changes in an MP's party affiliation, not only to changes from the governing party to the opposition and vice versa. The term is generally used to denote a situation in which members change their party affiliation before their term expires. Some countries allow such defections to occur (for example, South Africa, albeit for a limited period). In other countries, constitutional provisions prohibit defections altogether or stipulate that a change in party affiliation creates a vacancy in Parliament and thus forces the MP to face a new election (for example, Malawi).

The definition of floor crossing as used above leaves us with a number of questions. Some of these questions are relatively straightforward and have little relevance to relationships of vertical and/or horizontal accountability. Others seem to have a direct impact on the degree of the vertical accountability of elected representatives to the electorate and, to some extent, on the horizontal accountability of the executive to Parliament.

First is the question of the dissolution of Parliament. What happens if an MP's term has expired, Parliament has been dissolved and an MP decides to contest the elections for a different party? As mentioned above, 'floor crossing' generally refers to changes in party affiliation during an MP's term in office. Changing party affiliation after Parliament is dissolved to contest the new elections under a different party flag must not be regarded as floor crossing.

Second is the question of voting behaviour. An MP may abstain from a vote in Parliament while his or her party takes a particular position. Or, an MP may vote differently from his or her party. Historically, the voting behaviour of an MP has in itself not constituted an instance of floor crossing. The change in party affiliation needs to be more permanent than a specific vote and to be expressed in terms of party membership. This interpretation still holds in most countries.[2] Abstaining or voting against the wishes of one's party *per se* does not constitute an instance of floor crossing.

Third is the question of independent MPs. If an MP is elected as an independent and subsequently joins a political party, has he or she crossed the floor? What about an MP who belongs to a party and then resigns from that party and declares him or herself independent? In Malawi, these questions have been raised in court and answered in the affirmative by the MSCA.[3] As is clear from the judgment, these questions relate directly to the accountability relationship between an elected representative and his or her voters. Thus, they cannot be answered without considering the institutional architecture of representative democracy, in particular the nature of the electoral system (see section 4.2. of this chapter).

Fourth is the distinction between existing and new political parties and between parties inside and outside Parliament. Does an MP only cross the floor if he or she leaves his party and joins another party that already exists? What about joining or starting a new party? Similarly, does an MP only cross the floor if he or she joins another party that is already represented in Parliament or does an MP also cross the floor if he or joins a party that does not have any parliamentary seats? Related to these questions is the distinction between political parties and other political organisations. Does one cross the floor by joining a political organisation that has not (yet) been registered as a party? Again, these questions are directly relevant to the accountability relationship between MPs and the electorate and cannot be answered without taking into account the institutional architecture of representation, that is, the electoral and party systems.

Finally, there is the question of party coalitions, mergers and divisions. Floor crossing relates to individual MPs changing parties, while party mergers and divisions create new political parties out of existing ones and alliances or coalitions between parties often blur party boundaries and change party policies.

---

2   India is an exception: MPs need their party's permission to vote or abstain against the wishes of the party. Alternatively, the party needs to condone the MP's voting behaviour after the fact. If the voting behaviour is not permitted or condoned the MP is deemed to have crossed the floor.

3   *In the Matter of Presidential Reference of a Dispute of a Constitutional Nature under Section 89(1)(h) of the Constitution and In the Matter of Section 65 of the Constitution and In the Matter of the Question of the Crossing of the Floor by Members of the National Assembly*, MSCA Presidential Reference Appeal No 44 of 2006 (unreported).

They all give rise to similar questions of vertical accountability. Ideally, party members are involved in decisions about alliances, mergers and/or divisions and party leaders are accountable to their members and the electorate for major changes in the political landscape. The political developments in South Africa and Malawi that led to floor crossing (to be discussed in section 4) show how closely related floor crossing and party changes are. The South African example also demonstrates that the rules around party mergers and coalitions need to be consistent with the rules around floor crossing.

4.   Malawi and South Africa compared

4.1.   Legal framework: Enabling versus restrictive

The interim Constitution of South Africa[4] included an anti-defection clause, which stipulated that: 'A member of the National Assembly shall vacate his or her seat if he or she ceases to be a member of the party which nominated him or her as a member of the National Assembly.'[5] At the same time, the interim Constitution allowed for the easy removal of this ban on floor crossing by way of an Act of Parliament setting out how membership of the legislature could be retained after a loss of party membership, a party merger or a party subdivision. Such legislation to enable floor crossing was not expected to follow the procedure of a constitutional amendment provided that it was passed 'within a reasonable period'[6] after the final Constitution[7] took effect. As no such legislation was adopted, the anti-defection clause remained firmly in place until 2003 when it was removed by way of a constitutional amendment.[8]

The political developments that led to the removal of the anti-defection clause centred on the imminent demise of the New National Party (NNP) — the former ruling party of the apartheid era — and political alliances that were formed to gain control of the Western Cape. After the 1994 elections, the ANC became the ruling party in seven provinces; while the Western Cape was one of the two provinces not governed by the former liberation movement. The NNP took control of the Western Cape provincial government but lost its majority in the province in 1999, forcing it to enter into a coalition government. The NNP formed a coalition with the Democratic Party (DP) and the two parties subsequently decided to contest the local government elections in 2000 under the joint banner of the Democratic Alliance (DA). Because the ban on floor

---

4   Constitution of the Republic of South Africa Act 200 of 1993.
5   Section 43(b) of the 1993 Constitution.
6   Section 23A of Schedule 2 to the 1993 Constitution.
7   Constitution of the Republic of South Africa, 1996.
8   Constitution Tenth Amendment Act of 2003.

crossing prevented elected representatives of the two constituent parties in the national and provincial legislatures to change their party membership without losing their seats, a full party merger was impossible. In any event, soon cracks started to appear in the new political formation and the ANC saw an opportunity to split the DA and gain control of the Western Cape provincial government by entering into an alliance with the NNP. The NNP agreed and suspended its participation in the DA. At the provincial and national levels, this switch was possible because its representatives were elected on an NNP ticket, but at the local level, the NNP members were trapped. They were elected on a DA ticket and withdrawing from the new party would have meant losing their seats. Thus, in order to effect the new ANC-NNP agreement at all levels of government, the ban on floor crossing had to be lifted.[9]

In 2002, a package of laws[10] was passed amending the anti-defection clause for public representatives at the national, provincial and municipal levels. These amendments created a legal framework that enabled and regulated defections. Floor crossing would be permitted during two window periods of 15 days, one in the second and another in the fourth year after an election. Members would only be allowed to cross the floor if a 10 per cent threshold was satisfied. In other words, in order to defect, a Member would need at least 10 per cent of the elected representatives of his or her own party to cross with him or her. Thus, in a party with 30 elected representatives, 3 Members would have to defect in order for them to retain their seats. In a party with 10 elected representatives or less, a Member would be free to cross the floor without any support from colleagues. Obviously, this threshold protected the bigger parties from defections and left the smaller parties vulnerable.[11]

One of the smaller opposition parties, the United Democratic Movement (UDM), challenged this legislation in the Cape High Court, which halted the implementation of the legislation and referred the matter to the Constitutional Court. The UDM, joined by three other opposition parties — the African Christian Democratic Party (ACDP), the Inkatha Freedom Party (IFP) and the Pan Africanist Congress of Azania (PAC) — and two non-governmental organisations (NGOs) that intervened in the case as friends of the court, argued that the floor-crossing legislation was unconstitutional. Their main argument was

---

9   For more on these political developments, see Nijzink and Jacobs (2000), Nijzink (2005) and Booysen (2006).

10 This package consisted of the Constitution Eighth Amendment Act of 2002, the Constitution Ninth Amendment Act of 2002; the Local Government Municipal Structures Amendment Act 20 of 2002 and the legislation envisaged by section 23A of Schedule 2 to the 1993 Constitution, i.e. the Loss or Retention of Membership of National and Provincial Legislatures Act 22 of 2002.

11 The 10 per cent threshold would not be applied during the initial 15-day period of floor crossing that would begin immediately after the amendments came into force.

that the floor-crossing provisions were inconsistent with the founding values of the Constitution, because the purpose of the legislation was illegitimate — based on political expediency — and not in accordance with the constitutional commitment to multiparty democracy and proportional representation.

The Constitutional Court was not persuaded and ruled that the proposed floor-crossing legislation was consistent with the founding values of South Africa's Constitution.[12] It also found that defection in a PR system was not inconsistent with democracy and observed that 'the fact that a particular system operates to the disadvantage of particular parties does not mean it is unconstitutional' (para 47). The court did, however, uphold the UDM's challenge of the Loss or Retention of Membership of National and Provincial Legislatures Act 22 of 2002 on the technical ground that it amended the Constitution by means of ordinary legislation rather than by way of a constitutional amendment. While the interim Constitution allowed for the removal of the anti-defection clause by ordinary legislation within a reasonable period, the CC found that this provision had lapsed and required the change to be made by way of constitutional amendment. As a result, Parliament remedied the defect by passing the Constitution Tenth Amendment Act 2003, thus paving the way for floor crossing by Members of the provincial and national legislatures.

In contrast to South Africa's enabling regime, the 1994 Constitution of Malawi initially aimed to discourage floor crossing of MPs in section 65 (1) thus:

> The Speaker shall declare vacant the seat of any member of the National Assembly who was, at the time of his or her election, a member of one political party represented in the National Assembly, other than by that member alone but who has voluntarily ceased to be a member of that party and has joined another political party represented in the National Assembly.

At the same time, the Constitution ensured the right of MPs to exercise a free vote in parliamentary proceedings by stipulating that MPs cannot lose their seats solely because they have voted against the wishes of their political parties. Section 65(2) is clear: voting behaviour alone does not constitute a defection. What remains less clear is whether these restrictive floor-crossing provisions also apply to MPs who are the sole elected representative of their political party and to independent MPs, that is, MPs who are not affiliated to any particular political party.

As was the case in South Africa, certain political developments related to the realignment of party political loyalties led to a change in the floor-crossing provisions. In Malawi, these developments revolved around internal conflicts

---

12   *United Democratic Movement v President of the Republic of South Africa (No 2)* 2003 (1) SA 495 (CC); 2002 (10) BCLR 1086 (CC).

within the United Democratic Front (UDF), the party that won the 1994 and 1999 elections but failed to win an outright parliamentary majority. In order for the UDF to govern effectively, it had to enter into alliances with opposition parties. These alliances caused major frictions and tensions within the UDF. The tensions reached new heights when Brown Mpinganjira, a founding member of the UDF, resigned from the party and established a new party, the National Democratic Alliance. In an apparent bid to prevent him from holding on to his seat in Parliament and thus give the newly formed party instant representation in the National Assembly, the floor-crossing provision was amended to not only include defections to parties already represented in the National Assembly but to cast the net wider. The Constitution of Malawi Amendment Act 2 of 2001 amended section 65(1) to read as follows:

> The Speaker shall declare vacant the seat of any member of the National Assembly who was at the time of his or her election, a member of one political party represented in National Assembly, other than by that member alone but who has voluntarily ceased to be a member of that party *or* has joined another political party represented in the National Assembly *or* has joined any other political party, *or* association *or* organization whose objectives *or* activities are political in nature. (Emphasis added).

As in the South African case, this amendment was driven more by political expediency than by principle or policy considerations. It served to protect the interests of the UDF, at least in the short term.

The wider net that was cast by the new provision was first challenged in the High Court on the ground that it was inconsistent with the constitutionally guaranteed right to freedom of association. The court held that, because the amendment extended the concept of floor crossing to organisations and parties outside the House, it was indeed inconsistent with the right of MPs to freedom of association and therefore unconstitutional and invalid.[13] The effect of the judgment was that the floor-crossing ban as originally enacted in 1994 was again in effect. Although this case was not appealed against, the floor-crossing saga did not end here.

In 2005, the turbulence in Malawian party politics reached new heights when President Mutharika, elected in 2004 on a UDF ticket, left the party that brought him to power and formed his own new party, the DPP, which had no representation in the National Assembly. As a survival strategy, the President started to co-opt MPs not only to join his Cabinet but also to join his party. A wave of defections followed causing a grave deterioration in the relations

---

13 *Registered Trustees of Public Affairs Committee v Attorney General* Civil Cause No 1861 of 2003 (unreported).

between the executive and Parliament to the point of paralysis (see chapter 13 in this volume). In a bid to stop the Speaker from declaring the seats of as many as 85 of the 193 MPs vacant, the President brought the matter before the High Court, using his constitutional right to refer disputes of a constitutional nature to the High Court.[14] The President argued that section 65(1), as amended in 2001, was inconsistent with a number of constitutionally guaranteed political rights and freedoms.[15]

The High Court, sitting as a Constitutional Court, ruled against the President and held that section 65(1) was not inconsistent with any other provisions of the Constitution.[16] The President appealed against the decision. In its judgment of 15 June 2007, the MSCA upheld the decision of the Constitutional Court regarding the constitutionality of section 65 and held further, overruling the *Registered Trustees* case, that the amendment of 2001 was valid.[17] Thus, restrictions on floor crossing again applied not only to MPs defecting to another party in the House but also to MPs joining political parties not represented in Parliament or any organisation of a political nature.

Two issues are worth mentioning here because they were particularly relevant to the political predicament the President found himself in. In order to avoid having their seats declared vacant, MPs who wanted to support Mutharika declared themselves independent before pledging their support to the President's new party. Others simply took up a position in his Cabinet often against the explicit wishes of their own parties. Thus, the MSCA was also asked to determine the status of independent candidates with regard to floor crossing. Does it constitute an instance of floor crossing if independents cross to a party in or outside Parliament? What about MPs who leave their party, declare themselves independents, and then cross to a party outside Parliament? Similarly, is it floor crossing if an MP accepts a ministerial appointment from a President who belongs to another political party against the wishes of the MP's own party?

---

14 Section 89(1) of the Constitution of Malawi.

15 Section 32 of the Constitution (which protects freedom of association), section 33 of the Constitution (which protects freedom of conscience), section 35 of the Constitution (which protects freedom of expression) and section 40 of the Constitution (which guarantees political rights).

16 *In the Matter of a Presidential Reference of a Dispute of a Constitutional Nature Under s. 89(1) of the Constitution* Constitutional Cause No 13 of 2005 (unreported).

17 *In the Matter of Presidential Reference of a Dispute of a Constitutional Nature under Section 89(1)(h) of the Constitution and In the Matter of Section 65 of the Constitution and In the Matter of the Question of the Crossing of the Floor by Members of the National Assembly* (note 3 above). The MSCA ruled that the High Court in the *Registered Trustees* case (note 13 above) had in fact no jurisdiction to invalidate the 2001 amendment because it was effected 'following due parliamentary procedures'. This sparked a debate on judicial review in Malawi, see Matumbi (2007); Silungwe (2007).

On the first issue the MSCA ruled unequivocally:

A member of the National Assembly who was elected as a member of a political party and voluntarily decides to resign from that party thereby becoming independent or declaring himself or herself independent and later joins another party, whether that party is represented in the National Assembly or not, crosses the floor.

The second issue is a trickier one. Most MPs who supported the Mutharika government were ministers appointed from the two main opposition parties, the UDF and the Malawi Congress Party (MCP). In a political environment with less unilateral, top-down decision-making and more internal party democracy, this could simply have been regarded as a coalition government. Such appointments do not necessarily need to be restricted. This again shows that questions around party alliances, coalitions and mergers are closely related to questions around floor crossing and rules must be consistent. As it turned out, the MSCA held that the acceptance of a ministerial appointment *per se* did not constitute an instance of floor crossing. Additional evidence would have to show that the MP had defected. Thus, the MSCA wisely left it to the Speaker to determine on a case-by-case basis whether there is enough evidence establishing that an MP who accepts a ministerial appointment has indeed crossed the floor.

Partly because this judgment was advisory in nature, it did nothing to resolve the impasse between the executive and the legislature. It was expected that Parliament would be convened to decide on motions that would ask the Speaker to declare the seats of the affected MPs vacant. However, the President did everything to prevent Parliament from debating this issue, including limiting its sittings and dissolving it prematurely.

The elections of 2009 resulted in the re-election of Mutharika and a parliamentary majority for his DPP. Thus, the impasse around floor crossing resolved itself. However, although it is not as urgent as it was before 2009, the implementation of the restrictions on floor crossing remains problematic. As Patel (chapter 13) has pointed out, some of the 32 MPs who gained a seat in the 2009 elections as independent candidates have since crossed the floor to the DPP, but their seats have not been declared vacant by the Speaker.

4.2. Electoral systems: FPTP versus PR

The courts in Malawi and South Africa have been presented with arguments about the legality of the phenomenon of floor crossing in relation to the electoral system in which it occurs. Most of these arguments revolve around the notion that floor crossing is somehow more appropriate or acceptable in majoritarian systems with single member constituencies than in electoral systems based on proportional representation. A short comparison between the electoral systems of South Africa and Malawi demonstrates the key features that are relevant in this regard.

South Africa's electoral system is based on proportional representation with closed party lists. This means that voters do not vote for a particular MP but cast a vote for a particular party. Before the election, political parties decide on their list of candidates. The relative strength of the parties at the ballot box together with the order of the candidates on the various party lists determines who takes up the 400 seats in the National Assembly. The South African system is peculiar in that political parties allocate constituencies to their MPs after they have been elected. The parliamentary agenda allocates time for constituency work and MPs have set up constituency offices but their constituencies are not part of the electoral system and have no impact on the composition of the National Assembly. The voters in these constituencies do not elect 'their' MP.

In contrast, Malawi has the FPTP electoral system with single member constituencies. In other words, the 193 members of the Malawi National Assembly are elected in 193 constituencies. Voters cast their votes for a candidate in their own constituency. The candidate with the most votes in a particular constituency gets the parliamentary seat. This means that the voters in the constituency decide who gets elected as 'their' MP. Another important feature of the Malawian electoral system is that it allows for independent candidates to contest elections. These are candidates who are not put forward by a particular political party and once elected do not fall under party rules or discipline.

The argument that is advanced in both court cases is summarised by Choudry (2010: 42) as follows:

> Party-list systems of proportional representation fit poorly, at a conceptual level, with floor-crossing, because electoral mandates flow from voters to parties, not to individual members, who only sit in the legislature because of their membership in a party and relative placement on a party list.
>
> ...
>
> On the theory of representation implicit in Westminster parliamentary systems, a member represents, first and foremost, the residents of a geographic constituency. A party identity confers no electoral mandate *per se*, although it might have been critical in obtaining it. Thus, if that member crosses the floor, she has not lost her mandate to sit in the legislature, since that came not from her party, but the electorate.

This distinction suggests that, because constituency systems somehow keep the power of political parties in check, floor crossing may be allowed. Such an argument relies too heavily on a historical understanding of the Westminster system in which political parties play a limited role. This is no longer the case: even in the United Kingdom (UK), most MPs are completely dependent on their political party for selection and nomination as a parliamentary candidate and rely on their party for their election campaign. British MPs owe their election to their political party in much the same degree as MPs in established democracies with systems of proportional representation. Thus, floor crossing is as undesirable. In a situation of overall party discipline, it has only a limited function: to safeguard the freedom of conscience of MPs in exceptional circumstances.

The distinction made by Choudry and used by those who argue that floor crossing is more appropriate in FPTP than PR systems also suggests that there is no place for individual accountability of MPs in PR systems. This line of reasoning ignores the constitutional conventions and conceptual understanding of representation as they have evolved over time in the parliamentary systems of continental Western Europe. In Germany and the Netherlands, for example, which have a mixed and PR electoral system respectively, floor crossing is allowed as a measure of last resort. As in the UK, in a situation of overall party discipline, the freedom to cross the floor while retaining a seat is a last resort option for MPs who have failed to convince their party of their opinion but can, in all conscience, not comply with the party's directions.

So the empirical reality in European democracies shows that in different electoral systems political parties are the main vehicles of representation and floor crossing is allowed as a matter of last resort against overwhelming party discipline.

In all electoral systems (FPTP, PR or mixed), defections before an electoral term has expired must be regarded as a distortion of representation, that is, of the original voter preferences. Therefore, the key question is whether this distortion reflects a change in voter preferences or is at least condoned by the electorate thus making it democratically legitimate. Most MPs who cross the floor will probably claim that they have the support of their voters. The question really is how such claims can best be verified. Again, contrasting FPTP and PR is not helpful here. Electoral accountability demands that floor crossing is followed by a renewed mandate in all electoral systems. Thus, one would need to look at the specifics of the electoral system in question to judge its effect on the degree of vertical accountability. An FPTP system, which requires a by-election in the event of floor crossing, is obviously better for vertical accountability than a system in which voters have to wait until the next scheduled election to express their opinion about such a move.[18] Similarly, a PR party list system that allows voters

---

18   The MP who defected might not even contest the next scheduled election and/or the scheduled election can no longer be regarded as an expression of the voters' opinions about the defection because it is contested on the basis of other topical, nationwide issues.

to express their preference for a particular candidate on the list will leave more room to test whether individuals who cross have the voters' blessings.

In South Africa's PR system, political parties are the vehicles of representation. Voters cannot express a preference for a particular candidate on a party list. However, the legal framework that enabled floor crossing encouraged individual MPs to create new one-member parties in Parliament, thus severely compromising electoral accountability. While protecting the ANC from defections, the 10 per cent threshold left individual MPs from smaller parties free to cross the floor without restrictions. Their constituency allowances travelled with them. In addition, the Public Funding of Represented Political Parties Act 103 of 1997 did not exclude new political parties which gained their representation through floor crossing from the yearly allocations of funds and MPs who formed new one-member parties received additional financial support from funds allocated to party leaders in Parliament. In sum, the design of floor-crossing window periods with a 10 per cent threshold and certain financial advantages created incentives for individual MPs to distort representation without any regard for electoral accountability. As discussed above, there is a small role for floor crossing in PR systems in exceptional circumstances and limited individual accountability of MPs exists especially where voters are able to express their preference for a particular candidate on a party list. The South African mechanism that enabled floor crossing far exceeded that role and undermined rather than bolstered the limited individual accountability of MPs in PR systems.

In FPTP systems, the most effective way to ensure electoral accountability is to require a by-election in case of a defection. However, as the Malawian experience shows, this mechanism is not without its problems. Booysen (2006: 731) has observed that anti-defection limitations are frequently not upheld and often cause more problems than they solve: 'Prohibitions and constraints on floor crossing are often ineffective, if not farcical. Parties and representatives find loopholes and devise strategies to bypass legal and constitutional constraints'. The Malawi case clearly demonstrates how difficult it is to implement restrictions on floor crossing in the context of a highly charged political conflict. Although the court upheld the constitutional restrictions on floor crossing, the required by-elections did not occur and therefore electoral accountability was severely compromised.

Independent MPs in FPTP systems fall outside the realm of party politics and presumably have a direct and slightly different relation with their constituents. Their only mandate is from their voters; they are not at the same time accountable to a political party. Therefore, if they abandon their independent position by joining a political party, there is every reason to put this move to the test immediately and let them face new elections. Malawi has seen a significant rise in the number of independent MPs: from 4 in 1999 to 38 and 32 respectively in 2004 and 2009. Many of them were in fact disgruntled party members who did not get nominated by their parties and decided to stand as independent candidates. Once elected, some got back into the fold of their political party. This use of the position of the independent candidate was facilitated by a legal framework that raised doubt about whether floor-crossing restrictions apply to independents. When the MSCA subsequently clarified the matter, its judgment was not given effect—thus causing a major deficiency in electoral accountability.

All in all, considerations of electoral or vertical accountability are relevant to the issue of floor crossing in both PR and FPTP systems. While in South Africa the problem with electoral accountability mainly arose in relation to the enabling legislative framework of floor crossing, in Malawi the implementation of the floor-crossing legislation was the main obstacle. In both countries the role and strength of political parties and the party system in general is key to further understanding the impact of floor crossing on accountability.

4.3. Party systems: One-party dominance versus party system volatility

Examples in Western Europe show that where political parties are institutionalised and party systems are relatively stable, floor crossing is rare (Veen 2007). Disciplined, responsible and internally democratic parties ensure electoral accountability and, in both PR and FPTP systems, a parliamentary seat is only at the MP's personal discretion as a matter of last resort. It is, in principle, a party seat and floor crossing must be understood within this context. In Malawi and South Africa, however, floor crossing occurred in the context of major party realignments and party system volatility. In these circumstances, when MPs defect *en masse* or repeatedly within one term, ensuring electoral accountability is far more difficult.

Floor crossing can theoretically be democratically legitimate if it more accurately reflects voter preferences than the original election results. Thus, party realignment can, in theory, be a justification for floor crossing. However, in case of major changes in the party political landscape it would be best for reasons of electoral accountability to not resort to floor crossing but simply call new elections in order to put the new party configuration to the test. To design a system that allows for large scale party reconfiguration in a number of predetermined window periods, as happened in South Africa, not only encourages ongoing party system volatility rather than stability, it also shields defectors from accountability to the electorate that new elections would provide. Especially because the political realignment in South Africa was elite-driven rather than a reflection of important shifts in voter preferences, enabling floor crossing was a cynical exercise that compromised electoral accountability rather than enhanced the democratic legitimacy of the elected representatives.

The phenomenon of floor crossing in South Africa is in a number of respects determined by the context of its one-party dominant system. The ANC faced very little resistance when it decided to change the Constitution to allow floor crossing and was in a position to dictate the terms (window periods, 10 per cent threshold) that minimised negative effects to itself and ensured that it would benefit from floor crossing. When floor crossing turned out to be much more controversial than expected and generated negative public opinion, the ANC was also in a position to prohibit floor crossing just as quickly as it had allowed it by passing the Constitution of the Republic of South Africa Fifteenth Amendment Act of 2008. Thus, the context of one-party dominance certainly facilitated the South African experiment with floor crossing, but what was its effect on the party system?

The Constitutional Court observed in the case of *Ex-parte Chairperson of the Constitutional Assembly: In Re Certification of the Constitution of the Republic of South Africa* that the anti-defection clause

> prevents parties in power from enticing members of small parties to defect from the party upon whose list they were elected to join the governing party. If this were permitted it could enable the governing party to obtain special majority which it might not otherwise be able to muster and which is not a reflection of the views of the electorate.[19]

This observation was not too far off the mark. Overall, the ANC benefited the most from floor crossing. It obtained a two-thirds majority in the National Assembly allowing it to amend the Constitution without the support of any other party in Parliament. The DA initially also won MPs but later lost a few to floor crossing. In general, the smaller opposition parties lost MPs and the opposition as a whole was left fragmented. At the provincial level, floor crossing initially changed the balance of power in the two provinces where the ANC was not in power. In the Western Cape, the governing coalition of the ANC and the NNP took over but subsequently lost control of the province to the DA. In KwaZulu-Natal, the ANC acquired a majority and later took over from the IFP as the party in power. Thus, floor crossing enhanced the ANC's dominant status at the national and provincial level and undermined the horizontal accountability institutions that have the potential to keep an ANC-dominated executive in check: the checks and balances provided by the National Assembly and the provinces.

---

19 *In re Certification of the Constitution of the Republic of South Africa, 1996* 1996 (4) SA 744 (CC), 1997 (10) BCLR 1253 (CC), para 187.

Table 11.1: Effects of floor crossing in 2003 and 2007 on party representation in South Africa's National Assembly

	Seats after 1999 elections	Seats after 2003 floor crossing	Floor crossing gain/loss	Seats after 2004 elections	Seats after 2007 floor crossing*	Floor-crossing gain/loss
ANC	266	275	+9	279	287	+8
DA	38**	46	+8	50	47	-3
IFP	34	31	-3	28	24	-4
NNP	28	20	-8	7	-	-7
UDM	14	4	-10	9	6	-3
ACDP	6	7	+1	7	4	-3
FF+	3	3	0	4	4	0
UCDP	3	3	0	3	3	0
PAC	3	2	-1	3	1	-2
FA	2	2	0	-		
AEB	1	-	-1	-		
AZAPO	1	1	0	1	1	0
MF	1	1	0	2	2	0
ADP	-	1	+1	-		
IAM	-	1	+1	-		
ID	-	1	+1	7	5	-2
NA	-	1	+1	-		
PJC	-	1	+1	-		
NADECO					4	+4
APC					2	+2
FD					1	+1
PIM					1	+1
UIF					1	+1
UPSA					1	+1

* This list of seats per party after the 2007 floor crossing excludes the 6 vacancies that existed at the time.

** The DA contested the 1999 elections as the Democratic Party (DP) and changed its name to DA after the merger with the New National party.

Sources: Piombo and Nijzink (2005): *Procedural Developments in the National Assembly*, Issue 7, Item 21. Available at http://oldwww.parliament.gov.za/pls/portal/web.app.APP_NA_STATE_OF_PARTIES?p_page_name=PARLIAMENT_NA. Accessed 30 September 2007.

The table above shows the effects of the window periods for floor crossing in 2003 and again in 2007 on party representation in the National Assembly. During the first window period in 2003, one political party, the *Afrikaner Eendheidsbeweging* (AEB), disappeared from the NA and five new parties were created; all of them with only one member. Only one of these new parties, the Independent Democrats (ID), survived the subsequent 2004 elections. A total of 23 MPs crossed the floor. Comparing the 2004 election results with the seat allocation after the September 2007 window period shows similar results, with a total of 24 seats being affected by floor crossing. After the 2004 elections, one party with representation in the National Assembly disappeared altogether, the NNP. Six political parties represented in the National Assembly after the 2007 window period got their seats during the floor-crossing window period rather than through voter support; four of these newly created parties had only 1 member in the National Assembly. The National Assembly after the 2007 window period included six political parties with only one seat. Of these six one-member parties, only AZAPO and the PAC gained their representation at the ballot box.

As observed in section 4.2, the creation of one-member parties through the mechanism of floor crossing is highly problematic. Not only does this type of party fragmentation complicate the coordination of parliamentary business, it also puts unnecessary strain on the resources of the National Assembly. Moreover, it raises questions about the motives of those politicians who cross the floor to create a new one-member party. They seem to be motivated by financial or other personal advantages rather than ideological or policy considerations.

Interestingly, in the case of Malawi, which has a volatile party system and weakly institutionalised parties, the issue of access to state resources is equally prominent in the analysis of the effect of floor crossing. In Malawi, the first two democratic elections in 1994 and 1999 showed a picture of relative stability. Voting behaviour was largely determined by regional identities, with the UDF gaining its main support from the south, the Alliance for Democracy (AFORD) from the north and MCP finding its support base mainly in the central region (Ferree & Horowitz 2007). However, the seeds for the major turbulence that would follow were already sown because the largest party, the UDF, did not manage to win a parliamentary majority. Thus, a process of shifting party alliances and co-optation of MPs to support the government started. (See chapter 13 in this volume.)

This table shows that there has been a remarkable rise of independents and that the process of party political realignment has led to the demise of AFORD and a sharp decline in the size of the UDF and MCP in Parliament. The table does not show the numerous defections that happened after the 2004 elections when the President decided to defect from the party on whose ticket he was

Table 11.2: Number of seats in Malawi's National Assembly per party, 1994–2009

	1994	1999	2004	2009
DPP	-	-	-	113
UDF	84	93	49	17
MCP	55	66	59	27
AFORD	36	29	6	1
Mgwirizano	-	-	27	-
Independent	-	4	38	32
Invalid	2	-	-	-
Other	-	-	14	3
TOTAL	177	192	193	193

Sources: African Elections Database. Available at http://africanelections.tripod.com/mw.html and, for 2009 election results, *see* Malawi Election Archive of the Electoral Institute for the Sustainability of Democracy in Africa (EISA). Available at http://www.eisa.org.za/WEP/malelectarchive.htm. Both accessed 30 September 2010.

elected. Less unique and more structural circumstances for a wave of defections consisted of manifestations of the internal weakness of political parties: irregular party conventions, manipulated party constitutions and the imposition of candidates by party leaders.

The victory of Mutharika and the convincing majority of the DPP in the 2009 elections suggest that the floor-crossing phenomenon eventually benefited the President and his party. However, despite giving a degree of democratic legitimacy to the President who left his party and started a new one, the victory at the ballot box did nothing to repair the damage that the floor-crossing phenomenon did to the horizontal accountability relationship between the executive and the legislature.

The experience in Malawi shows that by-elections as a mechanism to ensure electoral accountability after floor crossing in FPTP systems is not effective in cases of party system change. One reason is the sheer number of by-elections required. In the context of many African democracies including Malawi, large numbers of by-elections might simply be unaffordable. On the other hand, the benefits of electoral accountability might still outweigh the costs and in the longer term, the disincentive of a by-election could prevent further floor crossing thus promoting party system stability. Another reason for the ineffectiveness of by-elections in situations of party reconfigurations is the implementation problem discussed above. Where major shifts in party loyalties occur the political environment is highly charged and implementation of the restrictions on floor crossing complicated. It may even hold the danger of weakening the rule of law and the position of the judiciary. In the case of Malawi, the floor-crossing legislation remained unimplemented and floor crossing was in the end unrestricted, which bolstered not so much the position of one political party but rather the position and power of the President. If the required by-elections had occurred, they would have provided a fair degree of electoral accountability. However, frequent or large numbers of by-elections resulting from party realignments could easily give rise to voter apathy and erode the trust of constituents in their MP, thus compromising vertical accountability in the long term. In fact, Chinsinga (2006:17) has identified the disenchantment of voters with floor crossing as one of the causes of increasing voter apathy in Malawi.

5. Conclusion

We have seen that the role of floor crossing in PR and FPTP systems is not necessarily different. Specifically in countries where party systems are stable, it serves as a measure of last resort. The phenomenon of floor crossing in South Africa and Malawi served a very different purpose: to accommodate party system change. In South Africa, floor crossing was designed to allow party realignment and gave misplaced opportunities to individual MPs to follow incentives that had little to do with political decisions of conscience. In Malawi, floor crossing was used to remedy internal party problems related to candidate selection in party primaries and to accommodate the establishment of a new governing party but without the mechanism that would ensure electoral accountability: by-elections did not take place. Thus, in both countries floor crossing compromised accountability.

South Africa remedied the situation by abolishing its flawed system and reintroducing the constitutional ban on floor crossing. This probably means that it will not easily consider re-introducing floor crossing as a measure of last resort, although this would introduce a limited degree of individual accountability that could be beneficial for democracy in the context of the country's one party dominant system. In Malawi, the legislative framework could be improved by clarifying the status of the independent MPs: do they cross the floor if they join a particular political party?

In addition to changes in the legislative framework that regulates floor crossing, there is the issue of constitutional implementation in the context of major party realignment. In both countries, this proved controversial and challenging. Constitutional provisions were being called into question and had to be implemented in situations where politicians faced various incentives to defect. In both Malawi and South Africa, the courts were called upon to resolve crucial problems of a political nature and in both cases the role of the court was a reason for cautious optimism. In the South African case, Parliament complied with the CC's judgment and remedied the unconstitutionality. The CC in turn did not get involved in political choices about allowing or prohibiting defections in a system of PR which can best be dealt with by Parliament passing the legislative framework it deems most appropriate. In the case of Malawi, there is also reason for cautious optimism about the role of the courts. Exposure of the courts to political pressure or even interference and a resistance to their rulings by government is a real danger (Von Doepp 2005) but the MSCA asserted itself in the face of the steadily growing power of the executive. This can only be regarded as a victory for horizontal accountability. The remaining problem is a political one in which the implementation of constitutional provisions confirmed by the Court is at stake.

Finally, it has been observed that floor crossing is democratically illegitimate, morally problematic, distorts representation and is an indicator of the weakness of political parties (Van Veen 2007). The developments in both Malawi and South Africa have shown that this is not an exaggeration. To change this, a combination of changes in political culture, conventions and legislative measures might be required. More clarity and perhaps regulation around coalition-building can prevent excessive floor crossing in a situation of minority governments. Strengthening intra-party democracy may assist in preventing floor crossing that is mainly driven by personal gain. Only under certain conditions is there a small but legitimate role for floor crossing in both PR and FPTP systems that can bolster rather than undermine accountability.

References
Legislation
Constitution Eighth Amendment Act of 2002 (South Africa).
Constitution Fifteenth Amendment Act of 2008 (South Africa).
Constitution Ninth Amendment Act of 2002 (South Africa).
Constitution of Malawi Amendment Act 2 of 2001.
Constitution of the Republic of Malawi, 1994.
Constitution of the Republic of South Africa, 1996.
Constitution of the Republic of South Africa, Act 200 of 1993.
Constitution Tenth Amendment Act of 2003 (South Africa).
Local Government Municipal Structures Amendment Act 20 of 2002.
Loss or Retention of Membership of National and Provincial Legislatures Act 22 of 2002.
Public Funding of Represented Political Parties Act 103 of 1997.

Cases

In re Certification of the Constitution of the Republic of South Africa, 1996 1996(4) SA 744 (CC), 1997 (10) BCLR 1253 (CC).

In the Matter of a Presidential Reference of a Dispute of a Constitutional Nature under Sections 89(1)(h) and 86(2) of the Constitution and in the Matter of Impeachment Procedures under Standing Order 84 Constitutional Cause No. 13 of 2005 (unreported).

In the Matter of Presidential Reference of a Dispute of a Constitutional Nature under Section 89(1)(h) of the Constitution and In the Matter of Section 65 of the Constitution and In the Matter of the Question of the Crossing of the Floor by Members of the National Assembly, MSCA Presidential Reference Appeal No. 44 of 2006 (unreported).

Registered Trustees of the Public Affairs Committee v Attorney General & Another Civil Cause No. 1861 of 2003 (unreported).

United Democratic Movement v President of the Republic of South Africa (No 2). 2003 (1) SA 495 (CC); 2002 (10) BCLR 1086 (CC).

Articles, books, chapters in books and other works

Booysen, S. 2006. The will of the parties versus the will of the people? Defections, elections and alliances in South Africa. *Party Politics,* 12(6): 727–746.

Bratton, M. & Van de Walle, N. 1997. *Democratic Experiments in Africa: Regime Transitions in Comparative Perspective.* Cambridge: Cambridge University Press.

Burnell, P. 2007. Political parties in Africa: different functional and dynamic? In Basedau, M., Erdmann, G. & Mehler A. (eds). *Votes, Money and Violence: Political Parties and Elections in Sub-Saharan Africa.* Uppsala: Nordic Africa Institute, 63–81.

Chabal, P. & Daloz, J.P. 1999. *Africa Works: Disorder as Political Instrument.* Indianapolis: Indiana University Press.

Chinsinga, B. (2006) *Voter Apathy in Malawi: A Critical Appraisal.* The Hague: Netherlands Institute for Multiparty Democracy.

Choudry, S. 2010. 'He had a mandate': The South African Constitutional Court and the African National Congress in a dominant party democracy. *Constitutional Court Review,* Forthcoming. Available at http://papers.ssrn.com/sol3/papers.cfm?abstract_id=1651332. Accessed 1 November 2010.

Erskine May, T. 2004. *Parliamentary Practice.* 23 ed. Butterworths: LexisNexis.

Ferree, K. & Horowitz, J. 2007. Identity voting and the regional census in Malawi. Afrobarometer Working Paper 72. Available at http://www.afrobarometer.org/papers/AfropaperNo72.pdf. Accessed 15 December 2007.

Gyimah-Boadi, E. 2007. Political parties, elections and patronage: Random thoughts on neo-patrimonialism and African democratisation. In Basedau, M., Erdmann, G. & Mehler A. (eds). *Votes, Money and Violence: Political Parties and Elections in Sub-Saharan Africa.* Uppsala: Nordic Africa Institute, 21–33.

Lindberg, S.I. 2010. What accountability pressures do MPs in Africa face and how do they respond? Evidence from Ghana. *Journal of Modern African Studies,* 48(1): 117–142.

Matumbi, B.P. 2007. The fallacy of the presumption of perfection: the presidential reference on section 65 and its ramifications. *Malawi Law Journal*, 1(2): 247–257.

Nijzink, L. & Jacobs, S. 2000 Provincial elections and government formation in the Western Cape: The politics of polarisation. *Politikon*, 27(1): 37–49.

Nijzink, L. 2005. Parliament and the electoral system: How are South Africans being represented?' In Piombo, J. & Nijzink, L. (eds). *Electoral Politics in South Africa: Assessing the First Democratic Decade.* New York: Palgrave Macmillan, 64–86.

Piombo, J. & Nijzink, L. (eds) 2005. *Electoral Politics in South Africa: Assessing the First Democratic Decade.* New York: Palgrave Macmillan.

Salih, M. 2003. *African Political Parties: Evolution, Institutionalism and Governance.* London: Pluto Press.

Salih, M. & Nordlund, P. 2007. *Political Parties in Africa: Challenges for Sustained Multiparty Democracy.* Stockholm: International Institute for Democracy and Electoral Assistance.

Silungwe, C.M. 2007. The courts' power of judicial review, composition of the National Assembly and the presidential reference on section 65. *Malawi Law Journal*, 1(2): 235–246.

Veen, H.J. 2007. Strong party system as a condition for representative democracy. In *The Impact of Floor crossing on Party Systems and Representative Democracy.* Johannesburg: Konrad Adenauer Stiftung, 11–18.

VonDoepp, P. 2005. The problem of judicial control in Africa's neo-patrimonial democracies: Malawi and Zambia. *Political Science Quarterly*, 120(2): 275–301.

Chapter 12

Democracy within political parties: The state of affairs in East and Southern Africa[1]

Augustine T. Magolowondo

1. Introduction

Today's representative democracy requires intermediary actors between the state and society as well as institutional mechanisms for the articulation of diverse views and policy preferences. Although there are a number of intermediaries that claim to connect the people to the state, it is becoming increasingly axiomatic that political parties are indispensable in contemporary democracies. Indeed, as Heywood (2002:73) has argued, political parties are 'so fundamental to the operation of modern politics that their role and significance are often taken for granted'.

Although the difference between political parties and other political interest groups is not always clear, political parties are distinguishable by their primary goal, which is to contest and capture state power through peaceful means (Matlosa 2007). It is this distinctive feature of political parties that makes them important institutions in a democratic society. They are the main vehicle for political representation, the primary mechanism for the organisation of government and an important channel for maintaining democratic accountability. Paradoxically, while political parties occupy a central place in contemporary democracies, their internal functioning and management has been under-researched. We do not know enough about the way political parties themselves are held to account: are they democratic in the way they run their affairs?

The question of the internal functioning and management of political parties is particularly pertinent in emerging democracies in Africa, where

---

1   This chapter is partly based on a report the author compiled for the Netherlands Institute for Multiparty Democracy (NIMD) in 2007 (Magolowondo 2007). An earlier version of this chapter was presented at the Regional Conference on the Functioning and Management of Political Parties in Eastern and Southern Africa, jointly organised by the Centre for Multiparty Democracy of Malawi and the NIMD on 13–14 March 2008, Blantyre, Malawi. The views expressed in this chapter do not in any way reflect the position or views of NIMD.

formal institutions co-exist with and often are subsumed by informal norms and power relations. In this context, how is the internal democratic life of a political party secured? To what extent do formal mechanisms to enhance intra-party democracy matter in the context of the pervasive leader-centred patronage networks that seem to characterise democratic politics in Africa?

2. The concept of internal party democracy

Like democracy in general, intra-party democracy is a concept that is difficult to define. Maravall (2008: 158) defines it as 'the capacity of party members to control their leaders'. According to Svåsand (2008: 5), this control is exercised 'prospectively, as in the selection of leaders and party policy, and retrospectively, when leaders are rewarded or sanctioned for past actions'. These definitions seem somewhat limited since democracy includes not only elections and holding leaders to account but also responsiveness.

Dahl (1971) defined democracy[2] as a political system in which those who govern are continuously responsive to the preferences and aspirations of those who are governed. Although Dahl was not specifically concerned with democracy within political parties, his definition is relevant here albeit with some modifications. According to Dahl (1971: 2), for a system to be democratic, it has to fulfil three fundamental conditions: citizens must be able to *formulate their preferences*, they must *express those preferences* freely among themselves and to the government either as individuals or in groups, and those *preferences must weigh equally* in the conduct of government.

Thus, internal party democracy could be defined as the extent to which a party subscribes to and abides by basic democratic principles. First, in a democratic party, party leaders are *responsive* and *accountable* to party members. Second, there is sufficient *internal political contestation* or *competition* as well as *participation* by members in the affairs of the party in order to enable party members to formulate their preferences and express those preferences both among themselves and to the party leadership. Third, a democratic party is *tolerant* of and *accommodates* divergent views and preferences in the conduct of party affairs.

Unlike democracy as such, intra-party democracy generates frequent questions about its desirability and feasibility. Is internal party democracy desirable? Is it a requisite for the effective functioning of a political party or merely an ideal to strive towards? If we agree that the primary aim of political

---

2   Dahl prefers to use the term *polyarchy*. He makes a distinction between the ideal democracy, and what exists in practice, *polyarchy*, and argues that the more a *polyarchy* will satisfy the necessary conditions, the more it will approximate the ideal democracy.

parties is to capture state power, is internal party democracy an asset or a liability? Svåsand (2008: 2) observes that scholars have long questioned both the desirability and feasibility of internal party democracy, arguing that 'oligarchic control by the party leaders of their party organisation is indispensable for the well-being of a democratic polity. ... leaders must escape control of their followers if they are to fulfil their broader role as the principal decision-makers in the political community'. Furthermore, the success of a party in terms of winning elections, it has been argued, does not necessarily depend on it being internally democratic. Intra-party democracy may in fact be a liability to electoral success.

However, precisely because the main concern of political parties is to win elections, a normative approach to intra-party democracy, which emphasises the educational and other beneficial effects of internal party democracy, seems to be more appropriate. If political parties are to be regarded as pillars of democracy and as a vital link between individual citizens and elected representatives, they must be democratic themselves (Magolowondo 2007; Teorell 1999). Political parties which are internally democratic are better able to aggregate and represent the interests of citizens, which in turn enhances the democratic system as a whole. Such political parties also serve as an arena where their members are able to learn and practise basic democratic tenets such as participation in decision-making and choice of leaders, electoral competition, and respect for the views of others. This, in turn, strengthens the political parties concerned. These benefits can then be transferred to other levels of society, thus strengthening the democratic system (Svåsand 2009; Scarrow 2005). In other words, democracy within parties should be regarded as a valuable asset for democratic societies. A normative approach seems to be especially relevant in Africa's emerging democracies, where it might assist in developing and deepening democracy.

3. Mechanisms to implement internal party democracy

What do we know about intra-party democracy in Africa? Political parties in Africa have only recently become the subject of academic inquiries (Erdmann 2005; Erdmann 2007; Salih & Nordlund 2007) and direct external support in development cooperation programmes (Burnell 2000a, 2000b; NIMD 2004; Carothers 1999). What follows is an overview of the formal mechanisms that shape the internal functioning and management of political parties in East and Southern Africa. The focus is mainly on political parties in Malawi, Mozambique, South Africa, Tanzania, Zambia and, to some extent, Kenya. This overview is partly based on work done by the International Institute for Democracy and Electoral Assistance (IDEA) in cooperation with the Electoral Institute for the

Sustainability of Democracy in Africa (EISA).[3] The analysis will focus on party constitutions, membership, decision-making, party leaders and party finances.

3.1. Party constitutions

All the political parties under review have written rules and regulations to govern their internal functioning. Key among these written rules are party constitutions. Some political parties also have codes of conduct to regulate the behaviour of party leaders and, in some instances, party members. Some party constitutions and regulations are rather extensive. The constitution of the African National Congress (ANC) in South Africa is one of the most extensive party constitutions in the region. It includes an oath of allegiance that party members swear before being accepted as full members. The ANC constitution also contains various procedures on party discipline and conflict management. In Tanzania, the ruling *Chama Cha Mapinduzi* (CCM) is also said to have 'well designed and elaborate regulations governing almost every aspect of the party' (Shayo 2005: 13).

While all political parties seem to have written rules and regulations, including party constitutions, the implementation and enforcement of these rules is not uniform. Some parties strictly implement their own rules while others do so selectively or fail to do so altogether. There are many incidences of political parties not respecting their own constitutions, especially when it comes to convening party conventions and procedures for candidate selection. A glaring example of the violation of a party constitution is what happened in Malawi when Chakufwa Chihana, president of the Alliance for Democracy (AFORD), died. AFORD's constitution clearly stipulated that in such a situation, the party's vice president automatically assumes the presidency until a party convention is held. However, the vice president in question hailed from the southern part of Malawi while the country's northern region is considered the party's stronghold. This caused senior party members to sideline the vice president. It took an intervention of the High Court to remind them that they were in violation of their own legally binding party constitution.

Such cases are not unique to Malawi. Whether these kinds of violations are challenged by party cadres depends on various factors, including the space that party leaders create for members to express themselves without risking negative consequences.

---

3   An important component of the IDEA-EISA Programme of Research and Dialogue on Political Parties focused on political parties' internal functioning and structure. The programme included a number of countries, but this chapter has primarily used the research reports on Malawi, Mozambique, South Africa, Tanzania and Zambia — see references.

3.2. Party members

Members are the foundation of a political party. They select party leaders who must be accountable to them for their actions. Curiously, accurate and reliable statistics on party membership are hard to come by in the region. Almost all political parties in East and Southern Africa claim to have national membership registers. Some parties also report having membership registers at a regional or district level. Membership is generally open. The most common restriction relates to age, as most parties restrict membership to adults (either 16 or 18 years and older). However, only political parties in South Africa and the ruling parties in Tanzania and Mozambique seem to have institutionalised membership registers. The ANC in South Africa, for instance, has computerised membership data capturing subscription payments and classifying members as being 'in good standing' or not. Given the general lack of accurate membership data elsewhere, it is difficult to establish the demographics of party membership, such as the number of women each political party has, or the ethnic or racial composition of each party. This, in turn, has important implications for the inclusiveness of the political parties in the region where gender, ethnicity, regionalism and race matter to democratic consolidation.

In terms of party members' rights and obligations, most political parties expect their members to make a contribution. This often takes the form of a fixed minimum fee per annum. In addition, members are expected to perform some voluntary work for the party and adhere to the party's rules, including rules on when and how to discipline members. In return, some parties have clearly set out members' rights, for example, in relation to voting at party meetings. However, political parties generally appear not to have any formal or written guidelines for party members on how to articulate their views and preferences on party matters.

Our overview further shows that the communication of political parties with their members is mainly top-down and mostly in the form of meetings and rallies where party leaders speak. Electronic communication via a website or an e-newsletter is also used, but this is largely limited to political parties in South Africa. The opposition Democratic Alliance (DA), for instance, publishes a weekly online letter, the *SA Today*, from the party leader. The ruling ANC publishes the *ANC Today* and *Umrabulo*. Individual correspondence of members with their political parties is rare. Political parties in countries with high illiteracy levels face a special challenge when it comes to connecting with their members, especially on issues of policy. Policy documents are predominantly written in English because many parties lack the resources to provide mother-tongue translations for their members. The limited use of policy documents within political parties further diminishes the extent to which party leaders can be held to account on key policy decisions.

3.3. Decision-making within parties

The highest decision-making body in all the political parties under study is the party convention, sometimes called national conference, party congress or general assembly. Generally, party conventions are made up of a wide range of delegates and, as such, are crucial for the democratic life of a political party. In most cases, decisions taken by party conventions are binding. In many political parties, the convention has the power to make policy decisions and amend the party's constitution. Furthermore, in many parties, the top leadership, often called the national executive committee, is elected at the convention.

For many political parties in East and Southern Africa, delegates to the party convention are selected based on two considerations: geographical balance, that is, representation across party structures (regions, districts, constituencies, wards/areas/branches) as well as demographic representation of different societal groups, most commonly women, the youth and professional affiliations. Among the parties reviewed, South Africa's DA adds a third consideration: the party's electoral strength across South Africa's nine provinces (Lodge & Scheidegger 2005). The party tries to ensure that the number of delegates from a specific province is proportional to the party's electoral success in that specific province in terms of its vote share in the elections preceding the party convention.

The frequency of party conventions varies, ranging from annually to once every four years. In practice, however, some political parties do not hold the conventions as required by their constitutions. As a matter of fact, some political parties have been founded and disbanded without holding a convention, while others have taken years to call a general national conference. Admittedly, party conventions are costly: they require finances and organisational skills and structures. The success of the ANC in holding national conferences has been attributed in part to the fact that delegates are financially supported by their respective party structures. In their study on political activism within the ANC, Lodge and Scheidegger (2005) found that local branches were engaged in fundraising activities in most cases to support the expenses of delegates travelling to provincial and national conferences. It appears that members see great value in the party convention and regard it as a way of influencing the policy direction and leadership of the party. Consequently, they are willing to contribute to party conventions in this way.

With regard to policy development, almost all parties have either specialised committees or think tanks that take the lead in policy-making. Party committees tend to have access to and make use of various sources of information and data, including surveys and opinion polls. Parties differ greatly as to who has the authority to make policy decisions. In some parties, such as the ANC, party policies need to be approved by the party convention in order to be binding. In other parties, including many breakaway or new political parties like the Democratic Progressive Party (DPP) of Malawi, the national executive has the final say.

3.4. Party leaders

Most party constitutions provide for elected party leadership, and require members of national executive or management committees and, in many cases, members of regional or district committees to be elected. Procedures for electing party leaders differ amongst parties, but the most common system is a simple majority system. Only a few parties require an absolute majority (50 per cent + 1 one vote) for election to the post of party president. As already observed above, in most cases national party leaders, including the party president, are elected at the party convention. It should however be pointed out that, especially in newly established parties, the tradition of electing people to senior leadership positions as prescribed in their respective party constitutions is yet to be institutionalised. Part of the problem lies in the fact that parties simply fail to hold conventions. Vacancies created by defections or deaths are often filled by appointment, which in turn strengthens the position of the party president or chairperson, who tends to fill the vacancies with his or her own loyalists. Unfortunately, these practices make it difficult for party members to question senior party leaders or to hold them to account.

Another important element of internal party democracy is the selection of a party's candidates for presidential, parliamentary or local elections. In all the parties under review, candidates for party electoral positions must fulfil a number of requirements. For example, candidates for presidential elections — in those countries where the President is directly elected — have generally to fulfil requirements related to age (often at least 35 years), educational qualification and party membership. In some parties, those wanting to contest presidential elections are further required to collect a certain amount of signatures — in the case of the CCM of Tanzania, for example, at least 25 signatures from 10 regions in Tanzania including two regions on Zanzibar are required (Shayo 2005). Party candidates for parliamentary or local elections must satisfy similar requirements, although the age limit is often lower (minimum of 21 years) and the number of signatures, where required, is lower. Although there appear to be no limits on the number of times someone can contest parliamentary or local elections for a political party, all countries included in this overview have constitutional term limits for the President. The presidential term limit relates to a candidate who successfully becomes President and serves the constitutionally prescribed maximum number of terms (usually two).

Even when a candidate has fulfilled all the requirements, many political parties have screening or vetting procedures either at the level of the national executive committee or the party convention. It is difficult to assess how transparent these screening processes are, when they actually occur and what happens when vetting authorities are not satisfied with a particular candidate. The experience in some countries shows that party screening creates an opportunity for party leaders to impose their preferred candidates on constituencies. In Malawi's 2004 and 2009 national elections, for instance, some party leaders imposed particular candidates on their parties which resulted in a number of disgruntled party members contesting and winning parliamentary seats as independent candidates (see chapter 13 in this volume). Similarly, the decision by the leader of Malawi's United Democratic Front (UDF) to unilaterally appoint the party's presidential candidate for the 2004 elections resulted in some senior members leaving the party to either form their own political parties or stand as independents (see chapter 13 in this volume).

It is clear that, generally, a position within party structures and good contacts with senior party leaders increase one's chances of becoming a candidate. Especially in countries with the first-past-the-post single member constituency system, a candidate's wealth is also an important factor.

Despite regional protocols on gender representation, very few political parties in East and Southern Africa have established quotas for women and/or youth. As an exception, the ANC has consistently applied a quota for women when preparing the list of candidates for parliamentary elections and ensured that every third position on the list is taken up by a woman candidate. By contrast, the DA in South Africa is generally not in favour of this kind of affirmative action (Lodge & Scheidegger 2005) although interestingly, both its current leader (Hellen Zille) and one of its three chairpersons (Anchen Dreyer) are women. Another South African party that has a quota for women is the United Democratic Movement (UDM), although the party reports that it has difficulties in filling its 50 per cent quota on the party list of candidates for parliamentary elections. In Zambia, the United Party for National Development (UPND) also decided on a 50 per cent quota for women. In Mozambique, *Frente de Libertacão de Moçambique* (FRELIMO)'s quota for women stands at 40 per cent of the party list for parliamentary elections. In addition, FRELIMO has a quota for the youth (20 per cent) and former combatants (10 per cent).

The degree of the inclusiveness of a political party is an important element of its internal democracy. It defines the extent to which a party takes deliberate measures to ensure the participation of less privileged groups such as women and young people in party affairs. While many political parties do not have official quotas for women and/or youth, they have within their organisations, structures like a women's league and a youth wing. The influence of women and youth leagues, however, varies considerably from party to party. The ANC Youth League, for example, is quite influential within the ANC. In other parties, the women and youth wings are largely symbolic as power remains with senior male politicians who, in some instances, paradoxically hold the position of 'Director of the Youth'.

3.5. Party finances

Party finances have a significant impact on the internal functioning of political parties. It is therefore important to establish the sources of funding that political parties have as well as how those funds are utilised and accounted for. With regard to funding sources, most political parties under review have access to state funding. In Malawi, Mozambique, South Africa, Tanzania and (in future) Kenya, the state provides financial support to political parties represented in Parliament. In Zambia, by contrast, the state does not provide public funds to parties. In the countries where state funding is available, political parties acknowledge that it constitutes a significant source of income.

Another important source of revenue is membership fees and donations. In most political parties, however, annual membership fees are very low and therefore more of a symbolic gesture on the part of members than a significant contribution to the financial survival of the party. Thus, it would appear that besides state funding, (private) donations constitute the main financial basis of many political parties in East and Southern Africa. These donations come in different forms. Some are voluntary contributions by individual party members, often those in leadership positions. Other donations are mandatory. Some political parties require that party members who are serving as cabinet ministers or Members of Parliament (MPs) make a financial contribution to the party. This is the tradition in the ANC and the DA in South Africa. In some political parties, for example the Movement for Multiparty Democracy (MMD) in Zambia and the UDM in South Africa, party members are obliged to make a donation if they want to stand as the party's candidate for elections. Whilst the mandatory contribution in return for a candidate position may be considered an innovative way of diversifying the party's sources of income, it can prevent deserving party members from contesting in elections on behalf of the party and promote factionalism, the buying of positions and corruption within the party.

It would appear that much of the funding that political parties raise or receive is spent on election campaigns and salaries for administrative staff and other salaried party positions. However, specific information on how parties spend their funds is hard to come by. In some instances, political parties are required by law to submit financial statements to designated public institutions in return for public funding. This can be the Electoral Commission, as is the case in South Africa, or the Ministry of Home Affairs, as in Tanzania. Internally, some parties submit financial reports to their party convention. In cases where conventions are not regularly held, it is unclear how party members get informed about party finances. In all cases, party finances are not administered and managed in a manner that is open even to party members.

4. The nature of African party politics

This overview of formal measures shows that many political parties in East and Southern Africa have established some structures, rules and mechanisms that could facilitate internal party democracy. However, the question arises: why are some parties more successful than others in building a culture of internal democracy?

An important consideration is the nature of the political parties in relation to their own history. The political parties under review can be divided into three categories. The first are parties that are closely associated with liberation or nationalist struggles in the countries concerned. These are the oldest political parties in the region, although some may have officially registered as political parties only at the beginning of the 1990s. These are *first generation* political parties. Today, the number of parties of this generation is diminishing. The once all powerful UNIP (United Independence Party) in Zambia, for instance, is on the verge of extinction, with only two MPs left. Similarly, the Malawi Congress Party (MCP), which led Malawi to independence and ruled the country for over 30 years, has seen its political dominance dwindle with each election since 1994 when it lost power. On the other hand, in Tanzania, Mozambique and South Africa, political parties of the first generation (CCM, FRELIMO and ANC respectively) continue to be in power and dominant.

The second category includes *second generation* political parties, that is, those that were formed in the period after independence but before the re-introduction of multiparty politics. Political parties in this category emerged as pro-democracy pressure groups, which in many instances were fighting the nationalist parties that had established authoritarian regimes. These pro-democracy pressure groups were operative either in exile or underground within their respective countries and turned into political parties during the wave of political liberalisation that hit the continent following the end of the Cold War. A number of these second generation parties won the general elections that were

Table 12.1: Categories of political parties in East and Southern Africa with selected examples

Category	Examples
First generation parties: liberation movements and nationalist parties	1. African National Congress (ANC), South Africa 2. *Frente de Libertação de Moçambique* (FRELIMO), Mozambique Liberation Front 3. Malawi Congress Party (MCP) 4. *Chama cha Mapinduzi* (CCM), Tanzania 5. United National Independence Party (UNIP), Zambia; 6. Kenya African National Union (KANU)
Second generation parties: post-independence, pro-democracy movements	1. Movement for Multiparty Democracy (MMD), Zambia 2. United Democratic Front (UDF), Malawi 3. Forum for Restoration of Democracy, Kenya (Ford-K) 4. *Chama Cha Demokrasia na Maendeleo* (CHADEMA), Tanzania
Third generation parties: breakaway parties	1. Democratic Progressive Party (DPP), Malawi 2. Congress of the People (COPE), South Africa 3. Foundation for Democracy and Development (FDD), Zambia 4. *União* Democrática (UD), Democratic Union, Mozambique

held to mark the re-introduction of multiparty politics. Nowadays, there are more second generation political parties in existence in the region than parties of the first generation.

The third category comprises *third generation* parties. These are breakaway parties formed as a result of factional infighting and rivalries within the established political parties of both the first and second generation. Many political parties in Africa fall in this category. The MMD in Zambia, for instance, is said to have given birth to more than five third generation parties since its own formation in the 1990s.

The table above shows examples of the political parties that fall within the three categories. A cursory look at the three generations of parties suggests a relationship between the nature of the party and the extent of its internal democracy, although there is a need to investigate further the exact dynamics of this relationship. The first generation political parties that have survived to date (ANC, CCM, FRELIMO) are well organised, have grass-roots party structures and display a notable degree of intra-party democracy. Their survival has not necessarily depended on a particular individual or group of individuals. Thus, they have been able to use institutionalised mechanisms to contain and accommodate internal factions. The ANC in South Africa, for example, managed to ensure a relatively smooth change of leadership after a bruising factional battle that resulted in the dramatic ousting of President Mbeki at the 2007 party conference in Polokwane.

As pointed out earlier, one of the basic principles of intra-party democracy is tolerance for and the accommodation of dissenting views and factions. This principle is difficult to adhere to in less institutionalised, emerging parties. Factions within new parties are difficult to manage and can easily threaten the survival of the party.

In addition to factionalism, membership poses another important problem for intra-party democracy, especially in second and third generation parties. It is often difficult in these parties to identify party members beyond those who hold party positions. In Malawi, for instance, no political party has party cards, because during the one-party era, these cards were an instrument of exploitation and oppression. In the absence of party cards, it is difficult to identify party members. Some parties have distributed T-shirts and party cloths to members but, in poverty stricken areas, many non-members receive such clothing. A survey of party membership in Malawi conducted in 1998 revealed that the total number of individuals who were registered as party members was 18 million, which was almost double the total population of Malawi (Kadzamira et al 1999). Likewise, where political parties have party cards which are sold or given to their members, such as in Tanzania and Kenya, there are no mechanisms to prevent or check dual or multiple memberships. Without reliable membership data, parties are not in a position to speak for an identifiable constituency, cannot benefit from the contributions of its members or facilitate the participation of its members in party activities.

In some of the countries under review, the legal and regulatory framework governing the functioning of political parties is either weak or non-existent. Until recently, there was no party law in Kenya. In Zambia, political parties continue to be registered as clubs or societies. In Malawi, the 1993 Political Parties (Registration and Regulations) Act[4] is more concerned with the registration of political parties than with regulating their functioning. Where relevant legal instruments do exist, they generally define what a political party is, what its functions are, how it can be (de)registered and how it may be funded, but little is stipulated about the internal functioning of political parties. It could be argued that the absence of an appropriate legal framework to foster and promote intra-party democracy is partly responsible for the lack of internal democracy in political parties in East and Southern Africa.

---

4   Chapter 2.07 of the Laws of Malawi.

However, to gain a deeper understanding of the state of intra-party democracy in Africa, there is a need to go beyond the formal aspects of rules, structures and mechanisms. This is particularly important in the light of what Chabal and Daloz (1999) describe as the informal character of African politics. As Bratton and Van de Walle (1997) have shown, political authority and institutions in sub-Saharan Africa are different and often overshadowed by informal power relations which affect the dynamics and outcomes of the democratisation processes on the continent. Their observation is equally true for the internal functioning and management of political parties.

Major challenges arise when political parties revolve around dominant personalities who are either party founders or financiers or both. A majority of the political parties of the second and third generation categories appear to be suffering from this 'big man' syndrome. In these cases, it is inconceivable that party followers would demand accountability from their party leader. Party leaders are regarded as the patrons of their followers who depend on their leaders for favours, material benefits and even jobs and income. These political parties do not have members but subjects, and it is erroneous to expect such members to hold their masters to account. Informal power relations determine the functioning of these parties which, despite formal rules and party constitutions, display a lack of internal democracy. Unless subjects turn into citizens and masters become democratically elected leaders, it is hard to see how democratic principles can be put into practice within these political parties. In this context, existing motives for party membership must also be challenged. Where individuals view political parties mainly as a source of personal gain, political activism will dwindle and, with it, the likelihood that the party and its leader will focus on policy preferences or party ideology rather than material benefits.

Unfortunately, African politics continues to be caught in a vicious cycle of patronage networks and clientelism. This is partly the reason why we see more members of the opposition crossing the floor to the ruling party than members of the governing party joining the opposition. Ruling parties enjoy the advantage of being able to offer dividends to their members in the form of access to state resources and positions. Similarly, when we see members failing to actively participate in party affairs, it is not necessarily due to a lack of formal mechanisms to facilitate their participation. Rather, it may simply be a matter of the cow no longer producing any milk. The lack of participation by women in party affairs may equally be a reflection of cultural norms rather than a lack of formal structures or rules to enhance internal democracy. In many African societies, women are generally discouraged to take up prominent roles in public life. It is probably for this reason that even when parties have seemingly progressive provisions in their rules to encourage women's participation, the effect is often minimal.

5. Conclusion

Considered from a formal perspective, it would appear that political parties in East and Southern Africa have established mechanisms, rules and regulations to facilitate internal democracy. However, implementation is uneven. Many parties struggle to comply with the basic requirements of intra-party democracy. Because parties are membership-based organisations, they cannot survive without organised membership recruitment campaigns. More importantly, they cannot meaningfully connect with their members and ensure member participation in party affairs without active party branches and an institutionalised membership register. With the exception of certain first generation parties, most second and third generation parties are fragile, without grass-roots structures, clear ideological positions, and established norms and practices for ensuring intra-party democracy, responsiveness and accountability.

In addition, political parties in East and Southern Africa need to create incentives for retaining members other than through material benefits and patronage networks. Ensuring members' meaningful participation in party activities is one thing. It is another thing for parties to develop an identity that both existing and future members want to be associated with, even if it does not provide direct personal benefits. Thus, the biggest challenge that many parties face is to go beyond the formal rules and structures and address informal norms and power relations that hinder intra-party democracy. It is hard to hold party leaders to account when they are actually sustaining the party financially. As the saying goes: 'You do not bite the hand that feeds you'. Ensuring that party finances do not rely on individuals and that parties have sustainable and diverse financial bases is therefore an important step in enhancing intra-party democracy in East and Southern Africa.

All countries in the region share a common history of oppression and autocracy which presents immediate obstacles to the development of a culture of internal party democracy. While colonialism created subjects instead of citizens (Mamdani 1996), the single party and other authoritarian political systems in East and Southern Africa, 'perpetuated a culture which cannot just be wished away' (Nyong'o 1997). This political culture included anti-democratic, egoistic, provincial, authority fearing, quite often insular, and ethnic-protective elements. The challenge, therefore, is to develop a political culture for democratisation. As Inglehart (1997) observed, democracy is not just a question of elite-level arrangements; the basic cultural orientations of the citizens also play a crucial role in its survival.[5] For this reason, there is a need for transformative political

---

5   The importance of culture for democratic consolidation has also been addressed by Diamond (1994).

education and innovative partnerships between political parties and civil society to affect cultural change.

Returning to the matter of intra-party democracy, the old debate between *universalists* and *relativists,* which is impossible to settle here, is resurfacing. An obvious response to this debate is to argue for a basic package of intra-party democracy while at the same time acknowledging that political parties, even in the same country, may be at different levels of institutional development. Our conceptual discussion has highlighted a number of democratic principles. The implementation of these principles is necessarily context-sensitive. While some parties are well established and institutionalised, others are just emerging and fragile. Therefore, one size may not fit all. Nevertheless, in the interest of the development of democracy on the continent, all political parties should adhere to basic democratic principles when it comes to their internal functioning.

References
Legislation

Political Parties (Registration and Regulations) Act, Chapter 2.07 of the Laws of Malawi.

Articles, books, chapters in books and other works

Bratton, M. & Van de Walle, N. 1997. *Democratic Experiments in Africa: Regime Transitions in Comparative Perspective.* Cambridge: Cambridge University Press.

Burnell, P. (ed.). 2000a. *Democracy Assistance: International Co-operation for Democratisation.* London/ Portland: Frank Cass.

Burnell, P. 2000b. Promoting parties and party systems in new democracies: Is there anything the international community can do? Paper for the Political Studies Association-UK 50th Annual Conference, 10–13 April, London.

Carothers, T. 1999. *Aiding Democracy Abroad. The Learning Curve.* Washington DC: Carnegie Endowment for International Peace.

Chabal, P. & Daloz, J.P. 1999. *Africa Works: Disorder as Political Instrument.* Oxford/ Bloomington: James Currey/Indiana University Press.

Dahl, R. 1971. *Polyarchy, Participation and Opposition.* New Haven/London: Yale University Press.

Diamond, L. (ed). 1994. *Political Culture and Democracy in Developing Countries,* Colorado/London: Lynne Rienner Publishers.

Erdmann, G. 2005. Hesitant bedfellows: The German Stiftungen and party aid in Africa. An attempt at an assessment. CSGR Working Paper No 184/05. Warwick: Centre for the Study of Globalisation and Regionalisation.

Erdman, G. 2007. Party research: Western European bias and the 'African labyrinth'. In Basedau, M. & Erdman, G. (eds). *Votes, Money and Violence: Political Parties and Elections in Sub-Saharan Africa.* Uppsala: Nordic Africa Institute.

Heywood, A. 2002. *Politics*. Houndmills: Palgrave.

Inglehart, R. 1997. *Modernization and Postmodernization: Cultural, Economic, and Political Change in 43 Societies*. Princeton: Princeton University Press.

Kadzamira, Z.D., Mawaya, A.D.G. & Patel, N. 1999. *Profile and Views of Political Parties in Malawi*. Harare: Konrad Adenauer Stiftung.

Lodge, T. & Schneidegger, U. 2005. Political parties and democratic governance in South Africa. EISA Research Report No 25. Johannesburg: Electoral Institute for the Sustainability of Democracy in Africa.

Magolowondo, A. 2007. Internal party democracy: The state of affairs and the road ahead. Results of a mini-survey commissioned by the Netherlands Institute for Multi-party Democracy Knowledge Centre, presented at the NIMD 2007 Partnership Days, The Hague, 11 September.

Mamdani, M. 1996. *Citizen and Subject: Contemporary Africa and the Legacy of Late Colonialism*. New Jersey: Princeton University Press.

Maravall, J.M. 2008. The political consequences of internal party democracy. In Maravall, J.M. & Sanchez-Cuenza, I. (eds). *Controlling Governments: Voters, Institutions and Accountability*. Cambridge: Cambridge University Press, 157–201.

Matlosa, K. 2007. Are political parties agents of democratisation in Southern Africa? Paper prepared for the International Conference on Sustaining Africa's Democratic Momentum, hosted jointly by the Independent Electoral Commission of South Africa, International IDEA and the African Union, International Convention Centre, Sandton, South Africa, 5–7 March.

Netherlands Institute for Multi-party Democracy — NIMD. 2004. *A Framework for Democratic Party-Building*. The Hague: NIMD.

Nyong'o, A.P. 1997. Institutionalisation of democratic governance in Sub-Saharan Africa. ECDPM Working Paper No 36, Maastricht: European Centre for Development Policy Management.

Salih, M. & Nordlund, P. 2007. *Political Parties in Africa: Challenges for Sustained Multiparty Democracy*. Stockholm: International IDEA.

Scarrow, S. 2005. *Implementing Intra-party Democracy*. New York: NDI.

Shayo, R. 2005. Parties and political development in Tanzania. EISA Research Report No 24. Johannesburg: Electoral Institute for the Sustainability of Democracy in Africa.

Svåsand, L. 2008. Internal party democracy: The case of the United Democratic Front in Malawi. Available at http://uit.n/getfile.php?PageId=1410@FileId=1353. Accessed 18 August 2011.

Teorell, J. 1999. A deliberative defence of intra-party democracy. *Party Politics*, 5(3): 363–382.

Chapter 13

Political parties in Malawi:
An accountability analysis

Nandini Patel

1. Introduction

It has been observed that the dawn of multiparty politics that occurred in the 1990s in sub-Saharan Africa has led to the emergence of dominant political parties (Van de Walle 2003; Bogaards 2004). In some countries, multiparty elections did not bring about a change in government as former ruling parties continued to cling to power. In countries where change did occur, the new incumbents proceeded to stay in power, thereby extending the relevance of the one-party dominant model. The case of Malawi is markedly different from this prevalent scenario. In 1994, the winds of change ushered in a new government under a new party, the United Democratic Front (UDF). However, since coming to power, the UDF has been reduced to a small entity. Instead of consolidating its political position, it was relegated to the position of third largest party in the 2009 parliamentary elections.

However, since the election of President Dr Bingu wa Mutharika in 2004 and the subsequent formation of his own party, the Democratic Progressive Party (DPP), there are signs of emerging one-party dominance in the Malawian political landscape, although it remains to be seen whether the DPP will maintain this dominance in the long-term. The DPP lacks internal democracy and accountability which are the main factors that contributed to the fall of the UDF. Moreover, the party revolves almost completely around its leader Bingu wa Mutharika.

The accountability role of political parties in Malawi, both within and outside the National Assembly, has varied from 1994 to the present. In the early years after the democratic transition, the opposition parties in Parliament, although not always consistent and effective, attempted to perform their oversight role by holding the party in power to account. However, this important role became diluted as opposition party leaders, without consultation or due process, switched sides in return for favours from the ruling party. Furthermore, as time passed, parties developed factions and fragmented due to a lack of intra-party democracy, thereby further reducing the effectiveness of their oversight role. The lack of adherence to democratic practices and norms within political parties exerted a weakening influence not only on the parties themselves but also on state institutions of governance.

2. Political parties and accountability

Accountability has two dimensions.[1] Horizontal accountability refers to the process whereby state institutions hold other state institutions, organs and agencies to account for their performance, actions and omissions. Vertical accountability relates to the means whereby ordinary citizens, mass media and civil society actors seek to enforce standards of good behaviour and performance upon public officials and state institutions (McNeil & Mumvuma 2006). Political parties play a crucial role in ensuring both dimensions of accountability.

Theoretically, democratic accountability is closely linked to the concept of political representation which focuses on whether elected representatives should act as delegates or as trustees of the people they represent. Representatives who are delegates simply follow the expressed preferences of their constituents, whereas trustees are representatives who follow their own understanding of the best action to pursue. Both viewpoints find support in the writings of eminent scholars like James Madison and Edmund Burke. In emerging democracies in Africa, where there is anxiety and deep fervour to safeguard the hard-won democracy, the electorate is keen to exact accountability upon elected representatives and thus prefer mechanisms through which they can directly hold their Members of Parliament (MPs) to account. The common understanding of accountability here is one related to the 'delegate' interpretation of representation. However, modern democracies require that representatives not only act in ways that safeguard the capacity of the represented to hold their representatives accountable but also to uphold the capacity of the representative to act independently of the wishes of the represented (Pitkin 1967). The complex and conflicting standards of representation make it difficult to bind all representatives to a fixed set of guidelines and prohibit a single understanding of what representatives must do.

In the African context, the difficulty of identifying representational roles that enhance accountability is further compounded by the behaviour of party leaders and their inner circle who, in a classic manifestation of neopatrimonialism, bind both elected representatives and the party rank and file in tightly controlled patronage networks. More often than not, party leadership can be equated with the wishes of one powerful individual within the party. Political parties in Africa

---

1   For a further discussion, see chapters 1, 15 and 16.

thus do not provide fertile grounds for inculcating principles of representation and accountability into their members.

In theory, political parties in multiparty democracies are important vehicles for political representation, political competition and democratic accountability. Their contributions range from linking the state and civil society, formulating public policy, engaging in political recruitment, structuring electoral choices and facilitating coalitions. Unfortunately, in most African democracies, political parties remain weak and poorly institutionalised despite having embraced and supposedly practised multiparty democracy for over two decades.

Lawson & Rakner (2005) have analysed how certain institutions of accountability operate in Tanzania and the extent to which they influence the quality and effectiveness of public policy. Amongst a range of institutions — such as local associations, traditional authorities, NGOs and religious bodies — opposition parties ranked lower on the list, whereas religious bodies emerged as the most effective. This pattern would not differ greatly in Malawi.

Generally in Africa, opposition parties are severely discredited, suffer from negative public opinion and are not seen as a viable alternative by the electorate (Olukoshi 1998). Ruling parties often resort to strategies of obstruction, harassment and division in order to weaken the opposition and are highly reluctant and resistant to accommodate dissent and diversity. This is true not only where the transition to multiparty democracy failed to bring about a change of government, but also in other transition scenarios. Generally, there is no level playing field in African politics and opposition parties lack funding, knowledge and skills, which tends to weaken them to the point of ineffectiveness.

In the African context generally and in Malawi in particular, both horizontal and vertical accountability mechanisms are weak due to a political culture that is characterised by an overwhelmingly powerful State President. Opposition parties have only limited space in which to perform their rightful role of holding the government to account. Their role is further weakened by a lack of intra-party democracy and leadership tussles. Weak vertical accountability relationships in turn undermine the level of public trust in elected officials. Against this general background, Malawian party politics since 1994 has followed an interesting trajectory, from relative stability to fragmentation and signs of emerging one-party dominance. This chapter describes this trajectory and analyses how it has influenced accountable governance in Malawi.

3. 1994–2004: From relative stability to fragmentation

3.1. The emergence of opposition parties in Malawi

Until 1993, the Malawi Congress Party (MCP) was the only officially registered political party in Malawi. The national referendum held on 14 June 1993 resoundingly endorsed a multiparty system and was followed by legal reforms which allowed underground pressure groups such as the UDF and the Alliance for Democracy (AFORD) to register as political parties. The 1993 Political Parties (Registration and Regulation) Act[2] laid down the requirements for an entity to register as a political party. The three major political groupings — MCP, UDF and AFORD — duly followed the requirements, such as holding a convention and nominating candidates for the forthcoming elections. Whilst rather basic, it is worth noting that these requirements were severely compromised in subsequent elections. Overall, eight political parties and 13 independents, comprising 614 candidates in total, contested the 177 parliamentary seats during the 1994 elections. Five candidates ran for the Presidency. In short, parties fully utilised the space for political competition that was opened up after 31 years of one-party rule.

The 1994 elections, which were contested mainly to bring about change, did indeed bring about a change of government. Muluzi of the UDF won 47 per cent of the votes, with former President Banda of the MCP getting 33 per cent, followed by Chihana of AFORD with 19 per cent (see table 13.1.). No single party achieved an absolute majority, which posed challenges to the new government. Paradoxically, it also resulted in the opposition having only limited space to hold the new government accountable, as will be discussed in section 3.2 below. The high voter turnout of 80 per cent across the country demonstrated the fact that political parties were able to mobilise the electorate in all parts of the country.

Table 13.1: Results of Malawi's presidential elections (in %), 1994–2009

	1994		1999		2004		2009	
DPP	-		-		-		Mutharika	66
UDF	Muluzi	47	Muluzi	52	Mutharika	36	-	-
MCP	Banda	33	-	-	Tembo	27	Tembo	31
AFORD	Chihana	19	-	-	-	-	Nyasulu	0.5
MCP/AFORD*	-	-	Chakuamba	45	Chakuamba	26	-	-
Other	Other	1	Other	3	Other	11	Other	2.5
Total		100		100		100		100

* In the 1999 elections, Chakuamba was the presidential candidate of both MCP and AFORD; in 2004, he contested the presidential elections for the Mgwirizano coalition.

Sources: African Elections Database. Available at http://africanelections.tripod.com/mw.html and, for 2009 election results, Malawi Election Archive of the Electoral Institute for the Sustainability of Democracy in Africa (EISA). Available at http://www.eisa.org.za/WEP/malelectarchive.htm. Both accessed 30 September 2010.

---

2   Chapter 2:07 of the Laws of Malawi.

Table 13.2: Number of seats in Malawi's National Assembly per party, 1994–2009

	1994	1999	2004	2009
DPP	-	-	-	113
UDF	84	93	49	17
MCP	55	66	59	27
AFORD	36	29	6	1
Mgwirizano	-	-	27	-
Independent	-	4	38	32
Invalid	2	-	-	-
Other	-	-	14	3
TOTAL	177	192	193	193

Sources: African Elections Database. Available at http://africanelections.tripod.com/mw.html and, for 2009 election results, Malawi Election Archive of the Electoral Institute for the Sustainability of Democracy in Africa (EISA). Available at http://www.eisa.org.za/WEP/malelectarchive.htm. Both accessed 30 September 2010.

The results of the 1994 parliamentary and presidential elections clearly demonstrated that region of origin and ethnicity were important factors in explaining voting patterns in Malawi (Chirwa 1995; Kaspin 1995). The electoral outcome showed strong regional and ethnic bases of support for the three main political parties: UDF in the south, MCP in the centre and AFORD in the north. This pattern in party support continued to dominate the political landscape of Malawi until the 2009 elections, when, to the surprise of many, the DPP won with an overwhelming majority across the country. Some commentators were quick to point out that the 2009 election had de-ethnicised and de-regionalised Malawian politics. This observation was perhaps too hasty given the return of regional/ethnic politics precipitated by the ruling party's reintroduction of the district-based quota system of admission to public universities.

3.2 Opposition parties as vehicles for accountability

In the first multiparty National Assembly of 1994, opposition parties were in the majority. The Speaker and both Deputy Speakers came from the opposition MCP and AFORD and all seven parliamentary committees were chaired by opposition MPs. This preponderance of the opposition made it difficult for the new UDF government to pursue its agenda in the legislature. As a result, the UDF resorted to an alliance with AFORD, offering key positions to AFORD President Chakufwa Chihana and a number of senior party members. In order to accommodate Chihana, the position of Second Vice President was created by way of an amendment to the Constitution. This amendment was subsequently challenged in court. Most members of AFORD were unhappy with the alliance hatched by party leaders but not democratically endorsed by party members. As it turned out, the alliance did not last long and was dissolved in 1996. However, during the two-year period of its existence, many Bills were passed without much deliberation. The alliance, though short-lived, proved to be a step towards weakening both political parties — a trend that only intensified in the run-up to the 1999 elections.

The demise of the controversial UDF-AFORD alliance gave rise to an MCP-AFORD opposition alliance, which performed commendably in its oversight role, raising fundamental concerns around constitutionalism and democracy. A case in point was the full-time attendance and participation of non-elected ministers in the proceedings of the House. Ministers who had not been elected as MPs were identified as 'strangers' in the House and the matter of their full-time attendance was referred to the Malawi Supreme Court of Appeal.[3] As a result, the trend of ministers without constituencies attending the House full time was reversed. Since then, they have only attended the House proceedings as and when required to do so.

However, the presidential nature of Malawi's political system combined with the political culture of neopatrimonialism proved not conducive to a strong oversight role for opposition parties. Ministers generally regarded themselves as being accountable to the President rather than to the legislature. Although opposition parties tried to fulfil their role of holding the government to account, they could not sustain these efforts because some of their own MPs, including some in leadership positions, shifted their loyalties to the government. The UDF lured opposition MPs over to its side in order to pass Bills, including some that had a direct bearing on constitutionalism and democracy, without much debate and dissent in the House. Parliamentary procedures and Standing Orders were compromised in the process and matters that were of an internal parliamentary nature were dragged before the judiciary. Not only did the practice of switching sides undermine the accountability role of political parties in Parliament, it also took a heavy toll on the party in power. What started with a few members leaving the UDF because of disagreements with the party's President soon after 1994, continued to increase and, by 2004, the trickle had turned into a torrent leaving the party in a dismally weakened state.

The alliances hatched virtually unilaterally by party leaders after the 1994 elections had an equally deleterious effect on the opposition parties. The number

---

3   *Attorney General v Dr Mapopa Chipeta* MSCA Civil Appeal No 33 of 1994 (unreported).

of opposition MPs ostensibly declaring themselves independent dramatically increased. In reality, these MPs were sympathising with and supporting the ruling UDF. This became clear during UDF's primary elections for the 1999 elections when 18 former MCP and AFORD parliamentarians, who had previously declared themselves independent, contested as UDF candidates in their constituencies (Kadzamira 1999).

With regard to the consequences of these and similar developments for vertical accountability, the right to recall MPs must be mentioned. Section 64 of the Constitution of the Republic of Malawi Act, 1994 (Constitution) originally provided for the recall of MPs by their constituents. However, this provision was repealed in 1995. Since then, a demand for the re-introduction of the 'recall provision' has featured on the agenda of many constitutional review fora, including the Constitutional Review Conference of 2007. The demand is based on a perception that MPs have thus far been more loyal to their party than to their constituencies. Political parties themselves are divided on the issue, but the right to recall is perceived by many as an important tool to secure the vertical accountability of MPs, especially in the context where MPs change their party allegiance quite regularly. Nevertheless, there are others who argue that this mechanism is difficult to implement in practice in a fair and just manner.

3.3. Accountability within political parties

The democratic practices displayed by political parties in the run-up to the 1994 elections unfortunately deteriorated dramatically thereafter, casting serious doubts on the existence of a culture of democracy and accountability within parties. The internal nomination process of the ruling UDF in the run-up to the 1999 elections was grossly flawed and marred by violence and high levels of intimidation. During the UDF's primary elections for parliamentary candidates, 13 former MPs including two cabinet ministers were physically assaulted by new candidates. There were instances of vote rigging and a general disregard for rules and procedures. While the irregularities concerning the nomination of parliamentary candidates generated a very negative public image, the nomination of the presidential candidate was not even contested in the UDF. The party simply failed to hold a convention, thus blatantly violating its own constitution. This high-handedness of UDF leaders and the lack of accountability to rank and file members cost the party dearly in the course of its second term in government. In the run-up to the 1999 elections, the MCP also experienced internal tensions and seemed to be heading for a split between two factions, led by John Tembo and Gwanda Chakuamba respectively.

The early 2000s began with an attempt by some in the UDF to seek a third term for President Muluzi. The third term issue subsequently led to the creation of splinter parties and the near disintegration of all three main parties. The MCP leadership dispute intensified with Tembo's support for Muluzi's third term bid. As a result, the MCP saw numerous defections of key party figures and the formation of two new splinter parties: the New Congress for Democracy (NCD) by the party's former publicity secretary, Hetherwick Ntaba, and the Republican Party (RP) by Gwanda Chakuamba, who went on to become the presidential candidate for the Mgwirizano Coalition in 2004.

Divisions in AFORD began when the party leader decided to rejoin the UDF as a coalition partner despite a party convention resolution not to support Muluzi in his third term bid. The party leadership refused to accept the view of the party members and forged ahead in its support for Muluzi. This intensified friction in the party and created a breakaway party, called the Movement for Genuine Democratic change (MGODE). Three MPs resigned from AFORD and joined other parties.

In the case of the UDF, many senior members were waiting for their chance to contest for the party's presidency. The third term bid by Muluzi was a threat to the leadership ambitions of many. It caused internal divisions leading to defections and the formation of two new parties: the National Democratic Alliance (NDA) and the People's Progressive Movement (PPM). When his bid for a third term in office failed, Muluzi subsequently compounded the damage by hand-picking an outsider, Dr Bingu wa Mutharika, as the UDF presidential candidate for the 2004 elections. This served to increase the number of senior members deserting the party.

In August 2003, the UDF amended its constitution to accommodate Mutharika who would otherwise not have been eligible to stand in the 2004 elections as the party's presidential candidate. The amendment was also tailored to accommodate Muluzi by creating the position of National Chairman of the party to be filled by him after stepping down as State President. Not having held a party convention for over ten years, the UDF subsequently held a highly stage-managed convention immediately before the 2004 elections in order to endorse Mutharika as its presidential candidate. In a similar move, the party called a convention in 2008 to 'elect' a presidential candidate for the 2009 elections. It was revealed during a UDF District Executive Committee that, before this convention, a meeting was convened for all UDF District Governors where they were instructed to ensure that all delegates to the convention would vote for the same, pre-chosen, candidate.

While democratic theory places emphasis on peoples' mandate to govern, the erratic, high-handed and undemocratic way in which party conventions were held indicates that political parties struggle to give effect to this ideal and to play a positive role in the democratisation process. Instead, party conventions were called to legitimise imposed candidates as the people's choice. While the issue of insufficient resources has been cited as an explanation, the reality is that there is a lack of political will to implement democratic accountability within political parties. For instance, during the ten years that the UDF was in government, the party did not hold one party convention despite the availability of funds for other party activities. Some senior members in the party apparently did not want to hold a convention for fear of losing their positions in democratic elections. Even in cases where people expressed their choice, the party set these decisions aside. The UDF leadership asked some parliamentary candidates who had won their candidacy to contest in the 2004 primary elections to withdraw because the party's National Executive Committee considered them to be unpopular.

3.4. The rise of independents

Since 1994, primary elections held to select candidates for parliamentary elections have been fraught with irregularities and unfairness, including the imposition of candidates by party leaders and the forced withdrawal of successful candidates to pave the way for hand-picked ones. Such instances were glaring and pervasive in all parties, but more so in the UDF. It resulted in a large number of candidates running for parliamentary seats as independents.

The number of independent candidates in the 2004 elections was three times larger than that in the 1999 elections. Some of these had ostensibly lost in the primaries, but decided to challenge the nomination outcome by running as independents. The selection of the candidates in the run-up to the 2004 elections also generated more court cases than any other part of the electoral process (Kanyongolo & Gloppen 2004).

Another reason for the increase in independent candidates was that the leadership of UDF and AFORD agreed not to compete against each other in the 2004 parliamentary elections as part of their electoral alliance. Thus, the UDF decided not to nominate candidates in most of the constituencies in the northern region, the stronghold of AFORD, while AFORD did the same in the southern region and other strongholds of the UDF. Within the UDF, however, this agreement was questioned at the constituency level by prospective candidates who, when denied nomination by the party, decided to run as independents. A large number of them emerged victorious and subsequently formed part of the third largest grouping in Parliament, the independents.

The rise of independents and the fragmentation of the main parties in Malawi as discussed above runs contrary to the democratisation theory which expects serious challenges to democratisation to occur in the early periods after the transition, and democratic consolidation to take place after two consecutive elections (Huntington 1991). In Malawi, however, major challenges were experienced by all political parties after the second elections. Perhaps a more appropriate observation is that multiparty elections do not automatically lead to stable multiparty systems (Bogaard 2004). This statement holds true in the Malawian case for three reasons: the fragmentation of the three main parties after two consecutive elections, the rise of independents and the emergence of numerous parties just before elections which disappear soon thereafter.

4. 2004–present: Emerging one-party dominance?

After the 2004 elections, Mutharika seemed to be keen to prove himself and to come out of Muluzi's shadow. Immediately after he took charge as President, he embarked on a massive anti-corruption drive. This scared many UDF stalwarts and friction soon began to mount between Muluzi and Mutharika, thereby expediting Mutharika's exit from the UDF. In 2005, Mutharika, perhaps fearing dismissal from the UDF, took the bold step of forming his own party, the DPP, which immediately went on to win by-elections in six constituencies. Nevertheless, the first four years of DPP rule were of a party in government with a very small presence in Parliament. As a result, the acrimony and tension between the executive and the legislature reached extraordinary heights. During this period, Parliament attempted to impeach the President, and the President in turn adjourned and prorogued Parliament. Whilst tensions and friction between the executive and the legislature are present in all democracies, the events in Malawi during this period were unprecedented.

4.1. The tug of war between the executive and the legislature

The incipient conflict between Mutharika and the UDF that emerged soon after the 2004 elections found its first expression in increasing tensions between the UDF in government and the UDF in the legislature. The conflict, which became more public and vicious with each passing day, led to a motion by a UDF MP for the adoption of impeachment procedures by Parliament. While the UDF explained that this motion was not necessarily targeted at the incumbent President, the commonly held view was that it was intended for the impeachment of Mutharika. This was soon proved correct when, after the general impeachment procedures were adopted, a motion was moved to summon the President before Parliament, citing seven grounds in support of his impeachment.

An injunction restraining Parliament from summoning the President for indictment was issued by the Constitutional Court, comprising three High

Court judges. They issued an order preventing the Speaker from implementing any impeachment procedures pending judicial review. The Constitutional Court effectively froze the parliamentary proceedings and debate on impeachment procedures pending completion of the judicial process. Whilst the Constitutional Court's injunction may be seen by some as a way of securing political stability, the other side of the coin is that it seemed to establish a dangerous precedent of the judiciary overextending its jurisdiction by directly impinging on the province of the legislature.

The lurking fear of impeachment compelled the Mutharika government to garner support in the House by any means including 'poaching' MPs from the opposition. At the same time, any move by the Speaker to make a ruling on instances of crossing the floor was countered by an immediate injunction, leading some to conclude that Malawi was developing an 'injunction culture'. Section 65 of the Constitution defines floor crossing as the voluntary decision of an MP to resign from the party that got him elected and explicitly states that the Speaker must declare the parliamentary seat involved vacant. This posed a serious problem for the Mutharika government. Determined not to allow any motions or rulings on section 65, the President prematurely adjourned and prorogued the House during the 2006/07 and 2008/09 budget sessions of Parliament.

In 2008, the UDF-MCP led opposition decided to block any debate on the budget until section 65 had been dealt with — either first or concurrently. The DPP-led executive insisted on passing the budget before any other discussions, thereby creating an impasse. Civil society joined the fray by pressuring the opposition into passing the budget. Underlying the ensuing polarity was a misconception that section 65 and the budget were two separate issues and that it was an 'either/or' situation. In reality, both were constitutional issues that were being manipulated to suit particular vested interests. This was further illustrated by the fact that the budget session was split into two segments in order to comply nominally with the constitutional requirement of a minimum of at least two sittings of the House per year. In the end, the executive promised to address the floor-crossing issue after the budget had been passed but promptly reneged by proroguing Parliament. Thus, Mutharika failed to take the opportunity to mend relations with Parliament as his first term in office was coming to an end.

At this juncture, it is important to highlight two events pertaining to section 65. During the opening of the Constitutional Review Conference in 2006/07, Mutharika publicly pronounced that *section 65 had to go*. Despite this pronouncement, the Conference fully endorsed the retention of the floor-crossing section in the Constitution. In addition, the Malawi Supreme Court in its 2007 ruling held that section 65 was an integral part of the Constitution.[4] Perhaps these endorsements of the validity and relevance of section 65 in Malawian politics increased the President's defensiveness and hardened his resolve to oppose its implementation. In the end, the tug-of-war around the floor-crossing issue and the related annual tussle about the adoption of the budget seriously eroded the capacity of Parliament to conduct its normal business, including that of holding the government to account.

During the period 2004–2009, the DPP-led executive and the UDF-MCP dominated legislature were engaged in a perpetual tug-of-war. As a result, Parliament only met for a total period of 30 weeks. In some years, particularly during the 2006/07 and 2008/09 fiscal cycles, Parliament stood virtually suspended and only met during the budget sessions which were tense and acrimonious.

In spite of the tense atmosphere and the paucity of parliamentary sittings, Parliament did carry out its oversight functions to some extent. The level of scrutiny of the national budget by experienced politicians from all parties was commendable and succeeded in trimming surplus fat off the government's budget proposals. Committee reports were received and debated, questions were presented to ministers and private member motions were presented and debated, all of which was impressive given the overall political climate. Parliamentary committees were fairly active although they functioned under enormous time constraints. The Public Appointments, Public Accounts, and Legal Affairs Committees in particular, deserve special mention for their diligence under the most trying circumstances. Concerns about a number of key public appointments were raised, and in some cases subsequently reversed. Parliament also successfully blocked the passage of the infamous Mozambique-Malawi Electricity Interconnection Bill.[5]

Despite the cold war between the two arms of government, it is heartening to note that the work on parliamentary reforms continued during the 2004–2009 term of Parliament. The Parliamentary Reform Programme identified the following six areas for reform:

1. A fixed calendar for parliamentary sittings
2. Parliamentary autonomy with regard to the management of its financial resources

---

4　See *In the Matter of Presidential Reference of a Dispute of a Constitutional Nature under Section 89(1)(h) of the Constitution and In the Matter of Section 65 of the Constitution and In the Matter of the Question of the Crossing of the Floor by Members of the National Assembly* MSCA Presidential Reference Appeal No 44 of 2006 (unreported).

5　Bill 8 of 2007. This Bill sought to authorise the government to embark on a World Bank-backed project involving the importation of electric power from Mozambique. Curiously, the President signed it into force believing that Parliament had already passed it, yet it had not.

3. Enhancing the status of the Speaker
4. Full observance of the provisions of the Parliamentary Service Act 35 of 1998
5. Creating new divisions in the Clerk of Parliament's department
6. A greater role for the National Assembly in the consideration of the nation's finances.

4.2. The DPP's rising popularity

The performance of the DPP government at the macro-economic level and particularly in the area of service delivery was a significant factor in the ground-breaking success of the DPP in the 2009 elections. A recent Afrobarometer survey comparing the performance of Mutharika's government in 2005 and 2008 with Muluzi's performance in 1999 and 2003 revealed that Mutharika's government outperformed its predecessor in public services such as sanitation, water and food security, and in combating HIV/AIDS, crime and corruption (Tsoka 2009a, 2009b). It further revealed a new trend that the DPP was gaining acceptance across ethnic and regional lines and growing in popularity in all regions. In the northern region, for example, AFORD had only 3 per cent support in 2008 compared to 10 per cent in 2005, whereas the newly formed DPP increased its support from 23 per cent in 2005 to 61 per cent in 2008. The same trend can be observed in the central and southern regions which were strongholds of the UDF and MCP respectively. The following table demonstrates the overall support for the DPP across the country.

Table 13.3: Parliamentary seats won by each party per region, Malawi's 2009 elections

	DPP	Independents	MCP	UDF	AFORD	MAFUNDE	NARC	MPP	Total
North	24	8	0	0	1	0	1	0	34
Centre	37	8	27	0	0	0	0	1	73
South	52	16	0	17	0	1	0	0	86
Total	113	32	27	17	1	1	1	1	193

Source: Malawi Electoral Commission, 2009 Presidential and Parliamentary Elections Results

The 2009 elections produced some unexpected outcomes for opposition parties. The DPP, contesting its first national election after only four years of existence, dominated the political landscape, gaining almost 60 per cent of the seats in Parliament. With the independents becoming the second largest group in Parliament, the UDF and MCP were reduced to 14 per cent and almost 9 per cent of parliamentary seats respectively. The DPP managed to win seats in almost all the districts, whereas MCP and the UDF only managed significant numbers in the central and southern regions respectively.

The popularity of Mutharika's government across the country was also reflected in the results of the 2009 presidential elections in which Mutharika secured the highest percentage of votes since 1994, 66 per cent. He had the largest share of the national, regional and district votes compared to the other candidates in the presidential race. The runner-up candidate, John Tembo of the MCP, despite competing strongly in some districts, only managed to get less than half of Mutharika's vote share. The overwhelming support for the DPP has been hailed as signalling 'de-regionalisation' and 'de-ethnicisation' and the beginning of the first truly national political party in Malawian politics. However, as will be argued below, the DPP's popularity may not last for the same reasons that led to the disintegration of the UDF and AFORD.

4.3. The DPP as a democratic and accountable political party?

The DPP's first convention was held on 17–18 January 2009. It was markedly different from the norm because no elections were held for positions in the party leadership. The party's constitution states that members of the National Governing Council shall be elected at the National Political Conference of the party for a period of five years (section 8(2)). It also states that the National Governing Council shall make appointments to all positions in the party which shall be endorsed by the National Political Conference (section 8(3)). Since no elections were held, the National Governing Council remains a body appointed by Mutharika.

At this convention, Mathurika, being the self-appointed president of DPP, was unilaterally endorsed as the party's presidential candidate. The party's justification of this appointment procedure was that it was consistent with the African style of leadership. No one came forward to contest against Mutharika and secrecy surrounded the selection of Mutharika's running-mate. The DPP's constitution is silent on the procedure for selecting a vice-presidential candidate. Whether it was because of this lacuna or some other reason, Mutharika's running-mate for the 2009 elections, Mrs Joyce Banda, was hand-picked by Mutharika at virtually the last minute.

Primary elections are the preferred mechanism for selecting party candidates for parliamentary elections and must in principle be managed at the grass-roots level of a political party. We have already noted that in all parties in Malawi, primaries are tampered with by the party leadership, and DPP's 2009 primaries were no exception. Primary elections often lack accountability and transparency because an 'inner circle' of party leaders favours influential incumbents and candidates with close personal links to the party leadership, thereby leaving very limited space for other aspirants. During the 2009 primaries, the DPP resorted to the imposition of candidates on local party structures, which was very similar to the practice in the UDF in the run-up to the 2004 elections. A large number of candidates in the 2009 elections lamented the unfair conduct of primaries and pointed to the heavy hand of party leaders in the candidate selection process. One candidate commented:

> ... there have been several instances where top party officials have openly displayed support for a particular candidate. This is done by giving party materials to such a candidate, thereby creating an unfair advantage. The party should not give materials to a candidate during primaries, but only after one has won the contest and is now standing on the party ticket. I was greatly disappointed and still feel cheated. As such, I have no desire to participate in the DPP's party activities unless most of the officials change their conduct (Interview with DPP's 2009 candidate, Ntcheu West Constituency).

A large number of aspirant DPP candidates decided to stand for parliamentary elections as independents in a show of protest against the irregular conduct of the primaries in their areas. A disproportionately large number of independent candidates were indeed disgruntled DPP aspirants. Interestingly, there were three categories of independents: those who were originally UDF members, independents aligned to the DPP and 'real' independents, who previously belonged to no party. Once elected to Parliament, many independents were seamlessly absorbed back into their previous parties. The 38 independents of 2004 lost no time in jumping back onto the party bandwagon. In 2009, Mutharika had, before the elections, labelled independent candidates as 'hyenas' and said that he did not recognise independent candidates campaigning for him but only candidates standing on the DPP ticket. This stance and language changed dramatically after the elections when he extended an olive branch to the former DPP aspirants who had won seats as independent candidates.

The DPP also followed in the footsteps of the UDF by using state resources for the campaign of the incumbent, thus displaying the same reluctance to levelling the playing field during election campaigns. In fact, the DPP even went a step further, especially with regard to access to public media. During the 2009 campaign, public media displayed a much stronger bias in favour of the incumbent than in 2004. Some media experts and political observers viewed the performance of the Malawi Broadcasting Corporation (MBC) and Malawi Television (TVM) in the run-up to the 2009 elections as the 'worst ever' (Chiyamwaka 2009). Funding of the two public broadcasters had been a critical issue during the 2004–2009 parliamentary term when the opposition refused to pass budgetary allocations for these institutions. During this time, these public broadcasters received funding from the state through covert channels despite Parliament's disapproval. The rejection of budgetary allocations to public broadcasters was later used by the DPP as a basis for pressurising the public broadcasters not to cover the campaigns of opposition parties. After his landslide victory, President Mutharika admitted that the two state-controlled broadcasters, MBC and TVM, were biased towards the ruling party during the election campaign (Chiyamwaka 2009). Unfortunately, this statement was not intended as an expression of regret or remorse, but to question the opposition's decision to deny funding to the two media houses. The President subsequently assured the two institutions that their funding would be assured now that the DPP commanded a majority in Parliament.

The election campaign of the DPP clearly revealed that its candidates enjoyed a disproportionate amount of access to state resources thereby creating an unequal playing field between contestants. A blatant display of abuse of public resources by the DPP was the use of vehicles of statutory corporations to ferry supporters to DPP rallies around Malawi in the weeks before the 2009 elections and DPP rallies were aired on local television daily.

4.4. No signs of improving accountability

One could argue that President Mutharika initially resorted to irregular actions, breaches of the Constitution and violations of the rule of law because the DPP government was paranoid about the opposition's strength and its intention to impeach him. In a desperate bid for survival, the executive, confronted with a minority status in Parliament, had little choice but to risk the integrity and jurisdiction of Parliament. However, as a result of the 2009 elections, the situation has changed dramatically with the DPP gaining an absolute majority while the fragmented opposition has been weakened further. Thus, with the government in a secure position, the current political landscape presents an opportunity to rectify previous wrongs and improve on democratic governance to the level of the government's impressive track record in economic governance. Unfortunately, the President has shown few signs of changing his *modus operandi* and has continued to interfere with the operations of Parliament.

Several incidents have occurred since the inauguration of the new government which give little hope of a healthy relationship between the two arms of government. Mutharika's second term began with assurances of not 'abusing his majority status in Parliament'. Although this expression was repeatedly used by members of the executive, it has hardly been observed in practice. According to the President, his party, after withstanding an uncompromising opposition, has now learnt to thrive. This stance is reminiscent of Mutharika's tit-for-tat politics during his first term in office.

Since 1994, there has been a tendency to increase the size of the Cabinet and this has become one of the key issues generating friction in executive-legislative relations. Generally, the Cabinet formed immediately after the elections is relatively small as promised to the electorate but becomes 'bloated' as the term progresses. For instance, immediately after the 1994 elections, the Cabinet had 22 members, which increased to 37 by 1998. The Cabinet formed after the 1999 elections had 30 members, which rose to 46 in 2003. The reason for the Cabinet to be inflated in 2003 related to Muluzi's failed attempt to gain a third term in office. He believed that a large executive would assist him in pushing through the necessary constitutional amendment in Parliament. After the 2004 elections, the 29-member Cabinet rose to 43 in 2006 as Mutharika sought to control the opposition-led majority in Parliament by awarding ministerial positions to some opposition members in order to induce their defection. In 2009, the Cabinet formed immediately after the elections already counted 45 members. This could be taken as a sign that Mutharika was seeking to dominate Parliament from the start of his second term in office.

Another telling sign is that section 65 continues to be ignored and floor crossing encouraged. Almost all MPs elected as independents in 2009 have joined the DPP. These MPs have crossed the floor and their seats should be declared vacant in accordance with the Constitution. It is highly unlikely that this will happen in the current political climate in which the power of the President seems to be increasingly unchecked and unchallenged. Another example is the recent constitutional amendment to allow the President to set the date for local government elections. Previously, the Constitution fixed the date of local elections, a year after holding parliamentary and presidential elections. And, in the 2010 budget session of Parliament, which lasted a mere 4 hours, over 400 budget votes were passed after only cursory scrutiny. In short, the opposition parties, the UDF and MCP, seem to struggle to find a voice. Opposition leaders are not standing up to provide alternative views on public policy. As a result, the President has virtually nobody who opposes him.

5. Conclusion

Since 1994, Malawi's political parties have performed their role of ensuring accountable government only partially and inconsistently. The personalisation of politics, leadership tussles and a lack of internal party democracy are the root causes of this uneven performance. Political expediency and narrow interests have seriously impeded the democratic functioning of both ruling and opposition parties.

In keeping with the waning public trust in political institutions, an appreciation of the role and relevance of political parties in democratic governance seems virtually non-existent. Collaboration and interaction between political parties and civil society tends to be confrontational and acrimonious, thereby restricting societal input in parties' programmes and policy formulation.

Fragile coalitions and weak party structures have brought the party system to breaking point and could ultimately derail the multiparty process if left unattended. Fragmentation on the one hand and emerging dominance — whether of one party or of the President — with blurred lines between state and party on the other hand are posing serious challenges to the sustainability of multiparty democracy in Malawi.

The lesson that can be drawn from the Malawian experience is that intra-party accountability is key to making holders of public power more accountable. Leaders appointed undemocratically by their parties and who are not accountable to their own political parties are unlikely to become paragons of accountability at the national level.

References

Legislation

Constitution of the Republic of Malawi Act 20 of 1994.
Mozambique-Malawi Electricity Interconnection Bill 8 of 2007.
Parliamentary Service Act 35 of 1998.
Political Parties (Registration and Regulation) Act, Chapter 2:07 of the Laws of Malawi.

Cases

Attorney General v Dr Papopa Chipeta MSCA Civil Appeal No 33 of 1994 (unreported).
In the Matter of Presidential Reference of a Dispute of a Constitutional Nature under Section 89(1)(h) of the Constitution and In the Matter of Section 65 of the Constitution and In the Matter of the Question of the Crossing of the Floor by Members of the National Assembly MSCA Presidential Reference Appeal No 44 of 2006 (unreported).

Articles, books, chapters in books and other works

Bogaards, M. 2004. Counting parties and identifying dominant party systems in Africa. *European Journal of Political Research*, 43: 173–197.
Chirwa, C.W. 1995. Elections in Malawi: The perils of regionalism. *Southern Africa Report Archive*, 10(2): 17.
Chiyamwaka, B. 2009. The role of the media. Paper presented at Election Evaluation Conference in Lilongwe, 23–26 June (unpublished).
Huntington, S.P. 1991. *The Third Wave: Democratizaton in the Late Twentieth Century*. Norman/London: University of Oklahoma Press.
Institute for Policy Interaction (IPI). 2009. *Malawi Parliamentary Observation Reports 2005–2008*.
Kadzamira, D.Z. 1999. *Management of the Electoral Process during the Second Multi-Party Elections*. Zomba: Kachere Series, Book No 10.
Kanyongolo, E. & Gloppen, S. 2004. The role of the judiciary in the 2004 general elections in Malawi. Paper presented at the NUFU workshop, Rosendaal, Norway, September 2004 (unpublished).

Kaspin, D. 1995. The politics of ethnicity in Malawi's democratic transition. *Journal of Modern African Studies*, 33(4): 595–620.

Lawson, A. & Rakner L. 2005. Understanding patterns of accountability in Tanzania. Final Synthesis Report. Unpublished commissioned report. Bergen: Chr. Michelsen Institute (CMI).

McNeil, M. & Mumvuma, T. 2006. *Demanding Good Governance: A Stocktaking of Social Accountability by Civil Society in Anglophone Africa*. Washington DC: World Bank.

Olukoshi O.A. 1998. *The Politics of Opposition in Contemporary Africa*. Uppsala: Nordiska Afrikainstitutet.

Pitkin, H. 1967. *The Concept of Representation*. Berkeley: University of California Press.

Tsoka, M.G. 2009a. Spot the difference: A comparison of presidents' and government's performance since 1999. Afrobarometer Briefing Paper No 74. Available at http://www.afrobarometer.org/papers/AfrobriefNo74.pdf. Accessed 30 October 2010.

Tsoka, M.G. 2009b. A country turning blue? Political parties and regionalism in Malawi. Afrobarometer Briefing Paper No 75. Available at http://www.afrobarometer.org/papers/AfrobriefNo75.pdf. Accessed 30 October 2010.

Van der Walle, N. 2003. Presidentialism and clientelism in Africa's emerging party systems. *Journal of Modern African Studies*, 41(2): 297–321.

Chapter 14

Family matters: The interplay between formal and informal incentives for accountability in Mali's local communities

Martin van Vliet

1. Introduction

The Malian government developed and implemented an ambitious decentralisation programme in the 1990s. Thousands of villages were regrouped into 703 municipalities and municipal councillors were elected. The central government was to transfer a considerable amount of authority and resources to these newly established municipal councils. The reforms were expected to strengthen local accountability and consequently spearhead local economic development and enhance local democracy.

This chapter examines the impact of Mali's decentralisation programme on local accountability mechanisms between 1999 and 2009. It is based on periods of extensive fieldwork following the first (1999), second (2004) and third (2009) local elections in Karan, a village some 90 kilometres south of Mali's capital city, Bamako. Following Oluwu (2001) and Ribot (2002), the central research questions are whether Mali's decentralisation programme has established municipal councils with sufficient powers to act within particular spheres of influence and to what extent the councillors are held accountable for their actions by ordinary citizens.

This chapter examines empirical data within the context of a theoretical debate around the relative importance of formal structures and informal power relations in shaping political behaviour. Ten years after the introduction of Mali's new governance institutions at the local level, informal power relations still influence their functioning to a large extent and hugely affect local accountability mechanisms. These informal relations, however, appear to be much more complex than the patron–client relations that dominate the academic literature on African political developments. A dynamic cultural perspective on informal political relations proves to be highly relevant.

2. Theories and concepts

2.1. Formal and informal approaches to democratic consolidation

A substantial group of scholars (including Huntington 1992; Diamond et al 1990) examines democratic consolidation processes by focusing on democratic institutions. Political and economic scientist Schumpeter is often referred to as an important source of inspiration in this respect. The presence of democratic institutions, such as elections, is considered to be the most important indicator of democracy (Van Cranenburg 2000; Schaffer 1998). Policy papers[1] and academic literature[2] focusing on formal aspects of governance processes are prominent in the debate around democratic consolidation in Africa. Rational-legal state-building models and formal democratic structures are used to analyse African state-building processes and prevail within international development cooperation practices. It is believed that by setting up new or strengthening existing governance institutions, rules and regulations, development can be spearheaded. The underlying assumption is that formal institutions shape individual behaviour to a large extent. Such institutional thinking also inspired a number of decentralisation programmes in Africa. The idea was that through new governance institutions such as municipal councils, democracy and accountable political behaviour could be generated.

In contrast, many studies on African governance processes are conducted on the basis of a neopatrimonial paradigm which has its roots in the 1970s and 1980s (eg, Eisenstadt 1973). It is argued that processes of state building and governance in Africa cannot be explained by focusing on formal state structures only. The African state has not institutionalised according to Weber's rational-legal form of domination but following the logic of neopatrimonialism. Political leaders, so-called *patrons*, provide a selected group of people, their *clients*, with personal gifts or services and obtain loyalty in return. These informal patron–client networks operate within the context of formal bureaucracies which are then referred to as 'hybrid regimes'(Médard 1982).

Recently, the neopatrimonial paradigm has been nuanced from different angles. Hagman (2006) argues that neopatrimonialism seems to have become a 'catch-all concept' that is used to explain political processes without always presenting the empirical evidence of the actual informal practices referred to. Others have denounced its usage for putting too strong an emphasis on informal dynamics to the detriment of formal rules and regulations that also seem influential in practice (Wiseman 1999; Engel & Olsen 2005; Lindberg 2006; Von

---

1   Notably reports on governance in Africa published by the World Bank (1989; 1993) and UNDP (1991).

2   Engel and Olsen (2005) provide a summary of formal approaches to governance in Africa.

Soest 2007). Thirdly, empirical studies (Therkildsen 2005; Hansen 2003) indicate that patronage is only one amongst many incentives African politicians face. Fourthly, the neopatrimonial approach tends to overestimate the influence of money or other advantages that are being exchanged between so-called patrons and their clients. Nugent (2001), for example, has demonstrated the need for Ghanaian politicians to transfer money into some kind of moral authority for it to become an effective campaign tool. Besides, numerous African politicians have lost elections despite having distributed large amounts of funds or other advantages within their support networks.

The institutional and neopatrimonial approaches have both been criticised for their lack of a culture-oriented perspective on democratic consolidation in Africa. Whereas Hyden (2008) indicates that institutions cannot be studied in isolation from the norms and values of the societies within which they develop, Schaffer (1998) concludes that democratic values which underpin specific institutions are not necessarily universal. Based on extensive fieldwork in Senegal he demonstrates that elections have a different meaning amongst Senegalese people as compared to citizens in the United States.[3] Reasoning along similar lines, Van Donge (2006: 97–98) notes that 'an emphasis on political culture should heighten awareness of the various forms which democratic values may take in different societies'. Besides the notion that democratic values take different forms, political and historical anthropologists have emphasised that 'multi-party democracy [in Africa] has simply been assimilated into a broader range of thought' (Abbink & Hesseling 2000; Geschiere 1997). Engel and Olsen (2005) conclude that examining popular notions of political concepts should be an integral part of empirical research. Recognising the importance of a culturally sensitive perspective on democratic consolidation, the question remains how political culture should be taken into account. Some scholars opted for a linguistic approach to political culture (Schatzberg 1993). Others regarded it as a set of historically grown symbols and values (Abbink 2006; Schaffer 1998). This chapter follows Chabal and Daloz's (2006) recent call for focusing on the meaning people themselves give to specific institutions.

Studying the new governance institutions as introduced by Mali's decentralisation programme thus needs to go beyond an analysis of their formal mandate. It is the complex interplay between formal and informal dynamics

---

3   In Senegal, many people exchanged their votes for material rewards or voted with the aim to strengthen personal relations with particular local leaders that could offer socio-economic protection in times of need. In the United States, the main focus of electoral participation lies in choosing between different sets of policies. In other words, Schaffer's research highlights the difference between voting in order to increase collective material welfare and reinforce bonds of local solidarity and voting as a choice between alternative policy positions.

that determines policy outcomes and has to be examined empirically.[4] The neo-patrimonial paradigm is certainly of use, although informal dimensions seem to be more complex than patron–client relations. A broader cultural perspective taking into account power relations at the local level as well as the meaning people give to political participation and representation would seem most relevant.

2.2. Accountability

Accountability has become a prominent concept in both academic literature and donor policies. Various authors have therefore recently warned against what Lindberg (2009) refers to as the 'inherent dangers of a Byzantine conceptual nightmare leading to [...] severe confusion about what the core meaning of accountability is'. Accountability is, by definition, relational. An agent, for example a political representative, performs a number of tasks in response to expectations held by another party, a group of citizens, for example. The political representative is first of all required to inform, explain and justify his actions to the citizens. In other words, the first component of an accountable representative is answerability to citizens. Secondly, the citizens must have the capacity to pass judgment and impose sanctions on the representative. Such enforceability is the second major component of accountability (Lindberg 2009; Hyden 2008; Burnell 2003; O'Neil et al 2007; Bovens & 't Hart 2005).[5] In this chapter, the impact of the introduction and subsequent functioning of the new municipal councils on both answerability and enforceability aspects of the accountability relationship between local political representatives and citizens will be assessed.

Based on a substantive review of literature dealing with the concept of accountability, Lindberg (2009) identifies three dimensions of accountability: the source of accountability (are representatives being held accountable internally, within an institution, or externally, by citizens), the degree of control that people have over representatives (although difficult to quantify) and the direction of accountability (vertical upwards, vertical downwards or horizontal). An important research question in this respect is whether Malian decentralisation policies have brought about a stronger degree of downward accountability of local representatives towards citizens. Reviewing much of the decentralisation literature, Ribot (2002) concludes that 'decentralization is not taking the forms

---

4   See Hagman (2006); Erdmann and Engel (2007); Hansen (2003); Carothers (2006); Booth (2008); Chabal and Daloz (2006).

5   Brinkerhoff (2001), quoted in Ribot (2002), considers answerability to be the essence of accountability. Burnell (2003) however clearly demonstrates that answerability is considerably reduced if the potential to sanction is limited.

necessary to realise the benefits that theory predicts, because it fails to entrust downwardly accountable representative actors with significant domains of autonomous discretionary power'. In order to examine the impact of Mali's decentralisation programme, specific attention will therefore be given to the new political representatives, the power they have obtained in practice, the domain over which they obtained influence and the direction of their accountability.

2.3. Decentralisation

Decentralisation is when a central government formally cedes powers to actors and institutions at lower levels in a political-administrative and territorial hierarchy (Rondinelli 1981). Various forms of decentralisation have been distinguished, although the main distinction that is often made is between deconcentration and devolution.[6] The latter refers to a process whereby responsibilities and financial means are truly transferred from the national government to lower, more or less autonomous, public authorities. Through deconcentration, a national government represents itself at the local level but remains in control of policies and budgets (thus creating forms of upwards accountability). This chapter builds on the definition of democratic decentralisation as highlighted by Olowu (2001) which 'occurs when powers and resources are transferred to authorities representative of and downwardly accountable to local populations'.

Various waves of decentralisation have spread over the African continent over the last decades. The objectives differed from controlling the rural areas from the centre (in colonial times and during one-party rule), and reducing national governments' expenditure (during the years of structural adjustment policies), to improving political participation and the accountability of local governments (during the last decade of democratisation).[7]

In Mali, the new political elites, that replaced the authoritarian regime which ruled for almost 25 years, needed to restore state legitimacy in the 1990s.[8] Decentralisation became an important strategy in this respect. Another motive behind the programme was the need to contain the secession struggle by Tuareg rebellion groups in the Northern regions. By allowing the Northern regions greater autonomy, the territorial boundaries of the country could be safeguarded (Sall 1993; Seely 2001). In 1993, a *Mission de Décentralisation*

---

6   Otto (1999) and Rondinelli (1981) distinguish devolution, deconcentration, functional decentralisation and privatisation whereas Kassibo (1997) makes a distinction between deconcentration and devolution only.

7   See Ribot (2002) and Olowu (2001) for an elaborate overview.

8   See speech by Konaré during the celebration of Mali's 37th year of independence; see also Traore and Ganfoud (1996), Kassibo (1997), Sy (1998).

(MDD) was established and mandated to come up with a legal framework for the implementation of Mali's decentralisation programme. Within a few years, legislation was drafted to restructure Mali's administrative hierarchy, to set up elected bodies in the provinces, districts and local communities[9] and to define the exact mandate of the new municipal councils.[10] The local administration teams were to include a mayor and three civil servants, ie secretaries to the municipality.[11] Subsequent to this preparatory legislative work, 683 new local communities, regrouping thousands of villages, were officially established in 1996.[12] The first local elections were scheduled for 1999.

The municipal councils were made responsible for service delivery in the areas of local infrastructure, education and transport (Centre Djoliba & KIT 2003). The mayors were to collect tax,[13] draft the annual budget in a participatory manner and present financial reports to citizens (Sy 1998; De Lange 2004). Citizens could demand clarifications from local government through the councillors they had voted for ('answerability') and, if they were able to mobilise a majority within the council, councillors could force the mayor to take specific actions ('enforceability'). The legislative context within which Mali's decentralisation policies were framed thus seemed to provide solid foundations for a stronger downwards accountable local government.

Following Ribot (2002), Hyden (2008) and Olowu (2001), three specific issues are of great importance to the proper functioning of democratic decentralisation at the local level. These concern the actors that take control of decentralisation, the power they obtain and the domain within which they obtain such power. When it comes to the actors, Olowu (2001) argues that 'many traditional rulers in different parts of Africa have used decentralised power to obstruct development of their people by diverting decentralised resources to personal uses [...] because of their fear that these may break their hold on local power'. In a recent article, Hyden (2008) emphasises the importance of addressing power relations when studying the performance of institutions in Africa. Policy outcomes are not only the result of institutional changes, but are also determined by informal power relations. Finally, Ribot (2002) holds that local representatives 'must have a domain of discretionary decision-making powers, that is, one of local autonomy. It is with respect to this domain of powers that decentralised actors represent, are accountable to and serve the local population'.

---

9   Directly elected at the community level; indirectly at the district and regional level.
10 N. 95-022, 95-34, 97-08.
11 In larger communities more civil servants were envisaged.
12 N. 96-059. This brings the total number of municipalities to 703.
13 67% of taxes were reserved for the municipal council, 15% for the district council, 5% for the regional council and 3% for the association of municipal councils.

3. Local accountability in Mande villages prior to decentralisation

It was noted above that informal local relations are broader than patron–client relations and often culturally shaped. We will now provide a brief description of the political culture, institutions and accountability mechanisms at the local level as they existed in the area under study prior to the implementation of the decentralisation programme.

This chapter presents results from extensive fieldwork conducted around the first (1999), second (2004) and third (2009) local elections in Karan, a village some 90 kilometres south of Mali's capital city, Bamako, close to the Guinean border. Karan is located in the second region of Mali, Koulikouro and the district of Kangaba. In cultural terms, it is part of the *Mande* region which stretches over parts of Senegal, Gambia, Guinea and Mali.

The most important political institution at the local level is the village council. The council meets on a weekly basis in the vestibule of the village headman and manages local economic, political and social affairs. Political representation and access to representative positions is based on a number of criteria: (1) claims of autochthony expressed through stories of origin, (2) patronymics (*jamuw*),[14] (3) *kabilaw*, (4) hierarchical status groups, (5) seniority and (6) gender. These criteria are not to be interpreted as 'predetermined cultural/ancestral patterns' (Olivier de Sardan 2008) which, in an objective and static manner, easily determine who becomes a local political representative and who is excluded. Rather, these are criteria used by different (groups of) people to present their — often contradictory — authority claims. As 'claims of autochthony' are important for gaining access to powerful positions, different (interest) groups portray themselves as the most autochthonous inhabitants of a particular village in order to claim their right to become a political representative.

The origin of a *Mande* village is usually presented (and as such still referred to by citizens today) as a pact between its first inhabitants and groups that arrived at a later stage. In Karan, the Keïtas are considered to be the most autochthonous inhabitants. According to their version of the 'myth of origin', their ancestor founded Karan and met two other families, the Traore and Dumbia, with whom he established a pact.[15] According to the pact, the function of village headman

---

14   'Patronymic' refers to a person's last name but also to a historical figure. Patronymics have a strong social meaning in *Mande* and specific relations exist between patronymics. For example, between certain patronymics a joking relationship exists which allows people to neglect certain moral codes and tell each other off.

15   Many different versions of the story of origin exist. The Traore and Dumbia, for example, claim that they had arrived in Karan before the Keïta but that the latter were more powerful and that is why the Traore and Dumbia could not maintain the position of village headman themselves. These stories of origin are therefore not to be analysed as true accounts of some ancient past, but more as a reflection of actual power relations in local society. By presenting themselves as autochthonous inhabitants, different groups make status claims in local society.

was to be taken up by the Keïta, whereas the Traore and Dumbia would become mediators in the village (locally referred to as the *furugnoko*). Today, this pact is still being referred to and the *furugnoko* indeed play a mediatory role. Although many other families arrived in the centuries following the establishment of Karan, up to 2009 the 11 village council members were descendants of these three most autochthonous families. The village council was in effect monopolised by the patronymics (*jamuw*) Keïta, Traore and Dumbia. Claims of autochthony thus highly influence one's access to representative functions. As Jansen (1995; 1996) and others have indicated, oral traditions in *Mande* are much more than storytelling about some ancient past. The stories are used as references which shape social life and justify powerful positions today.

Another criterion that influences one's chances to become a member of the village council is the *kabila* to which one belongs.[16] A *kabila* is one of the most important socio-political institutions at the local level. Its members work together on a communal field, put aside money collectively and meet on a regular basis to discuss internal and village affairs. A *kabila* groups together a number of families (and the migrants these host) that have a shared ancestor. In Karan, the sons and grandsons of the founder of the village established five different *kabilaw*. The selection of village council members is done on the basis of the existing *kabilaw* within the village. In other words, the village council members represent their *kabila*. But the number of representatives differs for the various *kabilaw*. The two *kabilaw* that were established by the sons of the village founder are awarded three seats in the village council, those established by his grandsons only two and the *kabila* founded by his great-grandson only one. Yet again, claims of autochthony expressed through genealogies appear to be an important factor determining one's access to representative positions. The earlier a *kabila* is founded, the more autochthonous it is and the more representatives it receives within the village council.[17]

The hierarchical set-up of *Mande* society, which echoes India's caste system, also influences the access to representative functions. Society is divided into noble people (*hooronw*), followed by craftsmen — usually bards and smiths — (*nyamakalaw*) and former slaves (*jonw*).[18] Access to the village council is limited to noblemen only. Representatives of the *nyamakalaw* and *jonw* 'caste' cannot become village council members. Lastly, all council seats are reserved for relatively old men, many of whom have been members since the early 1960s.[19] Seniority is

---

16   *Kabilaw* is plural and *kabila* singular.

17   In 2009, the number of seats was augmented from 11 to 15 and equal representation amongst the five *kabilaw* was being considered.

18   The social organisation is more flexible than in India as the social status of particular groups might change over time.

19   In 2009, an agreement was reached to renew the village council members.

still an important factor determining political authority. The village headman is always the oldest Keïta of the oldest generation alive. In daily life, norms prohibit people to publicly contradict older brothers or fathers. The political role of women is rather limited at the village level, although a number of women are very active in other domains of public life (such as in NGOs and women associations).

A last important local institution worth mentioning here concerns the *kare*, a generational group. A *kare* is formed by a generation of young boys who are together circumcised. They remain members of the same *kare* throughout their lives and donate funds to each other for marriages, support members if they fall ill and meet on a regular basis to discuss local events. Whereas a *kabila* provides vertical lines of solidarity (family ties crossing generations), a *kare* can be seen as a horizontal solidarity group (generational ties crossing family lines).

Although Karan's village councillors do inform, consult with and justify their actions towards members of their *kabilaw* (and are thus answerable), the opportunity to hold village councillors accountable is minimal. It seems almost impossible to pass judgment against or sanction village councillors that have been in office for 40 years. Therefore, enforceability is extremely limited and vertical downward accountability between village councillors, who have a wide sphere of influence, and citizens is relatively weak.

The next section of this chapter examines the extent to which the introduction of Mali's decentralisation programme has strengthened local mechanisms of accountability between 1999 and 2009.

4. The implementation of Mali's decentralisation programme: The case of Karan

4.1. The first local elections in Karan: Consensus-building instead of electoral competition

The establishment and subsequent functioning of the first municipal council was greatly influenced by existing notions of political representation and participation. This became apparent during the selection process of candidates in the run-up to the 1999 elections. Representatives of the *furugnoko*, the families that play a mediatory role according to Karan's pact of origin, met with the village council. They proposed to develop a consensus list containing representatives from the various *kabilaw* instead of organising competitive elections on the basis of party lists which could possibly generate conflict in the village.[20] The proposal was

---

20   The 1997 national elections had generated a lot of tensions in Karan between supporters of two rivalling candidates. Some people would no longer speak to each other, marriage proposals were refused on the basis of political affiliations and for some time the losing side refused to contribute to the development efforts of the village.

accepted and each *kabila* leader called for a meeting to identify representatives who would sit on the municipal council on behalf of the *kabila*. A consensus list was put together in accordance with the power-sharing arrangement between the five *kabilaw* in the village council. The list included only noble people and only descendants from the three families that claim to be the autochthonous inhabitants of Karan (Keïtas and *furugnoko*). Candidates were either Keïta, Traore or Dumbia. No other *jamuw* was represented on the list. On election day, Karanese citizens voted for the consensus list.

The newly elected municipal council differed from the village council in two respects, seniority and gender. The municipal councillors were all much younger than the village council members and included a female representative. The age difference enabled the village council to secure control over their 'younger brothers' in the municipal council, based on local seniority norms. In daily life, younger brothers are requested to conduct tasks away from home, whereas older brothers are responsible for internal (family) affairs (Jansen 1995; Van Vliet 2004). This division of labour was now also applied to the two institutions. According to the law, the municipal council was to become the main institution governing local affairs. In practice, however, the municipal council only maintained contact with the state bureaucracy, produced official state documents (birth and marriage certificates) and tried to attract foreign NGOs to invest in Karan. The municipal council was, in other words, used as a gateway to the world outside the village. The village council continued to dominate all internal affairs, notably tax collection, conflict management and decision-making over a wide variety of internal matters. All major decisions were taken in the vestibule of the village headman and not in the municipal town hall.[21]

Tensions between the village council and the municipal council arose during the first mandate of the municipal council. The first elected mayor of Karan had worked within the state bureaucracy and became frustrated with the gap between his extensive formal mandate and the limited powers he had in practice. The mayor was cut off from the two main local sources of finance, funds provided by the national cotton company on a yearly basis and local tax collection, because the village council continued to manage these funds. Yet, the village council had not kept financial records up to date and was unable to account for the manner in which these funds had been spent over the last years. More than 3 000 Euros were missing. The village councillors claimed that citizens had not yet paid their taxes, whereas many people indicated that they had paid the village council. No records were available for verification. The mayor continuously tried to persuade

---

21   A local survey conducted in 2002 confirmed popular views on this division of labour between the two institutions.

the village councillors and citizens to allow the municipal council to manage the funds (without which he could not execute any of his formal tasks). He also frequently pointed to the existing lack of financial transparency which greatly frustrated some of the village councillors. This issue would play an important role in the run-up to the second local elections organised in 2004.

Neither the 1999 elections nor the new municipal council were able to shape local political behaviour according to their formal mandate. Instead, the new formal structures were based on existing informal power relations shaped around cultural notions of political representation and loyalty. The immediate impact of Mali's decentralisation programme on local accountability was therefore minimal. The new political actors did not obtain sufficient power to act according to their formal mandate, were only engaged in an external sphere of influence and were primarily being held accountable by the village council rather than ordinary citizens. Instead of downwards accountability, a new form of upwards accountability from the municipal council towards the village council had arisen based on family ties and local norms of respecting seniority.

4.2. The second local elections in Karan: Informal power basis further reduces formal impact

In the run-up to the second local elections in 2004, a *furugnoko* proposal to allow for another consensus list and a second mandate for the incumbent mayor was rejected. The head of the village council was irritated by the mayor's ambition to control the local financial resources. He considered the elections as an opportunity to consolidate the supremacy of the village council over the municipal council. The head of the village council was also the leader of the largest *kabila* in Karan, called Dubala. One of the main political parties, called Alliance for Democracy in Mali (ADEMA),[22] was dominated by young members of Dubala. A pact was rapidly agreed upon: the head of the village council would mobilise the people of 'his' *kabila* behind ADEMA while the party, once elected, would safeguard the interests of the village council. The incumbent mayor, in turn, tried to mobilise his own *kabila*, called Kurula, behind the Party for Democracy and Renewal (PDR) in his ambition to become re-elected.

The election results led to a stalemate within the municipal council with regard to the election of the mayor. Both PDR (with strong support from Kurula) and ADEMA (with a firm support basis in Dubala) obtained five seats. The eleventh and last seat was won by Adama Keïta on behalf of the Union for the Republic and Democracy (URD). He had been able to secure support from his direct

---

22   Adema was the ruling party of Mali between 1992 and 2002 and is still the largest party in Mali's National Assembly.

family and part of the youth association. His vote for either ADEMA or PDR would determine which party would obtain the position of mayor.

Adama Keïta had been an active member and representative of the local branch of ADEMA in Karan. He had, however, left the party with two other rank-and-file members because of tensions with the local Secretary-General, Treasurer and Chairman of the party. Nevertheless, he supported ADEMA in the vote for the election of the second mayor of Karan.

> I wanted to vote for PDR. Prior to the elections, I had even reached an agreement with their leader. I didn't like the candidate from ADEMA nor the party. I had just broken away from it! After the elections, the leader of PDR offered me 250.000 Fcfa and a motorcycle in order to secure my support. As I come from the kabila Dubala, the leader of Dubala informed me that I would be suspended from the kabila if I didn't vote in favour of ADEMA. What could I do? It would complicate the rest of my life if I lost support from my kabila. It's my family. My life. I wasn't awarded a cent by ADEMA or Dubala, but I voted in favour of ADEMA.

Contrary to his own political preferences and despite the financial offers made to him, Adama Keïta voted in favour of ADEMA. This is just one example (out of many) of the way in which informal ties and family (*kabila*) pressure continue to strongly influence the selection of political actors at the local level. Such culturally shaped power relations can thus be much more influential than pure patronage and money politics. As it turned out, the leader of the *kabila* Dubala played a determining role in Adama Keïta's choice for an ADEMA mayor.

Once elected, the new ADEMA mayor indeed stopped the quest of the municipal council to gain control over local funds. He also refrained from competing with the village council, headed by the leader of his own *kabila*, nor did he criticise the village council for its failure to account for part of the tax money it had received from Karanese citizens. Under the new mayor, transparency of local affairs deteriorated. The mayor appointed young friends — mostly from ADEMA and Dubala — to head various local management boards. Although these boards are all formally required to report back to the municipal council on a regular basis, they only reported informally to the mayor in person. Municipal councillors of rival parties were left in the dark. The mayor himself refused to report to ordinary citizens. During his mandate, tax collection reduced from 3.9 million Fcfa to 2.3 million Fcfa, leaving the municipality unable to pay the salaries of municipal staff. The vast majority of local people suspected a rise in corrupt practices[23] but their biggest frustration was the lack of information provided by the mayor and his allies.

---

23 There were serious indications of corruption in the local health board, the management of the local granary and other institutions. The mayor also claimed to have lost more than 2 million Fcfa of public funds while driving with his motorcycle to a neighbouring village.

Public frustration with the performance of the mayor, certainly within the four other *kabilaw*, continued to grow. Interestingly, when asked why the police or regional authorities were not informed of the suspected corruption, almost all interviewees indicated that 'relations between our families never end; they are more important than money. This is between us here in Karan'.[24] A local cultural institution (*kare*) then started to lead a call for improved local governance, albeit outside the formal framework set out in the relevant local government legislation. In Karan, the Sobessi *kare* were considered to be the local police[25] but they decided to use their mandate in a larger sense. One of them expressed a widely shared feeling as follows:

> Karan has fallen into a well. We, as Sobessi, need to get Karan back out of there. The elderly people in the village council and the current mayor haven't managed the village well. Many projects that arrived in Karan already failed upon entry. They are responsible for Karan's decay. We have to change.

The Sobessi managed to build popular support for the removal of the corrupt management board of the local infirmary. They then initiated a quest to change the members of the village council which proved overambitious. The head of the village council started to put pressure on a number of Sobessi to stop their campaign for renewal. The case of Noumouri Keïta is illustrative:

> Our quest for renewal of the village council as Sobessi was not easy. When we started our opposition against the current members of the village council, my wife was taken away from me. She had to return to her hamlet where she was born. The leader of my kabila was behind all this. That is how he put pressure on me and tried to stop me from supporting the quest for renewal of the village council.

The mayor indicated that the Sobessi had no formal mandate to remove the village councillors. He continued to support the head of the village council and the Sobessi finally dropped their case. Not much later, a law was passed in the Malian Parliament which called for the renewal of village councils nationwide. This provided the formal grounds for renewal in Karan. Finally, in 2009, the village council was renewed. The mayor, however, refused to obtain the formal approval of the regional state authorities on the basis of which the new village council could start operating and the elderly continued to influence local affairs.

---

24 The former mayor had informed the authorities over alleged corruption by the current mayor with respect to his management of the local granary, but this was condemned by almost everyone, even those who believed the current mayor to be highly corrupt. Only 90 kilometres from the capital city, formal state institutions such as the police seemed to have little impact in this situation.

25 Members of the *kare* first and foremost mediate in conflicts between families if crops are being eaten by someone else's cattle.

Ten years after its introduction, the impact of Mali's decentralisation programme on local accountability continued to be limited. Although formal electoral competition now took place, the informal (*kabila* based) power basis of the new mayor limited his power to act once elected. Family ties proved more influential than patronage politics in shaping political behaviour during the second electoral mandate. The sphere of influence of the municipal council remained limited to external affairs and accountability relations were even strengthened upwards towards the village council to the detriment of ordinary citizens. The formally required renewal of the village council was blocked by the informal power arrangement between the mayor and the head of the village council. The downward accountability that was to some extent realised was shaped by a local cultural institution (*kare*) which held the village and municipal councils answerable for a lack of transparency and even enforced a renewal of the local infirmary board.

4.3. The third local elections in Karan: Alternation of power

Due to the informal deal between the head of the largest *kabila* Dubala and the mayor, opportunities for ordinary citizens to hold the poor performing mayor accountable were minimal during the second electoral mandate. The formal requirement to organise another local election in 2009 provided an opportunity to do so and ensure an alternation of power. However, a campaign strategy based on culturally shaped tactics and informal patronage was required in order to succeed.

In the run-up to the elections, two main competing blocks were formed. On the one hand, the *ben kan* list[26] was made up of PDR representatives who narrowly lost the 2004 elections and other (smaller) local parties. They were primarily supported by the *kabila* Kurula, the *kare* Sobessi, the Karanese people residing in Bamako and the village mediators (*furugnoko*). On the other hand, the incumbent mayor was supported by his own party ADEMA, by URD, the head of the village council, the *kabila* Dubala and the younger *kare* Sankassi. The campaign objective of the *ben kan* list was to maintain the support from its own electoral bases, while mobilising support within the Sankassi *kare* and Dubala *kabila*.

The electoral list of the *ben kan* group was put together in a clever way. Its main support basis (the *kabila* Kurula) was awarded two top positions but the other four *kabilaw* were also included.[27] The same applied to the different

---

26 Because their list was supported by the village mediators (who had tried to mobilise everyone behind the list), they referred to their alliance as the *ben kan* list, meaning the list of consensus.

27 As various group representatives explained, 'If you propose a list with people from just one, two or three *kabilaw*, the people will not accept it. You need to keep every *kabila* on board'.

generational groups (*karew*). The list only included people considered to be 'true autochthones'.[28] Another important criterion for being placed on the list was one's financial means. The *ben kan* list was headed by two men residing in Bamako. The number one, Djibril Naman, worked as a director for the National Railway Company, often travelled to Europe and had sound political contacts. This asset was successfully exploited during the electoral campaign period.

Obtaining support within the younger generations (notably the *kare* Sankassi) was judged crucial for *ben kan's* electoral success. According to one of the main campaign strategists,

> We knew URD and ADEMA had strong support in the Sankassi *kare*. The second mayor had awarded numerous local management positions to its members. We therefore decided that the head of our list should be someone from the Sankassi *kare*. We organised various informal meetings with all Sankassi in order to secure their support for Djibril because he was one of them.

Continued references to important cultural values was an important ingredient of the *ben kan's* campaign strategy. They stressed that the *furugnoko* supported their list and that, according to Karan's pact of origin, people needed to respect the wish of their mediators.[29] In addition, the large network and wealth of the leader of their list, Djibril Naman, was emphasised. During a rally, the campaign team stated:

> If everyone votes for Djibril Naman, we will mobilise the rich Karanese people residing in Bamako to come and invest in Karan. You have to vote for someone who has the capacity to build something for the entire community. You have to vote for us. We will build a community radio station here in Karan. We will also build a house within which the youth can gather.

Djibril Naman generated huge cheers from the crowd when he promised that the local mosque which the community had started to build would be finished quickly if he was elected. The message was clear. You either vote for the incompetent incumbent mayor or for someone who has the capacity to act as a patron for Karan and can guarantee a number of public goods.

Yet another successful campaign strategy was to put pressure on URD and ADEMA candidates not to campaign actively, by making use of informal

---

28 A comment by one of the non-autochthones who presented himself as a candidate in 2004 and invested a lot of money during his campaigns is illustrative in this respect: 'During the electoral campaigns in 2004, I offered local citizens a cow, 50 kilos of rice and spent 20.000 Fcfa for preparing the sauce. Some 150 people showed up and ate with me. Nevertheless, I only obtained 63 votes. My competitors had gone around the various hamlets saying that if I would be elected, I would take Karan's money to my own native town. People here prefer local candidates'.

29 Campaigning slogans used during their visits to the hamlets were: '*I fa boh ye*' (you respect the words of your father) and we are the group of *ben kan* or *ben makan* (consensus).

(and powerful) family ties. A striking example, amongst many, concerned the ambition of Naman Sidibé to become the leader of the ADEMA list.

> I wanted to become head of the list, but family pressure stopped me from doing so. The leader of my *kabila*, who supported the *ben kan* list, told me that I had to withdraw. My father told me the same. He said that if I didn't, the family would not support me if I ever got in trouble. That I would learn what life is like if you are not supported by your family. My room for manoeuvring was therefore rather limited. I could maintain a lower position on the list, but could not openly campaign or head the list.

On election day, the results were clear. Out of the eleven seats available, eight were won by the *ben kan* list, two by ADEMA and one by URD. The leader of URD responded: 'I have invested so much money and received only one seat in return. If it were not in politics, people would be jailed for such an offence'.

When the new mayor took office, the financial records indeed showed many irregularities. The former mayor, together with one of his allies, was obliged to pay back a percentage of the funds that had disappeared. The new mayor paid the rest from his own pocket and refused to inform state authorities of the matter in order to 'maintain social stability and avoid further tensions between families'. Transparency quickly improved. Management bodies of local institutions were replaced and reported on a regular basis to the municipal and village councils. The new municipal council also organised various public consultative meetings.

The new municipal council agreed upon a division of labour with the new village council. It would continue to focus on external matters and accepted the mandate of the village council to manage internal affairs 'because they would otherwise feel marginalised which would create problems for us', according to one of the municipal councillors. In the area of raising tax, the municipal staff would work closely together with the *kare* Sobessi (regarded as the local police).

The funds and network of the new mayor already proved valuable for Karan during the first six months of his mandate. He travelled to Spain in order to motivate the Karanese migrants living there to sponsor a Karanese development project, he paid a large share of the reparation costs of a path connecting Karan to the main road and he took a friend working for the National Media Institute to Karan in order to secure state assistance for a local radio station.

All in all, the formal requirement to organise local elections in 2009 opened up the possibility for people to sanction the second mayor of Karan. His political adversaries were well aware that in order to tap into his culturally shaped power basis, they had to come up with a culturally sensitive campaign strategy and present their candidate as a good patron for Karan. The patron had to obtain local cultural capital in order to win the elections. After the elections, the third mayor of Karan obtained much more power in practice than his predecessors primarily due to his own capital and network. In contrast to the competition between the municipal and village councils during the first mandate and the informal deal between the village headmen and the mayor which negatively affected the provision of public goods during the second mandate, a constructive agreement was now reached between the new mayor and the new village council. The sphere of direct influence of the municipal council would remain directed at Karan's external relations. The new municipal council greatly improved information provision and public consultation, thereby allowing ordinary citizens to hold them answerable. However, the dependence on the funds and network of the mayor and the top-down nature of these patron-client relations do not leave much room for strong enforceability mechanisms. Thus accountability only partially and gradually improved following the third elections, whereas the provision of public goods saw a rapid and dramatic improvement.

5. Conclusion

The case material presented above compels scholars and international development agents to be modest when it comes to expecting improvements in accountability through institutional change. New institutions encounter various existing informal institutions and are often incorporated within powerful informal relations that have a greater impact on their functioning than their respective formal mandates. Local elections create opportunities to bring about vertical accountability, but culturally shaped informal relations determine local citizens' ability to actually hold their representatives accountable. In practice, the powers, spheres of influence and degree of downward accountability of Karan's new municipal council are still lagging far behind its official mandate. Thus, this study confirms Ribot's (2002) conclusion that 'decentralisation is not taking the form necessary to realise the benefits that theory predicts, because it fails to entrust downwardly accountable representative actors with significant domains of autonomous discretionary power'. In other words, Mali's decentralisation programme does not seem to have affected the degree, source and direction of accountability in Karan in the ways its legal foundations stipulated.

The empirical data presented here indicate the need to refine the neo-patrimonial paradigm that dominates academic literature on African political developments. Powerful positions at the local level are strongly based on cultural values such as autochthony, seniority and family solidarity. Political support bases are primarily built within cultural institutions, notably the *kabilaw* and *karew*. Informal hierarchical family ties strongly influence an individual's political room for manoeuvring. In local politics, these ties are often much more influential than an exchange of goods, money and other favours between so-called patrons and clients. Even the 'patron of Karan' had to run a culturally sophisticated campaign in order to secure a victory at the third local elections.

In a somewhat unexpected manner, Mali's decentralisation programme does seem to have contributed to an improvement in the provision of public goods in Karan (and in many neighbouring villages); not so much as a consequence of the formal powers assigned to the new municipal council, but merely because local elections have offered successful people in Bamako an opportunity to invest in their villages of origin and start building a political support base. Informal family ties seem to have frustrated the functioning of the municipal council in Karan. However, based on the same informal family ties, a wealthy Karanese entrepreneur living in Bamako is now investing much of his private funds, time and network to improve the quality of life for the people in Karan.

References

Abbink, J. 2006. Discomfiture of democracy? The 2005 elections crisis in Ethiopia and its aftermath. *African Affairs*, 105(419): 173–199.

Abbink, J. 2006. Interpreting Ethiopian elections in their context — A reply to Tobias Hagman. *African Affairs*, 105(421): 613–620.

Abbink, J. & Hesseling, G. (eds.). 2000. *Election Observation and Democratisation in Africa*. Basingstoke: Macmillan.

Bovens, M. & 't Hart, P. 2005. Evaluating accountability. Paper presented at Accountable Governance: An International Research Colloquium, Queen's University Belfast, October 20–22.

Burnell, P. 2003. Legislative–executive relations in Zambia: Parliamentary reform on the agenda. *Journal of Contemporary African Studies*, 21(1): 47–68.

Booth, D. 2008. A research design fit for purpose. Discussion paper 3. London: ODI Africa Power and Politics Programme. Available at http://www.institutions-africa. org. Accessed 1 November 2010.

Carothers, T. 2006. *Confronting the Weakest Link: Aiding Political Parties in New Democracies*. Washington: Carnegie Endowment for International Peace.

Chabal, P. & Daloz, J.P. 2006. *Culture Troubles: Politics and the Interpretation of Meaning*. London: Hurst & Company.

Centre Djoliba & KIT. 2003. *Soutenir La Mise en Oeuvre de la Décentralisation en Milieu Rural au Mali: Tome 1, Thème d'Actualité; Tome 2, Boîte à Outils*. Amsterdam: KIT.

De Lange, M.S. 2004. *Rêves de Décentralisation et Réalités de Douentza, Etude Socio-juridique des Effets de la Politique de Décentralisation dans une Petite Ville au Mali*. Coopération Juridique Mali — Pays-Bas. Leiden: Van Vollenhoven Instituut.

Diamond, L., Linz, J.J. & Lipset, S.M. (eds.). 1990. *Politics in Developing Countries: Comparing Experiences with Democracy.* Boulder: Lynne Rienner Publishers.

Eisenstadt, S.N. 1973. *Traditional Patrimonialism and Modern Neopatrimonialism.* Beverly Hills: Sage Publications.

Engel, U. & Olsen, G.R. 2005. *The African Exception: Contemporary Perspectives on Developing Societies.* Farnham: Ashgate Publishing Limited.

Erdmann, G. & Engel, U. 2007. Neopatrimonialism reconsidered — Critical review and elaboration of an elusive concept. *Journal of Commonwealth and Comparative Studies,* 45(1): 95–119.

Geschiere, P. 1997. *The Modernity of Witchcraft: Politics and the Occult in Postcolonial Africa.* Virginia: University of Virginia Press.

Hagman, T. 2006. Ethiopian political culture strikes back: A rejoinder to J. Abbink. *African Affairs,* 105(421): 605–612.

Hansen, K.F. 2003. The politics of personal relations: Beyond neo-patrimonial practices in northern Cameroon. *Africa,* 73(2): 202–225.

Huntington, S.P. 1992. *Third Wave: Democratisation in the Late Twentieth Century.* Oklahoma: University of Oklahoma Press.

Hyden, G. 2008. Institutions, power and policy outcomes in Africa. Discussion paper 2. London: ODI Africa Power and Politics Programme. Available at http://www. institutions-africa.org. Accessed 1 November 2009.

Jansen, J. 1995. *De Draaiende Put. Een Studie naar de Relatie tussen het Sunjata-epos en de Samenleving in de Haut-Niger (Mali).* Leiden: CNWS.

Jansen, J. 1996. The younger brother and the stranger in search of status discourse for Mande. *Cahier d'Études Africaines,* 144 (46-4): 659–684.

Kassibo, B. (ed). 1997. La décentralisation au Mali: Etats des lieux. *Bulletin 14.* Hamburg/ California: Sage Publications.

Lindberg, S. 2006. *Democracy and Elections in Africa.* Baltimore: Johns Hopkins University Press.

Lindberg, S. 2009. Accountability: The core concept and its subtypes. Working paper 1. London: ODI Africa Power and Politics Programme. Available at http://www. institutions-africa.org. Accessed 1 November 2009.

Médard, J.F. 1982. The underdeveloped state in Africa: Political clientelism or neo-patrimonialism? In Clapham, C. (ed.). *Private Patronage and Public Power: Political Clientelism and the Modern State.* London: Frances Pinter.

Nugent, P. 2001. Winners, losers and also rans: Money, moral authority and voting patterns in the Ghana 2000 election. *African Affairs,* 100: 405–428.

Olivier de Sardan, J.P. 2008. Researching the practical norms of real governance in Africa. Discussion paper 5. London: ODI Africa Power and Politics Programme. Available at http://www.institutions-africa.org. Accessed 1 November 2010.

Oluwu, B. 2001. African decentralisation policies and practices from 1980s and beyond. Working paper 334. The Hague: ISS.

O'Neil, T., Foresti, M. & Hudson, A. 2007. *Evaluation of Citizen's Voice and Accountability: Review of the Literature and Donor Approaches.* London: ODI.

Otto, J.M. 1999. *Lokaal bestuur in Ontwikkelingslanden: Een Leidraad voor Lagere Overheden in de Ontwikkelingssamenwerking.* Bussum: Coutinho.

Ribot, J.C. 2002. African decentralisation: Actors, powers and accountability. Democracy, Governance and Human Rights Working paper 8. UNRISD Programme.

Rondinelli, D.A. 1981. Government decentralisation in comparative perspective. *International Review of Administrative Sciences,* 47(2): 133–145.

Sall, A. 1993. *Le Pari de la Décentralisation au Mali: (i) Contribution, (2) Textes Fondamentaux (1955-1993).* Bamako: Sodifi.

Schaffer, F.C. 1998. *Democracy in Translation: Understanding Politics in an Unfamiliar Culture.* London: Cornell University Press.

Schatzberg, M.G. 1993. Power, legitimacy and democratisation in Africa. *Africa,* 63(4): 445–461.

Seely, J.C. 2001. A political analysis of decentralisation: Co-opting the Tuareg threat in Mali. *Journal of Modern African Studies,* 39(3): 499–524.

Sy, O. 1998. *La Décentralisation et les Réformes Institutionnelles au Mali : Le Cadre d'une Nouvelle Dynamique de Démocratisation et de Développement.* Bamako: MDRI.

Therkildsen, O. 2005. Understanding public management through neo-patrimonialism: A paradigm for all African seasons? In Engel, U. & Olsen, G.R. (eds.). *The African Exception: Contemporary Perspectives on Developing Societies.* Farnham: Ashgate Publishing Limited.

Traore, O. & Ganfoud, B.O.A. 1996. *Problématique Foncière et Décentralisation au Mali.* Bamako: Centre Djoliba.

UNDP. 1991. *Human Development Report 1991: Financing Human Development.* Available at http://hrd.undp.org/en/reports/global/hdr1991. Accessed 6 September 2011.

Van Cranenburg, O. 2000. Democratization in Africa: The role of election observation. In Abbink, J. & Hesseling, G. (eds). *Election Observation and Democratization in Africa.* London: MacMillan.

Van Donge, J.K. 2006. Interpreting political culture: The Zambian presidential elections of 2006 (unpublished).

Van Vliet, M.T. 2004. *Het Malinese decentralisatiebeleid in cultureel-historisch perspectief.* University of Leiden: PhD Thesis.

Von Soest, C. 2007. How does neopatrimonialism affect the African state's revenues? The case of tax collection in Zambia. *Journal of Modern African Studies* 45(4): 621–645.

Wiseman, J.A. 1999. Book review of Africa works: Disorder as a political instrument. *Journal of Modern African Studies,* 37(3): 560–562.

World Bank 1989. *Annual Report 1989.* Washington DC: The World Bank.

World Bank 1993. *Annual Report 1993.* Washington DC: The World Bank.

Chapter 15

Understanding local forms of accountability: Initial findings from Ghana and Malawi

Diana Cammack

1. Introduction

Accountability — ensuring leadership compliance with expected standards of behaviour — is a central dimension of the essentially political processes that drive development outcomes in Africa. In the African context, accountability poses particular challenges going beyond the generic principal-agent problem. Generally, obedience is difficult to assure because of information asymmetries between leaders and service-providers on the one hand and their constituencies or clients on the other. In Africa, extremely large differentials in power often characterise accountability relationships, for example between officials and ordinary people, chiefs and villagers, and presidents and junior politicians. Moreover, when holding persons to account, actors apply norms or rules derived from a multitude of sources — legal, religious, cultural, professional and familial — in an often unsuccessful attempt to ensure that others perform as expected. The implications of these many different forms of accountability for development outcomes are a major topic of research in the Africa Power and Politics Programme (APPP)[1]. This chapter outlines the debate which has taken place within the APPP about the concept of accountability and presents some findings from research undertaken in 2008–2010 which illustrate the developmental consequences of patterns of accountability in sub-Saharan Africa.

2. Accountability in APPP

2.1. Background

In the 1990s, international donors delivered food aid to local communities, refugees and internally displaced people (IDP) through a variety of mechanisms, including food-for-work (FFW) projects and monthly distributions of relief

---

1   For more information about the Africa Power and Politics Programme, see http://www.institutions-africa.org/.

supplies. In the case of FFW projects, local leaders were asked to make a list of the most destitute in their villages that would be provided with work — building roads for instance — for which they would be paid by non-governmental organisations (NGOs) with bags of maize or rice. Evaluators found that many of these FFW programmes did not reach the most vulnerable people and that recipients often included relatives of the local headman. Similarly, researchers discovered, when evaluating refugee and IDP feeding programmes, that some ineligible beneficiaries, such as liberation army members, were prioritised in the allocation of aid. Women were often the least likely to receive a (fair) share.

The reason for such distortions in the distribution of aid lies in the perception that food is wealth and, as such, local power relations determine how new wealth is distributed. Those with control over food aid answer not to the weakest in their societies but to other powerful people. In other words, to whom they account is dependent to a large extent on power relations at the local level.

Experience such as this takes the concept of accountability out of the sphere of high-level political and legal theory and demonstrates its relevance to real-life, grass-roots behaviour. Specifically, the forms that accountability takes locally and nationally are contextually determined and subject to change over time, as power comes to be distributed differently, and this has significant implications for what can and cannot be achieved in development work. It is in this sense that accountability is of interest to the APPP.

The APPP is studying how accountability works under extant African institutions[2] because its researchers believe that existing norms may provide a better basis upon which to promote development than imposing foreign institutions (including some neoliberal good governance institutions) that do not 'go with the grain' of what already exists. The APPP's research is predicated on the belief, based on our reading of global political-economic history, that development is easier and more sustainable where local initiative is harnessed. APPP teams are looking for examples throughout sub-Saharan Africa where public goods[3] are provided more or less adequately by various types of leaders and communities and collective action problems are solved by institutions that are rooted in African realities.

The type of 'good outcomes' under study in the APPP is quite varied, as different research teams are dealing with different levels of action, from local governance or a single sector's business practices to the national political arena.

---

2   Here we are not talking about structures, but institutions as rules and norms that guide decision-making and behaviour.

3   Public goods are a 'large class of "good things" that are inherently liable to be under-supplied because … individuals, households and private organisations acting on their own have no interest in providing them' (Booth 2008a: 2–3). They include a sound enterprise environment, clean water and peace and public order.

Volunteers, entrepreneurs, farmers, courts, Members of Parliament (MPs), civil servants, Imams, chiefs and others actors are all included in the research.

The behaviour of these actors is obviously governed by different mixtures, or hybrids, of historically rooted norms and modern-day rules. Each institutional arrangement produces its own forms of authority and modes of governance. Nevertheless, the APPP expects to find some underlying causal mechanisms which operate across institutional spheres and countries, and which explain why some are able to produce public goods better than others. For instance, doing things in ways that conform to existing local practices may give leaders and their behaviours more legitimacy than if they behave like foreigners; they, more than outsiders, may have a better chance of overcoming collective-action problems and harnessing existing forms of social capital.

Additional hypothesising within the APPP has pinpointed other factors that some researchers suspect to have an important influence on outcomes. These are being explored in our field studies. It has been suggested that the African institutions that appear to be comparatively successful in solving collective-action problems and providing public goods are those which harness the motivating forces of family, ethnicity or religion (Kelsall 2008: 648–649); that ethnic networks endowed with mechanisms that discourage free-riding and reward cooperation will achieve better outcomes (Habyarimana et al 2007); that prevailing institutions that incentivise the adoption of innovative technical solutions to the undersupply of public goods will benefit communities; and that synergy between government and societal action is achieved when there is a clear division of labour, and the public actors are sufficiently enmeshed in networks of social relations at the local level to have the knowledge, contacts and respect to operate effectively (Booth 2009: 22–23). The importance of functioning regimes of sanctions and of agencies operating according to clear mandates is emerging from our fieldwork as well.

APPP researchers are aware that no purely traditional form of leadership or way of doing things exists in Africa (or anywhere for that matter) and that everywhere Africans have been the subject of imposed rule. Thus, in all cases it is hybrid forms of leadership and institutions that we are studying. Each APPP team, whether focusing on Islamic education or state-business relations, is documenting the manner in which specific blends of leadership and institutions have been constructed over time, and how and why they differ from place to place in their ability to generate positive outcomes.

Focusing on how power is used in Africa to either benefit or abuse communities, the APPP is naturally interested in forms of accountability. We expect that these will differ from place to place and from time to time as institutions and actors vary, and that, in each case, multiple overlapping forms will be evident. This is because, everywhere, people operate according to multiple registers; sometimes reacting as their ancestors might have done and other times using a mix of old and new, local and imported institutions to hold leaders or providers to account. It is expected that where several layers of accountability are found, each based in a different tradition, those relations which are rooted in local, practical norms will be more effective in generating responsiveness. Having more accountable leaders is generally expected to be more developmental.[4]

While there is no single, agreed position among APPP's 20-plus researchers about accountability, this chapter provides a brief overview of the concept as used by members of the programme, its relationship to other important issues such as power and legitimacy, and the role we feel it generally plays in promoting development. It then provides examples of how the concept is being utilised by APPP researchers in exploring the interaction of leaders and citizens and assessing whether their actions have positive outcomes that might be deemed developmental.

2.2. What is accountability?

Accountability is a form of interaction or relationship. It requires at least two actors, but often involves more. It is defined by an actor (A) being answerable to another (B) for behaving in a prescribed manner, responding to those prescriptions, justifying that behaviour, and being sanctioned if not performing as expected. When exploring accountability relationships it is therefore necessary to identify:

- A, the principal actor who is to be held to account
- The prescribed behaviour for which A is to be held accountable
- The individual or group (B) that is to hold A to account
- The actual response of A, including any decisions made, information shared or justifications given
- The sanctions that are to be enforced if performance is not deemed appropriate or adequate and the method by which enforcement is assured.

As should be clear from the example of food aid recipients mentioned earlier, the relationship between an actor and his or her expected behaviour need not be *formally* prescribed, for example, in the law, guidelines, regulations or the Constitution, though this is often the case. Instead, the relationship and

---

4   This does not assume democracy is developmental, for an autocrat who builds up his or her country's economy may feel more accountable to history than his or her contemporaries and may shun populist politics and democratic accountability. The question then to ask is who is accountable for what and to whom?

the expected action may be laid down historically, by tradition or culture, or by ideological conventions, for example, religious beliefs or shared ideals. As culture, ideologies, rules, and the bases from which these emerge (that is, social, economic and political conditions) change, so will accountability relationships. The informality of norms — the fact that they are not written down — does not make them any less powerful as parameters defining who are the responsible parties, how people are to act or what sanctions may be applied.

There is some debate within the APPP about what right B is invoking when he or she sanctions A — that is, does B possess only the right to have information and justification for actions and decisions made by A, or does B also have the right to sanction A for the content or effect of such decisions and actions? Lindberg (2009) argues that the meaning of the concept should be restricted to the former, the right to have information and justification. Others would argue that this is too restrictive, for people typically want more than excuses for another's non-performance or for their performance not resulting in expected, even promised, benefits. They want to hold A responsible for the actual delivery of benefits. Responsiveness is therefore central to the accountability relationship (Lange et al 2005; Kelsall 2008; Hyden 2010).

Another important issue when analysing accountability is the distinction between those who may benefit (or not) from the performance of actor A, and those who are in a position to sanction A's non-performance or non-delivery of benefits (Lindberg 2009). In many cases, the beneficiaries are not those with the power to sanction. For instance, if a doctor is to treat a child and fails, it will not be the child who punishes the doctor but the Medical Board or others in authority. In these three-cornered accountability interactions (see Figure 1), the rules or norms that guide performance and sanctions must be understood and accepted, and information must be shared by the key players for accountability to be effective.

When they are not, the recipient, in this case the child, may well be under-served by A because those meant to hold the physician to account (B) are unwilling or unable to sanction him or her. Then we would say the institutions — the norms and rules governing behaviour — are weak. This may be the case for many different reasons, mostly to do with incentives. For example, the board may be bribed by the doctor, or the dominant view of the board's members may be that relatively anonymous patients do not matter as much as a colleague's reputation and friendship. In such a case, it is also likely that the formal law and regulations are inadequately laid out or poorly enforced, or that information on the case is lacking.

It is for this reason that researchers need to explore the source of any accountability — that is, is it grounded in parchment institutions (laws,

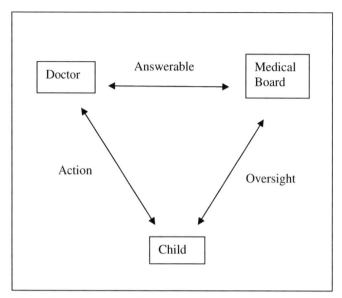

Figure 15.1: Accountability Interaction

constitutions, rules) or is it rooted in more informal, unwritten but shared understandings (culture, tradition, history, norms)? Both are likely to be involved, for there are often overlapping forms and sources of accountability. Also, changes in accountability relations must be explained. For instance, using the opening example again, the food-for-work projects of the early 1990s showed that kinship often trumped donor guidelines and villagers did not openly challenge a leader who distributed food aid to his or her family members first. With the advent of democracy and the introduction of human rights, local attitudes began to change and the most vulnerable, including women, were appointed to food-distribution committees and began to expect a more equal share of food aid. More often than before, leaders giving food aid to their relatives would be labelled corrupt.

Power lies at the heart of any accountability relationship. In the case of the child not receiving adequate medical care from a doctor, the power differential is all important. The child not only lacks information or the ability to understand any information he or she has, but also the capacity to sanction the doctor. His or her parents, if poor and uneducated or, interestingly, in situations where medical care is provided without charge, may be in a similarly weakened position. But if the child belongs to parents who are powerful through wealth or profession or who live where professionalism is prioritised, then they may hold the medical practitioner to account through formal means — via the courts or a medical board.

The poor as a group are often unable to hold their political representatives or their states to account—they lack information, they do not have access to enforcement mechanisms, they may be risk-avoiders or easily bought off, they may have a hard time forming and managing organisations with long-term goals and programmes of action. Social or societal accountability[5] is seen as the answer in such cases. Communities that are aware of their rights, have access to information, and know how to organise and campaign, have managed to hold their governments and service providers to account for their performance, especially the delivery of public goods.

Less successful in the long term are groups that come together and use violence or forms of criminal behaviour to force those in power to behave as desired. Social crimes are unlikely to establish new norms that take root, though their acts may be regarded as heroic by the populace (Hobsbawm 1965) and may force leaders to behave accountably for short periods of time.

Then there is so-called rude accountability, where individuals antagonise those in power through personal verbal abuse and the like, in order to change their behaviour. This has been documented in Bangladesh where it is based on a shared understanding of what is shameful but is thought to have limited impact (Hossain 2009). How willing people are to be rude to gain advantage probably depends on whether they feel vulnerable as individuals (and thus need at least a few others to stand with them when castigating service providers) or whether they fear retribution.

Power differentials between actors will affect the types of sanctions that can be used and how successfully they can be applied and, therefore, the outcome of any accountability relationship. Significant differences in power also seem to reflect the field of behaviour that an accountability relationship addresses. Very powerful individuals or agencies are unlikely to feel they should be held responsible for actions that they believe fall outside the purview of the least powerful. Social norms govern such situations, making some elites unpunishable. In such cases, ordinary people may well accept that a powerful group is justified to live by rules different from those that govern their own behaviour. Patrons in a patron–client system may live ostentatiously or corruptly and be forgiven—not held to account—because the norms governing the actions of elites legitimise such behaviour.[6]

---

5   'Societal accountability is characterised by actions taken by civil society and media aiming at forcing political, bureaucratic, business and legal decision-makers to give information on, and justifications for their actions. The strength of control is typically relatively weak in these cases but also varies with contextual factors such as legislation (e.g. freedom of information act or not)' (Lindberg 2009). Kelsall et al (2005) demonstrate that rural populations are less active at holding leaders to account, though some civic groups, especially the church, may be keener.

6   Such differential standards of behaviour are found in British 'upstairs–downstairs' situations, in Pakistan's rural areas where 'feudals' hold sway, and in African neopatrimonial societies. They deserve to be studied for they have development consequences.

There are various forms of accountability, including accountability between parents and children, accountability in business relationships, in electoral democracies and in patron–client systems. Each interaction has different agents, different concerns or fields of interest, different types of responses, sanctions, norms and rules. Moreover, accountability flows in various directions depending on relations of power.

In summary, there is no single model of accountability. As a system of interactions, it depends on the field of concern (whether business, government or family) and the specific behaviour for which agents are answerable (such as making profits, delivering public goods or cooking dinner on time). Accountability is a function of power differentials between actors, and of social norms, as well as the nature of information flows and the types of responses and sanctions built into the system.

3. Accountability in practice

APPP researchers are in the field exploring various institutions and modes of governance — from chiefs to cotton boards, Mullahs to MPs — and their contributions to the achievement of better social outcomes in sub-Saharan Africa. In each case, APPP researchers query the basis of a leader's authority — where does his or her power and legitimacy come from, and have these changed over time? For instance, a leader's authority may come from 'royal blood' (such as chiefs) or through elections (such as councillors and MPs); it may be derived from appointment (such as an official or Minister) or through individual achievement (such as a businessman or preacher). Authority may be ascribed by family ranking or by being close to a 'big man'.

We recognise that

> a leader who draws legitimacy from a patriarchal tradition, a tradition which views the family as a template for government, need not necessarily justify his decisions on grounds of reasonableness or rationality. While not entirely absent from familial governance, reasonableness and rationality are not at its core. Moreover, people are more likely to answer to him, than to make him answer' (Lange et al 2005).

Thus we have found examples of chiefs who display questionable moral behaviour but are not directly challenged by residents. On the other hand, we have identified self-styled leaders who are able to deliver goods and services and who as a result are gaining legitimacy and power locally though they have no standing in the law. How long the former is accepted by the community and the latter ignored by, say, city officials will depend on the norms governing how legitimacy and power are achieved and lost in each context. Ambiguities arise as different 'languages of accountability' are used by different actors, or as they change over time (Lange et al 2005). This has an impact on legitimacy.

When studying accountability in practice, these and other factors are taken into account by APPP researchers. We will now discuss two field studies which have explored these concepts directly.

3.1. MPs in Ghana

One stream of the APPP is inquiring into the accountability of African MPs — to whom do they account, for what, and how? The aim of this research is to look at how parliamentary governance works in practice, in an attempt to identify ways to improve MPs' actions and outputs. Field work is underway in Ghana — interviews with MPs have been done and questionnaires have been developed to collect answers to these and related questions from MPs. Constituents and other key actors, such as the Clerk of Parliament, have been interviewed and ethnographic data are being collected in Parliament and constituencies to corroborate the survey's findings. In due course, the work will be replicated in other African countries, and conclusions will be drawn about the nature of parliamentary representation in Africa and how MPs can be held more accountable (Lindberg 2008). The following discussion summarises the findings that have emerged thus far (Lindberg 2010a; 2010b).

As noted previously, accountability depends on the type of an accountability relationship. Thus, MPs in Ghana were asked whether and, if so, how eight different groups of people hold them accountable: (1) citizens in their constituencies; (2) the local party; (3) the national party; (4) the extended family; (5) chiefs; (6) religious leaders; (7) civil society organisations; and (8) businesses. A further component of this research will investigate how previous MPs in their constituency behaved, what current MPs promised during their campaign, and how powerful each actor is in relation to the other.

In general, MPs in democracies have four formal roles:

1. To enact, or contribute to the enactment of, *legislation*
2. To perform *executive oversight*
3. To *represent* their *constituencies* by voicing the concerns, problems and challenges of that particular area of the country and its people on the national political scene
4. To do *constituency service*, which may include the provision of public or private goods to individuals or groups at home.

How an MP balances his or her time to fulfil these roles will depend on a number of factors, including incentives or pressures coming from the eight groups mentioned above as well as his or her own goals, which are influenced by his or her values, psychology, and the culture of Parliament and of national politics generally.

It is at the level of national and local political culture that we see informal or local norms — those established by precedent, history and local values — influencing an MP's agenda. Kelsall (2008) argues that many Africans think about the relation between citizens and the state through the metaphor of an idealised extended family and its father — where a good father provides for his family.[7] Some voters in Zomba, Malawi, for example, told researchers that they thought it was the President's duty to deliver goods and services to all Malawians but their MP's job was to bring public goods home to them (Cammack et al 2007). It is within this fatherly role that many constituents hold their MP to account.[8] In other words, an MP hoping to be re-elected would have his or her behaviour shaped as much by his or her constituents' attitudes as by parchment institutions. Not surprisingly, as Lindberg (2010a) states, the hybrid configuration of the office of a Ghanaian MP puts enormous pressures on the office-holder to be responsive to constituents' needs and priorities.

And what is it that Ghana's MPs are asked to provide? This differs according to each of the eight sets of actors, though most common are personal benefits, usually in the form of 'monetary assistance — pocket money, for the payment of bills or school fees (very common), for the purchase of food items, monetary assistance for funerals and weddings, or towards start-up cost for small businesses or a farm' (Lindberg 2010a: 123). Less frequent but important are demands for jobs, typically requests for low skilled jobs in the army, police, fire services or immigration. Those asking for these are mostly constituents and local party officials. It is the chiefs who hold MPs accountable for the delivery of constituency development funds and development projects. Surprisingly, MPs claim that NGOs do not pressure them much for these. However, people, even those in rural areas, are aware of events in Parliament, and are keen to hear their MPs speak on their constituents' behalf (Lindberg 2010a: 125ff).

Surprisingly, evidence gathered in Ghana indicates that there is little pressure from the eight sets of actors for the passage of legislation. The legislative agenda seems to be of much more concern to the executive and the ruling party. In the past, the executive is said to have paid MPs to have certain laws enacted.

---

7   Rural informants in Tanzania talking about an MP told researchers, 'Do you want him to eat that money only with his children? We are also his children' (Kelsall et al 2005).

8   Recently the President of Malawi told voters at a by-election rally in Ndirande that MPs are not responsible for delivering goods to their constituents (*Nyasa Times*, 12 Aug 2009). This speech undoubtedly helped the candidate lose the by-election. Later, in the north in Rumphi, the ruling party regional chair was heard castigating voters who wanted their MP (also a cabinet minister) to tend to their local needs and telling them that they ought to approach him for these things instead (APPP Research Assistant Report, 1 October 2009).

Similarly, none of the eight groups pressed MPs to do executive oversight duties; nor were they held accountable for performing this role (ibid: 130–132). In other words, the data being collected in Ghana give us a picture of the role of parliamentarians that is somewhat inconsistent with the key functions of MPs listed above.

This is in part because MPs seem to be conforming to immediate incentives and long-term norms at both local and national levels rather than to expectations that emerge from the Constitution and the law. The more immediate pressures might include, for instance, the culture of Ghana's political parties, reflecting the relative power of party presidents and their MPs.

In sub-Saharan Africa generally, we know too that informal norms play a part in setting political agendas and that politicians at all levels are driven by a multitude of needs (Cammack 2007). For instance, running for office puts many parliamentary candidates deep into debt and repaying debts through clientelistic networks is frequent. Re-election has, since the transition to multipartyism, become of preeminent concern too. Importantly, then, providing private benefits or local collective goods to constituents may garner more votes than passing laws or pushing national development agendas. Performing oversight over the executive may hinder an MP's re-selection to run for Parliament in a system where party leaders choose candidates. That some Ghanaians believe that it is the President, not the public, who has the responsibility to hold MPs to account (Armah-Attoh 2006) helps to explain why MPs rarely perform executive oversight functions.

Finally, research in Ghana indicates that grafting of the 'family/father' institution onto the formal MP role has brought in an extra dimension for sanction:

> While sanction in the formal sense is possible at the ballot box every four years, the informal institution provides everyday tools of shame, harassment, collective punishment of the family, and loss of prestige and status. In effect, the accountability relationship between representative (agent) and citizens (principal) is much stronger than might appear from looking at the formal side of the institution only. (Lindberg 2010a: 136)

More on how people hold their MPs to account informally, through these family or locally based mechanisms, will be considered as the researchers move into the more ethnographic phase of the research. Qualitative information gathering at the local level will provide a more rounded picture of what MPs are being held to account for, and by whom. We hope that it will also explain the difference between what the public wants and expects from its MPs (as outlined by Armah-Attoh 2006) and what the public actually holds MPs to account for. The low level of MPs' interaction with their constituents outside of campaign times, the norms that govern MPs' behaviour and the incentives that spur them to action will be investigated to explain what makes MPs perform their expected roles (Lindberg 2008).

3.2. Town chiefs in Malawi

Research in the local governance and leadership stream of the APPP is currently underway in several countries, including Niger, Rwanda, Uganda, Tanzania and Malawi. The APPP is focusing on local leadership because it is at this level that community services and public goods are delivered, but are often not delivered well with devastating consequences for the poor especially. We aim to explain why this is, and to find successful African cases from which we can learn about hybrid institutions and local leadership forms. An initial paper on town chiefs in Malawi (Cammack et al 2009) is drawn upon here to explain how accountability operates at the local level.[9]

In Malawi, there are over 18 000 traditional authorities, formal chiefs (*mfumu*) of various grades from paramount chiefs down to village headmen. They are legally, culturally and historically rooted. The vast majority live and rule in rural areas, though some are found in towns and cities, where their claim to power is legally more ambiguous. Certainly that is the view of city and town authorities, most of whom are civil servants led by chief executive officers (CEOs) and district commissioners (DCs) answering to the national executive. Democratic decentralisation was introduced in the 1990s after the multiparty transition, but local councillors served only a single term (2000–2005) as party-politics and councillors' lack of qualifications and weak capacity made them dispensable. Meanwhile, urbanisation, delayed by former President Banda's policies, has taken hold of Malawi since the mid-90s, making its cities some of the fastest growing in Africa. Urban areas are expanding with little planning, funding or regulation, and slums are bourgeoning as heterogeneous populations flee rural poverty in search of opportunities and congregate in towns.

'Town chiefs' is the collective noun used to denote several types of urban leaders, including *capitawo* (captain), block leaders and (group) village headmen. They are largely male, may come from ethnic groups other than the hegemonic tribe in an area, are long-time residents with property, owners of businesses or otherwise relatively well-off, and are people of 'good character', 'hard working', 'respectable' and 'quiet'; individuals of 'good standing', who know 'how to stay

---

9   It should be noted that accountability was not the primary focus of that paper and that it is currently being updated on the basis of further research.

with people', 'understand the problems of the people', will 'help them', be 'good to them' and 'keep them well'. They are neither quarrelsome nor known 'drunkards' or 'womanisers'.

Town chiefs are a product of various institutional blends, with no clear cut boundary between them. Each is rooted in the local context and so slightly different from others. Some are 'royals', who, like rural chiefs, are paid by the state but the 'town has found them there'. Their authority and legitimacy are based on historical traditions and the law, though state officials deny that they have powers in town. Second are chiefs who use traditional titles (for example, group village headman) but have no 'royal blood'. Some have been appointed by the Traditional Authority (senior chief) for the area and serve as his 'ears and eyes'. Third, there are 'block leaders' who come to power in a variety of ways, such as by appointment by city or state authorities or political parties. Some have been elected, either as part of the 1990s decentralisation programme or through unrelated means, for example, at 'a funeral election' or informally by neighbours.

As the state is weak at the local level, town chiefs undertake a number of tasks that are locally expected. Foremost, they organise funerals, which includes granting access to graveyards, informing people when they can 'weep', and organising burial assistance. Their presence ensures deaths are not treated as unnatural, and that cultural practices to ward off evil spirits and witches are complied with. Secondly, town chiefs unofficially coordinate a variety of programmes. They say they do not sell or distribute land, but they undoubtedly do so when they can get away with it. Many hold court (*bwalo*) where disputes at neighbourhood level are settled and where fines can be imposed on any or all parties by the chief. Finally, town chiefs oversee the holding of political rallies, and may endorse candidates, and act as community entry points for NGOs and others wishing to work with urban residents. Except those who are 'royal' and are given state honoraria, town chiefs are not paid a wage. Some receive fees for their services to the community — from neighbours, MPs and on rare occasions from city officials. Why do they do this work? Because they are asked and it is expected, because they gain respect and insider knowledge of local affairs, including business opportunities, and collect some fees.

Their power varies from neighbourhood to neighbourhood. Generally, though, they oversee neighbourhood watch committees and report criminal activities, troublesome residents and incomers to the police. MPs work with them because some town chiefs belong to political parties but mainly because town chiefs ease politicians' access to constituents. Where public relief goods, such as fertiliser coupons, are being distributed, town chiefs are given the responsibility to hand them out to their people. They refer cases to magistrates, higher chiefs and the police. Generally town authorities and ministry staff do not acknowledge the authority of town chiefs but, informally, they recognise their importance in maintaining order and serving urban communities, and relate to them. Town chiefs hold court, levy fines, and some at least have the power to expel troublemakers and witches from their communities.

The legitimacy of town chiefs derives from various sources, depending on how they come to power. Those who are 'royal' are like chiefs in rural areas who are invested with legal and traditional rights to rule and it is difficult to remove them. Those who are appointed by senior chiefs or officials or elected by communities can be removed but not easily. Subsequent elections are rare. The fact that people come to their courts for judgments and pay them fines, and inform them whenever there are deaths and wait for them to authorise burials, is evidence of community respect. Those that actually deliver goods — such as peace, justice, relief and suitable burials — gain additional legitimacy. Few town chiefs say they are defied, though a small number acknowledges that 'characters' might reject their right to give orders and that sometimes youth in this post-transitional era, where there 'is too much freedom', will be disrespectful.

Chiefs have a variety of ways to deal with those who do not conform, but the ultimate sanction is threatening not to open a graveyard or help with burials when a family member dies. That they remove witches earns them additional respect in an era when Malawi's law on witchcraft, which does not recognise the existence of witches, means that the courts and police do not meet the public's demand to see these people punished.

There were historically, and continue to be, mechanisms for holding chiefs to account for their provision of public goods. One way is by working within the system. Subjects who believe that their chief is unresponsive might approach his or her senior chief, who in turn can ask the chief or his or her family to improve his or her leadership. The family might react by giving the chief better counsellors (*nduna*) and more day-to-day guidance. In the past, when there was more land, the easiest way of holding a bad chief to account was by moving out of his or her area and founding a new village with a new leader. As formal rule took hold and jurisdictions were demarcated, and as vacant land became scarce, moving away was a less likely option. But the public might in extreme cases go to the colonial administration and complain about an irresponsible chief with the hope he or she would be replaced. This was the case in Malawi after independence too, when the President took control of chiefly appointments.

It is not surprising that town chiefs in Malawi today find themselves the subject of actions similar to those noted historically. People in town can ask a senior chief to approach the family of the unresponsive sub-chief to replace him. Complaints to officials might work, though this is an indirect route because city administrators do not formally recognise town chiefs and would find it difficult to replace them. But if the chief were elected, city officials might intervene, and so too might the senior chief, especially if called upon to do so by residents. Still, if a chief were particularly troublesome, the Ministry of Local Government and other state actors, such as MPs, might intervene. On the other hand, a recent attempt by an MP to involve himself in a chiefly appointment in town was rebuffed by the Ministry on the grounds that the Ministry did not have jurisdiction over chiefs in urban areas.

Those who would have moved away in the past now can simply ignore the chief's orders and system. But a person doing this could find himself or herself labelled 'a character' and probably ostracised. Worse still, if they complained too much or pushed their independence too far they might find themselves evicted by the chief (sometimes with the connivance of the police) from the neighbourhood. Where town chiefs have come to power through elections, they might in theory be removed in future elections, though evidence of regular block-leader elections is scant. There will be a few residents who show their disapproval of a town chief by voting with their feet, that is, moving from one chief's jurisdiction to another. Finally, as witchcraft is an important part of everyday life for some Malawians, it is not uncommon to learn that a chief has been bewitched or accused of being a witch. In any event, town chiefs may be held to account in a variety of ways, some of which are not unlike those of the past.

4. Conclusion

In the APPP we are focusing on the relationship between power, institutions and public-goods provision, and are exploring the many ways by which people actually hold officials to account. Accountability is only one concept of interest to us, but it is central because it links leaders and subjects, and the social norms which govern it appear to vary in interesting ways through time and space.

It has long been understood that ensuring that leaders comply with rules and deliver public goods is more complicated than simply writing a liberal Constitution, passing good laws and drafting regulations. However, it is less clear whether there are viable alternative ways of approaching the matter. In Africa, people's willingness and ability to hold leaders to account is not only influenced by the weaknesses or strengths of the legal system and other formal arrangements. Clearly, jurisdictional confusion and weak regimes of sanction are key issues, but a range of other factors comes into play. On the negative side, these include poor information flows, large power differentials, clientelism, typical patterns of party politics, cultural norms that place elders and VIPs above the law and poor social networking. On the positive side, there seems to be an under-explored potential for hybrid forms of local leadership, and even quite clientelistic relationships, which have the potential to foster the accountability that can match that produced by formal accountability mechanisms.

In this chapter, we have advanced this idea with reference to two of the earliest pieces of APPP research, on MPs in Ghana and town chiefs in Malawi. Other APPP research — notably on the creation of an encouraging climate for investment (Cammack et al 2010; Kelsall & Booth 2010) and the provision of public goods at the local level (Booth 2010; Cammack & Kanyongolo 2010; Olivier de Sardan 2010) — is pointing in the same direction. It is providing further evidence in favour of grounding institutional improvements in what already exists, rather than resorting to standardised formulas based narrowly on recent Western experience. More specifically, studies are suggesting the need for a clearer distinction between those forms of neopatrimonial rule that centralise power and impose strong top-down performance disciplines and those that do not. This is emerging as a variable that is more important for public goods outcomes than the question whether the regime is formally democratic or complies in other general respects with the institutional orthodoxy on governance.

It might seem counter-intuitive to associate centralisation and top-down discipline with better development outcomes, but this is fully consistent with the central theme of this chapter, which is looking beyond formal mechanisms to discover informal or cultural norms and mechanisms that already exist and foster accountability in the actual context of African political systems.

References

Armah-Attoh, D. 2006. Political participation and popular perception of political accountability in Ghana. Open Society Institute, Afrimap, March. Available at http://www.afrimap.org/english/images/paper/Ghana%20popular%20perception(fin).pdf. Accessed 30 November 2010.

Booth, D. 2008a. The concept of 'public goods' and the APPP research design. London, ODI Africa Power and Politics Programme.

Booth, D. 2008b. A research design fit for purpose. Discussion Paper 3. London, ODI Africa Power and Politics Programme. Available at http://www.institutions-africa.org. Accessed 30 November 2010.

Booth, D. 2009. Elites, governance and the public interest in Africa: Working with the grain? Discussion Paper 6. London, ODI Africa Power and Politics Programme. Available at http://www.institutions-africa.org. Accessed 30 November 2010.

Booth, D. 2010. Towards a theory of local governance and public goods' provision in sub-Saharan Africa. Working Paper 13. London, ODI Africa Power and Politics

Programme. Available at http://www.institutions-africa.org. Accessed 30 November 2010.

Cammack, D. 2007. The logic of African neopatrimonialism: What role for donors? *Development Policy Review,* 25 (5): 599–614.

Cammack, D., Golooba-Mutebi, F., Kanyongolo, F. & O'Neil, T. 2007. Neopatrimonial politics, decentralisation and local government: Uganda and Malawi in 2006. Working Paper 2. Project on Good Governance, Aid Modalities and Poverty Reduction: Linkages to the Millennium Development Goals and Implications for Irish Aid. London & Dublin, Overseas Development Institute & Advisory Board for Irish Aid.

Cammack, D. & Kelsall, T. with Booth, D. 2010. Developmental patrimonialism? The case of Malawi. Working Paper 12. London, ODI Africa Power and Politics Programme. Available at http://www.institutions-africa.org. Accessed 1 October 2010.

Cammack, D., Kanyongolo, E. & O'Neil, T. 2009. Town chiefs in Malawi. Working Paper 3. London, ODI Africa Power and Politics Programme. Available at http://www.institutions-africa.org. Accessed 30 November 2010.

Cammack, D. & Kanyongolo, E. 2010. Local governance and public goods in Malawi. Working Paper 11. London, ODI Africa Power and Politics Programme. Available at http://www.institutions-africa.org. Accessed 30 November 2010.

Habyarimana, J., Humphreys, M., Posner, D.M & Weinstein J.M. 2007. Why does ethnic diversity undermine public goods provision? *American Political Science Review,* 101: 709–725.

Hobsbawn, E. 1965. *Primitive Rebels: Studies in Archaic Forms of Social Movement in the 19th and 20th Centuries.* New York: W.W. Norton.

Hossain, N. 2009. Rude accountability in the unreformed state: Informal pressures on frontline bureaucrats in Bangladesh. Working Paper 319. Brighton, IDS.

Hyden, G. 2010. Political accountability in Africa: Is the glass half-full or half-empty? Working Paper 6. London, ODI Africa Power and Politics Programme. Available at http://www.institutions-africa.org. Accessed 30 November 2010.

Kelsall, T. 2008. Going with the grain in African development? *Development Policy Review,* 26 (6): 627–655.

Lange, S., Kelsall, T., Mesaki, S. & Mmunya, M. 2005. *Understanding Patterns of Accountability in Tanzania, Component 2: The Bottom-up Perspective.* Oxford: Oxford Policy Management.

Kelsall, T. & Booth, D. 2010. Developmental patrimonialism? Questioning the orthodoxy on political governance and economic progress in Africa. Working Paper 9. London, ODI Africa Power and Politics Programme. Available at http://www.institutions-africa.org. Accessed 30 November 2010.

Lindberg, S.I. 2008. MPs, citizens, accountability and collective goods. University of Florida, APPP Project Proposal.

Lindberg, S.I. 2009. Accountability: The core concept and its subtypes. Working Paper 1. London, ODI Africa Power and Politics Programme. Available at http://www.institutions-africa.org. Accessed 30 November 2010.

Lindberg, S.I. 2010a. What accountability pressures do MPs in Africa face and how do they respond? Evidence from Ghana. *Journal of Modern African Studies*, 48 (1): 117–142.

Lindberg, S.I. 2010b. Variation in performance among Members of Parliament: Evidence from Ghana. Working Paper 7. London: ODI Africa Power and Politics Programme. Available at http://www.institutions-africa.org. Accessed 1 October 2010.

Olivier de Sardan, J.P. 2010. Local governance and public goods in Niger. Working Paper 10. London: ODI Africa Power and Politics Programme. Available at http://www.institutions-africa.org. Accessed 1 October 2010.

Chapter 16

External accountability meets accountability assistance: The case of legislative strengthening in Africa

Peter Burnell

1. Introduction

In a globalising world, power is often said to be shifting away from developing world states to institutions of global governance. Given its policy and institutional conditionalities, international development aid has been much criticised in this regard. The tendency towards external accountability prompted development aid partners in the Paris Declaration (OECD 2005) to resolve on establishing greater mutual accountability. The current age is one of international assistance to democratic governance. Accountability assistance is a specific component that merits examination as accountability is central to both democracy and good governance. This chapter inquires into whether governance-oriented accountability assistance for development risks furthering external accountability and lines of domestic accountability that do not optimise democratic accountability in partner countries. The argument is made with specific reference to the growing body of evidence supplied by reports on international support for legislative strengthening in Africa.

2. Forms of accountability
2.1. External accountability

The literature in international political economy is divided over how far power is leaking away from states and accruing to such international organisations as the World Bank and the International Monetary Fund (IMF) in consequence of global economic integration. A plausible view is that in the most powerful countries, like the United States, the state is not in decline but is being transformed. This may also be true of the larger emerging economies, in particular the so-called BRICs,[1] although none are in Africa. Many developing

---

1   Brazil, Russia, India, China.

countries, especially the smaller and poorer African countries, have seen power over decisions with important consequences for their citizens gravitate to multilateral institutions, where their voice is weak and over which they exert no control. Writing about these institutions, Grant and Keohane (2005: 37) say the problem is that they are accountable (in non-democratic ways) to only a few rich and powerful states. There appears to be a strong case for making such instruments of global governance more democratically accountable. At the same time, these very same bodies together with bilateral development aid agencies now stand at the forefront of international endeavours to encourage better governance in the developing world, arguing that greater governmental accountability is in the interests of development. Questions about whether the aid relationships that are influenced by this will actually reduce external accountability to the benefit of domestic accountability and, if so, whether democratic accountability is advanced as a result are worth investigating.

2.2. Domestic and democratic accountability

Definitions of government accountability customarily distinguish between *ex post* accountability (or accountability for policy implementation), achieved through oversight and scrutiny of performance after the event, and *ex ante* accountability (accountability for policy formation). This chapter dwells especially on the second of these, sometimes called responsiveness, which requires decision-making to be responsive to the opinions and expressed wishes of the constituents whose interests or needs are most affected. Put differently, it places at least as much value on making sure that elected representatives set out to do what society says they should do, as on arrangements for discovering how effectively they honoured their promises after the event. The quality of political representation is critical. In its most expansive sense, accountability demands not just transparency and answerability but also enforceability and the power to sanction.

Contemporary discourse makes little attempt to distinguish between *domestic* and *democratic* accountability. However, while the former may well be a necessary condition for the latter (and historically, democratic theory and practice have been premised on the national state), it is not a sufficient condition. Taking the idea of principal–agent relations as the context, the domestic versus democratic distinction revolves around the identity, nature and role of the principal. Domestic accountability can mean accounting to domestic actors and institutions without regard to whether or how far they enjoy or claim democratic credentials or are committed to values and objectives consistent with democracy. A principal's qualities can take many forms that are not intrinsically democratic, for example specialised knowledge and technical expertise or military power. In regard to relationships in world politics, Grant and Keohane (2005: 36) identified market accountability, peer/professional accountability and public reputational accountability, all of which might exist at national and sub-national levels too.

Identifying examples of what counts as non-democratic — or even anti-democratic — accountability either in external or domestic relations is easier than defining the accountability sub-set that comprises *democratic* accountability. But at minimum democratic accountability must mean, first, accountability to the expressed wishes of the whole *demos* — ultimately, control or rule by the people (the people are sovereign) — rather than to just one part. Note that this does not necessarily equate to ruling in the best interests of society objectively defined, where authoritarian paternalism conceivably might offer more. Secondly, democratic accountability is effected by instruments that are themselves democratically mandated or at minimum embody or respect democratic principles. Among other things, democratic accountability, also means acceptance of the rule of law. And although in liberal democracies an independent press and vigorous pressure groups representing big business and organised labour might be instrumental in making government more accountable, a situation where press barons or self-serving interest groups are the main principals would exhibit weaker democratic accountability than where government accounts to society as a whole.

3. Accountability assistance

3.1. What is accountability assistance?

Accountability assistance refers to international assistance that makes or is intended to make government more accountable. At least three different approaches and associated forms may qualify. One sets out to strengthen the capability of public institutions that hold government to account. Examples include the public institutions of vertical (electoral) and horizontal (intra-state) accountability that are often mandated in a country's Constitution. Here, legislatures occupy a special place by virtue of being at the nexus of the vertical and the horizontal.[2] Technical assistance to judicial and quasi-judicial institutions whose purpose includes ensuring respect for the rule of law by the executive, especially assistance that helps strengthening their autonomy of arbitrary political interference, provides a particular example.

---

2 Institutions of horizontal accountability include the judiciary, ombudspersons, anti-corruption bureaux, human rights commissions and national audit offices. The vertical dimension refers primarily to arrangements for submitting the rulers to popular election. In broad terms the vertical dimension appeals to *ex ante* accountability and the horizontal dimension to *ex post* accountability.

A second, perhaps longer term approach seeks to improve government's capability to respond to what society asks from government, by increasing the state's technical, managerial and financial capacity to deliver goods and services. This is the province of much development aid. But the outcome is not guaranteed. Government might see its capabilities increase but chooses to pursue different ends from society's expressed demands. So a third distinct approach comprises efforts to stimulate or support expressions of demand by society that government listens to society and then accounts to society for its actions afterwards.[3] This third approach, sometimes called 'demand-side' or 'bottom-up', contrasts with the largely supply-side orientation towards public institutions found in the first two approaches.

In practice much of what may be judged international accountability assistance according to these three approaches tends not to be formally labelled or presented as such. An example is the governance assistance that is designed to tackle corruption (the abuse of public office for private gain) and its causes, whose objectives clearly include securing improvements in public accountability. The accountability that inheres in relationships between domestic actors and institutions tends to cut across the sectoral and institutional dividing lines that structure most international assistance flows. A more integrated and less compartmentalised approach to framing international assistance would give a truer picture of how much democracy support and how much governance aid really is directed at furthering accountability,[4] although the political sensitivities that surround aid relationships could still prevent the label 'accountability assistance' acquiring official status.

As domestic and democratic accountability are not synonymous, the possibility exists that accountability assistance helps further the first more than the second. Moreover, not all of the accountability assistance which is delivered as an aid to good governance necessarily aims to advance *democratic* accountability. And not all of the democracy assistance which has that aim is bound to be successful. Accountability assistance itself is an external relationship. Whether it ends up reinforcing external accountability more than it helps to bring about domestic accountability, and whether by enhancing the latter it furthers democratic accountability in the country, cannot be presumed; the real outcomes must be established empirically.

---

3   A concrete example is the small Governance and Transparency Fund (GTF) of the United Kingdom's Department for International Development (DFID), established in 2007 to help citizens demand more accountability from their government. It invited social groups working on promoting democracy and strengthening Parliaments or parliamentary processes to apply.

4   The 'organisational silos' and 'tunnel behaviour' among Canada's democracy support efforts (Miller 2005: 8) is illustrative.

3.2. Enhancing mutual accountability?

Following years of criticism of mixed results from attaching policy and other conditionalities to development aid, most international development partners now agree that ownership by aid recipients is essential to achieving sustained support for the policy and institutional reforms that donors believe are essential to development. This understanding was enshrined in the 2005 Paris Declaration on Aid Effectiveness by a High Level Forum of the Organisation for Economic Co-operation and Development's (OECD) Development Co-operation Directorate in which African representatives took part.

Even so, as was noted at the time, the underlying power relationships were unlikely to change. 'If recipients do not match agreed performance, development partners can apply clear sanctions. However, if (international) development partners underperform, no such remedies are available to the recipient' (Rogerson 2005: 548–549). As Ebrahim and Weisband (2007: 11; 13) noted, asymmetries in resources 'become important in influencing who is able to hold whom to account' and 'only enforceability and rectification produce "strong forms" of accountability'. These observations are very relevant not just to *ex post* accountability but also to the power to set agendas in advance—which has a crucial bearing on the issue of responsiveness, and thereby on the possibility for aid partner countries to exercise democratic self-determination. As Hyden (2008) has more recently argued, the power to set agendas remains with the international partners notwithstanding Paris Declaration promises to enhance mutual accountability and all countries' respective accountabilities to their own citizens and Parliaments. The provision of accountability assistance to Africa, and support for legislative strengthening specifically, are a good test case.

3.3 Goals of accountability assistance

An assortment of international organisations, including large multilateral actors such as the World Bank and the United Nations Development Programme (UNDP), bilateral development agencies of governments like those of the United States, the United Kingdom and Sweden and autonomous but publicly funded non-profit democracy foundations and institutes, such as the National Democratic Institute for International Affairs (NDI) in the United States and the Parliamentary Centre of Canada (PCC), provide financial or practical support or both for objectives of accountability. Private contractors are also involved. The mission statements of the organisations vary. Some like NDI seek to help build democracy. UNDP's interest in assisting 'democratic governance' (and Parliaments in particular) can be traced partly to the United Nations' larger role in nation-building and conflict resolution (UNDP 2003: 7). Parliaments' role as places of dialogue to support national reconciliation occupies easily the largest global project under the UNDP Global Programme on Parliamentary Strengthening, with pilots in Algeria, Benin, Morocco and Niger and a regional programme in West Africa (Murphy & Alhada 2007).

However, the greatest single part of international accountability assistance is intended to improve governance for the purpose of advancing the prospects for development, understood in largely economic and socio-economic terms. This matters, because the choice of goal — whether securing peace, promoting democracy or alternatively furthering better governance as an essential condition for (pro-poor) development — influences ideas about why accountability is important, why it merits support, what kind of support is appropriate, and the kind of accountability that is furthered. For instance, support for building democracy suggests engaging across the entire range of state responsibilities, which might include making the security and law-enforcement agencies democratically accountable, whereas the cause of governance for development dictates a narrower focus — in the first instance a type of fiscal and audit accountability — and suggests different criteria for measuring performance.

The term 'good governance' has come to be almost universally accepted as an important, even defining condition of development. Clearly, this is analytically different from the idea of democracy, even if improving governance and building democracy are causally connected. The difference lies in the distinction between, on the one side, legitimate political authority resting on the consent of the people, which embodies rule by the people and such ideals as political equality, inclusiveness and freedom, and, on the other side, efficient and effective public administration, the government's ability to provide public goods and services free of corruption and at acceptable cost.[5] Within this general comparison the belief that stronger legislatures make for stronger democracies (Fish 2006) means Parliaments tend to feature more prominently in theorising about democratisation than in the governance debates. In democratic theory Parliaments' representational function is crucial (*ex ante* accountability), whereas in the governance discourse Parliament's role in overseeing the executive (*ex post* accountability) draws most attention, although this undeniably benefits democracy if it makes control of the state by society more feasible (Pelizzo et al 2006; Stapenhurst et al 2008).

4. Legislative strengthening in Africa

As the body that represents the people, makes laws and scrutinises the performance of the executive, the legislature is pivotal to democratic governance.

---

5   A systematic comparison of international development partners' ideas of 'good governance' and attitudes towards human rights and democracy can be found in Hoebink (2006).

In 2005, the Economic Commission for Africa (2005: 202) said: 'The executive in many African countries still largely overpowers the legislative'. More recently, Rakner and Van de Walle (2009: 113) said the modal legislature in Africa remains 'weak'. This suggests that Parliaments are obvious candidates for assistance, even if the real picture is not so uniform and some of Africa's legislatures are 'on the rise' (Barkan 2008), notably in their oversight function. In fact, half of Africa's Parliaments were already receiving some international donor-funded technical assistance quite long ago (IPU 2003: 11) and, of the 61 countries where Wehner et al (2007: 36) found 15 international organisations offering significant support for legislative financial scrutiny, Africa figures as the region of greatest activity.

Even so, the resources offered by international organisations to legislative strengthening are only a modest fraction of all support for democratic governance,[6] just as the amounts for improving governance are modest relative to development aid overall. And of course the very much larger amounts of development assistance that flow to governments, especially the growing proportion for direct general budgetary support, may also be thought to help domestic accountability in the long run if they increase states' capacity to deliver goods and services, so long as governments prove responsive to society's wishes. However, if development aid increases the executive's scope to allocate resources on a discretionary and neopatrimonial basis, development aid also boosts the power of the executive vis-à-vis the legislature. This creates a conundrum for accountability.

Partially reflecting this conundrum, the 2005 Paris Declaration made a donor commitment to help 'strengthen as appropriate the parliamentary role in national development strategies and/or budgets'. Since then, the idea of legislative strengthening does seem to have risen on the agenda of major international development cooperation organisations. This includes, in particular, the World Bank Institute (WBI), which calls itself the 'capacity development' arm of the World Bank. The WBI's Parliamentary Strengthening Programme, geared to improving the capacity to oversee the allocation and use of public funds, is a leading example. It helps international partners devise and administer parliamentary support programmes on the ground, like the PCC, currently

---

6   Legislative strengthening involves annual total expenditures of millions not billions of US dollars; democracy aid *tout court* is probably around US $5 billion, governance assistance is considerably greater. Inconsistencies over the coding and measurement of relevant activities thwart precise calculation. Generic support for values like public sector transparency might enhance executive accountability to legislatures without that being cited as a primary goal.

involved in nine African countries including Ghana since 1994.[7] The United Kingdom's Department for International Development (DFID) also expresses growing interest in offering parliamentary support, again with a special interest in financial oversight. Half of its 30 projects since 1998 are in Africa (Hudson & Wren 2007: 6).

As well as differences in the way the purposes and rationales are couched, the international actors committed to legislative strengthening also vary in the priority given to different legislative functions, in their approach and methods of support. Partly as a result of African voices contributing to the proliferation of reports on legislative strengthening, our knowledge of effectiveness has grown. The early emphasis on providing largely technical packages and material resources or 'institutional repair' (Hubli & Schmidt 2005: 17) is now supplemented by growing awareness of the need to understand the impact of a legislature's *political* environment (Hubli & Schmidt 2005; Wehner et al 2007; Hudson & Wren 2007; AAPPG 2008; Hudson & Tsekpo 2009). This can mean addressing the incentive structures that explain why parliamentarians behave the way they do, although progress so far in taking the lessons to heart and reaping benefits is debatable.

What still seems to be lacking is universal agreement on what defines a *democratic* legislature and how Parliaments contribute to the process of democratisation (as distinct from the role they play in established democracies).[8] This may be inevitable. International actors themselves represent different democratic traditions, expressed in different models of legislative–executive relations. Also, our understanding of why African legislatures are weak is imperfect, and the reasons probably vary across countries. Aside from inadequate parliamentary resources, weak qualifications, insufficient training and high turnover of elected representatives,[9] more deep-seated reasons might include feeble formal powers; limited autonomy (especially in presidential and semi-presidential systems); weak procedures and generally poor institutional design originating in the Constitution; effects of the political party system (whether

---

7   The WBI 'is seen as leader in the field of parliamentary support' (Johnston & Von Trapp 2008: 8; 14) and Africa accounts for over 40% of its work. Johnston and Von Trapp's positive account of parliamentary strengthening in Ghana identifies seven contributing factors, beginning with strong domestic political support. Wehner et al (2007: 49–50) are more critical. Lindberg (2009: 14) found oversight over the executive weak. Hudson and Tsekpo (2009: 3) contrast increased parliamentary oversight, mainly financial scrutiny, with poor representational performance.

8   CPA et al (2006) set out to develop common indicators of legislative performance and legislative development, while a separate UNDP initiative seeks distinct regional perspectives, reflecting for example views of the Southern African Development Community's Parliamentary Forum.

9   In Niger, the proportion of deputies in the National Assembly who are unable to play a major role because they are unschooled in French (currently 40%) has increased (Murphy & Alhada 2007: 80).

one-party dominant or, more rarely, a high fragmentation and flux); and the political culture, manifest in, for instance, strong patron–client traditions and a rational inclination for elected representatives to prioritise delivering public spending commitments to their constituents over holding government to account.[10] Poor relations between legislatures and other accountability institutions with whom cooperation is important, the national audit office for instance, may be another factor. Widespread indifference towards Parliament and mistrust of politicians also undermine the legislature's ability to promote democratic governance (on Africans' perceptions of their Parliaments, see Nijzink et al 2006).

Clearly, endeavours to build democracy through accountability assistance that is aimed at strengthening legislatures as instruments for holding the executive accountable, and complementary attempts to make Parliaments themselves properly accountable, invoke numerous and perhaps intractable issues. In contrast, much of the international attention to legislative strengthening has a narrower focus. This reflects the terms of reference and particular priorities of the international development community, rather than a goal of stronger democracy.

A recent contribution to an outpouring of literature on international legislative strengthening[11] by Hudson and Tsekpo (2009: 1) concluded that even now 'there is little systematic research or analysis about the effectiveness of Parliaments or about the effectiveness of parliamentary strengthening'. As with other kinds of support to democracy and governance, the designing of evaluation methodologies remains work in progress. Indeed, a report by the Africa All Party Parliamentary Group (AAPPG 2008: 21) surmised that if more effective approaches to legislative strengthening are to be devised, we must first learn more about Africa's Parliaments themselves, especially the impact of social and cultural norms and political networks.

That said, a frequent finding is that support for a stronger legislature can create friction between international partners. Usually, even in countries rated as democracies the executive opposes substantial efforts to make the legislature more powerful. Moreover, the officers of Parliament and even some parliamentarians appear suspicious of donor intentions or disagree over

---

10   This can mean loyalty to the executive (Barkan 2008: 127). Patron–client relationships between elected representatives and voters can resemble one kind of accountability relationship but do not embody the idea that society has an *entitlement* to receive public goods or that elected representatives have a duty to deliver services. Patron-client relationships are asymmetrical power relations that typically benefit the patrons disproportionately and in most reckonings ultimately harm democracy, governance and development.

11   Including Hubli and Schmidt (2005); USAID (2006); Hudson and Wren (2007); DFID-UNDP-WBI (2007); Murphy and Alhada (2007); Johnston and Von Trapp (2008); AAPPG (2008).

the best way forward.[12] At times, this seems to reflect government fears that parliamentary strengthening is aimed at strengthening the political opposition, and convictions that foreign connivance in this is unacceptable.

There are also suggestions that some parliamentarians believe the motive of international partners is to enlist their support for development policy initiatives the donors want to see adopted (Hubli & Schmidt 2005: 22; Eggers et al 2005: 58–59; Selbervik & Wang 2006: 15). If it is true that the 'fairly obvious' reason why DFID, for example, supports Parliaments' budgetary oversight function is to 'promote development and reduce poverty' and create 'the institutional conditions to make development aid effective' (Brösamle et al 2007: 19), it is not the same as a mission to promote democracy. Furthermore, while the overall goal of development prized by international development organisations can look unobjectionable, elected politicians inside the countries may harbour different views about development priorities and the most appropriate policies for achieving them. An examination of the two main features of international support for legislative strengthening that have come to the fore—how Parliaments can advance public financial accountability and endorsements of poverty reduction strategies (PRS)—offers elaboration.

4.1. Advancing public financial accountability

Control of the public purse is a key issue for democracy, and public financial accountability secured through fiscal oversight and scrutiny is central to making government accountable. Legislative participation in the budget process and, more especially, *ex post* scrutiny of government spending are a prime focus of the growing international interest in supporting legislative strengthening, including WBI initiatives to enlist legislatures in fighting government corruption.[13] An early example was WBI support for the African Parliamentarians Network against Corruption. In 2005, the Paris Declaration called on all international donors to use and strengthen their partners' systems for managing and overseeing the public finances. For a number of bilateral development agencies such as DFID, as well as for the WBI, this makes public accounts committees of Parliament an especially favoured object of support. DFID (2004: 36) has called an effective public accounts committee buttressed by an effective public audit 'Parliament's strongest anti-corruption weapon'. By comparison the application of legislative oversight to other areas attracts very little attention.

---

12 For example, Hudson and Wren (2007: 40) found wariness in Sierra Leone and Tanzania; Wehner et al (2007: 46) corroborated this for Sierra Leone and Hudson and Tsekpo (2009) for Tanzania.

13 Detailed accounts of programmes to improve fiscal scrutiny through legislative strengthening include Brösamle et al (2007); Wehner et al (2007); Stapenhurst et al (2008).

The rationale is clear. As development aid and the proportions of it allocated to direct budget support grow, donor concerns about corruption and political misuse still remain. The AAPPG report (2008: 7; 19) candidly acknowledges that direct budget support itself risks making governments 'more accountable to (international) development partners and less accountable to their people' and that Parliaments — and thereby international assistance to them — are 'potential allies in terms of monitoring the use and impact of aid monies'. On the other hand, there appears to be international anxiety that increased legislative involvement in budgetary matters could inflate demands for public spending, especially along clientelistic lines, rather than improve 'fiscal discipline' (Wehner et al 2007: 30–34). 'Legislative involvement can curb corruption but may increase pork-barrel politics' (Brösamle et al 2007: 69). However, Brinkerhoff and Goldsmith (2003: 697)[14], among others, argue that so long as government retains the power to determine overall spending and parliamentarians 'help citizens better understand the limits to resource reallocation', budget inflation need not materialise. The arguments advanced to allay fears of an increase in public spending provide additional evidence for concluding that the donors' main objectives, although defensible, do not equate to increasing responsiveness to the wishes of society.

4.2. The poverty reduction strategy process

The Poverty Reduction Strategy (PRS) process was introduced by the Bretton Woods institutions in the late 1990s as part of a deal on debt relief. Bilateral donors quickly aligned with it and have since joined in making the production of a poverty reduction strategy paper a routine requirement of development aid flows. By 2009, programmes had been formulated for around 70 countries, including 34 in Africa. Strategy papers must be written every three years. Uganda and Tanzania, for example, are now well into a second generation of poverty reduction strategies.

The PRS arrangements do not abandon the practice of attaching conditions to aid. Instead, they stipulate a process by which partner countries are supposed to acquire policy ownership, in addition to prescribing the policy content, namely take a pro-poor orientation within the familiar framework of a standard neo-liberal approach to growth and development.[15]

---

14   'The challenge is to protect aggregate fiscal discipline, while allowing legislative scrutiny of government priorities and implementation of programmes' (Wehner et al 2007: 34); for comparable reasoning regarding support for civil society's involvement in budgeting, see Krafchik (2005:5).

15   A critical review of PRS is Lazarus (2008); the country strategy papers are posted on the World Bank's website.

At first, governments were required to consult leaders of civil society and non-governmental organisations (NGOs), some of them involved in administering anti-poverty programmes funded in part by international aid. In 2005, a joint survey by the World Bank and International Monetary Fund (IMF) found that Parliament had been consulted in only around one-third of the countries that prepared poverty reduction strategies. Africa's parliamentarians voiced dissatisfaction. By 2009, some international development partners seem to have come round to the view that parliamentary involvement in the PRS process might help strengthen government commitments to implement pro-poor development policies, by broadening the base of country ownership.

However, it is clear that parliamentarians are not being invited to question the broad fundamentals of the PRS, in particular the macro-economic policy framework, orthodox monetary policy and the idea of fiscal discipline within which pro-poor initiatives must be contained. Indeed, the IMF, largely responsible for that overarching framework in consultation with ministries of finance and central banks, still has few dealings with Parliaments. Even contacts with civil society remain very limited (International Monetary Fund 2007: 25). Published sources drawing on voices in several countries, including Tanzania, Ghana, Uganda and Malawi, confirm that even where Parliaments are now included in the PRS process their involvement still tends towards tokenism and is, in extreme cases, akin to a rubber-stamp (Draman & Langdon 2005: 18; Hubli & Schmidt 2005: 23; Jones & Hardstaff 2005: 17–28; Whitfield 2005; Selbervik & Wang 2006; Zimmermann 2007: 5; Woll 2008; Hudson & Tsekpo 2009). These sources also confirm that the incentives both for governments and their international development partners to continue to cooperate free of the complications that a more assertive legislative involvement might bring remain strong. They similarly find that the reluctance of parliamentarians to rock the boat of donor relations is predictable, not just where the executive overpowers the legislature (such as through one-party dominance) but anywhere because the continued supply of international aid with which to lubricate their own patron–client relationships might be put at risk.

Findings like these do little to convince that democratic accountability is being advanced. However, does the picture change once we look at yet further new trends in accountability assistance that go beyond legislatures and, by trying to circumvent the obstacles that both the executive *and* Parliament might pose to better governance, pursue a bottom-up or demand-side approach?

5. Civil society's contribution to democratic accountability

Civil society's contribution to making governments accountable in the interests of more pro-poor development policy receives high-level encouragement from sources like the *African Governance Report 2005*. And with the exception of the IMF's (2007: 25) 'limited and ineffective' engagement with developing countries' civil society, there is growing international interest in such arrangements as public expenditure tracking and performance monitoring by civil society, social audits and citizens' report cards on corruption and public service delivery (McNeil & Mumvuma 2006). International support for strengthening what has come to be called *societal* (or social or society-driven) accountability, such as by assisting civic groups' efforts to render government transparent, has increased. A further development is support for *diagonal* accountability — the direct engagement of citizens not so much with the executive but with the workings of horizontal or intra-state institutions of accountability apart from the legislature. Examples include encouraging citizen action groups to cooperate with the courts and the national audit office, targeting executive negligence or misconduct. While these developments look very positive from the perspective of making governments more accountable domestically, especially if they do not crowd out parallel efforts to strengthen legislatures,[16] the net contribution to increasing democratic accountability could be less constructive, for several reasons.

First, civil society may become more divided between groups who adopt a confrontational stance and others who work harmoniously with the government and yet others who keep a distance from government and from donors too. A civil society that is fractured may be weaker, compounding divisions that the competition for donor poverty-reduction largesse already sows among NGOs.

Second, most democracy and democratisation analysts believe that well-functioning political parties in a competitive party system make a crucial contribution to the ability of legislatures to carry out their accountability and other functions.[17] Their comparative advantage in securing pro-poor public policies has also been noted (Bräutigam 2004). The international partners' preferment of civil society over political parties makes elected politicians resentful. As in Malawi and Tanzania, they see a recipe for domestic conflict (AAPPG 2008: 10;

---

16 Brösamle et al (2007: 15) document USAID and other support to civil society efforts to boost parliamentary commitment to legislative fiscal oversight. Robinson's (2006: 21–28) study of independent budget analyses and advocacy initiatives by civil society in South Africa, Uganda and elsewhere found they helped legislatures engage in the budget process and increased executive answerability but only modestly influenced budget allocations. Support to civil society that makes Parliament itself more accountable to the people (a bottom-up approach) in the course of strengthening Parliament's hands vis-à-vis the executive (demand-side approach to government accountability) achieves a double gain for democratic accountability. However, the evidence so far suggests this is atypical.

17 Rakner and Van de Walle (2009: 109) have argued that 'the continuing weakness of opposition parties presents a serious and complex problem. A stable and numerically viable opposition is a key requisite for horizontal accountability through legislative checks on executive power'.

Hudson & Tsekpo 2009: 16).[18] A mutually supportive relationship between political parties and civil society is generally regarded as more positive for democracy than where suspicions and rivalry exist. Krafchik (2005: 9) went so far as to suggest that a successful participative budget process 'may depend on a weak legislature or undermine the power of the legislature', because the executive might be driven to ignore established parliamentary procedures and override parliamentarians' objections in order to advance the involvement of civic groups.

Third, while elections in Africa are sometimes flawed (on average less so now than before) and public attitude surveys tell us that many people see Parliament as remote and politicians as self-serving, these are grounds for combating the causes and improving the quality of representation, not for turning away from legislatures (or parties) in favour of other institutions. Parliaments and not civil society actors have a durable constitutional mandate, powers and responsibilities to represent society as whole.[19] This includes passing laws that directly affect the rights and conduct of civil society organisations (CSOs). Civil society depends on safeguards that Parliaments can provide. Moreover, parliamentarians may be held to account — thrown out by the electoral sanction, which may change the overall composition of the government too. Between general elections, parliamentary action may secure high level ministerial resignations, albeit more so in parliamentary than presidential systems.

Many of the vast number of CSOs and NGOs that are now active in Africa are hardly more representative than Parliaments; many are self-appointed and some look elitist; most are urban-based. They have no formal powers to sanction government. Far from rising above what are often judged to be weaknesses shared by parties and parliamentarians, clientelism for example, civic groups may exemplify identical features because these come from the culture of society as a whole. And although not above the law, CSOs are not publicly accountable in the same way as elected Parliaments and politicians. While claiming to speak on behalf of groups in society, sometimes very effectively so, they are not the whole society's voice. Indeed, if Pender's (2007: 123) description of donor involvement in Tanzania is correct — 'civil society is deeply penetrated by international actors, both in terms of its resources and its authority, which derives at least as much from the civic actors' relationship with international agencies, as it does with Tanzanian society' — then civil society activities probably strengthen the lines

---

18 The Institute for Democracy in South Africa advised the AAPPG (2008: 34) relations between Parliament and civil society in South Africa 'are widely characterised by conflict, antagonism and mistrust'.

19 'Parliaments can get to the parts that development partners and civil society can't reach' (a PCC officer cited in AAPPG 2008: 19).

of *external* as much as domestic accountability. This is corroborated wherever civil society inclusion in pro-poor public deliberations at the international partners' behest amounts to just 'box ticking' (Zimmermann 2007: 4; Selbervik & Wang 2006). In addition to their vulnerability to excessive regulation and to co-optation — whereby they end up accounting to government or donors rather than holding either of these to account — CSOs depend on the arbitrary goodwill of the executive for being granted access to the foreign assistance they often come to rely upon (IMF 2007: 25).

For all these reasons, Hudson and Tsekpo's (2009: 5) findings about parliamentary strengthening in Uganda could have much wider application. If international actors mean to support the development of democracy understood to include competition between different ideas and agendas for society, emanating from society, and reflected in Parliament, then donors must engage more effectively with legislatures *and* with political parties.[20] This probably means helping to redefine relations between politicians and society away from patron–clientelism and towards a stronger focus on policy and national public goods.[21] More generally, whatever competes with efforts to build the strong parties and party system that can bridge the legislature and society, or whatever seems to reflect badly on that aim by appearing to downgrade the importance of electoral processes and the associated principle of representational accountability, does not serve democratisation well and goes against the grain of accountability assistance. Initiatives that have the effect of undermining the legislature or retard the quality of political representation invite similar criticism, even if they substitute a patchwork of more direct but still only partial and particularistic links between state and society maintained at the discretion of the government or donor. Whitfield (2005: 653) puts the point thus: 'There is a quagmire in not using the formal institutions because they do not function properly, but then subsequently undermining their development by sidestepping them.'[22] Furthermore, if Zimmermann (2007: 6) is right to say that country ownership of development policy 'would be much stronger if Parliaments had a greater role in overseeing development plans, policy frameworks and national budgets', then it is not just democracy but development too that would benefit from a stronger, more focused and undiluted international commitment to legislatures.

---

20   Burnell (2009) explores the dilemmas of combining the two.

21   Lindberg (2009: 13–14) provides evidence from Ghana that politicians engaged in this kind of 'strategic civic education' of the electorate can reduce the voters' emphasis on personalised and particularistic material favours.

22   Van Vliet (2009) expertly introduces the issues raised for democracy by competing claims by parties and civil society to represent the people's will in Zambia's deliberations on its new Constitution.

Neither democracy nor development will gain unreservedly from initiatives that on balance favour other actors, other institutions.[23]

6. Conclusion

Accountability has become a fashionable cause in the eyes of international organisations looking for better governance for the purpose of advancing development. Accountability is also central to ideas of democracy that inform international democracy promotion. Accountability support has become a noteworthy feature of Africa's international relations. However, it is important to distinguish among the different reasons why accountability is held to be important, and to ask questions about who is accountable for what and to whom. Increase in domestic accountability may not mean commensurate increase in democratic accountability. The 2005 Paris Declaration made 'mutual accountability' between international development partners and their recipient countries a shared goal. But as Meyer and Schulz (2008: 31) concluded from studying Mali among other countries, achieving this goal depends on how much policy space is conceded to governments and how much of it is shared downwards, beyond the executive, to society and its political representatives.

Apparently not all development practitioners and theoreticians yet see the importance of supporting elected legislatures. Murphy and Alhada (2007: 149) observed a 'broad-based tendency in both developed and developing countries to introduce managed public consultation and representation in discrete programme areas, often as an alternative to expanding the scrutiny and oversight roles of Parliament'. Some international partners now say that Parliaments merit more support but this seems to have come about less in response to requests coming out of Africa and more from changes in thinking and practice in the international development community. The international partners are looking for new ways of anchoring ownership of their ideas and practices concerning public financial rectitude and pro-poor development, as more aid takes the form of direct budgetary support amid lingering concerns about corruption.

Only time will tell whether and how donors come to terms with what Hudson and Wren (2007: 45) called 'the inevitable flip-side of real partnerships' — Parliaments that 'at times take positions which are uncomfortable for development partners'. It is also too soon to be confident that demand-led approaches to legislative strengthening aimed at raising governmental accountability will be

---

23 Of course democracy assistance must be held accountable for largely neglecting political parties, even more so than Parliaments, enabling civil society to gain disproportionately from governance-oriented development aid *and* from democracy support.

effective in countering executive domination and will undercut unreasonable influence by donors. The Accra Agenda for Action (2008) agreed in Ghana by ministers of developing and donor countries urged Africa's governments to work more closely with Parliaments over development policies. But at the same time it earmarked more international support for civil society organisations and did not undertake to reduce aid conditionality or to end the policy conditions. There is still no sea change underway.

Turning to the bigger picture, arguments that say greater democratic accountability in Africa is worthless as long as states are losing power to global institutions possessing few, if any, democratic credentials themselves may be defeatist or overblown. Even so, how relations of mutual accountability can be constructed between international development organisations and African governments in ways that are guaranteed to advance democratic accountability inside their countries, rather than strengthen relations of external accountability or domestic accountabilities that do not advance democracy, remains hugely challenging. And on this the prospects of development as well as democracy depend in the longer run.

References

Africa All Party Parliamentary Group. 2008. *Strengthening Parliaments in Africa: Improving Support.* London: House of Commons AAPPG.

Barkan, J. 2008. Legislatures on the rise? *Journal of Democracy,* 19(2): 124–137.

Brinkerhoff, D. & Goldsmith, A. 2003. How citizens participate in macroeconomic policy: International experience and implications for poverty reduction. *World Politics,* 31(4): 685–701.

Bräutigam, D. 2004. The people's budget? Politics, participation and pro-poor policy. *Development Policy Review,* 22(6): 653–668.

Brösamle, K., Dimsdale, T., Mathiesen, M. & Merz, T. 2007. Improving fiscal scrutiny through legislative strengthening. Report to the UK Department for International Development. Available at http://sdnhq.undp.org/governance/parls/docs. Accessed 1 November 2010.

Burnell, P. 2009. Legislative strengthening meets party support in international assistance: A closer relationship? *The Journal of Legislative Studies,* 15(4): 460–480.

Commonwealth Parliamentary Association (with UNDP, WBI & NDI). 2006. Benchmarks for democratic legislatures. Available at http://sdnhq.undp.org/governance/parls/docs/CPA. Accessed 1 November 2010.

Department for International Development. 2004. Helping parliaments and legislative assemblies to work for the poor. A guide to the reform of key functions and responsibilities. Available at http://www.dfid.gov.uk. Accessed 1 November 2010.

DFID-UNDP-WBI. 2007. Democratic governance. Consultation on parliamentary development and financial accountability. Available at http://sdnhq.undp.org/governance/parls/agenda. Accessed 1 November 2009.

Draman, R. & Langdon, S. 2005. *PRSPs in Africa: Parliaments and Policy Performance.* Eschorn: Deutsche Gesellschaft für Technische Zusammenarbeit.

Ebrahim, A. & Weisband, E. 2007. Introduction: Forging global accountabilities. In Ebrahim, A. & Weisband, E. (eds). *Global Accountabilities.* Cambridge: Cambridge University Press, 1–23.

Economic Commission for Africa. 2005. *African Governance Report 2005.* Addis Ababa: ECA.

Eggers, A., Florini, A. & Woods, N. 2005. Democratizing the IMF. In Carin, B. & Woods, A. (eds). *Accountability of the International Monetary Fund.* Aldershot: Ashgate, 38–61.

Fish, S. 2006. Stronger legislatures, stronger democracies. *Journal of Democracy,* 17(1): 5–20.

Grant, R. & Keohane, R. 2005. Accountability and abuses of power in world politics. *American Political Science Review,* 99(1): 29–43.

Hoebink, P. 2006. European donors and 'good governance': Condition or goal? *European Journal of Development Research,* 18(1): 131–161.

Hubli, K. & Schmidt, M. 2005. *Approaches to Parliamentary Strengthening. A Review of SIDA's Support to Parliaments.* Stockholm: SIDA Evaluation 05/27.

Hudson, A. & Tsekpo, A. 2009. Parliamentary strengthening and the Paris principles: Synthesis report. Overseas Development Institute & the Parliamentary Centre of Canada. Available at http://www.odi./org. Accessed 1 November 2010.

Hudson, A. & Wren, C. 2007. *Parliamentary Strengthening in Developing Countries: Final Report for DFID.* London: Overseas Development Institute.

Hyden, G. 2008. After the Paris Declaration: Taking on the issue of power. *Development Policy Review,* 26(3): 259–274.

Inter-Parliamentary Union. 2003. *Ten Years of Strengthening Parliaments in Africa, 1991–2000. Lessons Learnt and the Way Forward.* Geneva: IPU.

International Monetary Fund. 2007. *The IMF and Aid to Sub-Saharan Africa: Evaluation Report.* Washington, DC: IMF Independent Evaluation Office.

Johnston, N. & Von Trapp, L. 2008. Strengthening parliaments — Strengthening accountability. The World Bank Institute's parliamentary strengthening program. Retrospective. Available at http://siteresources.worldbank.org. Accessed 1 November 2010.

Jones, T. & Hardstaff, P. 2005. Denying democracy: How the IMF and World Bank take power from the people. London: World Development Movement.

Krafchik, W. 2005. *Can Civil Society Add Value to Budget Decision-Making? A Description of Civil Society Budget Work.* Washington, DC: International Budget Project.

Lazarus, J. 2008. Participation in poverty reduction strategy papers: Reviewing the past, assessing the present and predicting the future. *Third World Quarterly,* 29(6): 1205–1221.

Lindberg, S. 2009. Member of the Parliament of Ghana: A hybrid institution with mixed effects. Working paper 2. London, ODI Africa Power and Politics Programme. Available at http://www.institutions-africa.org. Accessed 1 November 2010.

McNeil, M. & Mumvuma, T. 2006. *Demanding Good Governance. A Stocktaking of Social Accountability Initiatives by Civil Society in Anglophone Africa*. Washington, DC: World Bank Institute.

Meyer, S. & Schulz, N. 2008. Ownership with adjectives. Donor harmonisation: Between effectiveness and democratisation: Synthesis report. Madrid, FRIDE Working paper 52.

Miller, R. 2005. The role of NGOs in international democratic development. The case of legislative development. Montreal, Institute for Research on Public Policy. Available at http://www.irpp.org. Accessed 1 November 2010.

Murphy, J. & Alhada, A. 2007. Global programme for parliamentary strengthening II: Mid-term evaluation report UNDP. Available at http://sdnhq.undp.org. Accessed 1 November 2010.

Nijzink, L., Mozaffar, S. & Azevedo, E. 2006. Parliaments and the enhancement of democracy on the African continent: An analysis of institutional capacity and public perceptions. *The Journal of Legislative Studies*, 12(3–4): 311–335.

Organisation for Economic Co-operation and Development. 2005. Paris Declaration on Aid Effectiveness. Available at http://www.oecd.org. Accessed 1 November 2010.

Pelizzo, R., Stapenhurst, R. & Olson, D. 2006. *Parliamentary Oversight for Government Accountability*. Washington, DC: World Bank.

Pender, J. 2007. Country ownership: The evasion of donor accountability. In Bickerton, C., Cunliffe, P. & Gourevitch, A. (eds). *Politics without Sovereignty*. London: UCL Press, 112–130.

Robinson, M. 2006. Budget analysis and policy advocacy: The role of non-governmental public action. University of Sussex, IDS Working paper 279.

Rakner, L. & Van de Walle, N. 2009. Opposition weakness in Africa. *Journal of Democracy*, 20(3): 108–121.

Rogerson, A. 2005. Aid harmonisation and alignment: Bridging the gaps between reality and the Paris reform agenda. *Development Policy Review*, 23 (5): 531–552.

Selbervik, H. & Wang, V. 2006. In pursuit of poverty reduction: What have parliaments got to do with it? Bergen: CMI Report 13.

Stapenhurst, R., Pelizzo, R., Olson, D. & Von Trapp, L. (eds). 2008. *Legislative Oversight and Government Accountability*. Washington, DC: World Bank.

United Nations Development Programme. 2003. Parliamentary development. Practice note. Available at http://www.undp.org. Accessed 1 November 2010.

USAID. 2006. *International Legislative Strengthening: Alternate Approaches*. Washington, DC: USAID.

Van Vliet, M. 2009. The politics of constitutional reform processes in Zambia. In Sachs, A. et al. *Writing Autobiographies of Nations: A Comparative Analysis of Constitutional Reform Processes*. The Hague: NIMD Knowledge Centre, 39–58.

Wehner, J. with Brösamle, K., Dimsdale, T., Mathiesen, M. & Merz, T. 2007. Strengthening legislative financial scrutiny in developing countries. Final report to DFID. Available at http://www.internationalbudget.org. Accessed 1 November 2010.

Whitfield, L. 2005. Trustees of development from conditionality to governance: Poverty reduction strategy papers in Ghana. *Journal of Modern African Studies*, 43(4): 641–664.

Woll, B. 2008. Donor harmonisation and government ownership: Multi-donor budget support in Ghana. *European Development Research*, 20(1): 74–87.

World Bank and International Monetary Fund. 2005. Synthesis 2005 review of the PRS approach: Balancing accountabilities and scaling up results. Available at http://siteresources.worldbank.org. Accessed 1 November 2010.

Zimmermann, F. 2007. Report on ownership in practice. OECD Development Centre. Available at http://oecd.org. Accessed 1 November 2010.

Table of Cases

Index